Philosophical Foundations of the Law of Express Trusts

Philosophical Foundations of the Law of Express Trusts

Edited by

SIMONE DEGELING, JESSICA HUDSON, AND IRIT SAMET

OXFORD
UNIVERSITY PRESS

OXFORD
UNIVERSITY PRESS

Great Clarendon Street, Oxford, OX2 6DP,
United Kingdom

Oxford University Press is a department of the University of Oxford.
It furthers the University's objective of excellence in research, scholarship,
and education by publishing worldwide. Oxford is a registered trade mark of
Oxford University Press in the UK and in certain other countries

First Edition published in 2023

Published in the United States of America by Oxford University Press
198 Madison Avenue, New York, NY 10016, United States of America

British Library Cataloguing in Publication Data

Data available

Library of Congress Control Number: 2023944951

ISBN 978–0–19–284493–4

DOI: 10.1093/oso/9780192844934.001.0001

Printed and bound by
CPI Group (UK) Ltd, Croydon, CR0 4YY

Contents

List of Contributors

Sinéad Agnew, Fellow of Newnham College and Catherine Seville Associate Professor of Law, University of Cambridge

Hanoch Dagan, Distinguished Professor of Law and Director, Berkeley Center for Private Law Theory, Berkeley Law School

Simone Degeling, Professor of Law, School of Private and Commercial Law, UNSW Law & Justice

Simon Douglas, Fellow of Jesus College and Associate Professor of Law, University of Oxford

David Foster, Lecturer in Law, University College London

Matthew Harding, Dean and William Hearn Professor of Law, University of Melbourne

Jessica Hudson, Associate Professor of Law, School of Private and Commercial Law, UNSW Law & Justice

Ben McFarlane, Professor of English Law and Fellow of St John's College, University of Oxford

Paul B. Miller, Professor of Law, Notre Dame Law School

Charles Mitchell, KC (Hon) FBA, Professor of Law, University College London

Ann Mumford, Professor, Dickson Poon School of Law, King's College London

Irit Samet, Professor, Dickson Poon School of Law, King's College London

Express Trusts: Concepts, Justifications, and Boundaries

Simone Degeling, Jessica Hudson, and Irit Samet[*]

The express trust is seen by many as the most important innovation of the law of Equity. In his *Lectures on Equity*, Maitland described the trust as equity's 'largest and the most important ... invention and development' and a 'distinctive achievement of English lawyers'.[1] Lionel Smith has described trusts law as 'the signal contribution of Equity jurisprudence to the legal landscape of the world'.[2] While not all jurisdictions have express trusts and trusts law, it is a popular framework in those that do.

Within these jurisdictions, trust law generates a range of legal relations that apply to control how the trustee uses the legal entitlements held on trust, and also impacts the positions of the settlor, beneficiary, and third parties. As such, trust law has consequences for the application of a variety of laws that generate the subject matter of an express trust, such as property law, contract law, tort law, a range of statutory regimes, and other equitable rules. Further, trust law influences the operation of a range of statutory regimes such as taxation, personal bankruptcy, and corporate insolvency and trust law has also informed the origins and development of a range of other significant areas of law, such as fiduciary law and corporations law.

Trust law remains, nevertheless, under-theorised. While its technical and purely doctrinal aspects are being studied fairly intensively, investigation of the foundational questions to which it gives rise is largely missing. The trust presents the jurist with numerous conceptual, doctrinal, and ethical challenges. It is an '"institute" of great elasticity and generality'[3] that has been deployed towards a variety of personal and commercial pursuits, including family wealth distribution, charities, pensions, personal and commercial investments, and government purposes. In addition to being

* This collection arose from a workshop on the Philosophical Foundations of the Law of Express Trusts held at Kings College London in late 2021. We are in awe of the courage and resilience of those who contributed despite the long months of Covid lockdowns all over the world. We also offer our sincere thanks to workshop participants for their comments, and to all who Zoomed in at what may, for them, have been very late into the night or early in the morning. We are indebted to our research assistants Louis Triggs and Jack Zhou for their extraordinary work in assisting with the preparation of the chapters for publication and to our editor Rebecca Lewis for stewarding the book through to publication.

1 FW Maitland, *Lectures on Equity* (JH Chaytor and J Whittaker eds, CUP 1936) 23 (hereafter Maitland, *Lectures on Equity*).

2 Lionel Smith, 'Equity is Not a Single Thing' in D Klimchuk, I Samet and H Smith (eds), *Philosophical Foundations of the Law of Equity* (OUP, 2020) 144, 145.

3 Maitland, *Lectures on Equity* (n 1) 23.

Simone Degeling, Jessica Hudson, and Irit Samet, *Express Trusts: Concepts, Justifications, and Boundaries* In: *Philosophical Foundations of the Law of Express Trusts.* Edited by: Simone Degeling, Jessica Hudson, and Irit Samet, Oxford University Press.
 DOI: 10.1093/oso/9780192844934.003.0001

used towards the pursuit of good, it has also been used for ill, and the interaction of trusts law with other laws (both judge and parliament-made) agitates numerous conceptual and moral quandaries about its essence (as an equitable body of law), the nature of the relationship it creates (between trustee and beneficiaries, as well as vis-à-vis third parties), and its value to society.

The chapters in this book explore some of these quandaries with a view to initiating and encouraging further engagement and learning. They identify different challenges and adopt a variety of methodological approaches and perspectives towards their resolution, ranging from conceptual questions about what is 'the trust' and 'trusts law', chapters analysing the legal and/or moral statuses of each of the settlor, trustee, and beneficiary, to chapters questioning the moral foundations of different trusts and range of pursuits towards which parties have deployed them. Three broad themes emerge from the chapters presented. The first is a consideration of the ways in which conceptual, historical, and doctrinal analyses impact upon the ways in which we understand and justify the law of express trusts. The second theme is about justifications. It asks about the ends achieved by trusts, despite the risk that the trust form may be abused for illegal or illegitimate ends. The third and final theme returns to this risk of abuse and considers some of the justificatory challenges presented for trusts. Each theme will be considered in turn.

I. Conceptual Analyses of Trusts

A familiar and specific aspect of this theme is the analytical debate about whether the trust relationship and a beneficiary's interest thereunder should be characterised as *in personam*,[4] or *in rem*.[5]

While different views have been expressed in favour of the *in personam* or *in rem* classifications, as well as other characterisations such as right against a right, all sides agree as to the significance of this debate. How we characterise the trust and the beneficiary's interest has influenced how we understand and rationalise various rules of trust law, as well as the availability of certain equitable remedies against the trustee and third parties.[6] It is important beyond our understanding of the express trust, and has implications for understanding the interconnections between trust law and other rules,[7]

[4] See, eg, ibid, chs 9–11; HF Stone, 'The Nature of the Rights of the Cestui Que Trust' (1917) 17 Col L Rev 467. For a modern version of this view see Ben McFarlane and Robert Stevens, 'The Nature of Equitable Property' (2010) 4 J Eq 1; Robert Chambers, *An Introduction to Property Law in Australia* (2nd edn, Lawbook Co 2008) [13.90].

[5] As in JE Penner, 'The (True) Nature of a Beneficiary's Equitable Proprietary Interest under a Trust' (2014) 27 Can J Law Jurisprud 473; Hanoch Dagan and Irit Samet, 'The Beneficiary's Ownership Rights in the Trust *Res* in a Liberal Property Regime' (2023, forthcoming) MLR.

[6] Such as a beneficiary's entitlement to recover misapplied trust property (or its traceable substitute) from third parties. See, eg, *Westdeutsche Landesbank Girozentrale v Islington LBC* [1996] AC 669 (HL) 705 (Lord Browne-Wilkinson); *Foskett v McKeown* [2001] 1 AC 102 (HL) 108–10 (Lord Browne-Wilkinson), 127–30 (Lord Millett).

[7] Such as tort law, see generally: J Edelman, 'Two Fundamental Questions for the Law of Trusts' (2013) 129 LQR 66; and conflict of laws, see generally: Sinéad Agnew and Ben McFarlane, 'The Nature of Trusts and Conflict of Laws' (2021) 137 LQR 405.

and that between equity and law more generally.[8] Resolution of this analytical debate is also complicated by the reliance upon prior assumptions about the categories of *in personam* and *in rem*, and the particular context and purpose for which any classification is made.

The chapters by Ben McFarlane, David Foster, Simon Douglas, and Jessica Hudson and Charles Mitchell all explore various conceptual analyses of the trust and their analytical and justificatory implications. Each chapter asks questions such as what is a trust, and the nature of the rights created thereunder, and explores how the answers to some of these questions matter for how we justify trust law. A range of methodological perspectives are also employed to answer these and other questions, including historical, moral, doctrinal, comparative, and conceptual analyses.

Some chapters engage with the specific debate of how to characterise a trust as *in personam* or *in rem*, such as that by David Foster, who does so from a historical perspective, asking how analytical conceptions of the trust have evolved in the period *c* 1600–1900. Foster shows that particular emphasis was placed on the trust as a 'confidence annexed in privity' at the start of the period, and this highly personal conception of the trust emphasised the reposing of trust in an identified individual and the binding of their conscience to perform the trust. Such a personal conception tended towards some significant limitations on the enforceability of the trust but, as the trust concept evolved over the course of the seventeenth century, many of these limitations began to fade from the case law. Foster goes on to show how the trust came to be conceived as attaching not merely to the trustee's conscience, but to the trust property itself. This shift in emphasis from 'confidence' to 'property' had a number of consequences for the creation, administration, and enforceability of trusts, and also encouraged a reconceptualisation of the trust in explicitly proprietary terms. Foster goes on to show how analytical jurisprudence turned to classical Roman law concepts on '*in personam*' and '*in rem*' conceive of the trust, and in particular the beneficiary's interest thereunder. In so doing, the chapter bridges a gap between historiography and jurisprudence on the express trust in highlighting the role historical conceptions of the trust have, and should continue to play in shaping legal thought.

Ben McFarlane also engages with the intricate relationships between the trust and concept(s) of property. To date, much scholarly debate has focused upon the nature of the beneficiary's rights under a trust to analyse the trust as *in personam*, *in rem*, or something else. McFarlane introduces a new approach by focusing on the nature of the *trustee's* rights under a trust. He starts by asking what we can (and cannot) learn about the trust if we look at it through the lens of property rights. In contrast with Hanoch Dagan and Irit Samet, McFarlane is fairly sceptical about the extent to which the concept of property can help us understand and justify the enforcement of trusts. Looking at various examples—eg recent case law on the complex issue of what can be the subject matter of a trust—he finds that 'right' is a much more fertile and precise conceptual

[8] See, eg, Ben McFarlane, 'The Persistence of Equity: Lessons from the Trust' in S Elliott and B McFarlane (eds), *Equity Today: 150 Years After the Judicature Reforms* (Hart 2023).

anchor from which to explore the trust relationship, as references to property (in case law and scholarly work) often use the concept as a proxy to right. It would be a mistake, however, to think about the extent to which the trust is being informed and defined by the concept of property without recognising the profound way in which recognising the trust shapes, in its turn, the concept of property in such legal systems. This influence, McFarlane argues, is made most clear when we think about the undisputed legal fact that trustees are owners of the trust property; without the right to benefit from it, or use it as the trustee sees fit (unless authorised to do so by the trust terms), the trustee's right challenges our most basic notions of ownership. The two-way interaction between the property regime and the trust therefore has profound ramifications for how we understand these relationships.

Simon Douglas' chapter focuses less on the specific debate whether to analyse the trust as *in personam* or *in rem*, and offers a novel way of analysing the trust via the legal concepts of estate, patrimony, and legal personality. In so doing, Douglas addresses a fundamental question about the nature of the express trust as a creation of the legal system, namely, whether it can be said to have a legal personality. The received wisdom according to which the trust does not have a legal personality, and only the trustees—who own the trust property—can therefore be properly said to execute powers, take on liabilities, enjoy immunities, etc., is in tension with the way trusts function as legal entities. Thus, recent legislation introduced registration for trusts, duties to pay tax that are directed at the trust, and other requirements that characterise (natural and artificial) legal personalities. The way in which popular express trusts, like the charity or the open-ended discretionary trust, operate without a beneficiary also demonstrate that the trust cannot be reduced to a web of jural relations between the relevant parties. Douglas therefore proposes to analyse the trust as having a 'weak estate' defined as a legally distinct pool of assets each of which is available to meet only and any of the estate's liabilities, when a person closely connected with the estate stands as a surety for its liabilities. This analysis explains a central aspect of the trust, namely, the way in which trust assets can and should always be used to pay the trust's debt (eg indemnity to trustees), while they are never unavailable to creditors of an insolvent trustee, and may or may not be available to the *beneficiary's* creditors. According to Douglas' account, therefore, the conceptual building blocks that make or break the trust as a legal entity are taken from the property discourse, but they are deployed in by reference to the unique notion of the 'estate'.

Taking a broader conceptual approach again, Charles Mitchell and Jessica Hudson explore the analytical utility and justificatory implications of conceptualising the trust as secondary or meta-law, and using complex adaptive systems theory. They examine 'the trust' and 'trusts law' as objects for justification, asking what, exactly, is being justified by the body of theoretical literature seeking to justify 'the trust' and 'trusts law'. They argue that the rules of 'trusts law', like some other equitable rules, operate as 'meta-law', meaning that they are rules about rules, the point of which, in this context, is to control the way in which the trustee uses the legal entitlements afforded to them by law. In assessing the effect of 'trust law' as 'meta-law', they utilise ideas from complex adaptive systems theory to suggest that 'the trust' and 'trusts law' make up a complex adaptive system made up of a set of individual legal propositions defined by multiple legal rules. Further that these individual legal rules work together, and interact with other legal rules generating the subject matter of the trust, such as contract law and property law, to produce an overall system-level effect they identify as being to redefine the trustee's authority as titleholder. As such, 'trusts' and 'trusts law' present multiple interrelated objects for justification. Hudson and Mitchell discuss how conceiving of 'trusts' and 'trusts law' in these ways can enable theorists to gain a more finely textured understanding of how a jurisdiction's commitment to 'the trust' may or may not be justified, illustrating this point with examples of how autonomy theory might support different features of 'trusts' and 'trusts law'.

II. Justifying the Trust by Reference to its Ends

In an exploration of the philosophical foundations of a body of law, conceptual questions naturally lead to lead questions of justification. For some writers in the volume, most explicitly Hudson and Mitchell, the justification work cannot start before a conceptual clearing is done. For others, notably Dagan and Samet, these investigations must be taken together as a reflective equilibrium process. But everyone agrees that in law (at least) questions of concept are intimately connected to justificatory principles. And so, the second, but closely related, theme we identify in the chapters is a quest after the reasons that can be cited in favour of having, keeping, and nurturing the trust in our law books. Attempts have been made, especially in the United States, to justify the trust as a promoter of economic efficiency. In difference from analyses of other staples of private law like contract or tort, the conceptualisation of trust as yet another legal relationship whose justification lies solely in its potential to increase efficiency did not pick up many advocates.[9] The chapters in this volume are therefore tackling the justification challenge from a normative perspective: taking the trust as a private law device for achieving an end (or ends) and asking whether these ends instantiate a value in a way that makes the trust a worthwhile part of the law in spite of a non-negligible abuse (see the third theme of this Introduction).

Dagan and Samet take a robust view about the way in which the trust can be justified as a means to promote the autonomy of settlors and beneficiaries. While they agree that trust sceptics are correct to revolt against the increasing abuses of the trust, they argue that those who deem the express trust beyond redemption are wrong. The authors develop a sympathetic interpretation of trust doctrine and of the legacy of the trust that offers a happy *raison d'être* around which it can, and should, be reconstructed. The trust, they argue, plays a distinctive role in a system of liberal (that is autonomy-enhancing)

[9] See, for example, John H Langbein, 'The Contractarian Basis of the Law of Trusts' (1995) 105 Yale LJ 625, and criticism in Henry Hansmann and Ugo Mattei, 'The Functions of Trust Law: A Comparative Legal and Economic Analysis' (1998) 73 NYULR 434.

property law, as it allows settlor(s) to set up the beneficiaries' entitlements in ways that diverge from state sponsored types of property-holding. The authors explore the diverse and sophisticated ways in which the trust enhances the autonomy of beneficiaries and settlors, interpret the legal rules that apply to the formation and running of the trust in ways that highlight this contribution, and make suggestions on how they should be developed in the future. Finding a justificatory principle for trusts within the framework of liberal property also enables the writers to delineate the boundaries of the legitimate trust, for the liberal state should only sanction property-holding forms that enhance autonomy and *also* satisfy the minimum requirements of relational justice. This move allows the writers to explain, for example, why discriminatory terms of trusts—a problem that blighted the scholarship and jurisprudence of trusts for many years—are *ultra vires* the trust.

In a different take on the justificatory question, Paul Miller examines a more concrete way in which trusts serve an end. Highlighting the way in which trusts are perceived in the United States as focused on the settlor, in distinction from other common law jurisdictions in which the beneficiaries are seen as the focal point of the trust, Miller critically assesses the trust as a vehicle for passing property to the next generation. Given the popularity of trusts to achieve this end, the justification of the trust as a legal device is dependent on us finding a good reason for allowing such transfers in spite of the way in which they may enshrine gaps between owners and the propertyless. To do that, Miller examines trusts as vehicles for testamentary freedom of disposition, addressing the tension between US trust law's commitment to the promotion and nurturing of freedom of testamentary disposition and the great difficulty in finding a sound normative defence for this common characteristic of legal concepts of ownership. The trust is conceived by US jurists as very much focused on the wishes of the settlor (in contrast with the preservation of the beneficiaries' interests). Given the sheer volume of trusts that are testamentary in nature, the justifying principle behind the trust must include a defence of owners' freedom to determine how exactly will the property be used after their death. Mainstream justifications are, alas, disappointing as Miller shows. The chapter therefore sets out to offer a nuanced defence of an owner's power to set the agenda for their property beyond the grave by focusing on the gift-giving nature of testamentary disposition. Miller argues that the legal focal point of the testamentary trust tracks the moral sense in which gift-giving expresses socially valuable virtues like care, benevolence, sense of duty, and affection. Taking its rootedness in gift-giving practices/rituals seriously enables the author to draw carefully the legitimacy boundaries of the testamentary trust and thus offer a critical view of current practices. Miller's analysis thus takes the justification for (a considerable chunk of) express trusts out of the range of run-of-the-mill justifications for private property rights, and sets it on the independent ground of the morality of gift-giving. The vision he has for the trust is therefore not as a continuation, or equitable extension of property and/or contractual right. Rather, he highlights the *sui generis* nature of the express trust as embedding in the law some moral practices that are essential for healthy communal and familial relationships.

Sinéad Agnew in her chapter examines the novel question: what significance does the *settlor's* status have for the way we justify elements of the trust? Interrogating the under-examined idea of the settlor's conscience, she argues that this idea is relevant to self-declared trusts and trusts by transfer, utilising the autonomy rationale to explain the significance of, and limits to, the settlor's conscience as applied knowledge. Agnew draws on moral philosophy to explain the idea of conscience, its relevance to equity and to assessing the moral significance of a settlor's actions in self-declaring a trust and the ensuing assumption of responsibility. Agnew looks to the autonomy rationale to explain why the settlor's conscience is bound by the duties of an express trustee, looking to the circumstances in which a settlor's conscience will be bound by a custodial duty in order to rescue an express trust which would otherwise fail due to incomplete constitution or disclaimer. Agnew argues that although the idea of conscience as applied knowledge is relevant, the settlor's actions are crucial as well. The courts are engaged in a balancing act between respecting a settlor's dispositive autonomy by giving legal effect to her performative utterances and external acts and protecting those who rely on them. Agnew makes these arguments by reference to various contexts, such as the creation of self-declared trusts and the rescue of express trusts by transfer which would otherwise fail because of inadequate constitution or disclaimer. Agnew observes that it remains to be seen whether the courts have struck the right balance arguing that justifications based upon conceptions of 'unconscionability' can raise more questions than they answer.

The justificatory question with reference to the trust ends, and the conceptual question whether it is the beneficiary or the trustee that are the focal point of the trust also plays out in Matthew Harding's chapter. In a call to radically change the way trusts tend to be conceptualised in Australia, England, and other jurisdictions as centred upon the beneficiary (as expressed in the semi-sacred 'beneficiary principle'), Harding challenges the usefulness of non-charitable purpose trusts. If such uses can be identified, and the value attached to them is high enough to overcome the dangers they pose, common law jurisdictions that disallow them should rethink this dogma. Common law jurisdictions typically recognise trusts for public charitable purposes.[10] Additionally, charitable purpose trusts attract particular legislative fiscal and regulatory regimes, which may be advantageous and confer privileges or immunities on the trustee. As explored by Matthew Harding, such trusts bring into sharp relief the normative justifications for private express trusts in general and purpose trusts in particular, and the doctrinal question of what will count as a purpose trust and the mechanisms for the enforcement of such trusts.

In his chapter, Harding takes a stepwise approach, first asking, as an institutional form, how may purpose trusts be justified? He considers this question against the backdrop of the trust as an important element in a liberal property regime. Drawing on the work of Irit Samet, Hanoch Dagan, and Rosemary Teele Langford, the author observes

[10] *Income Tax Special Purposes Commissioners v Pemsel* [1891] AC 531 (HL) 580 (Lord Macnaghten); Charities Act 2011; *Charities Act 2013* (Cth). As discussed by Harding, there are also exceptional cases such as *Re Denley's Trust Deed* [1969] 1 Ch373 (Ch D) which put under pressure the maintenance of a distinction between beneficiary and purpose trusts.

that not only does the trust enable settlors to craft bespoke arrangements (within limits) within which they and others may enjoy the benefits of property in multiple ways, but that purpose trusts make a further distinctive contribution. This contribution is that they permit purpose-based governance. Unlike other institutional forms which may be available to settlors, such as charitable corporations or gifts to unincorporated associations, purpose trusts offer not only purpose-based governance but also a high degree of fidelity to settlor intentions. As a matter of default law, the trust terms do not permit variance from disponor intentions and, ultimately, a court exercising its supervisory jurisdiction will execute the terms of the trust. Thus, Harding identifies purpose trusts as a sub form of trust which offer a distinctive mode of governance and enforcement which are autonomy enhancing and facilitative private law structures.

Given this conclusion, the author then moves to consider the existing distinctions between valid charitable purpose trusts and largely invalid non-charitable purpose trusts. The author suggests that private purpose trusts may similarly hold autonomy enhancing and facilitative capacity for their settlors and asks whether such private purpose trusts should also be valid. Leaving to one side the question of enforcement, the author tentatively proposes that, to the extent that purpose-oriented trusts satisfy an overriding requirement of public benefit,[11] all purpose trusts should be recognised as valid. On the question of enforcement the author argues that despite the absence of beneficiaries, a trust enforcer could be appointed to fulfil this function in a private purpose trust and cautions against overstating the concern for a lack of motivation or accountability. He points to s 115 of the Charities Act (UK) as a template for an enforcer model, the legislation conferring standing on 'any person "interested in" the trust' while also acknowledging that further questions remain on how to motivate and supervise the enforcer.

Simone Degeling examines the use of trusts for settlement distribution regimes. Degeling shows that the fund of settlement monies ('the recovery') in an Australian federal class action will likely be held subject to a private express trust. The court appoints an 'Administrator' who holds the recovery on trust for eligible group members according to the terms of the court approved settlement deed and settlement distributions scheme. The office of Administrator is not provided for in the *Federal Court of Australia Act 1976* (Cth) Part IVA ('Part IVA'). Rather, the office is one recognised or created by the parties in their settlement agreement and recognised and approved by the court in approving the terms of any class action settlement where a trust is contemplated or declared in the settlement distribution scheme.

Attempts to justify the trust as instantiating a value—be it morality, justice, welfare, or what have you—tend to rely on familiar, traditional trusts. However, given the increasingly sophisticated ways in which trusts are being used in the commercial setting, these justificatory projects would be significantly enriched if we examine their

[11] Matthew Harding, *Charity Law and the Liberal State* (CUP 2014), especially ch 3; Matthew Harding, 'Independence and Accountability in the Charity Sector' in John Picton and Jennifer Sigafoos (eds), *Debates in Charity Law* (Hart Publishing 2020); Matthew Harding, 'Charity and Law: Past, Present and Future' [2020] SJLJ 564.

application to the new cutting-edge ways in which trusts are used today. In her chapter, Degeling embarks on such mission. Degeling seeks to understand the distinct contributions made by the express trust relationship to the administration of class actions. She argues that various interlinked and interdependent justifications may be offered. Moreover, while other institutional forms such as a company or contract may deliver some of these benefits, none contain the entire package offered by the trust. Most importantly, a trust of the recovery ensures that the monetary settlement approved by the court actually reaches the hands of group members. This is because the trust permits a particular structure of court supervised delegated decision-making and distribution pursuant to which the Administrator is the Court's delegate and allows the Administrator to assume responsibility for administering the recovery. The trust offers a direct line of reporting and responsibility facilitating close supervision by the court yet also permits the delegation of appropriate powers to the Administrator. However, the trust is not simply a structure of delegated decision-making. Crucially, in its supervisory jurisdiction, the trust also carries with it a standard default; a set of rules which ensure that the Administrator as trustee adheres to the terms of the court approved settlement distribution scheme and the ability of the court directly to carry into execution the terms of the settlement distribution scheme should the Administrator fail to do so.[12] The flexibility of the trust form also itself facilitates the enrolment of suitable actors as Administrator, thus facilitating the administration of the class action. Moreover, the trustee sits at the apex of a 'matrix of accountabilities'[13] which means that an external regulatory body or a court administering Part IVA is able to focus on the trustee as the primary object of regulation.[14] The trust form thus simplifies and facilitates the setting and supervision of required conduct under class actions regimes.

III. Drawing the Boundaries of Legitimacy

A justificatory principle for any human artefact cannot work without checking for possible abuses that may undermine the value it instantiates. A few chapters in the volume look at the legitimacy limits of trust, or the ends for which it cannot be justly employed.

Ann Mumford's chapter considers the intersection of express trusts and tax law, and the use of trusts to obstruct tax law, drawing on the facts of *Hniazdzilau v Vajgel*.[15] This was a dispute about the beneficial ownership of shares in a company incorporated in England, albeit that the main protagonists, and many of the key events, were sited in Belorussia. Applying *Tinsley v Milligan*,[16] the English court held that Hniazdzilau did not need to rely on any alleged illegality to make out his beneficial title to the shares in the company. That he might have 'misled'[17] tax authorities in Belorussia and Russia

[12] See also J Hudson and C Mitchell, 'Justificanda' in this book.
[13] M Scott Donald, 'The Pension Trust: Fit For Purpose?' (2019) 82(5) MLR 800, 807.
[14] ibid
[15] [2016] EWHC 15 (Ch) (hereafter *Hniazdzilau*).
[16] [1994] 1 AC 340 (HL).
[17] *Hniazdzilau* (n 15) [228] (Mr Jeremy Cousins QC).

was not relevant to this question. Mumford asks whether the fact of tax abuse may justify defeating a beneficial interest under a private express trust, even when, as in *Hniazdzilau*, the abuse is only tangential to the trust. The author invites us to consider whether continuing to provide state recognition and enforcement of trusts is justified in those cases where trusts are used as vehicles to undermine taxation, given that taxation is as an instrument of social and legal policy, and thus carries social justice considerations. Moreover, as in *Hniazdzilau*, the tax abuse may involve an international element. Starting from the position of comity between nations, the author points to the possible argument that 'if it is a tax law, it should be enforced, by all states'.[18] However, as she demonstrates, this quickly breaks down when we consider the enforceability of a tax law from a state which does not respect human rights. Further, as the author points out, it is unclear how much scrutiny we may legitimately place on the content of foreign law. For example, does scrutiny also extend to a consideration of the economic content of the taxation law and the ends which the revenue raised by taxation law permits in those societies it serves? The author concludes that a broader lens is required to integrate a wider range of considerations in balancing the freedoms of choice offered by trusts law with the obligations of taxation law. She argues that existing legal frameworks are not adequate to do this job.

Other chapters mentioned above also engage and explore this theme. Dagan and Samet argue that the trust plays a distinctive role in a liberal property regime as it permits the settlor to create bespoke property arrangements which takes on the stable form offered by the trust yet also reflects the particular self-determining ends of the settlor. However, this choice is not unconstrained. The authors point to the very foundations of autonomy as an internal limitation on what securing the settlor's autonomy entails. Put another way, the trust carries internal limits, so that when parties attempt to use a trust to achieve ends which infringe this internal limit, this is an abuse which must be considered *ultra vires*. So how may *ultra vires* be demonstrated? Dagan and Samet argue that one pillar on which trust law's legitimacy is contingent is that the private authority conferred by trusts should be circumscribed to meet their instrumental role. Thus, the background property regime which guarantees all the material, social, and intellectual preconditions of self-authorship is actually undermined by trusts which perversely permit parties to subvert their duties as owners.[19]

Dagan and Samet identify another limit in the prescriptions of relational justice, which is to ensure that the trust does not offend the maxim of reciprocal respect for self-determination. The authors argue that a particular instance of impermissible dispositions is private express trusts which discriminate *against* potential beneficiaries on the basis of religion, race, or ethnicity.[20] Testamentary or settlor freedom does not entail a freedom to distribute benefits on a discriminatory basis; to hold otherwise would be tantamount to disrespecting the self-determination of others.

[18] A Mumford, 'Illegality, Tax in Another Jurisdiction, and an Express Trust' in this book, 269.
[19] See also Hanoch Dagan and I Samet, 'What's Wrong with Massively Discretionary Trusts' (2022) 138 LQR 629.
[20] See, for example, *Re Donn's Will Trusts* [1944] Ch 8 (Ch D); *Re Selby's Will Trusts* [1966] 1 WLR 43; *Re Abrahams' Will Trusts* [1969] 1 Ch 463 (Ch D); *Blathwayt v Baron Cawley* [1976] AC 397 (HL).

Paul Miller advances a thesis which highlights the *sui generis* nature of the express trust as a vehicle for the morally sound social practice of gift-giving. According to this view, trusts enable well-motivated choices to give to others, and which are oriented towards the wellbeing of others and support human flourishing. In making this argument Miller also acknowledges that the law tolerates callous motivations (eg calculative gift-giving) and malevolent motivations (eg gifts motivated by malice, spite, envy, and jealousy). However, the author argues that if the law is to enable well-motivated conduct, it must provide freedom of choice as will occasionally permit amoral or immoral motivations for the sake of securing greater prospects for morally motivated choice: 'the law must tolerate vice within fairly wide margins if it is to elicit virtue'.[21] Miller argues that this tension is particularly acute with testamentary dispositions as these are often substantial gifts and are (one of the final) dispositions of the testator during life.

The justificatory challenges presented by trust law's ends are also considered by Matthew Harding who tentatively proposes that, subject to satisfying an overriding requirement of public benefit, all purpose trusts should be valid. The consequences of this validity should, suggests Harding, be dealt with independently, such that regulatory and fiscal regimes be calibrated to their own particular criteria and would not themselves affect the anterior question of whether a purpose trust was valid. Thus, for example, the tax consequences would not turn on the question of whether the trust was a purpose trust, but some other criterion. However, the important point to observe is that subject to public benefit, all purposes are valid.

[21] PB Miller, 'Freedom of Testamentary Disposition' in this book, 197.

1
Justificanda

*Jessica Hudson and Charles Mitchell**

I. Introduction

Law should be justifiable on the basis that it achieves some good.[1] Scholars working from various standpoints have argued that different goods are secured by 'express trusts' and that these justify the choices made by some jurisdictions to 'recognise' versions of the 'express trust' and to develop rules of 'trusts law'. Express trusts are not a feature of every jurisdiction, of course, and they may not be needed for the protection of basic individual rights and interests. However, in the jurisdictions which choose to 'recognise' them, this choice has consequences. Typically, the law of these jurisdictions provides that the trust parties have rights and powers and correlative duties and liabilities and that various forms of relief may be granted against trustees and third parties. All of these consequences should be amenable to justification.

In this chapter, we examine 'express trusts' and 'trusts law' as objects of justification. Foundational to every justificatory project is a clear conception of its object. Unless we know what is being justified, we cannot tell if the justification holds. Yet scholars who propose justifications of 'express trusts' and 'trusts law' often pay scant attention to what these are. Some, indeed, proceed as though the details of this were distracting and unimportant. As scholars with a background in interpretative doctrinal analysis we find this surprising, but we acknowledge that it is attributable, at least in part, to differences of disciplinary methodology. We are most familiar with an approach that identifies the content of law as a first step and then asks if this can be justified. This differs from the approach that is typically taken by law and economics scholars who start by positing justificatory hypotheses and then test these using models which are not meant to correspond to the law of any jurisdiction.[2]

Simplified constructs of 'express trusts' and 'trusts law' are also used by scholars who argue that these are justified because they promote some moral or political value. Most

* An earlier draft of this chapter was presented at the Property Connections Workshop, 22 June 2021, hosted by the Oxford Law Faculty. We thank the organiser, Ben McFarlane, and the participants for their comments. All errors are our own.

[1] J Raz, *Between Authority and Interpretation: On the Theory of Law and Practical Reason* (OUP 2009) 177–78, 180.

[2] See, eg, H Hansmann and U Mattei, 'The Functions of Trust Law: A Comparative Legal and Economic Analysis' (1998) 73 NYULR 434; T Merrill and H Smith, 'The Property / Contract Interface' (2001) 101 Columbia LR 773, 849; R Sitkoff, 'An Agency Costs Theory of Trust Law' (2004) 89 Cornell LR 621; R Sitkoff, 'An Economic Theory of Fiduciary Law' in A Gold and P Miller (eds), *Philosophical Foundations of Fiduciary Law* (OUP 2014) ch 9.

Jessica Hudson and Charles Mitchell, *Justificanda* In: *Philosophical Foundations of the Law of Express Trusts*. Edited by: Simone Degeling, Jessica Hudson, and Irit Samet, Oxford University Press.
DOI: 10.1093/oso/9780192844934.003.0002

commonly this is done as a simple one-off exercise.[3] However, some scholars begin by asking how models of the 'express trust' and 'trusts law' might be justified before moving on to examine legal doctrine, their interpretation of which is informed by justificatory precepts derived from their initial analysis, followed by further discussion from a justificatory standpoint and further interpretation of legal doctrine in an ongoing iterative process.[4]

We acknowledge that insights can be derived from all these approaches, but we consider that paying closer attention to the content of 'express trusts' and 'trusts law' has the potential not only to bring the scholarship into closer alignment with law as it is understood in practice, but also to enrich the justificatory projects in which theorists of 'express trusts' and 'trusts law' are engaged. In our view, 'express trusts' and 'trusts law' are not essential to the implementation of any given moral or political commitment or value and so one cannot define 'express trusts' and 'trusts law' by reference to a predetermined moral or political norm on the basis they are necessary to the fulfilment of this norm. At most, one can only ask whether pre-existing legal constructs of 'express trusts' and 'trusts law' might be justifiable on the basis they contribute to such norms, and to do this one must first understand these constructs on their own terms.

The goal of this chapter is therefore to develop conceptions of 'express trusts' and 'trusts law' that we believe to be more promising objects for justification than the simplified versions used as starting points in much of the scholarship.[5] We argue that an 'express trust' is a set of legal propositions concerning the trust parties' rights, powers, permissions, constraints, and duties, that these propositions are centred on the trustee's title to specific property, and that their combined effect is to redefine the authority over trust property that would otherwise devolve on the trustee.[6]

[3] See, eg, J Langbein, 'The Contractarian Basis of the Law of Trusts' (1995) 105 Yale LJ 625; J Langbein, 'Mandatory Rules in the Law of Trusts' (2004) 98 Northwestern University L Rev 1105; N McBride, *The Humanity of Private Law* (Hart 2018) ch 5 pt 3; M Bennett and A Hofri-Winogradow, 'Use of Trusts to Subvert the Law: An Analysis and Critique' (2021) 41 OJLS 692; E Hudson, 'A Normative Approach to the *Quistclose* Trust' (2017) 80 MLR 775; S Agnew and S Douglas, 'Self-Declarations of Trust' (2019) 135 LQR 67; YK Liew, 'Trusts: Modern Taxonomy and Autonomy' (2021) 35 TLI 27; YK Liew, 'Justifying Anglo-American Trust Law' (2021) 12 William & Mary Business L Rev 685; J Penner, 'Justifying (or Not) the Office of Trusteeship with Particular Reference to Massively Discretionary Trusts' (2021) 34 Can J Law Jurisprud 365. Similarly, but with particular reference to charitable trusts; M Harding, *Charity Law and the Liberal State* (CUP 2014) ch 2. And cf J Penner, 'An Untheory of the Law of Trusts, or Some Notes Toward Understanding the Structure of Trusts Law Doctrine' (2010) 63 CLP 653, who argues that 'trusts law doctrine' is not susceptible to, and does not require, any justification.

[4] H Dagan and I Samet, 'What's Wrong with Massively Discretionary Trusts' (2022) 138 LQR 624; H Dagan and I Samet, 'The Beneficiary's Ownership Rights in the Trust Res in a Liberal Property Regime' (2023) 86 MLR 599; H Dagan and I Samet, 'Express Trust: The Dark Horse of the Liberal Property Regime' in this volume.

[5] We include in our analysis the situations where a trustee holds property for a legal person or a charitable purpose in response to the parties' volitional actions. For the sake of succinctness, we do not specifically distinguish the situation where the right to due administration is held by a legal person on their own behalf from that where the right is held by the Attorney-General on behalf of the Crown. Also, we have excluded other situations where a 'trust' is said to arise in response to other reasons, such as a resulting trust or constructive trust. There are difficult questions about how the line is drawn between these different trusts, but we will only discuss the conceptually preliminary question of what an 'express trust' is.

[6] Parts of what we label as 'property' and 'property law' in this chapter might be labelled differently by others, who may prefer to describe these as falling within the categories of, eg, 'contract' or 'debt' or 'contract law': see, eg, S Douglas and B McFarlane, 'Defining Property Rights' in J Penner and H Smith (eds), *Philosophical Foundations of Property Law* (OUP 2013) ch 10. We have used the label of 'property' to denote everything which can be the subject of an express trust as per the rules for trust creation, according to which '[t]here can be a trust of a chattel or of a chose in action, or of a right or obligation under an ordinary legal contract, just as much as a trust of land'. See

We also unpack what it means to say that a jurisdiction 'recognises' the 'express trust' and 'trusts law'. This language is often used rather loosely to describe the collective effect of different rules. Some of these provide for the creation of 'express trusts', others provide for their operation. It is not wrong to suggest that they work together to produce 'express trusts', but caution is needed when saying that they entail the 'recognition' of 'express trusts' within any given jurisdiction, or this language will conceal more than it reveals about the purposes and content of the rules and how they work.

Further, and returning to our earlier point, we do not believe that it is illuminating to treat the choice made by a jurisdiction to 'recognise' the 'express trust' as an object for justification in itself. We consider that it is more helpful to conceive of 'express trusts' and 'trusts law' as multiple objects for justification: there are the individual legal rules that provide for the creation and/or operation of 'express trusts', as well as the 'express trust' as the set of legal propositions which apply between the trust parties and which interact with one another, and with the rules of property law that specify the trustee's rights and powers as the owner of the trust property, to redefine the trustee's authority as titleholder. This means that for any justificatory project which concerns 'express trusts' and 'trusts law' the question arises: which, if any, of these rules and propositions are the justificanda, ie the object(s) for justification?

In this chapter, we suggest that the 'express trust' and 'trusts law' make up a complex adaptive system, using this term to denote a set of phenomena, the properties of which are emergent— meaning that they result from the interactions between parts of the system with one another and with their environment, sometimes in unpredictable ways, and always in ways that produce higher level system effects that would not be produced by any part of the system operating alone. Different versions of complex adaptive systems theory have been used to explain and interpret various phenomena by scientists and social scientists,[7] and Henry Smith has proposed that scholars may find it fruitful to draw on these ideas as a source of insights into private law—[8]a proposal which we have taken up here.

Applying complex adaptive system theory to 'express trusts' and 'trusts law' suggests that the 'express trust' can be understood as both (a) a set of individual legal propositions defined by multiple legal rules, all of which work together to produce (b) an overall system-level effect which we identify as being to redefine the trustee's authority as titleholder. Consistently with this, we argue that 'express trusts' and 'trusts law' present multiple interrelated objects for justification, being both the individual legal propositions and rules, as well as system-level effects produced by their interactions with one another and with background rules of property law. We also argue that the

Lord Strathcona Steamship Co Ltd v Dominion Coal Co Ltd [1926] AC 108, 124 (Lord Shaw); *Ultraframe (UK) Ltd v Fielding* [2005] EWHC 1638 (Ch) [1523]–[1547] (Lewison J).

[7] For a bibliography, see JB Ruhl, 'Complex Adaptive Systems Literature' (*The Society for Evolutionary Analysis in Law*, Vanderbilt Law School) <https://www.vanderbilt.edu/seal/scholarly-resources/complex-adaptive-systems-literature/>.

[8] H Smith, 'Systems Theory: Emergent Private Law' in A Gold and others (eds), *The Oxford Handbook of the New Private Law* (OUP 2020) ch 9.

rules of 'trusts law', like some other equitable rules, operate as 'meta-law', meaning that they are rules about rules, the point of which, in this context, is to control the way in which people use legal entitlements they have been given by the common law.

In the final part of the chapter, we discuss how conceiving of 'express trusts' and 'trusts law' in these ways can enable theorists to gain a more finely textured understanding of how a jurisdiction's commitment to the 'express trust' may or may not be justified, and we illustrate this point with examples of how autonomy theory might support different features of 'express trusts' and 'trusts law'.

Before we begin, we should stipulate that there are two things that we are not trying to do. *First*, we believe that complex adaptive systems theory may help trust lawyers to answer many questions of interest, such as the effect on an 'express trust' of a change to a jurisdiction's background property law regime, to give just one example. However, exploring every possible question of this kind is not the project of this chapter. Our goal is only to give an outline sketch of what a complex adaptive system theory of 'express trusts' and 'trusts law' might look like and how such a theory might enrich analytical and justificatory studies of these topics. On this approach, the overall effect of 'the trust' is not just an aggregate of the effects of the individual legal propositions that make up the 'express trust', but additionally depends on the interactions between the constituent legal propositions and the interactions between these propositions and the trustee's title to the trust property. We argue that this insight may furnish trusts law theorists with a more accurate conception of what they seek to analyse and justify. We go no further than this, however, and if our argument is accepted, it will be obvious that there remains a good deal of conceptual analytical and justificatory work to be done. Further questions also present themselves, which we do not consider here, for example how complex adaptive systems theory might assist with analytical and justificatory projects focused on other areas of law, such as property law and contract law; and also, how the propositions and rules which collectively make up each of these areas of law interact with and respond to one another.

Second, we illustrate our system-based conceptions of 'express trusts' and 'trusts law' with examples of constituent legal propositions and rules that form part of the laws of Australia and England. These are the jurisdictions with which we are most familiar, but we do not claim that the content of the 'trusts law' systems which we find in these jurisdictions is more (or less) justifiable than the content of the 'trusts law' systems which can be found elsewhere. Our goal is only to describe a system-based conception of 'express trusts' and 'trusts law' which we believe holds good for the Australian and English jurisdictions, and which we also believe holds good for other common law jurisdictions where 'express trusts' and 'trusts law' exist, although we do not attempt to prove this.

II. 'The Express Trust'

A. Identifying the Objects for Justification

How we understand the 'express trust' matters for how we justify it. Yet the 'express trust' and 'trusts law' are rarely unpacked in the law and economics literature or in work by other private law theorists and they are often presented as conceptual black boxes. However, an 'express trust' is not a tangible thing or physical phenomenon, nor is it a legal person with the capacity to own rights and owe duties.[9] Common law jurisdictions which 'recognise' express trusts have developed equitable and statutory rules concerning the creation, constitution, administration, enforcement, variation, and termination of 'the trust'. These rules are capable of affecting the legal positions of the settlor, trustee, beneficiary, and third parties in many different ways. This means that for any given justification of 'express trusts' and 'trusts law' the question arises: which, if any, of these rules are the justificanda?

Scholars working in this field often have very loose conceptions of what they seek to justify. For example, it has been said that an 'express trust' is a 'facility', a 'legal structure', an 'amenity', or a 'device' that permits the pursuit of certain ends, and little attempt is made to go beyond these labels to identify particular legal rules as the objects of justification. Even when an effort is made to do this, convincing conceptions of these rules are not always forthcoming. For example, the objects for some justificatory projects have been identified as (i) a settlor's option or power to create an 'express trust', without any thought being given to the legal consequences flowing from an exercise of this option, (ii) a facility that produces 'outcomes' which, as a factual matter, may or may not flow from any given instance of an 'express trust', or (iii) a legal relation that is described in reductive and underinclusive terms. The problems with each of these approaches will be outlined in turn.

1. The settlor's power to create an 'express trust'

Sometimes, the object for justification is said to be the choice afforded to settlors and/or the power conferred on settlors to create an 'express trust'. A jurisdiction's 'recognition' of 'express trusts' and 'trusts law' is then said to be justified, for example, because settlor autonomy is promoted by giving her a choice as to how she deals with her property and giving legal effect to the choice that she makes. In some versions of this argument, the approach taken can be underinclusive and misunderstand the 'express trust' and the rules for trust creation.

[9] *Investec Trust (Guernsey) Ltd v Glenalla Properties Ltd* [2018] UKPC 7, [2019] AC 271 [59](i) (Lord Hodge). See also *Kelly v Mina* [2014] NSWCA 9 [103] (Leeming JA); *ACES Sogutlu Holdings Pty Ltd (in liq) v Commonwealth Bank of Australia* [2014] NSWCA 402, (2014) 89 NSWLR 209 [15]–[20] (Leeming JA, with whom Beazley P and MacFarlan JA agreed); *Agricultural Land Management Ltd v Jackson (No 2)* [2014] WASC 102, (2014) 285 FLR 121 [302] (Edelman J).

These rules define the existence and scope of the settlor's power to create an 'express trust' and they prioritise the choices she makes as a party who has the 'power to direct how [her] ... property should be dealt with'.[10] The rules typically require the settlor to define, while allowing her to choose, the content and detail of (a) what property will be held on trust, (b) who will have or eventually acquire an entitlement to the benefit of this property, or at least who will be given the opportunity to disclaim such an entitlement, and (c) who will be the trustee, or at least who will be given the opportunity to accept or disclaim that role.[11]

We agree that the priority afforded to the settlor's choices about these matters may be justified on the basis that it is her property which is being settled on trust. As we discuss further in Part III, we also consider that settlor autonomy may be enhanced rather than subverted by rules which invalidate attempts to create trusts that fail to comply with the foregoing requirements.

However, we would add that trust creation is not a wholly unilateral act of the settlor[12] and the existence of an 'express trust' and its terms can depend upon the actions of others. In saying this, we acknowledge that the rules for trust creation do not require a beneficiary's actions in manifesting her assent[13] and a settlor can unilaterally create an 'express trust' for unborn[14] or unknowing[15] beneficiaries, or for a charitable purpose. Nonetheless, there are other situations where the existence of an 'express trust' depends on the actions of others, and the terms are not solely determined by reference to the settlor's actions.

[10] *Re Duke of Norfolk's ST* [1981] 3 All ER 220, 229 (Fox LJ; Brightman and Cumming-Bruce LJJ agreeing). See also *Fitzpatrick v Waring* (1882) 11 LR Ir 35, 44 (Law LC): *Letterstedt v Broers* (1884) 9 App Cas 371 (PC) 386 (Lord Blackburn); *Nguyen v Phan (No 2)* [2015] VSC 634 [232] (Elliott J); M Bryan 'The Inferred Trust: An Unhappy Marriage of Contract and Trust?' (2016) 69 CLP 377, 395. There can be later settlors who choose to settle their property under the terms as pre-determined by the original settlor. A trust pension scheme, for example, will have multiple settlors, being the employers and/or employees as they contribute funds to the scheme. For each contribution, the imposition of the trust terms is a result of each settlor's exercise of power to settle their property on terms, even if these terms are pre-determined.

[11] For which see, eg, *Knight v Knight* (1840) 3 Beav 148, 172–74; 49 ER 58 (Lord Langdale MR); *Garrett v L'Estrange* (1911) 13 CLR 430, 433–34 (Griffith CJ; Barton and O'Connor JJ agreeing); *McPhail v Doulton* [1971] AC 424; *Byrnes v Kendle* [2011] HCA 26; (2011) 243 CLR 253 [49]–[65] (Gummow and Hayne JJ).

[12] There are judicial dicta to the contrary, eg 'trusts can be created (and often are created) by the unilateral act of the settlor without any involvement on the part of the beneficiaries': *Pleshakov v Sky Stream Corp* [2021] UKPC 15 [47] (Lord Sales). Scholars have also said that the intention to which an express trust responds is a 'unilateral' one: eg C Rickett, 'Instrumentalism in the Law of Trusts: The Disturbing Case of the Constructive Trust upon an Express Trust' (2016) 47 VUWLR 463, 466; Liew, 'Trusts: Modern Taxonomy and Autonomy' (n 3).

[13] *Lady Naas v Westminster Bank Ltd* [1940] AC 366 (HL) 403 (Lord Wright): 'the declaration of trust by the settlor depended not on the other party's consent any more than on mutual consideration. It depended on the act of the settlor in executing the settlement. The beneficiary might, it is true, disclaim but her acceptance was immaterial except perhaps as ruling out disclaimer'; see too 402 (Lord Wright), and 389 (Lord Russell). Different views have been expressed as to whether this is because a beneficiary's assent is an essential condition to trust creation that is presumed by law (see, eg, *Smith v Michelmores Trust Corp Ltd* [2021] EWHC 1425 (Ch), [2021] WTLR 1051 at [64]–[72] (HHJ Matthews); *Commissioner of Taxation v Carter* [2022] HCA 10; (2022) 399 ALR 521 [27]–[31] (Gageler, Gordon, Steward and Gleeson JJ)), or is not a condition to trust creation and is relevant only to show the absence of disclaimer (see, eg, *Carter* [33]–[48] (Edelman J)). On either view, the settlor does not have a unilateral power to create a trust and define its terms as a beneficiary's disclaimer will retrospectively apply to 'defeat' the legal consequences of the settlor's actions, *Commissioner of Taxation v Ramsden* [2005] FCAFC 39; (2005) 58 ATR 485 [45] (the Court), and see notes 18 and 19 below and accompanying text.

[14] *Mansell v Mansell* (1732) 2 P Wms 678, Cas t Talb 252; *Savage v Taylor* (1736) Cas t Talb 234, 239.

[15] *Rose v Rose* (1986) 7 NSWLR 679, 686.

Consider, for example, a trust by transfer, which cannot be created by the settlor unilaterally. The putative trustee must not disclaim her title and must also accept her role as trustee on the terms as defined by the settlor.[16] In the situation where a court appoints a new trustee to act instead,[17] the existence of the trust and its terms providing for who is the trustee depend on actions of those other than the settlor. Also, a settlor cannot force a beneficiary to accept, and a beneficiary has a power to disclaim her interest(s), an exercise of which retrospectively 'defeats [the settlor's] intention'.[18] Indeed, if all beneficiaries disclaim, the settlor's actions will be ineffective to create a trust.[19] The putative trustee and beneficiary accordingly have a say in the creation of a trust and its terms, *as between them*, and it follows that any justification of 'express trusts' which refers only to a settlor's power to create one is too narrowly focused.

There is an additional problem. Powers to create 'express trusts' (and rules of trust creation that define these powers) present one set of objects for justification. But whatever the justification(s) for these, a separate set of objects for justification must also be considered, namely, the *consequences* which flow from the parties' exercise of their powers: the 'express trust' and the legal rules that apply to the parties *after* the trust has been created. It cannot be assumed that whatever justifies the rules for trust creation also supports the rules which detail the legal results of this, on the basis that the parties implicitly choose these 'downstream' rules whenever they choose to create a trust. In other words, proving that the rules which define the existence and scope of powers to create 'express trusts' are justified does not also automatically prove that the rules which follow as a consequence of trust creation are also justified. The latter set of rules must be considered as part of a related but distinct justificatory exercise.

2. A 'facility' that produces desirable outcomes

Sometimes scholars speak of the 'express trust' as a 'facility' or 'legal framework' that produces a social effect or outcome, and/or a legal effect, such as benefiting some person (or purpose); affording the settlor choice(s) not otherwise available, such as splitting legal and equitable title to separating the 'benefit' of the trust property from its control and management. There are problems with this as well.

[16] If the settlor complies with the rules for transfer of title to the putative trustee title will pass, and in the event of disclaimer of title or non-acceptance of trusteeship, title will be held on an automatic resulting trust. See further: *A-G v Lady Downing* (1767) Wilm 1, 23–25, 97 ER 1, 9–10 (Wilmot CJ); *Townson v Tickell* (1819) 3 B & A 31, 37–40; 106 ER 575; *Mallott v Wilson* [1903] 2 Ch 393; *Raftland Pty Ltd v Commissioner of Taxation* [2006] FCA 109 [66] (Kiefel J).

[17] In addition to the court's inherent jurisdiction, there is a statutory power: see, eg, Trustee Act 1925 (UK), ss 36–41; Trustee Act 1925 (NSW), s 70.

[18] *Ramsden* (n 13) [45]. As to disclaimer by a beneficiary, see generally: *Lady Naas* (n 13) 396; *Federal Commissioner of Taxation v Cornell* (1946) 73 CLR 394, 401–02 (the Court); *Stratton v IRC* [1958] ch 42 (CA) 54–55; *Re Paradise Motor Co Ltd* [1968] 1 WLR 1125 (CA) 1143; *Carroll v Toronto-Dominion Bank* [2021] ONCA 38, (2021) 63 ETR (4th) 1 [27] (Paciocco JA); *Smith* (n 13) [64]–[72]; *Carter* (n 13) [46]–[48]. Discretionary objects have the same power of disclaimer; *Re Gulbenkian Settlements (No 2)* [1970] ch 408 (Ch) 418. See further: P Matthews, 'The Constitution of Disclaimed Trusts Inter Vivos' [1981] Conv 141; N Crago 'Principles of Disclaimer of Gifts' (1999) 28 UWALR 65.

[19] See also YK Liew and C Mitchell, 'The Creation of Express Trusts' (2017) 11 J Eq 133, 152–55. Albeit in the case of a transfer from the settlor to putative trustee, the settlor's actions may mean the transferee holds on an automatic resulting trust for the settlor.

First, justifications that rest on the desirability of social outcomes and legal effects necessarily depend on a balancing exercise that weighs up both the desirable *and the undesirable* outcomes that may be produced by any given 'express trust'.[20] Typically, however, it is left unexplained whether any such calculation has taken place and, if so, what yardstick has been used to measure the relevant outcomes and weigh them off against one another. Typically, also, scholars who make such arguments do not identify any particular legal rule as their justificandum. The implicit assumption is that the stated outcomes produced by 'the trust' justify, or fail to justify, some unspecified legal rules and their effect. But it is hard to accept that these outcomes are produced by 'express trusts', let alone their relative desirability, without knowing which rules of 'trusts law' are said to produce which outcomes.

A second problem is that the outcomes identified by scholars may not be unique to 'express trusts'. There are a range of other power relationships, such as that between a principal and an agent with a power of attorney, or some other power over the principal's property, that can produce the same outcomes of affording choices to property owners, including a choice to confer some sort of 'benefits' from property onto people other than the titleholders, or of separating the beneficial enjoyment from the control or management of property. To the extent that an 'express trust' produces effects that are also produced by other legal relations, 'arrangements' or 'facilities', the question arises whether a jurisdiction's 'recognition' of 'the trust' is justified as well.

A third problem concerns the focus on the 'benefits' which are often said to flow from 'the trust' or define its overarching purpose. 'Benefit' is an elusive concept. Not all 'express trusts' necessarily benefit a person (or a purpose) in any of the ways assumed by scholars, leaving a justificatory lacuna for trusts which fail to do this. For example, 'express trusts' do not all benefit a beneficiary in the sense that she receives title to property from the trustee (accepting—which is not a given—that a beneficiary would be 'benefited' by receipt). Whether a trust confers a 'benefit' in this sense may depend on the size of the trust fund. For example, if a trust fund depreciates in value to the extent that it becomes impossible to distribute property, any justification of 'the trust' that depends on this outcome being achieved does not apply.

Nor will every trust 'benefit' a beneficiary in the sense of creating an entitlement to the benefit of trust property. Some trusts must eventually create this entitlement (assuming the sufficiency of the trust fund).[21] In the meantime, however, an entitlement to benefit will depend on the parties' actions in defining the trust terms, which may *or may not* create this entitlement at any given moment. This is explained in *DKLR Holding Co (No 2) Pty Ltd v Commissioner of Stamp Duties*[22] where Hope JA states that the beneficiary's 'interest is essentially a right to compel the trustee to hold and use his

[20] See, eg, Bennett and Hofri-Winogradow (n 3); Dagan and Samet, 'What's Wrong With Massively Discretionary Trusts' (n 3).

[21] As the rules against remoteness of vesting will require an entitlement to the benefit of trust property, eventually, to vest in a beneficiary's favour: eg *Cadell v Palmer* (1883) 1 Cl & Fin 372, 6 ER 956, as modified by statute, eg the Perpetuities and Accumulations Act 2009 (UK) and the Perpetuities Act 1984 (NSW), unless an exception applies, such as for charitable trusts and pension trusts.

[22] [1980] 1 NSWLR 510, 518–20.

legal rights *in accordance with the terms of the trust*' and a beneficiary will only have an entitlement to the benefit of trust property *where the trust terms so provide*.[23] Any justification that depends on the existence of the latter entitlement cannot apply for so long as it is suspended under the terms of a given trust.[24]

Hope JA's dicta also point up an important difference between the beneficiary's right to receive property and the beneficiary's right to due administration of the trust, meaning a right to compel the trustee to hold and use her legal rights *in accordance with the terms of the trust*.[25] The latter right is held by the beneficiary *for her own benefit*, or *beneficially*, in the sense that she need not use it in any particular way but can exercise the right, or not, as she likes, including in a self-interested way. In this respect, the beneficiary's position differs from that of a trustee who has the same right to due administration against a co-trustee, or a former trustee, but does *not* hold this 'beneficially' because she must exercise it in accordance with the trust terms, and may also be unable to exercise it in a self-interested fashion.[26]

All of this suggests that justifications of 'express trusts' which identify their object of justification as a 'facility' to produce 'benefits' lack force if they do not explain clearly which 'benefits' produced by trusts are being referred to and how this effect is achieved.

3. A relationship based on rights and duties

A third approach is to settle on a conception of the 'express trust' as *a legal relationship* between the trustee and beneficiary. Of the three approaches we have discussed, we believe that this is the most promising. At least in the majority of common law jurisdictions, it is a good fit with the way that judges, practitioners, and doctrinal scholars think about 'express trusts',[27] and in fact we argue for a more complex version of the basic idea in later parts of this chapter. However, we consider that this idea is under-developed in the theoretical literature, and there are some problems with the way in which versions of it have been presented.

[23] ibid 520 (emphasis added). See too the Trusts Act 2019 (NZ), s 26.

[24] For example, where there is a non-exhaustive power of appointment and in default of appointment an exhaustive power to appoint to an open class of objects: J Hudson 'Mere and Other Discretionary Objects in Australia' in YK Liew and M Harding (eds), *Asia-Pacific Trusts Law: Theory and Practice in Context* (Hart 2021) ch 2.

[25] For the principle see, eg, *Youyang Pty Ltd v Minter Ellison Morris Fletcher* [2003] HCA 15, (2003) 212 CLR 484 [32]; *AIB Group (UK) plc v Mark Redler & Co Solicitors* [2014] UKSC 58, [2015] AC 1503 [64]; *Akers v Samba Financial Group* [2017] UKSC 6, [2017] AC 424 [82]. For judicial descriptions of the principle as one that imposes a 'duty of due administration' on trustees and gives beneficiaries 'rights of due administration' see, eg, *Spellson v George* (1987) 11 NSWLR 300, 315–16; *Chief Commissioner of Stamp Duties (NSW) v Buckle* (1998) 192 CLR 226, 242; *ASIC v Carey (No 6)* [2006] FCA 814, (2006) 233 ALR 475, [30]; *Whaley v Whaley* [2011] EWCA Civ 617, [2011] 2 FCR 323 [112]. On behalf of the Crown, the Attorney-General holds the right to due administration of charitable trusts.

[26] *Young v Murphy* [1996] 1 VR 279, 281–83 (Brooking J).

[27] See, eg, *Royal Brunei Airlines Sdn Bhd v Tan* [1995] 2 AC 378, 386 (Lord Nicholls); *Lewis v Condon* [2013] NSWCA 204, (2013) 85 NSWLR 99 [84] (Leeming JA); *Aussiegolfa Pty Ltd (Trustee) v Commissioner of Taxation* [2018] FCAFC 122, (2018) 264 FCR 587 [140] (Moshinsky J); *Valard Construction Ltd v Bird Construction Co* 2018 SCC 8, [2018] 1 SCR 224 [58] (Brown J); M Leeming, 'What is a Trust?' (2008) 31 Aust Bar Rev 211; R Chambers, 'Distrust: Our Fear of Trusts in the Commercial World' (2010) 63 CLP 631, 637–38; D Coshott, 'Understanding and Reforming the Trustee's Rights of Indemnity' (2019) 33 TLI 45. cf *In re Scott, decd* [1948] SASR 193, 196 (Mayo J): a trust is '[a] ... duty or ... aggregate accumulation of obligations that rest upon a person described as a trustee'.

Some scholars have focused on a particular feature of the legal relationship between trustee and beneficiary such as the 'trustee's obligation of confidence' or 'the trustee's obligation to benefit the beneficiary' and the beneficiary's correlative right to 'enforce the trust'. However, the rights and duties on which such arguments are focused are not always described with enough specificity for the discussion to be illuminating. Whether or not it is justified to fix a trustee with a 'duty of confidence' or a duty to supply the beneficiaries with 'benefits' can be imponderable if it is left unclear what these duties entail and how they are enforced.

Another point is that an idea of the 'express trust' as a legal relationship necessarily entails the existence of enforceable rights and duties between the trustee and the beneficiary, but in that respect 'the trust' is no different from other right-duty relationships such as those between contracting parties or those between tortfeasors and tort victims. Hence, something more needs to be said about the content of the rights and duties that are understood to make up 'the trust', and the interplay between these, if 'the trust' is to appear as a distinct object for justification. Accordingly, the question arises, of what this 'more' might be?

B. What 'Express Trusts' Are

'The express trust' is not a single legal proposition, nor even several legal propositions working independently of one another, but (i) a set of legal propositions concerning the trust parties' rights, powers, permissions, constraints, and duties; (ii) which interact with one another and with the background rules of property law to produce the system-level effect of redefining the trustee's authority as titleholder; (iii) the existence of which depends on the voluntary actions of the settlor, trustee, and beneficiary and the legal rules that give legal effect to these parties' actions. We discuss each of these aspects of our conception of 'express trusts' further in the rest of this Part II.B.

1. A set of legal propositions

An 'express trust' is a set of legal propositions that interact with one another, and with the background rules of property law which establish the trustee's title to property, to produce an overall system-level effect. To perceive that effect, one needs to have an idea of the constituent set of legal propositions. However, if one tries to identify a minimum set that must be true for any and all 'express trusts', this turns out to be a difficult project. This is for two reasons.

First, the propositions that collectively constitute an 'express trust' vary from one jurisdiction to the next.[28] Jurisdictions take different views about what 'express trusts' are and what propositions must hold good for such 'trusts' to work effectively. A set of

[28] Penner 'An Untheory' (n 3) 664–66 argues that the 'core' and 'constituent' principles that make up 'the trust' are almost never in dispute because it is an 'artificial facilitative construct'. We agree with Professor Penner that 'the trust' is a set of legal propositions, but we part company from him insofar as we say that jurisdictions can and do differ on what they think 'the trust' is and on which propositions are necessary to its construct.

propositions that counts as an 'express trust' in one jurisdiction may not count as an 'express trust' in another.[29]

Second, even within a single jurisdiction like Australia or England, 'express trusts' arise across a wide range of social, economic, and relational contexts, and there are differences in the number and content of the legal propositions that must hold good for particular types of trust to exist. This variety is reflected in the range of labels used to identify different combinations of legal propositions, examples being: 'simple' or 'bare'[30] express trusts, 'fixed trusts', 'discretionary trusts', 'active trusts',[31] 'unit trusts', 'commercial trusts',[32] 'traditional trusts',[33] 'trading trusts', and 'family trusts'.[34] While they are pervasive, these descriptive labels do not assist in identifying any given minimum set of legal propositions that must be present for each type of trust. The labels lack a 'constant, fixed normative meaning'[35] and are sometimes 'plagued with terminological indeterminacy'.[36]

For these reasons, we do not attempt to describe the minimum set of legal propositions that must be true for an 'express trust' to exist in every jurisdiction. Instead, we make the different point that whatever propositions must hold good in any jurisdiction, an 'express trust' always presents multiple objects for justification, because a trust is always a set of legal propositions that interact with one another, and with the rules of property law which establish a trustee's title to property, to produce a particular effect.

To illustrate this point, we will describe the legal propositions that are generally agreed to make up an 'express trust' in Australia and England.[37] They are (a) the trustee holds title to specified property and as a consequence 'has all the powers [and other

[29] A point frequently made in relation to the conception of 'the trust' endorsed by various offshore jurisdictions. See, eg, D Waters, 'Reaching for the Sky: Taking Trust Laws to the Limit' in DJ Hayton (ed), *Extending the Boundaries of Trusts and Similar Ring-Fenced Funds* (Kluwer Law International 2002), 243; DJ Hayton, 'Developing the Obligation Characteristic of the Trust' (2001) 117 LQR 96. This point also has implications for whether a jurisdiction will recognise a given legal arrangement as a 'trust' that is recognised as such in another jurisdiction: DJ Hayton, '"Trusts" in Private International Law' in *Collected Courses of the Hague Academy of International Law*, vol 366 (Brill, Nijhoff Leiden 2014); D Waters, 'The Institution of the Trust in Civil and Common Law' (1995) 252 Recueil des cours 117, 427–35; 'The Distinctive Characteristics of the Anglo-Saxon Trust', in STEP France, *Trust et fiducie: concurrents ou compléments* (Academy & Finance, Geneva 2008) 23 et seq; 'The Future of the Trust from a Worldwide Perspective' in DJ Hayton (ed), *The International Trust* (3rd edn, Jordans 2011) ch 17; see also M Lupoi, *Trusts: A Comparative Study* (CUP 2000).

[30] See, eg, *Christie v Ovington* [1875] 1 Ch D 279, 281 (Hall VC); *Morgan v Swansea Urban Sanitary Authority* (1878) 9 Ch D 582, 585; *Herdegen v FCT* (1988) 84 ALR 271, 281–82 (Gummow J).

[31] *Chief Commissioner of Stamp Duties v ISPT Pty Ltd* (1998) 45 NSWLR 639, 651–52 (Mason P).

[32] *Target Holdings Ltd v Redferns* [1996] AC 421, 434–36 (Lord Browne-Wilkinson); *AIB* (n 25) [70] (Lord Toulson), [127] (Lord Reed).

[33] *Target* (n 32) 434–36; *AIB* (n 25) [70], [127].

[34] We could add to this list various statutory definitions of specific forms of trusts, such as a 'trading trust' under section 102N and a 'unit trust' under section 202A of the Income Tax Assessment Act 1936 (Cth).

[35] *CPT Custodian Pty Ltd v Commissioner of State Revenue* [2005] HCA 53; (2005) 224 CLR 98, [15] (the Court) in relation to a 'unit trust' and 'discretionary trust'. See also M Leeming, '"Chameleon-hued Words": A Note on Discretionary Trusts' (2015) 89 ALJ 371. Similar comments have been made in relation to a 'bare trust' in *Fischer v Nemeske Pty Ltd* [2016] HCA 11, (2016) 257 CLR 615 [118] (Gordon J), and a 'fixed trust' in *ElecNet (Aust) Pty Ltd v Commissioner of Taxation* [2016] HCA 51, (2016) 259 CLR 73, [88] (Nettle J).

[36] *Fischer* (n 35) [118] (Gordon J) in relation to a 'discretionary trust' and 'bare trust'. A 'bare trust' is described as being subject to 'academic controversy' in *ISPT* (n 31) 651–52 (Mason P). See also *Byrnes v Kendle* (n 11) [21] (French CJ).

[37] As we have said in the introduction of this volume 'Express Trusts: Concepts, Justifications and Boundaries', we are not engaged in a prescriptive exercise here: we are merely describing what lawyers in our jurisdictions generally understand to be necessary for an express trust to exist.

legal entitlements] incidental to ownership';[38] (b) the trustee is not free to use those legal entitlements for her own benefit in the way she could if no trust existed as she must 'preserve the assets of the trust except insofar as the terms of the trust permit [her] to do otherwise',[39] and the trustee must exercise, or not exercise, those entitlements in specified ways,[40] and account for her stewardship of the trust property;[41] and (c) a beneficiary has a 'basic right ... to have the trust duly administered in accordance with the provisions of the trust instrument, if any, and the general law',[42] sometimes called a right to due administration.

The detailed content of these propositions can vary with the parties' intentions as manifested by their actions. Depending on these, further legal propositions may also hold good, including: (d) the trustee's conduct may be constrained by additional requirements, for example, she may owe a duty of care, a fiduciary duty, and/or a duty to consider the exercise of her powers; (e) a beneficiary may have an entitlement to the benefit of trust property,[43] and the trustee may owe a correlative duty to give effect to that entitlement; (f) beneficiaries may[44] also have a power to call for the trust property, the exercise of which power requires the trustee to transfer title to the trust property to them; and (g) a trustee, beneficiary, or third party may have a power to re-define the existence or content of the constituent legal propositions, eg by changing the trustee or beneficiaries, by varying or ending a beneficiary's entitlement to the benefit of trust property, or by authorising actions by the trustee that would otherwise be unauthorised.

The existence and content of these further propositions depend on choices made by the settlor, trustee, and beneficiary and the legal meaning which is attributed to their actions. For example, a trustee's fiduciary duties can be excluded or modified by the parties.[45] Similarly, and as noted in Part II.A.2, a beneficiary's

[38] *Carter Holt Harvey Woodproducts Australia Pty Ltd v Commonwealth* [2019] HCA 20, (2019) 268 CLR 524, [82] (Bell, Gageler and Nettle JJ); *DKLR Holding* (n 22) 518 'the trustee has ... all the rights of the absolute owner in fee simple ...'.

[39] *AIB* (n 25) [51].

[40] cf *Harries v Church Commissioners* [1992] 1 WLR 1241, 1246 (Nicholls V-C): 'It is axiomatic that charity trustees, in common with all other trustees, are concerned to further the purposes of the trust of which they have accepted the office of trustee. That is their duty. To enable them the better to discharge that duty, trustees have powers vested in them. Those powers must be exercised for the purpose for which they have been given: to further the purposes of the trust.'

[41] *Doss v Doss* (1843) 3 Moo Ind App 175, 196–97; 18 ER 464; *Associated Alloys Pty Ltd v ACN 001 452 106 Pty Ltd (In Liquidation)* [2000] HCA 25, (2000) 202 CLR 588 [54]–[56].

[42] *Target* (n 32) 434.

[43] This entitlement *may* mean an object has a right to possession: J Penner 'The (True) Nature of a Beneficiary's Equitable Proprietary Interest Under a Trust' (2014) 26 CJLJ 473. This entitlement is sometimes referred to as 'equitable ownership'.

[44] Under the rule associated with *Saunders v Vautier* (1841) 4 Beav 115; 41 ER 482. This power depends on other conditions, such as the trustee's indemnity for expenses being satisfied, the beneficiary/ies being sui juris (*CPT* (n 35) [42]–[44], [47]; J Harris 'Trust, Power and Duty' (1971) 87 LQR 31), and the nature and type of trust property allowing for division without prejudice to the interests of another beneficiary; *Beck v Henley* [2014] NSWCA 201 [37]–[38]. This proposition does not form part of the 'trust' in other jurisdictions, eg many American states which have followed the decision in *Claflin v Claflin* 149 Mass 19, 20 NE 454 (1889).

[45] *Space Investments Ltd v Canadian Imperial Bank of Commerce Trust Co (Bahamas) Ltd* [1986] 1 WLR 1072 (PC) 1075; *Re Beatty (deceased)* [1990] 1 WLR 1503, 1506; *Citibank NA v MBIA Assurance SA* [2007] EWCA Civ 11, [2007] 1 All ER (Comm) 475, 497; *Re Lehman Brothers International (Europe) (in administration)* [2010] EWHC 2914 (Ch) [225](iii) and [227]–[247]; *Whalley v Whalley* [2011] EWCA Civ 617, [2011] WTLR 1267 [51]; *ElecNet* (n 35) [50]; *Barnsley v Noble* [2016] EWCA Civ 799, [2017] ch 191 [16].

entitlement to the benefit of trust property will exist only when the parties so intend.[46]

Two bodies of scholarship discussing the nature of 'express trusts' in common law jurisdictions also have a bearing on how these legal propositions are understood, but neither is directly relevant to our question, namely, what is being justified by those who seek to justify 'the trust'. First, there is a debate about whether an 'express trust' should be conceived in wholly obligational terms or as a proprietary right or as some hybrid interest.[47] This is an interesting question but deciding how one should classify the legal relations that constitute 'the trust' is a project which presupposes that one has already identified these relations and the rules that give them shape and effect—and it is this work in which we are engaged here.

Second, it has been discussed whether there is an 'irreducible core' of trustee duties and correlative beneficiary rights, a proposition which was originally floated by David Hayton,[48] has been explored by other scholars,[49] was endorsed by Millett LJ in the course of adjudicating on the validity of a trustee exemption clause,[50] and fed into the two-fold classification of 'mandatory' and 'default' trustee duties that appears in the New Zealand Trusts Act 2019.[51] Proponents of this idea have not argued, however, that an 'irreducible core' of trustee duties and beneficiary rights (whatever the content of this may be) is coterminous with 'the express trust'. They argue that such rights and duties are necessary for a 'trust' to exist, but they accept that more is needed and so the question remains of what this is.

(a) The 'trust terms'

Pausing here, we must distinguish the legal propositions which form part of an 'express trust' from the 'trust terms'. When courts and commentators refer to the 'trust terms' they usually have one of two things in mind: either (i) the detailed content of the legal relations which the trust parties intend should exist between them or (ii) statements of this content which appear in written documentation.[52] The first of these usages is

[46] *DKLR* (n 22), 520. See also *Carter* (n 38) [82] (Bell, Gageler and Nettle JJ) [emphasis added]; see also [27] (Kiefel CJ, Keane and Edelman JJ).

[47] A Scott, 'The Nature of the Rights of the Cestui Que Trust' (1917) 17 Columbia L Rev 269; H Stone, 'The Nature of the Rights of the Cestui Que Trust' (1917) 17 Columbia L Rev 467; D Waters, 'The Nature of the Trust Beneficiary's Interest' (1967) 45 Can Bar Rev 219; B McFarlane and R Stevens, 'The Nature of Equitable Property' (2010) 4 J Eq 1; S Gardner '"Persistent Rights" Appraised' in N Hopkins (ed), *Modern Studies in Property Law*, vol 7 (Hart 2013); Penner, 'The (True) Nature of a Beneficiary's Equitable Proprietary Interest'(n 43); EC Zaccaria, 'The Nature of the Beneficiary's Right under a Trust: Proprietary Right, Purely Personal Right or Right Against a Right?' (2019) 135 LQR 460.

[48] DJ Hayton, 'The Irreducible Core Content of Trusteeship' in AJ Oakley (ed), *Trends in Contemporary Trust Law* (Clarendon Press 1996) ch 3.

[49] JH Langbein, 'Mandatory Rules in the Law of Trusts' (n 3), esp 1121–26; AS Butler and DJ Flinn, 'What is the Least that We Can Expect of a Trustee? Exclusion of Trustee Duties and Exemption of Trustee Liability' [2010] NZLR 459; D Fox, 'Non-excludable Trustee Duties' (2011) 17 T&T 17; C Mitchell, 'Good Faith, Self-Denial and Mandatory Trustee Duties' (2018) 32 TLI 92; G McLay, 'How to Read New Zealand's New Trusts Act 2019' (2020) 13 J Eq 325.

[50] *Armitage v Nurse* [1998] Ch 241, 253–54; *Segelov v Ernst & Young Services Pty Ltd* [2015] NSWCA 156; (2015) 89 NSWLR 431 [145]–[146]; *Crossman v Sheahan* [2016] NSWCA 200; (2016) 115 ACSR 130 [307]–[308].

[51] Trusts Act 2019 (NZ), ss 22–39.

[52] Nor are they a written representation in the case of an oral declaration that is later represented in writing.

illustrated by the statement that '[perhaps the] ... most important duty of a trustee is to obey the terms of the trust',[53] the second by the dictum that '[t]he basic right of a beneficiary is to have the trust duly administered in accordance with the provisions of the trust instrument'.[54]

Although they are easily confused, these are different ideas. An 'express trust' and its terms are constituted and defined by the parties' actions and given legal effect by the rules which govern the creation and operation of the trust. The meanings of the parties' actions in expressing their intentions for how the trustee should and should not hold and use her title are not the same as the documentary evidence of those actions. The trust and its terms do not cease to exist, for example, on the destruction of a trust deed (or any other documentary evidence) recording what the settlor intends and what the trustee and beneficiary give their consent to.

In cases such as *Target Holdings Ltd v Redferns* and *Youyang Pty Ltd v Minter Ellison Morris Fletcher*, the 'trust terms' are understood to define a sphere of permission within which the trustee is permitted to exercise her powers as titleholder.[55] This effect can be achieved in different ways. The trustee may be *directed* to exercise her power as titleholder to distribute trust property to a beneficiary on a certain date;[56] or she may be *prohibited* from transferring property to a named person;[57] or she may be *permitted* to exercise her power as a titleholder in particular ways, for example to transfer trust funds to a beneficiary or to a third party to pay trust expenses. The sphere of permission may be very wide, as occurs in many discretionary trusts;[58] or it may be very narrow as in the case of 'bare trusts' where the trustee is effectively holding title to trust property at the direction of the beneficiary. The rule that a trustee owes a 'duty to obey the trust terms'[59] thus operates as a general principle of trust law that is given detailed content on a case by case basis according to what the parties intend and consent to: as stated in *ElecNet (Aust) Pty Ltd v Commissioner of Taxation*, the parties' legal relations are 'not determined by ... [a] general designation, but by the operative terms' of the trust.[60]

There are different ways in which trust terms may come into existence. Sometimes the parties may expressly state what they intend and consent to, and indeed there are some terms which *must be* expressly stated or there will not be a trust at all, owing to the

[53] *Youyang* (n 25) [32].

[54] *Target* (n 32) 434.

[55] See too *Head v Gould* [1898] 2 Ch 250, 268 (Kekewich J); *Ali v Dinc* [2020] EWHC 3055 (Ch), [2021] 2 P & CR 19 [318] (Sarah Worthington QC (Hon)): 'Consider trustees holding property for X on trusts which expressly allow, or oblige, the trustees to give the property to Y or sell it to Z. If the trustees act according to those powers or duties, X will have no proprietary claims to priority against Y or Z: X's prior interests will have been overreached, perhaps replaced by interests in the sale proceeds from Z, but all will depend on the terms of the trust'; *CPT* (n 35) [10]. See also the *Hague Trusts Convention*, art 2, 'the trustee has the power and the duty, in respect of which he is accountable, to manage, employ or dispose of the assets in accordance with the terms of the trust and the special duties imposed upon him by law'.

[56] Whether these are derived from the settlor's intention, an exercise of power by a beneficiary to call for the trust property, or rules against perpetuities and accumulations requiring the eventual vesting and transfer of trust property.

[57] *Gadsdon v Gadsdon* [2003] WASC 48 [61], [86], [101].

[58] L Smith 'Massively Discretionary Trusts' (2017) 70 CLP 17.

[59] *Space Investments* (n 45) 1075.

[60] *ElecNet* (n 35) [50]. See also *Kauter v Hilton* (1953) 90 CLR 86, 98; *Segelov* (n 50) [130]; *Valard Construction* (n 27) [58]–[60].

rules of trust creation that require a settlor to define the content of certain propositions, and the trustee and beneficiary to consent to these, such as the identity of the trust property, the object(s) of the trust and trustee(s).[61] Other terms, though, are supplied by the operation of statutory or equitable rules that require or permit a trustee to do certain things with the trust property. These are not terms to which the parties expressly consent, but arise as a result of actions taken by the parties which bring trusts into existence and thereby engage the application of general law to their arrangements in the absence of further actions to exclude or modify the default propositions.[62] Examples are statutory rules[63] which provide that a trustee has powers to invest trust property or may use trust property to pay trust expenses: whenever an express trust is created these powers will vest in the trustee unless the parties state otherwise.

It seems that the distinction between these two modes of creating trust terms is what Lord Browne-Wilkinson had in mind in *Target Holdings Ltd v Redferns*[64] when he distinguished between legal propositions flowing from 'the provisions of the trust instrument' and propositions arising out of the 'general law'. The means by which particular trust terms are created differ, and they covary to differing extents with the actions taken by the parties, and the way in which they express their intentions. But the common thread that runs through all 'trust terms' is that they define the ways in which a trustee should and should not exercise her power as the titleholder of trust property.

2. That operate as system

We think it is helpful to understand the operation and effect of the set of legal propositions that we have identified as the 'express trust' by employing the idea of a complex adaptive system. As noted in the introduction of this book 'Express Trusts: Concepts, Justifications and Boundarie', the potential of this idea to support conceptual analysis of private law rules and propositions has been explained by Henry Smith. A system is composed of two or more constituent parts. It is an adaptive system if one or more of these parts interact(s) with other parts and/or with the environment within which the system exists. A system is complex, and not merely complicated, when these interactions produce system-level effects which may be unpredictable and which cannot be identified merely by asking what is the aggregate sum of the effects of each constituent part acting on its own. It is therefore said that the properties of a complex adaptive system are 'emergent', meaning that they emerge from the constituent parts and the interactions between these, and sometimes also from their interactions with their environment, which may itself comprise another system or systems. When analysing

[61] These rules for trusts creation are discussed further in pt II.B.3 below.

[62] In the contractual context, the terms are described as being 'synthesised' from general law, rather than from social facts, such as the parties' actions: F Wilmot-Smith 'Term Limits: What is a Term?' (2019) 39 OJLS 705, 708–12.

[63] Trustee Act 2000 (UK), ss 3 (trustee may invest trust property), 31 (trustee's indemnity for expenses); Trustee Act 1925 (NSW), ss 14 (trustee may invest trust property), 59(4) (trustee's indemnity for expenses).

[64] *Target* (n 32) 434. See also *Hague Trusts Convention*, art 2, '... the trustee has the power and the duty, in respect of which he is accountable, to manage, employ or dispose of the assets in accordance with the terms of the trust and the special duties imposed upon him by law'.

complex adaptive systems it may be an error to focus too narrowly on the properties of their component parts because the complexity of the system means that such a reductionist assessment will fail to account for its emergent properties.

Applying these ideas to the 'express trust' and 'trusts law', one might therefore say that their system-level effect is a product of the interactions between each constituent legal proposition and rule that affects the trust parties and other parties with whom they deal, *as well as* the interactions between all of these propositions and rules and another legal system, which consists of the rules of property law which generate the trustee's legal entitlements as titleholder. It is not possible to understand the effect of each component of the 'trust system' by examining it in isolation and without considering its interactions with the others. Nor can the effect of the whole 'trust system' be understood merely by identifying and aggregating the individual effects of each constituent proposition and rule of trusts law. This is because the overall or system-level effect is emergent: it is a product of each proposition, the interactions between them, and the interactions between the trust system and the underlying system of property law that generates the trustee's title.

The system-level effect of the propositions and rules which we identify in Part II.B.1 as forming the 'express trust' and rules of 'trusts law', and their interactions with one another and the rules of property law, is *the redefinition of the trustee's authority as titleholder.* This effect is what people refer to when they speak of an 'express trust' being 'annexed', 'impressed', or 'engrafted' on to (and not out of) the trustee's title to trust property.[65] These descriptions do not mean that the existence of the trust redefines or limits the trustee's *powers or other legal entitlements as titleholder*. The legal propositions that constitute the 'express trust' do not change the rules of property law which define what the trustee can and cannot do, or the legal rights or privileges that the trustee holds in her capacity as owner of the trust property. An 'express trust' does *not*, for example, change the rights and privileges that the trustee holds as titleholder, or the scope of the trustee's powers as titleholder so as to require her compliance with the trust terms in order to deal with her title. The scope of the trustee's power(s) to deal with her title, for example, remains defined by the relevant principles of law, equity, and statute that determine the assignability of the subject property. A trustee can exercise her powers as titleholder even in ways that are contrary to the trust terms,[66] with the result that a third-party recipient can acquire title to trust property which has been transferred to her in an unauthorised transaction provided that the trustee satisfies the background rules of property law pertaining to the transfer of the subject property.

[65] Language used in, eg, *DKLR* (n 22) 519, reversed on other grounds, (1982) 149 CLR 431, where the trust obligations are described as being 'impressed' upon the trustee's title to trust property, 474; *Re Transphere Pty Ltd* (1986) 5 NSWLR 309, 311 (McLelland J); *First City Monument Bank Plc v Zumax Nigeria Ltd* [2019] EWCA Civ 294, [2019] WTLR 511 [16] (Newey LJ); *Commissioner of State Revenue v Rojoda Pty Ltd* [2020] HCA 7, (2020) 268 CLR 281 [44] (the Court); *Chalcot Training Ltd v Ralph* [2021] EWCA Civ 795, [2021] BTC 18 [62] (Lewison LJ).

[66] The trustee's ability to exercise her power as titleholder despite non-compliance with the trust terms is noted in: *Rolled Steel Products (Holdings) Ltd v British Steel Corp* [1986] Ch 246, 303 (Browne-Wilkinson LJ); *Akers* (n 25) [51] (Lord Mance).

While the 'express trust' does not affect the trustee's title and incidental legal entitlements, it may mean that sometimes the legal consequences of a trustee's exercise of power as titleholder are susceptible to equitable relief, including against a trustee or third-party recipient. This is because the overall effect of the trust is that the trustee's *authority as titleholder* is redefined.[67] Like other equitable rules that can be understood as meta-law,[68] the legal propositions that constitute any given 'express trust' control how the trustee uses the legal entitlements she holds as the titleholder of the trust property. It is in this sense that the trust is 'annexed to', 'impressed onto', or 'engrafted onto' the trustee's title.

The trustee is thus in a different position from other titleholders whose authority is not conditioned by compliance with a set of terms and who are free to exercise their legal entitlements in any way they wish and for purposes of their own choosing. The trustee is different because her authority, understood as her ability to lawfully exercise her legal entitlements as titleholder, is circumscribed. A trustee cannot not lawfully exercise her rights, powers, or other legal entitlements in whatever way she chooses, because she must hold and use her title in compliance with the trust terms. The trustee's compliance is enforced by her duty to account and the personal and proprietary liabilities she can incur in cases of non-compliance, and third parties may also incur liabilities in cases where a trustee exercises her legal entitlements as titleholder in an unauthorised way.

In referring to the 'lawfulness' of a trustee's action, we are not saying that the trust impacts upon the legal effectiveness of the trustee's exercise of her powers and other legal entitlements as titleholder. As mentioned in this Part already, an 'express trust' does not impact on the content and operation of the rules that provide for how a trustee can exercise her legal entitlements as titleholder and does not impact upon the lawfulness of a trustee's action in this sense. The trust does not, for example, disable or disempower the trustee from exercising her power to transfer title to the trust property. Indeed, equity's remedies are needed precisely because the trust does not redefine the powers, rights, and other legal entitlements that constitute the trustee's title. The trust (only) affects the lawfulness of a trustee's action insofar as it is a set of legal propositions that 'governs the exercise of [the trustee's] legal capacity as legal owner of the property'.[69]

'Express trusts' and 'trusts law' do not constitute a wholly self-contained system, but one that exists within and alongside other systems of legal propositions and rules. Like other systems generated by equitable rules that operate as meta-law, the trust system

[67] The core conceptual distinction between a power-holder's ability to effect an intended change to the legal status of another and the lawfulness of the power-holder's action(s) in the exercise of a power is obscured when a '(legal) power' is confused with 'authority'. This distinction is discussed in: W Seavey, 'The Rationale of Agency' (1920) 29 Yale LJ 859, 861; A Corbin, 'The Authority of an Agent: Definition' (1925) 34 Yale LJ 788, 794; M Raczynska, *The Law of Tracing in Commercial Transactions* (OUP 2018) pt 1.4.3; J Hudson, 'Equity's Gloss on Authority' in S Elliott and B McFarlane (eds), *Equity Today: 150 Years After the Judicature Reforms* (Hart 2023).

[68] See, eg, B McFarlane, 'Form and Substance in Equity' in A Robertson and J Goudkamp (eds), *Form and Substance in the Law of Obligations* (Hart 2019) ch 9; H Smith, 'Equity as Meta-Law' (2021) 130 Yale Law Journal 1050, 1054; J Hudson, B McFarlane and C Mitchell, *Hayton, McFarlane and Mitchell on Equity & Trusts* (15th edn, Sweet & Maxwell 2022) ch 1.

[69] *Wellington Capital Limited v Australian Securities and Investments Commission* [2014] HCA 43; (2014) 254 CLR 288 [60] (Gageler J), see also [40] (French CJ, Crennan, Kiefel and Bell JJ).

is parasitic insofar as it 'depends upon',[70] and cannot exist without, the rules of property law which generate the trustee's title to property. The 'express trust' is a means of controlling how a holder of legal entitlements, the trustee, holds and uses her legal entitlements as the titleholder of trust property and as Frederic Maitland famously explained, '[i]t's of no use for Equity to say that A is a trustee of Blackacre for B, unless there be some court that can say that A is the owner of Blackacre'.[71] This does not mean, however, that the best approach is to treat 'trusts law' as part of property law, or the 'express trust' as a type of property right, for the purposes of any justificatory project. A more illuminating conception is of the 'express trust' as a set of legal propositions which interact with another set of legal propositions generated by an underlying body of law, ie property law, to redefine the trustee's authority as titleholder.

Another way of expressing the point we make here is that the legal propositions and rules which constitute the 'express trust' and 'trusts law' are a kind of mini-complex adaptive system which interacts with other sets of rules, such as those of property law, for example. However, while we certainly consider that this is an important feature of the 'express trust' and 'trusts law', we do not argue, and we do not think, that 'express trusts' and 'trusts law' are the *only* areas of private law of which this can be said. 'Property law' itself, for instance, can be understood not only as a complex adaptive system[72] but also as one that interacts with and is premised on the existence of law and legal systems more generally. Nor do we believe that the interactions between the rules of 'trusts law' with one another and with, eg, the rules of property law necessarily work in the same way as the interactions between other parts of the law which can also be understood in the terms of complex adaptive systems theory. Indeed, we would say that 'trusts law systems' possess a feature that is not shared by other systems of private law rules, such as the rules of contract law and property law, for example. Unlike these other systems, the rules of 'trusts law' have a meta-law function, the concern of which is to ensure that legal entitlements generated by other legal rules are not abused—a point we have made already.

An 'express trust' does not exist between the parties *ex ante*. It is brought into existence by the parties' actions with the help of the broader legal system that gives legal consequence to those actions. Common law jurisdictions typically have rules affirming that the legal propositions that collectively form an 'express trust' will come into existence only if the parties perform the actions needed to achieve this in particular ways. These rules for trust creation define when and how a settlor can create a trust, the existence and terms of which may also depend on the beneficiary's and putative trustee's

[70] N Jones, 'Trusts in England After the Statute of Uses: A View from the 16th Century' in R Helmholz and R Zimmerman (eds), *Itinera Fiduciae: Trust and Treuhand in Historical Perspective* (1998) 173, 190; C Rickett, 'Completely Constituting an Inter Vivos Trust: Property Rules?' [2001] Conv 515, 518; 'it should not be forgotten that the trust is a relationship concerning property, and property law rules need to be respected too'; L Smith, 'Scottish Trusts in the Common Law World' (2013) *Edinburgh Law Review* 283, 287.

[71] F Maitland, *Lectures on Equity* (CUP 1929) 19. Maitland makes this same point in relation to equity generally, stating, '[e]quity was not a self-sufficient system, at every point it presupposed the existence of common law ... Equity without common law would have been a castle in the air, an impossibility'.

[72] As argued in Smith (n 8).

actions as well, and, generally speaking, the actions that the parties must take to create the trust are (a) an externally manifested, conceptually coherent and precise statement of intention by the settlor to create a trust by bringing into force the legal propositions which are needed to achieve this, examples being the propositions that the trustee's powers as owner are constrained in certain ways and that the beneficiary has a correlative right to due administration; (b) the giving of consent by the trustee to the acquisition of ownership subject to the limits placed on her authority; and (c) at least one beneficiary not disclaiming her entitlement(s) on the terms as otherwise defined by the settlor and trustee.

By conditioning the existence of trusts on choices made by the parties, the rules of trust creation effectively give them the power to create trusts, and therefore exemplify the facilitative aspect of equity and demonstrate that it is not just a body of legal principles that restrain the exercise of powers.[73] As we shall see in a moment, this facilitative aspect is also shown by many rules governing the operation of trusts since these also give legal effect to the trust parties' wishes. However, it would be historically inaccurate to identify the origins of every rule of Australian and English 'trusts law' in a decision taken by the jurisdiction to support the choices of settlors, trustees, and beneficiaries. Plenty of examples can be given of this, of course, but the history of 'express trusts' and 'trusts law' in these jurisdictions is also the history of a dialectical tussle between drafters who have pressed against the boundaries of the legally and conceptually possible and legislatures and courts who have yielded to or resisted this pressure for reasons which may or may not have been tied up with the desire to further the needs of property owners.

The parties' actions in constituting an 'express trust' are necessary to bring the trust into existence and also explain why it possesses many of its features. To explain these phenomena, however, we must also take note of other legal rules that provide for the operation of the trust. These *operation* rules give legal effect to the parties' actions because they constitute the trust as a set of legal propositions. The rules apply between the parties as a result of the parties' exercise of power to create the trust. They define how the trust should operate and how a trustee is to duly administer the trust.

As we have said, the content of many of these propositions, for example what the trustee is and is not permitted to do, will vary with the parties' actions insofar as they are expressions of the parties' intentions and consent. In addition, there are 'gap filling', or 'default' rules, which as mentioned above, supply a default set of legal propositions which will apply between the parties unless, and to the extent that, they opt out of or modify them; and 'validation rules' that provide that third parties have the security of knowing that their dealings are legally effective when there is an authorised transaction. There will also, sometimes, be rules that apply in response to some mandatory policy that is external to the function and operation of the trust.[74]

[73] On the power conferring aspect of equity, see also M Harding 'Equity and Institutions' in D Klimchuk and others (eds), *Philosophical Foundations of the Law of Equity* (OUP 2020) ch 16.

[74] Such as Pensions Act 1995 (UK), s 67, which sets out certain restrictions and procedures for an exercise of a power to amend the terms of a pension scheme to affect a member's accrued right under the scheme; and Pensions Act 1995 (UK), s 40, which restricts a trustee from investing trust funds in employer-related investments.

In addition to the rules that provide for the due administration of the trust are the operation rules that provide for the court's assistance in securing the due administration of the trust.[75] For example, a court may provide judicial advice to a trustee as to how she should administer a trust, either to prevent a breach of trust, or to address one. Another example is the availability of a suit for general administration. In addition are rules that facilitate the supervision of the trustee and make available various forms of equitable relief in the event that due administration has not occurred. The trustee's accounting liability, for example, requires the trustee to provide the records of her dealings with trust property and to produce the trust property (or its value) in accordance with the records *corrected* as necessary to ensure all exercises of power *are authorised*.[76] These facets of the trustee's accounting liability are enforced through equity's accounting procedures and orders for consequential relief[77] all of which facilitate the supervision of the trustee and due administration of the trust.

Further examples include a range of other personal and proprietary remedies that are potentially available against the trustees (and their creditors and trustees in bankruptcy) and third parties in the event of an unauthorised execution. These include a beneficiary's or trustee's claim for recovery of misapplied trust property or its traceable substitute, which can be asserted against the (former) trustee, her trustee in bankruptcy, and third-party recipients.[78] Liabilities may also be incurred by knowing recipients and knowing or dishonest assistants.[79] There are also rules affecting a trustee's power to recoup against a beneficiary or co-trustee.[80]

As mentioned already, the trust and the legal rules that affect it presuppose the existence of other legal propositions, relevantly those defining the trustee's title to the trust property. A trustee's authority as titleholder cannot be subjected to restrictions and duties if the trustee is not a titleholder in the first place. This means that, outside of the situation in which the settlor self-declares a trust and the putative trustee already has title to the subject property, the settlor must transfer the subject property to the putative trustee, who must accept such title, in addition to the parties taking the other actions needed to constitute the trust. The existence of the trust thus depends on the actions taken by the parties *and* on there being a pre-existing legal system that creates a system of title to property upon which the trust can operate.

[75] *Duke of Norfolk's ST* (n 10) 230. Equity's inherent jurisdiction is today complemented by statute, see, eg, Trustee Act 1925 (UK); Trustee Act 1925 (NSW).

[76] *Doss* (n 41) 196–97; *Head* (n 55) 266.

[77] See generally: *Libertarian Investments Ltd v Hall* [2013] HKCFA 94; (2013) 16 HKCFAR 681 [167] (Lord Millett NPJ); *Agricultural* (n 9) [333]–[349] (Edelman J); S Elliott, 'Personal Monetary Claims' in J McGhee (ed), *Snell's Equity* (34th edn, Sweet & Maxwell 2020) ch 20.

[78] See, eg, *Foskett v McKeown* [2001] 1 AC 102; *Independent Trustee Services Ltd v GP Noble Trustees Ltd* [2012] EWCA Civ 195, [2013] Ch 91.

[79] *El Ajou v Dollar Land Holdings Plc* [1993] BCC 698, 715–16; *Bank of Credit and Commerce International (Overseas) Ltd v Akindele* [2001] Ch 437; *Fistar v Riverwood Legion and Community Club Ltd* [2016] NSWCA 81, (2016) 91 NSWLR 732 [45]. Australian and English law differ in their formulation of the fault element for assistance liability.

[80] See further: J Hudson and C Mitchell, 'Trustee Recoupment: A Power Analysis' (2021) 35 TLI 3.

III. Implications

A. Justificanda

A recurring feature of private law theory is that the content of the law is put to one side, sometimes on the basis that the details vary from one jurisdiction to the next. Some theoretical accounts start with a reduced or simplified construct of an area of law as their object for justification. This disciplinary methodology may be more or less convincing depending on whether the object itself is amenable to such reduction, and the degree of fit between the law and the construct. All this may be easier to do for some bodies of legal rules, such as contract, for example, which are less complicated in the sense that they determine the existence and content of the primary legal relations between the parties.

The added aspect of complexity for the rules that constitute 'trusts law', like other equitable rules that operate as meta-law, is that they control how the holder of a legal entitlement may hold and enjoy that entitlement. The rules of 'trusts law' thus necessarily presuppose and respond to the complexities of the property law rules that generate the relevant entitlement, which themselves therefore need to be understood in addition to the rules of 'trusts law' itself.

It is hardly surprising, therefore, that there is no single rule that can be identified as the object of justification in any project which purports to justify 'express trusts' and 'trusts law'. The content of 'trusts law' comprises much more than the rules for trust creation, and the content of the 'express trust' comprises much more than the choice presented to the settlor by rules governing trust creation. Once made, this choice entails a further commitment to rules that give legal consequence to the parties' choices to create the 'express trust' through those rules that provide for its operation.

A jurisdiction's commitment to the express trust, thus, is implemented through multiple types of legal rules that provide for the *creation* and *operation* of the trust. These legal rules, and the power they confer on the parties to create the 'express trust' and the consequent set of legal propositions that apply between the parties, are all discrete objects for justification that impose their own justificatory burdens.

We think that it is important for these objects to be carefully identified and delineated from one another. We demonstrate this by exploring the implications for autonomy-based justifications and other justificatory projects that relate to the individual legal rules providing for the creation and operation of 'express trusts' (Part III.B), as well as a jurisdiction's commitment to the whole of 'trusts law' that, in one way or another, affords the parties the power to create a trust (Part III.C).

A further implication of our approach to conceptualising 'express trusts' and 'trusts law' is that a previously unrecognised means of justifying these exists, namely, that a given jurisdiction's conception of 'the trust' may make some legal rules necessary and/or contributory to 'the trust' so conceived. This may offer a more promising means of justification for certain rules affecting trust creation and operation as we discuss further in Part III.D below.

B. Justifying the Legal Rules for the Creation and Operation of 'Express Trusts'

The individual legal rules that provide for the creation and operation of 'express trusts' are all potential objects for justification. In saying this, however, we do not think it is helpful to isolate one legal rule and ask whether it can be justified as a standalone rule without any consideration of its contribution to the creation or operation of the trust. If it is desired to justify any particular rule a more promising approach is to consider as a first step how it can be understood in light of its interactions with other rules that provide for trust creation and operation, and/or the rules that provide for the trustee's title to trust property, and also to consider how the rule contributes to the system-level effects of the trust. Of course, the answers to these questions will depend upon a given jurisdiction's conception of the 'express trust' and the legal rules which are taken to be necessary or contributory to producing its effects. As will be discussed in Part III.D below, any justification for an individual legal rule is therefore dependent on a jurisdiction's conception of the trust, and also assumes the justification(s) for the jurisdiction's commitment to the trust in the first place, as discussed in Part III.C next.

Assuming these matters, a clear conception of the contribution that a legal rule makes to the creation and/or operation of the 'express trust' facilitates a more accurate and fine-grained analysis of how a given justification for that legal rule can or cannot work. We will demonstrate this in relation to an autonomy-based justification for some of the rules for trust creation and operation. In summary, we argue that our approach makes it possible to explain more clearly how the rules that prioritise the parties' choices are autonomy enhancing, and additionally helps to explain why rules that are sometimes considered autonomy limiting are in fact autonomy enhancing.

As discussed in Part II.A.1 above, there are rules for trust creation that prioritise the parties' choices by conditioning the existence of the trust between the parties on their volitional actions. These rules give primacy to the settlor's choices, as it is the settlor who determines whether her property will be settled upon trust, and the constituent terms and some autonomy-based justifications sometimes focus on how the settlor's unilateral power to create an 'express trust' enhances the settlor's autonomy. However, the beneficiary and the trustee, where a trust is created by transfer, also have the power to determine the existence of the trust as between them. All parties to the trust are afforded an option for decision in relation to how they structure their relationship(s) between themselves in relation to the subject property. As we discuss in Part III.C below, whether or not this option can be justified as autonomy enhancing depends on an evaluation of whether the *particular* option offered by the trust is a meaningful option for decision. As we explain below, the strength of that evaluation, and ensuing justification, will depend on an accurate understanding of the trust and the precise option it affords the parties.

Also, there are the rules for trust creation and operation that limit the parties' choices in some way. For example, the beneficiary principle[81] prevents the parties from creating a trust other than as between two or more legal persons. The so-called 'illusory trusts' doctrine and 'the irreducible core' doctrine both prevent the parties from creating a trust where the trustee is not in substance bound by any obligation to obey the trust terms at all.[82] Similarly, other rules for trust creation require the settlor to define the subject property, the trustee, the object, and the terms upon which the trustee's authority depends.[83]

All these rules could be understood as limiting the parties' options for how they create a trust. Against this, some of these so-called mandatory rules have previously been rationalised as being autonomy enhancing on the basis that these rules protect party autonomy by preventing the parties from entering self-defeating arrangements that undermine the trust, and/or implement and respond to the parties' intention to create a trust, and only that intention.[84] John Langbein has argued, for example, that some 'mandatory rules', such as those preventing terms abrogating all trustee duties, authorising bad faith execution or abrogating a duty of disclosure, are intent serving or protecting the settlor's autonomy because all of these rules remove the risk of the trust being 'unenforceable and … illusory'.[85] Further, these rules require the settlor to be clear and precise in articulating her intention, and 'have only the modest aspiration of truth in labelling'.[86]

We agree that some of the legal rules that condition the parties' power to create the trust upon them taking certain actions can be understood as autonomy enhancing for these reasons. Our additional point is that this type of argument depends upon a so far unarticulated assumption about what an 'express trust' is. Any argument that a given legal rule ensures that the settlor intends to create a trust, and/or prevents the settlor from taking meaningless or self-defeating actions, and/or preserves the trust as a meaningful option for decision, depends on some conception of the 'express trust' such that there are specific legal rules necessary to it.

Our conception of the 'express trust' means that we can more precisely explain what it is, and how and why certain legal rules are necessary to its creation and operation. For

[81] *Morice v Bishop of Durham* (1804) 9 Ves Jr 399, 404–05; 32 ER 656 (Sir William Grant MR); *Morice v Bishop of Durham* (1805) 10 Ves Jr 522, 539–40; 32 ER 947 (Lord Eldon LC).

[82] The settlor could not create a trust where the trustee could do as they wish with the subject property, *Pearson v Lehman Bros Finance SA* [2010] EWHC 2914 (Ch), [275] (Briggs J); *Clayton v Clayton* [2013] NZHC 309; [2013] 3 NZLR 236 [90]; *Clayton v Clayton* [2016] NZSC 29; [2016] 1 NZLR 551 [126]; *JSC Mezhdunarodniy Promyshlenniy Bank v Pugachev* [2017] EWHC 2426 (Ch); (2017) 20 ITELR 905 [246], [267], [278] (Birss J); *Webb v Webb* [2020] UKPC 22, [2021] 1 FLR 448 [78]–[89] (Lord Kitchin). Similarly, even when the label of 'trust' is used the court will still look to whether or not the parties intend for the putative trustee to obey a set of terms in her exercise of power as titleholder, see, eg, *National Stadium Project (Grenada) Corp v NH International (Caribbean) Ltd* [2020] UKPC 25, (2020) 194 Con LR 1 [36]–[38] (Lord Briggs and Lord Sales).

[83] See note 11 and accompanying text above.

[84] L Fuller 'Consideration and Form' (1941) 41 Columbia Law Rev 799; Langbein, 'Mandatory Rules in the Law of Trusts' (n 3).

[85] Langbein, 'Mandatory Rules in the Law of Trusts' (n 3) 1120–27.

[86] ibid.

example, the parties cannot create a trust that purports to confer an entitlement to the trustee's due administration on anything other than an individual or entity with legal personality. This is because the trust is constituted by a set of legal propositions that necessarily exist between the trustee and at least one other legal person. Any one or all of the constituent legal propositions that redefine the trustee's authority cannot operate with only one legal person in the picture.

In the situations of an illusory trust or purported exclusion of the irreducible core, the parties cannot create a trust because they do not intend for the trustee to comply with a set of terms in her exercise of power as titleholder. In other words, the parties do not intend to redefine the trustee's authority as titleholder. They do not intend there to be a trust at all.

Underpinning these arguments is a conception of the 'express trust' and its overall effect. As we discuss in Part III.D below, a jurisdiction's conception of the 'express trust' can itself be a source of justification, assuming the justification(s) for a jurisdiction's commitment to the trust in the first place, and which we discuss in Part III.C below.

Before doing this, we point out that another influence upon the rules for trust creation and operation is a jurisdiction's underlying conception of and commitment to the rule of law. That commitment will mean that the existence and content of some legal rules will also be informed by the requirements for legal rules to be predictable, transparent, and understandable to those subject to them. We can observe these influences in the rules for trust creation that demand conceptual certainty in relation to the parties to the trust, the subject property, and the content of the propositions concerning when the trustee may and may not lawfully exercise her powers as titleholder. The same is true of the rules preventing the parties from creating internally inconsistent or meaningless legal relations that would make compliance and court supervision and enforcement difficult or impossible.

C. Justifying a Jurisdiction's Commitment to the 'Express Trust'

Another object for justification is a jurisdiction's commitment to the parties' power to create an 'express trust', implemented through all of the rules for trust creation and operation. There are a range of different justificatory methodologies and perspectives that might be adopted to justify this commitment. Some prominent justifications, such as those based on law and economics or individual autonomy, in one way or another, justify a legal rule by reference to the effect(s) produced. Different perspectives will focus on different effects and will have different types of reasons why one effect or another does, or does not, justify the trust.

Leaving aside the empirical question as to the extent that certain social effects are or are not produced, those effects cannot be ascertained without first having a clear understanding of the rules providing for the creation and operation of 'express trusts' and their legal effect(s). For example, a justification of the 'express trust' that is based on its economic efficiencies will depend on identification and evaluation of those efficiencies.

That evaluation cannot be undertaken in relation to an unspecified conception of 'the trust' as some vaguely described facility or other legal device. Nor can it be undertaken on the (incorrect) premise that 'the trust' permits the settlor to do whatever they want with their property. In addition to the complex questions as to how economic efficiencies are to be ascertained and measured, that evaluation will also depend on some understanding of the trust and its legal effect.

Similarly, the valency of any autonomy-based justification will depend on the accuracy with which its object is defined. The parties' choice is not enough to show the trust is autonomy enhancing. Individual autonomy does not require the State to present any and all options for decision, only an adequate range of meaningful ones.[87] An autonomy-based justification for a jurisdiction's commitment to the trust will depend on some evaluation of it being a meaningful option for decision. Again, this entails some conception of the trust and its overall legal effect.

We hope that our conceptions of 'express trusts' and 'trusts law' will assist future justificatory projects in this regard. We have shown that the option with which 'trusts law' presents trust parties is the power to create a defined system of legal propositions with a specific legal effect.[88] As we have said the content of 'express trusts' and 'trust laws' may vary between jurisdictions. In relation to Australia and England at least, the legal effect produced by the rules for trust creation and operation is to confer on the parties a *power to redefine the trustee's authority as titleholder*. An autonomy-based justification of the rules enabling parties to do this might explain why the redefinition of a trustee's authority over trust property is a *meaningful* option for decision. Similarly, a justification from a law and economics perspective might consider the economic efficiencies produced by allowing the parties to redefine the trustee's authority.

It is beyond the scope of this chapter to provide these explanations, save to point out how our conceptions of the 'express trust' and 'trusts law' will also assist future justificatory projects to articulate why these afford parties with an option that is *distinct* from that afforded by other bodies of law such as the rules of contract law and property law. Some scholars have already argued that the rights generated by 'trusts law' differ from those generated by property law or contract law, and that this provides parties with more efficient or meaningful options. We hope that our analysis will enable scholars to develop such arguments by defining more precisely what it is that the 'trust option' affords the parties.

For example, our conception of 'express trusts' distinguishes them from contractual rights. 'Express trusts' have previously been justified as functional equivalents to contracts on the basis that there are similarities between the two, such as consensual formation and the covariance between the parties' actions and the terms.[89] Despite these parallels, our analysis suggests that the system-level effects produced by 'express trusts' and 'trusts law' are distinct from those produced by the rules of contract law.

[87] On the general significance of this condition, see J Raz, *The Morality of Freedom* (Clarendon Press 1986) 371–77, 390–95.

[88] See generally in relation to the power conferring nature of equity, Harding 'Equity and Institutions' (n 73).

[89] Langbein, 'The Contractarian Basis of the Law of Trusts' (n 3) pt IV.

A contract may allow the parties to make binding promises about how one party may or may not exercise her powers in relation to subject property, but a contract and its constituent propositions do not redefine the titleholder's authority in the same way as the trust. The rules of trust law, like the rules of contract law, respond to unauthorised exercises of power by imposing liability on those who knowingly interfere with another party's rights.[90] But trusts law goes further, recognising that a proprietary claim against *un*knowing recipients lies to recover trust property (or its traceable substitute).[91] Contractual rights are not protected in the same way. In addition, the trust is protected by equity's administrative jurisdiction which affords a unique form of support to trustees. A party to a contract cannot, for example, seek the advice of the court as to the interpretation of the contractual terms, nor the performance of her contractual duties. A court may assume the administration of a trust. A contractual parallel is not possible.

Further, the option presented by the 'express trust' is more flexible than that provided by contract in that the rules for trust creation allow the settlor to choose the party who owes an obligation of due administration, the trustee, as well as the party to whom the trustee owes her obligations, usually referred to as the beneficiary or object (subject to a beneficiary's disclaimer, and trustee's acceptance if a trust by transfer). Parties to a contract can create an obligation to benefit a third party, although privity of contract means they cannot choose who owes the duty of performance and to whom the right to performance is owed save for some limited statutory exceptions in some jurisdictions. Finally, the scope of the parties' power to create the trust is broader than their power to create a contract in that an express trust can be created voluntarily, that is without consideration, something not possible for contract.

A better understanding of the 'express trust' may also provide a justification for the unique form of protection afforded it as compared to that afforded other relational systems, such as contract. As noted above, equity provides protection against third party *knowing* interference with both relational systems, but it also provides a further form of protection for the trust against *innocent* recipients, to the extent they still have the trust property or the traceable substitute. This additional protection may be justified in the future having regard to the different features, and concomitant vulnerabilities, of the trust itself.

Finally, our conception of 'express trusts' may mean that justifications offered for system-level effects will necessarily presuppose the justification(s) for the rules of property law which generate the trustee's title to property. Various justificatory perspectives may have a role in this regard, although we do not think that the trust can be subsumed

[90] The similarity in equity's protection against wrongful interference with obligations, whether trust or contract, has been observed before, see L Smith, 'Transfers' in P Birks and A Pretto (eds), *Breach of Trust* (Hart 2002); L Smith, 'Philosophical Foundations of Proprietary Remedies' in R Chambers, C Mitchell and J Penner (eds), *Philosophical Foundations of Unjust Enrichment* (OUP 2009).

[91] The recipient's knowledge is not an element to the proprietary claim in, *Re Montagu's ST* [1987] 1 Ch 264, 271–72, 276–78 (Megarry VC); *Foskett* (n 78); *Krnjulac v Lincu* [2015] NSWCA 367 [2]–[6], [18] (Bathurst CJ, Leeming JA agreeing). But compare: S Agnew and B McFarlane, 'The Paradox of the Equitable Proprietary Claim' in S Agnew and B McFarlane (eds), *Modern Studies in Property Law* (10th edn, Hart 2019) ch 17.

within the law of property and justified as such. The trust, as an object of justification, is not property law itself, nor is it a type of property.

D. The Significance of a Jurisdiction's Conception of the 'Express' Trust

The 'express trust' is a legal construct. It is the product of a jurisdiction's conception of what 'express trust' means and the rules considered necessary or contributory to this conception. Jurisdictions can differ in relation to these matters, and a jurisdiction's conception of 'express trust' can be a source of explanation, if not justification, for one or another legal rule pertaining to trust creation or operation. This is implicit in the irreducible core jurisprudence, such as *Armitage v Nurse*[92] where Millett LJ reasoned that certain legal rules apply between a trustee and beneficiary because they are 'the minimum necessary to give substance to the trust ... '. The trustee's duties to obey the trust terms, act honestly and in good faith, to account for her stewardship of the trust property, and the beneficiary's correlative entitlement to due administration, all apply *because* they are essential to the operation of the trust.

This justificatory methodology is also implicit in those cases that rationalise a trustee's duty to account as being a 'basic principle ... on which trusts rest' because without this duty 'the trustee could do as he pleases with the trust property and commit any breach of trust that he cared to commit'.[93] In other words, a trustee's accounting liability is justified on the basis that it is an essential means by which the operation or due administration of the trust is secured. Likewise, the rules for trust creation, including certainty of object, have also been justified on the basis of what is necessary to permit the trustee to carry out their duties as such.[94]

In addition to legal rules that apply because they are *necessary* to the operation of the trust, there are rules that apply because a jurisdiction has taken the view that a given rule somehow *contributes*, even if it is not necessary, to the due administration of the trust. The trustee's indemnity for properly incurred expenses, for example, is not necessary and thus not mandatory. Sometimes these rules apply because the parties have chosen them. Otherwise, the rules providing for trustee's indemnification for properly incurred expenses apply not because the settlor, or other parties, chose them, but by operation of equitable or statutory principle, and on the basis that the trustee's indemnity for expenses ensures 'the trust is efficiently and properly administered'.[95] The rationale

[92] *Armitage* (n 50) 253–54.

[93] *Randall v Lubrano* (Supreme Court of New South Wales, Holland J, 31 October 1975), published as an annexure to *McDonald v Ellis* (2007) 72 NSWLR 605, 621, [7].

[94] *McPhail* (n 11) 455–56 (Lord Wilberforce).

[95] *Price v Saundry* [2019] EWCA Civ 2261, [2020] WTLR 233 [23] (Asplin LJ). We could point to other legal rules that apply on the basis they further the due administration of the trust in some way, such as the rules that permit a trustee to recoup against a beneficiary, see further: Hudson and Mitchell, 'Trustee Recoupment: A Power Analysis' (n 80).

for this is that it saves the trustee from personal liability arising in the due administration of the trust.

We could point to other legal rules that apply on the basis they further trust administration in some way, such as the rules that permit a trustee to recoup against a beneficiary.[96] These rules are justified on the basis they are necessary or desirable to trust administration. This justification depends on a jurisdiction's conception of the trust such that one or more rules are necessary or desirable. All of these justifications assume that a jurisdiction's choice to recognise 'the trust' and enforce its due administration is itself justified in the first place, whether that be by autonomy or other perspectives.

As we have said, different jurisdictions can differ in relation to what a trust is, and they can also differ in relation to what rules are considered necessary or ideal to trust administration. Hence, it matters how a jurisdiction conceives 'express trusts' and the ways in which particular rules contribute to these because these conceptions provide (i) a stronger basis upon which to explain some default rules as autonomy enhancing, (ii) a justification for some jurisdictional and/or historical differences, and (iii) a map of future lines of inquiry in relation to some of the rules that respond to problems in trust administration. Each are explored in turn.

1. Default rules

A more convincing justification for some default rules may be given in light of each rule's contribution to the 'express trust'. We have outlined already how some default rules, such as the trustee's indemnity for expenses, can be understood as contributing to trust administration. Further, the default nature of these rules allows the parties to adopt a sophisticated and functional system of legal propositions through relatively simple or unsophisticated actions, and potentially make the trust a more easily accessible option for decision. The significance of this other means of justification may be important to the extent that there are limits to the extent autonomy can be relied upon to justify rules that apply in default of the parties' excluding or modifying them and as opposed to the parties having positively chosen for the rules to apply.[97]

2. Jurisdictional and historical differences

Some jurisdictional variations may be justified by reference to a jurisdiction's conception of the 'express trust' and the underlying system of property law, both of which may also change over time. With each change, there may be correlative change in the legal rules that are thought to be necessary, or to contribute, to that system. For example, the 'express trust' is sometimes understood as creating an entitlement to the benefit of trust property. One consequence is that the rules considered necessary for trust creation condition the existence of the 'express trust' on the parties' creating this entitlement for

[96] See further: Hudson and Mitchell, 'Trustee Recoupment: A Power Analysis' (n 80).

[97] J Raz, 'Promises and Obligations' in P Hacker and J Raz (eds), *Law, Morality and Society, Essays in Honour of HLA Hart* (OUP 1977) 228 [emphasis added]. Professor Raz has explained that the enforcement of voluntary obligations that are positively assumed is justified on the basis of respecting the promisor's choice, without more. A negatively assumed obligation, on the other hand, requires something more than the promisor's negative choice.

a beneficiary.[98] Conversely, for those jurisdictions that take a different view of the trust there are also different views about the rules for trust creation. For example, in other jurisdictions an entitlement to benefit, sometimes referred to as 'equitable ownership', is not taken to be a necessary feature of 'express trusts'.[99] Correlatively, the rules for trust creation in these jurisdictions do not make it necessary for the parties to intend for such an entitlement to exist at all points in time during the existence of the trust.

As we have said already, the bounds of possibility are not static, and have evolved over time as jurisdictions change and refine their conception of the 'express trust'.[100] Our point is that historical and jurisdictional deviations in relation to individual rules of 'trusts law' can be partly justified by reference to a jurisdiction's conception of the 'express trust' and that jurisdiction's views about the rules which are needed to sustain or support this conception.

A well-known difference between the rules of 'trusts law' in England and Australia, on the one hand, and the rules of most American states, on the other hand, relates to the beneficiary's power to call for the trust property. The so-called rule in *Saunders v Vautier*[101] applies to some 'express trusts' in the former jurisdictions, but not to their equivalents in the latter.[102] We suggest that our approach to understanding the rules of 'trusts law' and their interaction with background rules of property law helps explain this difference. It is a result of jurisdictions taking different views about which legal rules are necessarily incidental to a beneficiary's entitlement to the benefit of trust property, as informed by the underlying system of property law.

In Australia and England, for example, a beneficiary's power to call for the trust property arises *in response to the settlor's choice* to create an absolute entitlement to the benefit of trust property in that beneficiary's favour,[103] and assuming other conditions are met.[104] This rule has been described by Mummery LJ in *Goulding v James*[105] as recognising '… the rights of beneficiaries … to exercise their proprietary rights to overbear and defeat the intention of a testator or settlor …'.[106] It may sometimes be difficult to construe the meaning of the settlor's actions, in relation to whether or not the settlor

[98] Smith 'Massively Discretionary Trusts' (n 58); P Matthews, 'From Obligation to Property, and Back Again? The Future of the Non-Charitable Purpose Trust' in D Hayton (ed), *Extending the Boundaries of Trusts and Similar Ring-Fenced Funds* (Kluwer Law International 2002).

[99] See, eg, *Glenn v Federal Commissioner of Land Tax* (1915) 20 CLR 490, 497 (Griffith CJ); Harris, 'Trust, Power and Duty' (n 44) 47.

[100] Some of these changes have been commented upon in Smith 'Massively Discretionary Trusts' (n 58); J Palmer and C Rickett, 'The Revolution and Legacy of the Discretionary Trust' (2017) 11 J Eq 157; R Nolan, 'Trustees and Third-Party Powers', K Low, 'Non-Charitable Purpose Trusts', in R Nolan, K Low and T Wu (eds), *Trusts and Modern Wealth Management* (CUP 2018) ch 2. For an example of a jurisdiction's consideration of reforms to trusts laws, see, eg, the initiation of a Law Commission project titled 'Modernising Trust Law for a Global Britain' as described on: https://www.lawcom.gov.uk/project/modernising-trust-law-for-a-global-britain/.

[101] *Saunders* (n 44).

[102] *Claflin* (n 44).

[103] *Sainsbury v IRC* [1970] Ch712 (Ch D) 724–25 (Ungoed-Thomas J); *CPT* (n 35) [43]–[44], [47].

[104] See note 44 above.

[105] *Goulding v James* [1997] 2 All ER 239 (CA) 247.

[106] This theme is continued in other cases and academic commentaries, see eg, *Re Tracey* [2016] QCA 194, [2017] 2 Qd R 35 [72] (Boddice J); *CPT* (n 35) [48]. The 'mandatory' nature of this rule has been criticised: J Langbein 'Why the Rule in *Saunders v Vautier* is Wrong' in PG Turner (ed), *Equity and Administration* (CUP 2016) 189; J Penner, *The Law of Trusts* (10th edn, OUP 2016) 82.

intends for a beneficiary to *have* an absolute entitlement and incidental power, which might be defeasible on certain conditions, or whether the settlor intends the existence of this entitlement and power to be conditioned on certain events. Leaving aside that issue, the settlor may choose *not* to confer such an entitlement for a period, such that no-one may have a power to call for the property from the outset. A beneficiary's power to call for the trust property does not 'override the trust terms' or defeat the settlor's intention. The power is a response to that intention.

Not all jurisdictions have made the same choice to respond to the settlor's intention for a beneficiary to have an absolute entitlement to benefit, and a notable example is provided by the laws of many American states.[107] This difference shows how jurisdictions take different views about how to give effect to an entitlement to benefit, and, further, how those views might be affected by a jurisdiction's conception of the 'express trust' and/or its underlying property system. As has been argued by other scholars,[108] the unavailability of the power to call for the trust property in many American states can be understood as reflecting the relevant jurisdiction's view that this power is not necessary or facilitative of an entitlement to benefit in light of the underlying property system that recognises a different form of absolute ownership to that recognised in England, for example.

3. Responding to problems in trust administration

Finally, we briefly consider how a jurisdiction's conception of the trust can provide a justification for the rules that respond to problems that arise in trust administration, such as the rules that require a trustee, or third parties, to restore the trust fund when certain of the operation rules have not been complied with. These, and other, rules have been understood and justified from a range of different perspectives, including the protection of (equitable) proprietary interests, protection against knowing interference with obligations, and restitution for unjust enrichment. Space does not permit us to work through the implications of our analysis for these arguments save to notice that the relevant rules may also stand to be justified, or not, according to a jurisdiction's conception of the 'express trust' and the contribution made by a rule to that jurisdiction's system of 'trusts law'.

Along these lines the argument could be made that rules that provide a response to an unauthorised execution can be justified by an autonomy-based perspective. This might be because the parties did not intend for an unauthorised execution and rules that provide for a response to an unauthorised execution give effect to the parties' intentions and thus are autonomy enhancing. However, we think this is too simplistic a view of the express trust and particularly the legal rules that affect third parties. The individual autonomy of third parties demarcates the work to be done in justifying the legal rules that create third-party liabilities in response to unauthorised transactions.

[107] *Claflin* (n 44).
[108] P Matthews, 'Why the Rule in *Saunders v Vautier* is Wrong: A Commentary' in P Turner (ed), *Equity and Administration* (CUP 2016) ch 11.

Here, it may be helpful to draw on ideas of relational respect and a third party's duty to respect relationships and institutions that also facilitate her own individual autonomy. Observe that this line of inquiry will depend on some explanation of how the rules for third-party liability facilitate or support the due administration of the trust, and in turn some conception of the 'express trust' itself.

These inquiries must also take account of the trust's existence within a broader system of law such that some legal rules are required to mediate the interactions between trust rules and other legal rules and their underlying policies.[109] A balance needs to be struck between the due administration of any given trust and one or another policy that is external to it. For example, the various situations in which a third party's claim against a trustee is subordinated to the due administration of the trust, either because a trustee cannot be ordered to act contrary to the trust terms, or because a beneficiary has a proprietary claim against a third party, can be understood as involving a complex balancing exercise between a jurisdiction's commitment to the 'express trust' (which itself may promote the autonomy of the settlor, trustee, and beneficiary) and the protection of third-party interests and perhaps also a wider social interest in promoting the certainty of property transactions.

IV. Conclusion

Writing extra-judicially, Justice Leeming[110] has described one approach to understanding the 'express trust' in the following terms:

> [On] one view, the answer to the question 'what is a trust?' is that given by Professor Scott:
>
> The trust is the whole juridical device: the legal relationship between the parties with respect to the property that is its subject matter, including not merely the duties that the trustee owes to the beneficiary and to the rest of the world, but also the rights, privileges, powers and immunities that the beneficiary has against the trustee and against the rest of the world.
>
> That is to say, the answer to the question is the whole body of the law of trusts.

Our conception of 'express trusts' and 'trusts law' as a set of legal propositions and rules that constitute a complex adaptive system is not far from Scott's view. We have also emphasised the importance of understanding the system-level effects that emerge from the interactions between these propositions and rules inter se, and with the background rules of property law.

[109] See also S Gardner, *An Introduction to the Law of Trusts* (3rd edn, OUP 2011), pt 2.2.

[110] Leeming, 'What is a Trust?' (n 27) 211 (quoting A W Scott and W F Fratcher, *The Law of Trusts* (4th edn, Little Brown 1987), vol 1, §2.4.

We hope that our discussion will assist future justificatory projects focusing on the 'express trust' and 'trusts law'. Having described some of the ways in which our conceptions of these can help those projects, we conclude this chapter by suggesting that our approach may also have relevance to other areas of private law. Similarities between the 'express trust' and various forms of property or other consensual arrangements, such as contract, have been made before. We speculate that our conception of the 'express trust' as a system of legal propositions that produces certain legal effects may be applicable to other areas of law, each of which might usefully be understood as an interconnected system of legal propositions that stand to be justified or not by reference to the system-level effect(s) they produce. This might be helpful not only for understanding other areas of law as objects for justification and the consequent justification(s) but would also assist the broader justificatory project of understanding the roles played by discrete systems within private law, such as those constituted by the rules governing trusts, property, contract, tort, and unjust enrichment, within a broader legal system.

Finally, a further implication of our discussion is to close off an analytical and justificatory approach that treats 'express trusts' as property and 'trusts law' as being a part of property law. As we have said, an important feature of 'trusts law' is that it is designed to support other legal rules, such as the title-conferring rules of property law, by preventing people from abusing the entitlements they acquire by application of these other rules. Hence, we consider that it would be a false step to collapse 'trusts law' into property law, the central concerns of which are different, namely, to define how people should relate to each other in relation to things and their physical surrounds. We acknowledge there are differing accounts of property law and how its boundaries should be drawn,[111] but on any view, property law is not meta-law and does not have the same concern as 'trusts law' of preventing the abuse of legal rules or a person's power to hold and use her legal entitlement to property.

[111] See note 6 above.

2

Trusts, Property, and Rights

*Ben McFarlane**

This chapter begins to grapple with two related questions. First, what can the concept of property tell us about the operation of the trust? Second, what consequences does the existence and operation of the trust have for a particular legal system's concept of property? As to the first question, the chief argument is that great care must be taken in using the concept of property to understand the operation of the trust. The key point is that references to property within a trust structure can often better be understood as references to rights. As will be shown, this has a number of practical and conceptual consequences. For example, the focus of analysis should often be the nature of the rights held on trust, and the question of how different legal relations are packaged together to form a 'right'. A key aspect of the trust's operation, it will be argued, is that the integrity of such packages of legal relations is respected. So, while the possibility of setting up a trust does usefully add to the autonomy of a right-holder, it does not do so by allowing her to fragment, or redistribute parts of, the 'bundle' of legal relations that constitute that right.

As to the second question, it will be argued that the existence of the trust and its effect on trustees may have significant consequences for how we should think of property. For example, where the right held on trust is a freehold of land, the trustee has a property right; yet, many of the features usually associated with ownership are absent. Considering the position of the trustee may therefore be useful in establishing what is, and what is not, essential if a party's right is to be regarded as a property right. Indeed, as there are limits placed on both the trustee's ability to benefit from the right held on trust and the trustee's freedom to choose how to exercise powers arising from that right, it may further be said that the trustee's position forces us to reconsider some formulations of what it means to have a right at all. This is one example of a wider methodological point: while much attention has of course been directed to examining the nature of beneficiaries' interests under a trust, it is just as important to consider the impact of a trust on the interests of trustees. Indeed, this is a point which courts have recently had to face in considering, for example, the nature of a trustee's rights of retention and indemnity.[1]

* I have benefitted from comments received at the Philosophical Foundations of the Law of Express Trusts Workshop, and also from earlier discussions with Robert Stevens and Jessica Hudson, as well as with graduate students, including Giuseppe Jafari and Zach Pullar.

[1] See, eg, *Carter Holt Harvey Woodproducts Australia Pty Ltd v Commonwealth of Australia* [2019] HCA 20, (2019) 368 ALR 390 (hereafter *Carter Holt*), discussed below, and *Equity Trust (Jersey) Ltd v Halabi; ITG Ltd v Fort*

Ben McFarlane, *Trusts, Property, and Rights* In: *Philosophical Foundations of the Law of Express Trusts*. Edited by: Simone Degeling, Jessica Hudson, and Irit Samet, Oxford University Press. © Ben McFarlane 2023. DOI: 10.1093/oso/9780192844934.003.0003

I. The Subject Matter of a Trust

It is very common, of course, to consider a trust as an arrangement whereby one or more trustees hold property for the benefit of one or more beneficiaries, or for a permitted purpose.[2] Indeed, an obvious sense in which the idea of property can be relevant to the law of express trusts is the requirement that there must be certainty as to the subject matter of the trust, often expressed as a need for the 'trust property' to be identified.

In most cases, this formulation is unlikely to cause any difficulties. An exception occurs, however, if undue weight is put on the term 'property' in deciding if a particular right can be the subject matter of a trust. For example, in each of *AA v Persons Unknown*[3] and *Ruscoe and Moore v Cryptopia Ltd*,[4] a court had to consider if particular digital assets, such as cryptocurrencies, were capable of being held on trust. In each case, in justifying its conclusion that such a trust was possible, the court relied in part on the analysis of Lord Wilberforce in *National Provincial Bank v Ainsworth*,[5] as 'the classic statement of the characteristics of "property"'.[6] Such an approach is dangerous as it overlooks the different contexts in which the term 'property' can be used.

In the *Ruscoe* case, one issue was as to the application of section 2 of the Companies Act 1993 (New Zealand). Like section 436 of the Insolvency Act 1986 (UK), it adopts, for the purposes of interpretation of particular statutory provisions, a very broad definition of property. As has been noted in relation to the United Kingdom Act, such a definition includes a simple contractual right, such as a right to be paid a specific sum, or a licence to make use of another's property.[7] This wide definition makes sense if, for example, there is a question as to which rights form part of a 'bankrupt's estate' and so are prima facie available for distribution to the bankrupt's creditors. In contrast, in *Ainsworth*, the 'property' issue, and hence Lord Wilberforce's analysis, arose in a quite different context. The question was not whether the right in issue, Mrs Ainsworth's 'deserted wife's equity', would pass to a trustee in bankruptcy of Mrs Ainsworth. Nor was the question whether such a right was capable of being held by Mrs Ainsworth on trust for another party. It was rather whether her right was capable of binding a third party (the bank) that had acquired a charge over the matrimonial home from its sole registered proprietor, Mr Ainsworth. The features identified by Lord Wilberforce as necessary before a right 'can be admitted into the category of property' were thus chosen with

Trustees Ltd [2022] UKPC 36 (hereafter *Equity Trust*). The judgments in *Equity Trust* were delivered too late for consideration in this chapter.

2 See J McGhee and S Elliott (eds), *Snell's Equity* (34th edn, Sweet & Maxwell 2020) 21-001: 'The general feature of an English trust is that a person in whom property is vested (called the "trustee") is compelled in equity to hold the property for the benefit of another person (called the "beneficiary"), or for some legally enforceable purposes other than his own.'

3 [2019] EWHC 3556 (Comm) (hereafter *AA*).

4 [2020] NZHC 728 (hereafter *Ruscoe*).

5 [1965] AC 1175, 1248 (hereafter *Ainsworth*).

6 *Ruscoe* (n 4) [75]. See too *AA* (n 3) [59] and *B2C2 Ltd v Quoine PTC Ltd* [2019] SGHC (I) 3 [142] (reversed on appeal: [2020] SGCA (I) 2).

7 See, eg, *Akers v Samba* [2017] AC 424 (PC), [60] (Lord Mance), [87] (Lord Sumption) (hereafter *Akers*).

this specific question of third-party effect in mind; indeed, they have been criticised as being so linked to that effect as to be circular.[8] Even if Lord Wilberforce had been seeking to identify what is sufficient, rather than merely necessary,[9] for a right to have such third-party effect, it is misguided to use those features as a test for the quite different question of whether a right is capable of being held on trust.

This can be demonstrated very simply by considering a standard contractual chose in action, such as a bank account. Lord Wilberforce's criteria aim to make sense of the division between 'property rights on the one hand, and personal rights on the other hand'.[10] A customer's right against her bank is clearly in that sense a personal right, not prima facie binding on any party other than the bank, yet, this does not prevent bank accounts forming the subject matter of a trust. As Briggs J, as he then was, put it in *re Lehman Bros International (Europe)*,[11] 'no-one doubts the beneficial interest of clients in a solicitor's client account. Yet the subject matter of that fund consists entirely of the solicitor's purely personal rights as a customer of the client account bank or banks'.[12] Such clarity as to the position in relation to bank accounts was absent from the Court of Appeal's analysis in *Trustee of the Property of F C Jones v Jones*.[13] Sums credited to the bank account of Mrs Jones were the traceable proceeds of a disposition of partnership assets made to her. That disposition was void as made after an initial act of bankruptcy. It could therefore be said that Mrs Jones held the bank account, her chose in action against the bank, on trust for the trustee in bankruptcy of the partnership. Millett LJ, however, regarded that chose in action as one which 'in reality belonged to the trustee [in bankruptcy]', so that trustee in bankruptcy was 'entitled to the money in [Mrs Jones's] account'.[14] In that case, the need for precision was, in practice, reduced by the fact that the bank had interpleaded, asking whether it should pay the sums credited to Mrs Jones's account to Mrs Jones herself, or to the trustee in bankruptcy. Nonetheless, it is important to note that the dispute was not as to the 'ownership' of the proceeds of the void disposition. Indeed, where a chose in action such as a bank account is concerned, 'ownership' is immediately a difficult concept, as there is no specific independent resource to which the chose relates. It may be possible to talk of a party 'owning' a right, but it is not clear that the term 'ownership' adds anything of value to the concept of simply holding, or having, a right.[15] In *Jones*, the chose in action comprised by the bank account was necessarily held by Mrs Jones, as it was she who entered

[8] See, eg, K Gray and S Gray, 'The Rhetoric of Realty' in J Getzler (ed), *Rationalizing Property, Equity and Trusts* (LexisNexis 2003).

[9] The fact that the criteria identified by Lord Wilberforce are not sufficient for the recognition of a proprietary right can be seen by, eg, the refusal to recognise positive freehold covenants as capable of binding third parties: see, eg, *Rhone v Stephens* [1994] 2 AC 310. For difficulties with using the *Ainsworth* test in the context of asking if cryptocurrency can be held on trust, see too K Low, 'Bitcoins as Property: Welcome Clarity?' (2020) 136 LQR 345, 348–49 and 'Trusts of Cryptocurrency' (2021) 34 TLI 191.

[10] *Ainsworth* (n 5) 1248.

[11] [2010] EWHC 2914 (Ch).

[12] ibid [241] (Briggs J).

[13] [1997] Ch 159 (CA) (hereafter *Jones*).

[14] ibid 170.

[15] This point is very well made by G Gretton, 'Ownership and its Objects' (2007) 71 RabelsZ 802, see especially at 834, where 'titularity' is used to refer to the 'relationship of the right-holder to the right held' and it is noted that: 'Ownership and titularity are different: one word should not cover both.'

the contractual relationship with the bank. The real question was whether, because of the circumstances in which she had acquired that right, she was under a duty in relation to that right. The success of the trustee in bankruptcy, it is submitted,[16] depends on showing a trust of the chose in action comprised by Mrs Jones's account, rather than on simply 'locating'[17] money which it owned.

The publication by the European Commission of a draft Data Governance Act in 2020, with suggested limits on how an individual can deal with General Data Protection Regulation rights,[18] is linked to a different usage of 'property' which may also cause confusion in this context. The power of a party to transfer a particular right may sometimes be seen as characteristic of property, and so limits on transferability might then be seen as denying the possibility of a right's being held on trust.[19] It is possible that a particular reason for denying the power to transfer a right may also extend to denying the power to declare a trust of that right,[20] but there is, again, no general conceptual reason why the question of whether a right can be held on trust should be linked to a distinct question, such as that of whether a right can be transferred.[21] This is demonstrated by the willingness of the Court of Appeal to recognise a trust of a right which, either because of its inherent nature, or because of the terms of the contract in which it arises, is non-assignable.[22]

The requirement of 'trust property' can therefore best be understood as a requirement that a specific, identified right or rights be held on trust. It is significant, for example, that in their joint judgment in *Carter Holt Harvey Woodproducts Australia Pty Ltd v Commonwealth of Australia*,[23] Kiefel CJ, Keane and Edelman JJ refer consistently to 'rights held on trust',[24] rather than 'trust property', noting for example that the expression 'trust assets' is simply shorthand for 'the rights held on trust by the trustee'.[25] Where the right constituting the supposed subject matter of a trust is itself ownership of goods, then the requirement for certainty of subject matter of the trust will apply in exactly the same way as the need, in a sale, for goods to be identified before title can pass to a buyer. As a result, a buyer who is unable to satisfy that identification requirement, and so has not acquired the seller's title to the goods, will not be able to show that such a title is instead held by the seller on trust for the buyer.[26] In such a case, the

[16] See too B McFarlane and R Stevens, 'The Nature of Equitable Property' (2010) 4 J Eq 1, 21–22. See too L Smith, 'Simplifying Claims to Traceable Proceeds' (2009) 125 LQR 338, 347.

[17] The language used by Millett LJ in *Jones* (n 13) 170.

[18] See Recital 24 of the draft Data Governance Act 2020/0340 (COD).

[19] See, eg, Draft Common Frame of Reference Book X.–3:102: 'Trust assets may consist of proprietary or other rights, so far as these are transferable.' For discussion, see, eg, B McFarlane, 'An English Perspective: Two Cheers for Book X' (2011) 15 Edin L Rev 471, 473.

[20] See, eg, R Goode, 'Contractual Prohibitions against Assignment' [2009] LMCLQ 300.

[21] Similarly, as noted by, eg, S Delacroix and N Lawrence, 'Bottom-up Data Trusts: Disturbing the "One Size Fits All" Approach to Data Governance' (2019) 9 Int Data Priv Law 236, the fact that data in some contexts does not count as property is not inconsistent with specific data rights being the subject matter of a trust.

[22] See, eg, *Don King Productions Inc v Warren* [2000] Ch 291 and *Barbados Trust Co v Bank of Zambia* [2007] EWCA Civ 148.

[23] *Carter Holt* (n 1) discussed further below.

[24] See, eg, ibid [24]–[28].

[25] ibid [24].

[26] See, eg, *re Goldcorp Exchange Ltd* [1995] 1 AC 74 (PC).

requirement of 'trust property' does match the need for property, in the sense of an identifiable physical thing, but only because the subject matter of the claimed trust is, on the facts, title to goods. There is, nonetheless, a broader analogy which can be made between claiming title to goods in a sale and claiming a right under a trust. In each case, the claimant needs to show not merely that another party has come under a duty to her, but rather that the duty relates to something independent of the two parties: in the case of sale, specific goods; and, in the case of trusts, specific rights.

It is not, therefore, surprising that there is often said to be a need for 'trust property'. First, as in the case where T holds a freehold on trust for B, the subject matter of a trust may well be a property right. Note that, in such a case, it is the freehold, rather than the land itself, which is the subject matter of the trust. This point can also be seen where a relative title, such as that acquired by a thief of goods, is held on trust: it is that title, rather than the thing itself, which is the subject matter of the trust.[27] Identifying a specific right (rather than a thing itself) as the subject matter of a trust is therefore important even beyond cases where a chose in action is held on trust. Second, even where the right held on trust is a chose in action, as where T holds a bank account on trust for B, the existence of the trust depends on the fact that T is not simply under a duty to B to act or not act in a particular way; rather, T's duty must relate to a specific right held by T. In each case, then, there must be something independent of the two parties that is capable of being seen as subject to B's right. In that way, there is an analogy between the positions of B, and of O, a party with an unencumbered title to goods. Each can identify an external subject matter of her right: in O's case, the physical goods; in B's case, the right of T.[28] As shown by, for example, Lau, Penner, and Wong's examination of data trusts,[29] B's task where a trust is claimed is to show that there is an identifiable right of T which forms the subject matter of the trust. Further, it is this requirement that a trust must relate to an identifiable right, rather than any question of policy, which rules out many possible claims to constructive trusts: a tort victim of the defendant, or a party with a simple debt claim, cannot show that the defendant's duty to her relates to any specific right held by the defendant, and thus a trust is conceptually impossible.[30]

Of course, it is not suggested that the move from 'property' to 'rights' solves all difficulties in relation to the permitted subject matter of a trust. Indeed, it opens up some challenging questions, and forces us to consider the broader question of how we identify and distinguish particular rights. As noted by, for example, Webb,[31] the term 'right', no less than the term 'property', can have multiple competing meanings. In the context of a trust, however, it is clear that our focus is not on what Webb refers to as R-rights:[32]

[27] There is controversy over whether a theft can give rise to a constructive trust in favour of the victim of the theft: see, eg, R Chambers, 'Trust and Theft' in E Bant and M Harding (eds) *Exploring Private Law* (CUP, 2010) 223 discussing, inter alia, *Black v S Freedman & Co Ltd* (1910) 12 CLR 105. The point however is that, *if* such a trust arises, it is the thief's relative title which is held on trust: see Chambers (ibid) at 229–30. Moreover, a thief (or other party with relative title) can simply set up an express trust in the usual way.

[28] See further: B McFarlane and S Douglas, 'Property, Analogy, and Variety' (2022) 42 OJLS 161.

[29] J Lau, J Penner and B Wong, 'The Basics of Private and Public Data Trusts' (2020) Sing JLS 90.

[30] For discussion, see B McFarlane, 'The Centrality of Constructive and Resulting Trusts' in C Mitchell (ed), *Constructive and Resulting Trusts* (Hart 2010).

[31] C Webb, 'Three Concepts of Rights, Two of Property' (2018) 38 OJLS 246.

[32] Webb (n 31) 253, referring to 'the concept of a right as a reason (R-rights)'.

interests that provide a ground for duties on others, such as an interest in bodily security or reputation. It is more promising to see the subject matter of a trust as consisting of rights in the sense of specific legal relations, which is consistent with what Webb refers to as C-rights:[33] conclusions that one party has a claim-right correlating to a duty of another. This also fits well with the equitable origins of the trust, and the secondary nature of equitable intervention: once a particular set of legal relations has been recognised, it is then possible for a secondary system to recognise duties that relate to those very legal relations. At the first stage, we might think of, for example, physical things, or particular actions of others, as providing the content of rights and duties; once legal relations have been established, however, such relations can then themselves provide the content of such rights and duties. So, for example, O's ownership of a car instructs others how to behave in relation to that car; whereas, T's holding ownership of car on trust instructs T as to how to behave not in relation to the car as such, but rather in relation to *T's right* to the car. This is why, as noted by Penner,[34] T's duties as trustee extend not only to T's claim-rights against third parties not physically to interfere with the car, but also to the powers T holds as a result of title to the car, such as the power to transfer that title, or to license particular uses of the car.

Henry Smith has argued that the law of property, in managing the complex interactions between strangers in relation to resources, makes use of the idea of a 'thing' as an organising module.[35] So, for example, rather than enumerating different possible uses of an object, such as a car, and then allocating those uses to particular parties, the physical object itself can be used as the unifying source of parties' duties—they need only to know that they should not interfere with that physical thing. In the law of trusts, it can be argued, the organising modules are made up not of things but of rights. On such a view, the duties of the trustee relate to the right, or rights held on trust; and the third parties against whom an equitable 'proprietary' or knowing receipt claim can be made are those who have acquired those rights, or their traceable proceeds. It seems then that setting up a trust permits a settlor to deal in a particular way with those packages of legal relations that can be regarded as independent and distinct 'rights'. On this view, the trust does not allow a settlor to fragment such existing packages, or to deal separately with legal relations which are not severable from a particular package. This point can be underlined by considering the nature of the rights of a trustee.

[33] Webb (n 31) 253, referring to 'the Hohfeldian concept(s) of a right (C-rights)', which 'operate as practical conclusions, identifying the concrete demands we can make of one another' (ibid 252).

[34] J Penner, 'The (True) Nature of a Beneficiary's Equitable Proprietary Interest under a Trust' (2014) 27 Can J L & Juris 473.

[35] H Smith, 'Property as The Law of Things' (2012) 125 Harv L Rev 1691. See too T Merrill and H Smith, 'The Architecture of Property' in H Dagan and B Zipursky (eds) *Research Handbook on Private Law Theory* (Elgar, 2020) 134, 138–41.

II. The Rights of a Trustee: General Position

As was noted by Hohfeld,[36] much attention is directed to understanding the nature and proper characterisation of the rights of a beneficiary of a trust. Much less effort has been devoted to analysing the rights of a trustee. This is unfortunate, not least because the resolution of the second question has important consequences for the first. It will be argued here that there is an important continuity between the position of O, a party who simply has an unencumbered right which she is free to use for her own benefit, and that of T, a party who holds the same type of right on trust. This can be seen, for example, by considering the Supreme Court's analysis, in *Akers*,[37] of the position where T, acting without authority under the trust, transfers shares held on trust to C, a third party who, as a bona fide purchaser for value of those shares, takes free of any claim of B, the beneficiary. It is not the case that, through an exception to the *nemo dat* rule, T has transferred to C B's interest in the rights held on trust: there is no 'disposition' of B's rights to C.[38] Yet, C is now in the same position as O, a party who simply has an unencumbered right which she is free to use for her own benefit. C acquired that right, and the package of legal relations that go with it, from T: indeed, C's acquisition of the right held by T is central to C's ability to make out the bona fide purchaser defence. Contrary to the analysis of Birks,[39] C does not need to invoke any *nemo dat* exception, as C acquired the right from T, who did indeed hold that right.[40] The difference between the position of C and T, like that between O and T, is simply that the former, unlike the latter, is not under any duty to B in relation to that right. This analysis is consistent with the treatment of T, prior to statutory intervention, in a case where the right of the sole beneficiary of a trust is lost by B and does not pass to any other party: the duty owed by T to B disappears, and with it the encumbrance on T's right, so T is now free to assert the underlying right T has held all along.[41]

This analysis is also consistent with the unavailability of a strict liability restitutionary claim to B in a case where T, without authority under the trust, transfers the rights held on trust to C, and C then disposes of those rights and their traceable proceeds before acquiring knowledge of the trust. The point in such a case is that C's initial gain came at the expense of T, not B, as it consisted of rights formerly held by T, and transferred to C by T. The law on the availability of restitutionary claims is also of note when it comes to the position of a defendant who receives rights, as a result of a flawed transfer, and receives those rights in the position of a trustee. In *Skandinaviska Enskilda Banken AB*

[36] W Hohfeld, 'Some Fundamental Legal Conceptions as Applied in Judicial Reasoning' (1913–14) 23 Yale LJ 16, 16.

[37] *Akers* (n 7).

[38] ibid [54] (Lord Mance), [72] (Lord Neuberger), [88] (Lord Sumption).

[39] P Birks, 'Notice and Onus in *O'Brien*' (1998) Trusts Law Int 1.

[40] See too B McFarlane and A Televantos, 'As Complex as ABC? Bona Fide Purchasers of Equitable Interests' in P S Davies and Cheng Han Tan (eds), *Intermediaries in Commercial Law* (Hart 2022).

[41] *Burgess v Wheate* (1759) 1 Wm Bl 123, 96 ER 67; 1 Eden 177, 28 ER 652. For discussion, see P Matthews, '*Burgess v Wheate* (1759)' in C Mitchell and P Mitchell (eds), *Landmark Cases in Equity* (Hart 2012).

(Publ) v Conway,[42] for example, a liquidator attempted to recover the value of payments made to investors who had held redeemable shares, where those payments were invalidated by statute.[43] One such investor was the defendant, which had held those shares on trust for the beneficiaries. The Privy Council rejected the defendant's argument that its position as trustee meant that it did not itself benefit from the payment, and so was not liable. It also rejected the view that the trustee received the payment merely as an agent of the beneficiaries: even in the case of a bare trust, it is not the case that the beneficiaries are the true owners of the rights held on trust, and the trustees are mere agents. As noted by Lord Reed, it was the trustee, not the beneficiary, who held the rights to the shares and so was 'owed the redemption monies'.[44] Lord Reed went on to say that: 'A trustee who is not acting as agent is enriched at common law by the payments which he receives, since the common law ignores the equitable interest of the beneficiaries.'[45] The language used is unfortunate: it would be odd if, so long after the Judicature Acts, the courts were to show wilful blindness to equitable rights. And, clearly, there are instances where the common law has for many years taken account of such rights.[46] The conclusion is better seen as resting on the fact that the position in equity, and indeed the equitable interest of the beneficiaries, *depends* on the trustee's holding of the rights forming the subject matter of the trust. As it is the trustee who, in *Conway*, acquired rights as part of the immediate transaction with the claimant, the trustee is the appropriate defendant in a strict liability restitutionary claim. The fact that the defendant was also under a duty to the beneficiaries in relation to the right received is not ignored because the duty is equitable; rather, it has no effect as it is not relevant to the reasons behind the particular claim. The awkwardness of Lord Reed's formulation is related to his interpretation of enrichment, which is linked, as in the usual sense of that word, to the acquisition of an overall benefit. It may be, however, that at least in relation to a strict liability restitutionary claim as made in *Conway*, it is the acquisition of rights, rather than the general freedom to benefit from holding those rights, that is critical.[47]

The *Conway* decision forms an interesting parallel to that of the United States Supreme Court in *Sprint Communications Co v APCC Services Inc*.[48] In that case, the question was whether the plaintiff aggregators, to whom payphone operators had assigned their statutory claims against carriers, had standing under Article III of the Constitution to pursue those claims. The defendants' argument was that, as the plaintiffs had promised (in return for payment of a fee) to remit all sums thus recovered to the payphone operators, no 'injury in fact' would be suffered by the plaintiffs if their

42 [2019] UKPC 36, [2020] AC 1111 (hereafter *Conway*).
43 Companies Law (2013 rev), s 145(1) (Cayman Islands).
44 *Conway* (n 42) [89].
45 ibid
46 See, eg, *Carter Holt* (n 1) [25] (Kiefel CJ, Keane and Edelman JJ), discussed further below. For discussion of the consequences for equity more generally of the analysis of the trust proposed in this chapter, see B McFarlane, 'The Persistence of Equity: Lessons from the Trust' in S Elliott and B McFarlane (eds), *Equity Today: 150 Years After the Judicature Reforms* (Hart 2023).
47 See, eg, B McFarlane, 'Unjust Enrichment, Value and Rights' in D Nolan and A Robertson (eds), *Rights in Private Law* (Hart 2010); R Chambers, 'Two Kinds of Enrichment' in R Chambers and others (eds), *Philosophical Foundations of the Law of Unjust Enrichment* (OUP 2009).
48 *Sprint Communications Co v APCC Services Inc*, 554 US 269 (2008) (hereafter *Sprint Communications*).

claim were denied. It is true that, under its arrangements with the operators, the plaintiffs could be said to lack an ongoing interest in the *value* of the right it sought to assert. The majority, however, found that a claim could be made: the fact that the plaintiff was obliged to pay over any sums recovered to a third party did not change the fact that the plaintiff was simply attempting to enforce a duty owed to it by the defendant. Such enforcement of a duty could hardly be seen as beyond 'the traditional concern of the courts at Westminster'[49] and thus outside the scope of Article III. The majority drew on the position of a trustee,[50] who can enforce rights held on trust against third parties even though she is under a duty to use that power (and any proceeds obtained through it) only according to the terms of the trust. Indeed, as will be discussed below, if the trust property consists of a property right in a physical thing, then it is *only* the trustee, and not any beneficiary, who can pursue a claim against a stranger who physically interferes with that property. The key point in each of *Conway* and *Sprint Communications* is that it is an error to regard the existence of the trust as meaning that the rights of the trustee have somehow been lost or reduced, rather than simply encumbered by the duties arising under the trust.

These similarities—between the position of a trustee and the position of a party who simply has a right and is not subject to any duties in relation to it—assist in explaining the lack of specific formality or registration requirements in relation to the creation of an express trust.[51] If O holds a right, and then declares a trust of that right in favour of B, this does not have significant, immediate effects on the duties of third parties. Here, again, the modular aspect of the trust is to the fore: the specific internal complexities of the trust, including the individual entitlements of particular beneficiaries, do not have a significant effect on the duties of third parties.[52] Consider the case where the right held on trust is a right to a physical thing, such as a freehold of land. If X then deliberately or carelessly damages the land, including buildings or equipment attached to it, X breaches a duty owed to T. Similarly, if C wishes to make a particular use of the land, or to acquire a property right, such as a lease of the land, it is the trustees with whom C must deal, as the trustees have the power to license uses or to grant a property right. Two key attributes of property—the 'right to exclude' and the power to allow uses of the resource or transfer or grant interests in it—thus remain with T, notwithstanding the existence of the trust. This is consistent, of course, with analyses which emphasise that the creation of a trust does not involve fragmenting T's rights, but rather keeps

[49] To adopt the words of Justice Frankfurter interpreting the art III judicial power in *Coleman v Miller*, 307 US 433, 460 (1939).

[50] *Sprint Communications* (n 48) 287–88.

[51] In English law, for example, there is of course a formal requirement in relation to a declaration of a trust of land (see Law of Property Act 1925, s 53(1)(b)) but it is notable that the requirement is less demanding than that generally applying to the creation of legal estates and interests in land (see Law of Property Act 1925, s 52 and Land Registration Act 2002, s 4).

[52] See, eg, F Maitland, *State, Trust and Corporation* (D Runciman and M Ryan eds, Cambridge 2003) 105, referring to the 'hard, exterior shell for whatever lies within' that the trust provides, and, at 106, referring to the 'trustee wall' behind which the varied arrangements of 'unincorporated bodies' can exist.

those rights (ie the packages of legal relations) intact and instead encumbers them with duties, owed both to the beneficiaries and to any co-trustees.[53]

This analysis also shows why the approach of the Court of Appeal in *Shell UK Ltd v Total UK Ltd*[54] is difficult to defend.[55] It was accepted by the judges that, where X carelessly damages buildings or equipment attached to land, consequential loss suffered by a beneficiary of a trust of that land is purely economic loss. This is consistent with the view that the duties of third parties in relation to a physical thing that correlate to an owner's 'right to exclude' are owed to the trustees and not the beneficiaries. At the same time, however, it was said that the case fell within one of the special categories where recovery for carelessly caused economic loss is possible, as the existence of the trust provided the required 'special relationship'. On its own terms, of course, the reasoning is fallacious, as the special relationship required for recovery must be between the claimant (here, Shell as a beneficiary of the trust) and the defendant, whereas the trust shows only a special relationship between the beneficiary and the *trustee*. The motivation for the conclusion was that Shell, on the facts, was regarded as, in substance, the owner of the land, entitled to its economic benefits.[56] Such reasoning, however, is far too simplistic as it overlooks the context in which Shell's right arose, and the significant differences, substantive as well as formal, between that right and legal title.

First, as discussed above, the minimal controls on the circumstances in which a right under a trust can arise, and on the content of the right of any individual beneficiary, make it very hard to justify the potentially hidden and far-reaching liability arising if a defendant has to meet the consequential losses of all beneficiaries. Second, as will be discussed further below, it is simply incorrect to see a beneficiary, even under a simple trust structure such as that in *Shell*, as holding the same economic benefits as an unencumbered owner of property: the rights of a beneficiary, unlike those of such an owner, are subject to the trustee's rights of indemnity and, in substance as well as in form, this places an important limit on the beneficiary's rights.

The analysis in *Shell* can also be seen as exemplifying a more general type of misstep. It consists of extracting one aspect of a party's position under a trust, comparing that aspect to other positions which have a very similar practical effect, and then seeking to apply the same or similar rules as regulate that analogous position. Such a misstep can occur for the best of reasons, such as a recognition of the need for coherence in the law, and the importance of treating like cases alike. It can, however, have exactly the opposite effect, if it depends on mischaracterising a party's position by failing to see that position within the broader context of the whole set of rules that apply to a trust. In *Shell*, the problem comes from evaluating the position of a beneficiary of a trust, noting,

[53] See, eg, P Matthews, 'The Compatibility of the Trust with the Civil Law Notion of Property' in L Smith (ed), *Worlds of the Trust* (CUP 2013).

[54] [2010] EWCA Civ 180, [2011] QB 86 (CA) (hereafter *Shell*).

[55] For criticisms of the decision, see, eg, J Edelman, 'Two Fundamental Questions for the Law of Trusts' (2013) 129 LQR 66; B Häcker, '"Substance over Form": Has the Pendulum Swing Too Far?', W Swadling, 'In Defence of Formalism', and B McFarlane, 'Form and Substance in Equity', all in A Robertson and J Goudkamp (eds), *Form and Substance in the Law of Obligations* (Hart 2019).

[56] *Shell* (n 54) [143].

for example, the duty of the trustee to use the rights held on trust for the benefit of that and other beneficiaries, and drawing an analogy to the position of an unencumbered holder of a property right, who also has access in practice to the value of a resource. The assumption then is that coherence is promoted by giving the beneficiary, as closely as possible, the same protection as that unencumbered holder. This overlooks, however, the key point that the beneficiary's rights arise as part of a much broader set of rules, including, for example, the trustee's right of indemnity and the general absence not only of formality and registration rules but also of limits on the content of the individual beneficiary's right. Once the beneficiary's position is seen within that broader set of interconnected rules, it is clear that there is a risk in drawing an analogy with the position of a party whose right arises beyond the law of trusts, and thus beyond the scope of those rules. This same type of error, it can be argued, lay behind Birks's argument that a strict liability restitutionary claim should be prima facie available to a beneficiary of a trust against a recipient of the rights held on trust or their traceable proceeds.[57] The beneficiary's right is not treated differently merely because of its equitable origins, no more than the result in the *Conway* case[58] depends on the common law 'ignoring' equity; rather, its treatment depends on the nature of the right, and the important differences between that right and its supposed common law 'equivalents'.[59]

A key feature of the trust, of course, is that a beneficiary's right can have an effect on successors in title to the trustees. Again, however, it is dangerous to extract this aspect of a beneficiary's position and to argue, as Birks did, that, where a 'proprietary' claim can be made against such a successor, equity is recognising a form of *vindicatio*, involving the direct assertion of an ownership interest.[60] First, as noted by Lord Sumption in *Akers*, the third party's liability depends on her conscience being affected by knowledge of the trust[61]—the beneficiary's claim does not have the distinctive 'That's mine!' form, focused simply on the connection between the claimant and the asset, which, on Birks' view, characterises a *vindicatio*. Second, it is again important to think of the common situation where there are different beneficiaries, with distinct entitlements under the trust—a particular beneficiary, B1, can make a claim against the recipient, but it is not a claim that the recipient must simply hand over the rights acquired to B1. The claim rather is that the recipient must give up the rights, by returning them to identified parties who will then hold the rights on the terms of the initial trust—the aim is to restore the 'trust estate' rather than to make the specific claimant whole.[62] Third, and related to this, that type of claim, recognising a liability of a third party to respect a pre-existing structure under which rights are held subject to duties, is not unique to trusts, and can

[57] See, eg, P Birks, 'Receipt' in P Birks and A Pretto (eds), *Breach of Trust* (Hart 2002).

[58] *Conway* (n 42).

[59] See, eg, L Smith, 'Unjust Enrichment, Property, and the Structure of Trusts' (2000) 116 LQR 412.

[60] P Birks, 'Personal Property: Proprietary Rights and Remedies' (2000) 11 KCLJ 1, 4: 'Equity does have a *vindicatio*'.

[61] *Akers* (n 7) [89]. See further: S Agnew and B McFarlane, 'The Paradox of the Equitable Proprietary Claim' in B McFarlane and S Agnew (eds), *Modern Studies in Property Law: vol X* (Hart 2019).

[62] See, eg, *Akers* (n 7) [46] (Lord Mance); *Target Holdings v Redferns Ltd* [1996] AC 421, 434 (Lord Browne-Wilkinson): in each case, it is noted that, in the case of a bare trust to which the rule in *Saunders v Vautier* (1841) 4 Beav 115 applies, the beneficiaries can instead claim payment directly to themselves.

be made even where there is no party who can be identified as an equitable 'owner'. In *Commissioner of Stamp Duties v Livingston*,[63] for example, it was held that a residuary legatee has no 'beneficial interest' in rights making up a testator's estate during administration; yet, where an unauthorised disposition is made by an executor, such a party *does* have the power to make a claim against a third party.[64] Such a claim clearly cannot be seen as a *vindicatio*, yet its essential structure is the same as the 'proprietary' claim of a beneficiary of a trust.

III. The Rights of a Trustee: Insolvency and Rights of Indemnity

The foregoing analysis has attempted to show first that, in analysing the operation of trusts, it is better to see trusts as a way of dealing with rights rather than with property; and, second, to the extent that having 'property' consists of having particular rights, there is a significant and not merely technical sense in which a trustee is entitled to the trust 'property'. There are at least three reasons, however, why it may seem counter-intuitive to think of the trustee as having 'property'. First, as noted in, for example, *Shell*,[65] the characteristic duty of trustees not to use the rights held on trust for their own benefit (unless and to the extent permitted by the terms of the trust or by rights of indemnity) means that, in the final analysis, once that duty is taken into account, it is other parties who will benefit from the value of those rights. As noted above in relation to the *Conway* and *Sprint Communications* cases, the existence of such a duty, owed to specific individuals, does not, however, impede the legal relations between the trustee and third parties that arise from the trustees' having the rights that form the subject matter of the trust. On one view, in seeking to define and distinguish property rights, it is the *general* position applying, prima facie, between a party and the rest of the world that is crucial, rather than the *particular* position applying as between that party and specific other parties. On that view, for example, the existence of the trustee's duty to certain others not to use a right for her own benefit does not, in itself, prevent the trustee being seen as having 'property', if such a term is otherwise applicable to someone holding the same rights as held by the trustee.

Second, trustees are liable, under certain conditions, to be removed from their position, and can thus be made to give up the rights that they hold. They therefore lack the same type of 'immunity against divesting' that Honoré identified as characteristic of property rights.[66] The vulnerability is not, however, of the same kind as that of, for example, a contractual licensee, who can lose her practical freedom to make a particular

[63] [1965] AC 694 (PC).

[64] See C Mitchell, '*Commissioner of Stamp Duties (Queensland) v Livingston* (1964)' in B Sloan (ed), *Landmark Cases in Succession Law* (Hart 2019). See too cases where a 'proprietary claim' is available to a beneficiary under a discretionary trust, or an object of a power, as discussed by, eg, J Hudson, 'Mere and and Other Discretionary Objects in Australia' in YK Liew and M Harding (eds), *Asia-Pacific Trusts Law: Theory and Practice in Context* (Hart 2021). See too *Serious Fraud Office v Litigation Capital* [2021] EWHC 1272 [205] (Foxton J).

[65] *Shell* (n 54) [132].

[66] A Honoré, 'Rights of Exclusion and Immunities Against Divesting' (1960) 34 Tul L Rev.

use of land if the licensor divests her of it by means of a transfer of the licensor's freehold. The liability of trustees to be removed is instead a feature of the need to ensure due administration of the trust and is linked to the trustees' performance of their role under the trust. This feature is thus a consequence of the fact that trustees hold particular rights subject to duties; it does not deny that they hold those rights.

Third, and most significantly for present purposes, rights held on trust are not available to meet claims of the trustees' creditors. This is, of course, a crucial feature of the modern operation of the trust: it breaks a fundamental rule by allowing a party to hold rights while insulating those rights from the claims of that same party's creditors.[67] This allows parties to achieve asset-partitioning effects without the creation of distinct legal personalities.[68] This feature has been identified as making the trust heretical from a civilian perspective, as it conflicts with the basic model of one person, one patrimony;[69] yet, it is just as challenging in English law, which also seems to adopt the general, prima facie position that all of one's rights are available to meet all of one's debts.[70] This point is an important one as it means the existence of the trust does not simply affect a trustee's legal relations with beneficiaries and co-trustees, but also has an immediate effect on the trustee's general legal relations with all other parties.

Certainly, if such liability to execution is an indispensable aspect of having 'property', then it follows that rights held by a trustee, whatever their nature, cannot, without more, be regarded as property of the trustee. The meaning to be given to 'property of' the trustee is not a purely academic question, of course, as that term is used in statutes and therefore must be interpreted by the courts. Indeed, while it was noted above that academic attention to the 'proprietary' aspects of the trust has focused largely on the position of beneficiaries, rather than of trustees, some recent litigation has led to closer scrutiny of the rights of trustees. In *Carter Holt*,[71] for example, the High Court of Australia had to consider whether rights held on trust could be seen as 'property' of the insolvent company (which had traded as the trustee of a trading trust) or its receivers within the meaning of the term used in the Corporations Act 2001 (Cth); this was relevant to triggering a provision ensuring that employees of the company could receive payment prior to holders of a 'circulating security interest' in the company's assets, as would have been the case if the company had not operated through a trading trust structure.[72] In examining this question, the court very usefully highlighted some 'fundamental principles of trust law'.[73] For example, it was noted that common law courts had for centuries taken 'notice of a trust' by holding that 'rights held by a bankrupt on trust do not generally form part of the bankrupt's estate that is available for general

[67] See, eg, *Investec Trust (Guernsey) Ltd v Glenalla Properties Ltd* [2018] UKPC 7, [2019] AC 271 [59] (Lord Hodge).

[68] See, eg, H Hansmann and U Mattei, 'The Functions of Trust Law: A Comparative Legal and Economic Analysis' (1998) 73 NYULR 434.

[69] See, eg, N Kasirer, 'Translating Part of France's Legal Heritage: Aubry and Rau on the *Patrimoine*' in R Valsan (ed), *Trusts and Patrimonies* (Edinburgh UP 2015).

[70] See, eg, B McFarlane, 'The Trust and its Civilian Analogues' in L Smith (ed), *Worlds of the Trust* (CUP 2013).

[71] See *Carter Holt* (n 1) above.

[72] Corporations Act 2001, s 433, as amended 2012.

[73] *Carter Holt* (n 1) [23].

distribution amongst creditors'.[74] Legislation such as the Bankruptcy Act 1966 (Cth) then followed this approach by 'excluding from the property divisible among creditors all property held by the bankrupt on trust for another person'[75] but even if a particular statute, such as the Corporations Act, did not expressly make such an exclusion, it had to apply 'by undisputed analogy'.[76] The explanation given for this position by Kiefel CJ, Keane and Edelman JJ,[77] quoting from *Gladstone v Hadwen*,[78] is the simple and persuasive one that, given the power of a beneficiary to make a claim against a donee successor in title to the trustee, it would be 'absurd', on bankruptcy, for rights to vest, or be controlled by, a party who could then be ordered not to use those rights for the very purpose for which it is to act: to benefit the creditors of the insolvent party.

That joint judgment then states that 'rights held on trust were, and are, generally excluded from inclusion in the statutory concepts of the "property" of the bankrupt or the "property" of the insolvent company'.[79] However, some care must be taken here. The technique used by the express statutory provisions is not to deny that rights held on trust are the property of the insolvent trustee; rather, it is accepted that those rights form part of the property of the trustee but stated that those rights do not form part of the property available to be realised and/or distributed to creditors. So, technically then, the rights held on trust are, for the purposes of the statute, property of the trustee; it is just that, like other excluded categories of the insolvent's property (such as, eg, tools of the insolvent party's trade), those rights are not available for distribution. By itself, however, this point would not have been decisive in *Carter Holt*, as the priority for the employees depended on whether, in making a payment to employees out of trust assets, the receivers could be said to make payment 'out of the property coming into his, her or its hands' as specified by section 433(3) of the Corporations Act 2001. It could be argued then that property 'comes into a party's hands', within the meaning of that provision, only to the extent that a party is, overall, free to use that property for its own benefit.[80] On that view, although rights held on trust are property of the trustee, the particular duties owed by the trustee to beneficiaries and co-trustees prevent those rights being seen as 'coming into the hands of' the receivers.

Even if that interpretation of the provision were to be accepted, however, a trustee is free, even as against beneficiaries and co-trustees, to use rights held on trust for its own benefit if this is permitted by the structure of the trust. Trustees' rights of indemnity have long been a crucial aspect of the smooth operation of trusts. As a trust is not

[74] ibid [25]. Compare the discussion above of Lord Reed's reasoning in *Conway* (n 42).

[75] *Carter Holt* (n 1) [25]. See Bankruptcy Act 1966 (Cth), s 116(2)(a): 'property divisible amongst the creditors of the bankrupt' as defined by section 116(1), does not extend to 'property held by the bankrupt in trust for another person.'

[76] *Carter Holt* (n 1) [26]. The position seems to be the same in English law: section 283(a) of the Insolvency Act 1986 expressly states that 'property held by the bankrupt on trust for any other person' does not form part of the bankrupt's estate and the same result applies to companies in the absence of an express provision: see, eg, *Barclays Bank v Quistclose Investments* [1970] AC 567; W Swadling, 'Property' in A Burrows (ed), *English Private Law* (3rd edn, OUP 2013) 4.152.

[77] *Carter Holt* (n 1) [27].

[78] (1813) 1 M & S 517, 526.

[79] *Carter Holt* (n 1) [27].

[80] ibid [54].

a separate entity, trustees carrying out their duties in a manner authorised under the trust will incur personal liabilities, so it is necessary for trustees to have the authority to meet those liabilities by directly using the value of rights held on trust (a right of exoneration), or by having access to that value to indemnify themselves for payments made from their own pocket (a right of reimbursement). As seen in the language used by the joint judgment of Kiefel CJ, Keane and Edelman JJ in *Carter Holt*, the right of exoneration can be described as a 'power to use trust funds to discharge debts that were properly incurred by the trustee in the course of the trust business'.[81] As discussed by Hudson and Mitchell,[82] this power should be distinguished from the general power of a trustee, simply as a holder of the rights held on trust, to transfer those rights to a third party. Such a transfer can of course take effect, and be valid in the sense of conferring rights on the third party, even if the trustee does *not* have authority to make the transfer under the terms of the trust.[83] This is consistent with the analysis above: the terms of the trust depend on, and cannot deny, the powers trustees have within the package of legal relations that constitute the rights held on trust. So, the power of exoneration refers specifically to the power that a trustee has, as against beneficiaries and co-trustees, to alter their legal relations by reducing the scope of the rights held on trust. In the context of the analysis here, it is more pertinent to see the right of exoneration as a liberty: the trustee does not owe a duty to the beneficiaries or co-trustees not to use the rights held on trust in that specific way.[84] The 'right' of exoneration, therefore, is not an *additional* general right, given to a trustee on top of the package of legal relations constituted by the right held on trust; it is rather a consequence of (i) the trustee's holding that right, and (ii) a limit on the scope of the duties owed by the trustee in relation to that right. This explains the sense in which, as confirmed in *Carter Holt*,[85] a beneficiary's interest is subject to the right of exoneration: that interest depends on the scope of the duties of the trustee, overlaid on the rights held by the trustee, and the limit on those duties leaves the trustee free to use the rights in a particular way. So if, for example, a right held by a receiver counts as property coming into its hands, and so is caught by section 433 of the Corporation Act 2001, only if the receiver is free from any duty to another not to use that right for its own benefit,[86] then, to the extent of the liberty of exoneration, a right held on trust does so qualify.

[81] ibid [31].

[82] J Hudson and C Mitchell, 'Trustee Recoupment: A Power Analysis' (2021) 35 Trust Law Int 3, 8 (hereafter Hudson and Mitchell, 'Trustee Recoupment').

[83] See, eg, *Rolled Steel Products Ltd v British Steel Corp* [1986] Ch 246, 303 (Browne-Wilkinson LJ): 'If two trustees convey trust property in breach of trust, the conveyance is not void. As human beings they have the capacity to transfer the legal estate: their capacity to transfer flows from their status as human beings, not from the powers conferred on them as trustees. Even if their powers under the trust instrument did not authorise the conveyance, the legal estate will vest in the transferee.'

[84] Note that where the trustee has a 'right' of reimbursement, the liberty is somewhat different in content, as the trustee is then free to use the trust rights, to that extent, in any way that the trustee wishes; whereas with a 'right' of exoneration, the liberty is confined to making an authorised use of the trust rights.

[85] See too *Chief Commissioner of Stamp Duties (NSW) v Buckle* (1998) 192 CLR 226.

[86] See too *Carter Holt* (n 1) [84], where Bell, Gageler and Nettle JJ find that the trustee's right of exoneration can be described as 'constituting a beneficial interest in the trust assets'.

This analysis also means that care must be taken in describing the trustee's right of exoneration as a charge or lien over the trust assets. As noted in the joint judgment of Bell, Gageler and Nettle JJ in *Carter Holt*, the trustee's right 'is not, however, a charge or lien comparable to a synallagmatic security interest over property of another. It arises endogenously as an incident of the office of trustee in respect of the trust assets.'[87] It would, again, be a mistake to think of the trust assets as in some sense belonging to the beneficiaries, and thus constituting property of another over which a trustee needs a secondary right. In fact, this is to have things precisely the wrong way around.

This terminological point may seem to be of limited interest but, as recently noted by Hudson and Mitchell,[88] it is important when considering the position of a former trustee who remains liable for authorised debts incurred as trustee. In such a case, there is a question as to the nature and protection of the former trustee's right of indemnity and, as seen by recent litigation in the Privy Council,[89] there can be an issue of priority as between that right of indemnity and the rights of other parties who have claims against the current trustees. As a former trustee no longer holds the rights that are the subject matter of the trust, it is possible for such a party to have a charge over those rights in the standard sense of an equitable security right relating to the right of another party. As Hudson and Mitchell argue,[90] it would be a mistake to think that, because a current trustee's right of indemnity can be said to arise under a charge or lien, in the loose sense noted above, it is *necessarily* the case that the former trustee must have a genuine security interest over the trust assets.

IV. Wider Consequences of the Argument

This section will briefly consider, by way of conclusion, some possible consequences of the argument made here for three much-debated questions in the law of express trusts and beyond.

A. The Nature of a Beneficiary's Interest

The focus of this chapter has been on the nature of the interest of a trustee, partly because this aspect of the foundations of the trust has been overshadowed by discussion of the nature of the interest of a beneficiary. Nonetheless, it is worth briefly noting that the argument made here has important consequences for that question. The first and perhaps simplest point is one that has been made by, for example, Maitland[91] and

[87] ibid [83].
[88] Hudson and Mitchell, 'Trustee Recoupment' (n 82) 16–17.
[89] *Equity Trust* (n 1).
[90] Hudson and Mitchell, 'Trustee Recoupment' (n 82) 16–17.
[91] FW Maitland, *Equity: A Course of Lectures* (A H Chaytor and W J Whittaker eds, revised by John Brunyate, 2nd edn, CUP 1936) lectures 9–11 (hereafter Maitland, *Equity: A Course of Lectures*).

Hackney:[92] it is a mistake to see the interests of trustee and beneficiary as competing or opposed.[93] It is not the case that each party makes distinct claims to the same resource; rather, a trustee has an initial package of legal relations, and a beneficiary then has the ability to insist that those rights are administered in accordance with the duties attaching to them. It is in the interests of a beneficiary for the trustee to have a strong package of legal relations with respect to third parties: to that extent, the strength of a beneficiary's rights lies in the strength of the trustee's rights. This suggests that there is no need for equity to set up a second law of property; it can rather protect a beneficiary by giving that party not only a claim against the initial trustees, but also against recipients of the rights held on trust, where their conscience is affected by knowledge of the trust. Third parties potentially liable in this way are identified not by their dealings with specific resources, but rather by their acquisition, from the trustee, of particular rights. Further, as noted in the discussion of *Livingston* above, this liability of third parties does not depend on a beneficiary being seen as an owner of the trust assets—it rather arises from an insistence on respecting the pre-existing structure subject to which a party, such as a trustee or executor, held specific rights. Moreover, as seen in the analysis of Kiefel CJ, Keane and Edelman JJ in *Carter Holt*,[94] the protection of a beneficiary in the insolvency of the trustee (another attribute shared with a legatee of an unadministered estate) can also be seen as flowing from this insistence, rather than on any pre-existing ownership of assets by a beneficiary.

Second, and linked to this point, the creation of a trust, as has been judicially noted,[95] does not involve the fragmenting, as between trustee and beneficiaries, of the legal relations constituted by a pre-existing right: rather, the right remains intact and a beneficiary's right can better be seen as arising from duties imposed on the trustee in relation to that right. As shown by the impact of the trustee's rights of indemnity, any limit to those duties necessarily limits the rights of a beneficiary and so further distinguishes the position of a beneficiary from that of an owner of a resource. Simply put, the nature and scope of the trustee's rights means there is less scope to see a beneficiary's rights as amounting to ownership.

B. The Nature of Property

There is, of course, a wide variety of views as to the best way to approach the legal concept of property. The point to be made here is essentially a methodological one: to what extent should an analysis of that concept be able to explain the position of a trustee? One would expect that such an analysis should account for the position of, for example,

[92] J Hackney, *Understanding Equity and Trusts* (Fontana 1987) ch 1.

[93] See too H Smith, 'Equity as Meta-Law' (2021) 130 Yale L J 1050, 1098–100 (hereafter Smith, 'Equity as Meta-Law').

[94] *Carter Holt* (n 1) [27].

[95] See, eg, *DKLR Holding Co (No 2) Pty Ltd v Commissioner of Stamp Duties* [1980] 1 NSWLR 510, 518–19 (Hope JA) (hereafter *DKLR Holding*); *Carter Holt* (n 1) [82] (Bell, Gageler and Nettle JJ).

O, a party with an unencumbered title to a physical thing such as a car. Should the analysis also be able to account for the position of T, a party who holds title to a car on trust? On the argument made in this chapter, there are very important continuities between the legal relations of each of O and T against parties other than beneficiaries of the trust. These continuities are easier to explain on some views of property than on others. For example, models which focus on the general third-party effects of particular claim-rights and powers[96] can incorporate the position of T within the concept of property, as T's claim-rights and powers in relation to third parties, as discussed above, are essentially the same as those of O.

Models which instead focus on the *overall* position of a party, and which would therefore have to consider limits on T's position arising under the trust, cannot include T's position within the scope of property in the same way. For example, if a model emphasises the role of property in enhancing autonomy,[97] or the ability of an owner to set the agenda for the use of a resource,[98] then it seems that T is placed outside that model by the particular limits imposed by the trust on T's choice as to how to exercise the claim-rights and powers that form part of the subject matter of the trust. Similarly, in providing a Kantian analysis of the differences between property and sovereignty, Ripstein emphasises that whereas there are internal limits to the authority of a sovereign, based on the reasons for which that sovereignty is held, the 'owner of property can use it for any purpose whatsoever, subject only to external restrictions'.[99] Of course, this point is not by any means suggested as a fatal flaw in such models of property, but rather as raising the methodological question of how the position of T should be handled. For example, it could justifiably be seen as an exceptional case, which does not have to fall within the core meaning or function of property. Or T's duties could be seen as 'external restrictions', perhaps by making a distinction between the overall, general and particular positions: it is true that, *overall*, T is not free to use the resource to which the trust relates as T wishes, but that is simply a consequence of the duties T is under to *particular* parties, rather than being a *general* limit on T's choices. Such a view is easier to adopt if the limits on T are seen as flowing from the particular duties of T, rather than any general proprietary entitlement of the beneficiaries. If, however, as suggested by Samet and Dagan in their chapter,[100] the trust is seen as a way of enhancing the autonomy of an owner by allowing her to confer what is in effect a proprietary entitlement on beneficiaries, then it becomes harder to explain the continuities between the position of T and that of O.

[96] For example, by seeing property in its core sense as recognising duties not to interfere with physical things (see, eg, S Douglas and B McFarlane, 'Defining Property Rights' in J Penner and H Smith (eds), *Philosophical Foundations of the Law of Property* (OUP 2012); or, by emphasising property's role in managing complexity by adopting a notion of a physical or legal 'thing' as a module around which particular uses of a resource can cohere, thus limiting information costs imposed on strangers (see, eg, H Smith, 'Property as The Law of Things' (2012) 125 Harv L Rev 1691); or by analysing property as based on a right to immediate exclusive possession accompanied by powers to permit interference and to transfer ownership (see, eg, J Penner, *Property Rights: A Re-examination* (OUP 2020)).

[97] See, eg, H Dagan, *A Liberal Theory of Property* (CUP 2021).

[98] See, eg, L Katz, 'Exclusion and Exclusivity in Property Law' (2008) 58 U Toronto L J 275.

[99] A Ripstein, 'Property and Sovereignty: How to Tell the Difference' (2017) 18 Theor Inq in Law 243, 244.

[100] H Dagan and I Samet, 'Express Trust: The Dark Horse of the Liberal Property Regime' in this book.

C. The Nature of Rights

In the discussion above of *Sprint Communications*, it was argued, consistently with the majority view in that case, that T can have a right (and a power to enforce it) even if T will not in the end benefit, overall, from D's performance of the correlative duty. This can be seen as providing some support for the objections made by Hart to Bentham's analysis of a right-holder as being the party who benefits from another's duty.[101] Hart's preference is, in general,[102] to identify the right-holder as having powers of control over the duty, including the choice as to whether or not to waive, extinguish, or enforce that duty, so that rights can be seen as consisting of a party's legally respected choices. It is not clear, however, how this analysis deals with the position of a trustee. On the one hand, as argued above, where a freehold is held on trust by T, T does have the power, as against a third party, to choose whether to waive, extinguish (or suspend), or enforce that party's duty not to physically interfere with the land. However, in his analysis, building on that of Bentham, Hart generally regards rights as conferring 'bilateral liberties': that is to say, the right-holder is free from both a duty to act and a duty not to act.[103] That is not the case for T, where the trust imposes a duty on T to exercise or not exercise her power to waive, extinguish, or enforce another party's duty.

Indeed, in his analysis, Hart refers at two points to the position of a trustee. In each case, it is to give an example of a case where a party is commonly said to have a right even though she does not have a bilateral liberty. It is first stated that a trustee who has a duty under the trust to put a resource to a particular use is said to have a right to make that use of the resource as 'the equitable duty is for historical reasons conceived as something distinct grafted on to his still persistent legal bilateral liberty-rights, although its actual effect is to render the liberty unilateral'.[104] Hart gives this as an example of the phenomenon, noted by Bentham, where duties are 'super-added'[105] to liberty-rights. Hart later states that the same pattern can occur in relation to a power held by a trustee, as a trustee's 'legal rights are theoretically distinguishable from his equitable duties and are thought of as co-existing even where they in fact conflict'.[106] This reference to there in fact being conflict, and T's liberty being rendered unilateral, echoes Hohfeld's rejoinder to Maitland's analysis of the interaction between common law and equity: in a case, for example, where T's holds a freehold of land on trust, T's common law liberty as against trust beneficiaries and co-trustees to cut down ornamental trees on that land conflicts with T's equitable duty to those parties not to do

[101] H Hart, *Essays on Bentham* (OUP 1982) ch 7 (hereafter Hart, *Essays*). Hart at 187–89 cites contracts intended to benefit third parties as a case where the party intended to benefit from the performance of a duty is not a right holder as 'he has no legal control over the duty'.

[102] See ibid 188–90 for limits on the theory.

[103] ibid 171–74. A liberty is unilateral in this sense if a party has only one of the freedom to act in a particular way, and the freedom not to act in that way.

[104] ibid 174, n 56.

[105] Bentham, *Of Laws in General*, in *Collected Works* (Athlone Press 1970) 270–71, 296.

[106] Hart, *Essays* (n 101) 188, n 93.

so.[107] It also suggests, consistently with Hart's analysis of when a party benefits or not from another's duty, that Hart is adopting an *overall* analysis of T's position, which does not separate the *general* position as against the rest of the world from the *particular* position as against beneficiaries and co-trustees. The difficulty with adopting such a view, however, is that T does not then have a bilateral liberty to waive, extinguish, or enforce another party's duty not to interfere with the land, and so T's position does not fall within the analysis of rights preferred by Hart.

One way to avoid this problem would simply be to say that the standard model of rights cannot apply to T's position, but that would seem to be a problem for a model which in Hart's words, is intended to be satisfactory at the 'level of the lawyer concerned with the working of the "ordinary" law'.[108] A different response would be to distinguish between the overall, general and particular views of T's position and to dispute Hart's assumption that it is only for 'historical reasons' that T's duty as trustee is conceived as 'something distinct grafted on to'[109] T's still-existing right. It can instead be argued that such a view is not purely historical, and that T does indeed have a general bilateral liberty, as against parties other than beneficiaries,[110] to choose whether to waive, extinguish, or enforce the duties of such parties. It is necessary to separate that *general* position from the *particular* position as between T and the beneficiaries who, after all, would not wish to dispute the view that T has a genuine right against the third parties, as they can then benefit from the existence of that right. Such a separation is far from being a relic of history, as it instead reflects the distinct nature and structure of trusts, and recognising it is necessary to avoid the errors which come from 'flattening'[111] the distinction between common law and equity by failing to recognise the secondary nature of a beneficiary's rights, which have as their subject matter the rights of the trustee.[112]

This approach can also be used to limit the divergence between the views of Maitland and of Hohfeld. Whereas Hohfeld was correct to argue that, at the level of the legal relations between trustee and beneficiary, there is a conflict between the position at common law and in equity, Maitland's more significant point was that, in a case where, for example, a freehold is held on trust, this conflict does not involve the 'civil war and utter anarchy'[113] that would result from the two systems disagreeing on the fundamental

[107] Hohfeld, 'The Relations Between Equity and Law' (1913) 11 Mich L R 537, 555.

[108] Hart, *Essays* (n 101) 193.

[109] Compare the similar language used in, eg, *DKLR Holding* (n 95) 518–19 (Hope JA); *Carter Holt* (n 1) [82] (Bell, Gageler and Nettle JJ).

[110] Where there is more than one trustee, T will also be under duties to the co-trustees: for simplicity, the discussion here assumes there is a sole trustee.

[111] H Smith, 'Fusing the Equitable Function in Private Law' in K Barker and others (eds), *Private Law in the 21st Century* (Hart 2017); Smith, 'Equity as Meta-Law' (n 93).

[112] See, eg, B McFarlane and R Stevens, 'What's Special About Equity? Rights About Rights' in D Klimchuk and others (eds), *Philosophical Foundations of the Law of Equity* (OUP 2020).

[113] Maitland, *Equity: A Course of Lectures* (n 91) 17.

question of who is the owner of the land.[114] The crucial point is that, in such cases, the trust does not deny, but rather depends on, the freehold, the package of legal relations equated with ownership, belonging to T, who has 'all the powers incidental to ownership subject only to the power of the beneficiaries to compel [T] to exercise [T's] powers in accordance with the terms of the trust'.[115]

[114] See further: B McFarlane, 'Avoiding Anarchy? Common Law v Equity & Maitland v Hohfeld' in P Turner and others (eds), *Equity and Law: Fusion and Fission* (CUP 2018).

[115] *Carter Holt* (n 1) [82] (Bell, Gageler and Nettle JJ): note that, where there is more than one trustee, T's position will also be subject to the powers of co-trustees to enforce the terms of the trust.

3

The Settlor's Conscience

Sinéad Agnew[*]

I. Introduction

In the context of trusts law, discussions of conscience tend to focus on the conscience of the trustee (T). Any mention of the settlor's conscience is rare. There is a tendency to assume that if anyone's conscience is relevant in the context of express trusts, it is that of a person *other* than the settlor (S)—eg the alleged trustee or a third-party recipient of trust assets—and so the idea of the settlor's conscience does not receive much attention at all. However, as this chapter will show, the settlor's conscience is relevant in various contexts, such as the creation of self-declared trusts and the rescue of express trusts by transfer which would otherwise fail because of inadequate constitution or disclaimer.

II. Conscience and the Law of Trusts

Before considering the relevance of the settlor's conscience in the law of express trusts, it is necessary to consider what 'conscience' means and its place in English equity.

A. The Concept of Conscience

The roots of the word can be found in the Greek and Latin terms for 'I know' or 'I know together with', which meant that, historically, *conscience* could be understood in two senses: first, as a form of private knowledge; and secondly, as involving 'a community of knowledge', whereby one could bear witness (*conscire*) to one's own acts or the acts of others.[1] Collectively, these meanings suggest a narrow view of conscience, which does not necessarily involve any moral judgement.

The development of conscience as a concept was influenced by Catholic casuistry. Late medieval scholastic philosophers, such as Aquinas,[2] conceived of conscience

* I am grateful to Charles Mitchell, Lusina Ho, all the participants at the Philosophical Foundations of Trust Law workshop and the editors for their helpful comments on this chapter.

[1] CS Lewis, *Studies in Words* (2nd edn, CUP 1967) 181, 184–87; D Marietta Jr, 'Conscience in Greek Stoicism' (1970) 17 Numen 176, 177.

[2] For Aquinas' reflections on conscience, see: St Thomas Aquinas, *Summa Theologica* (Fathers of the English Dominican Province tr, Benziger Bros 1947) pt 1(1), q 79, arts 12–13, pt II (1), q 91, arts 1–2 (hereafter Aquinas, *Summa Theologica*); St Thomas Aquinas, *Opera omnia*, vol 22, *Quaestiones disputatae de veritate* 16-17 in *Conscience in Medieval Philosophy* (T Potts tr, CUP 1980) 124–35.

Sinéad Agnew, *The Settlor's Conscience* In: *Philosophical Foundations of the Law of Express Trusts*. Edited by: Simone Degeling, Jessica Hudson, and Irit Samet, Oxford University Press. © Sinéad Agnew 2023. DOI: 10.1093/oso/9780192844934.003.0004 (*conscientia*) as an act of applied knowledge, which involved the application of *synderesis* (an innate ability to identify certain basic moral truths derived from divine law) in individual cases. By combining her moral understanding with her knowledge of the facts of a particular situation, an individual could judge what she ought to do now or in the future and evaluate the moral quality of her past actions.

Three features of the Thomist idea of conscience are worth noting, as they connote a wider sense of conscience with moral reasoning at its core. First, it presupposes an 'external, objective moral law',[3] which was accessible to all through *synderesis*. Secondly, it admits of the possibility that errors of conscience arising from non-culpable ignorance of relevant facts could be excused.[4] The idea of culpable ignorance is reflected in modern philosophical arguments to the effect that we are all subject to 'epistemic obligations', the purpose of which is to enable us to acquire the information necessary to enable us to satisfy our primary moral duties.[5] Thirdly, the Thomist idea of conscience works syllogistically to enable individuals to combine known moral precepts with factual knowledge to reach a moral judgement.[6]

B. Conscience in Equity

The idea of conscience in both senses described above has been relevant to the development of English law. The procedural distinction between the early equitable and common law jurisdictions could be said to be based on conscience in the narrow sense, as equity admitted proof of private knowledge of facts (and subjective intentions), which could not be proved so easily, if at all, at common law.[7] The late scholastic idea of conscience as applied knowledge appears to have been substantively influential in the development of *both* the common law[8] and equity[9] during the late medieval and

[3] See, eg, D Klinck, *Conscience, Equity and the Court of Chancery in Early Modern England* (Ashgate 2010) 32 (hereafter Klinck, *Conscience, Equity and the Court of Chancery*); M Drakopolou, 'Equity, Conscience and the Art of Judgment as Ius Aequi et Boni' (2000–2001) 5 Law Text Culture 345, 351–52 (hereafter Drakopolou, 'Equity, Conscience and the Art of Judgment').

[4] Aquinas, *Summa Theologica* (n 2) pt II (1), q 6, arts 1 and 8, and q 19, art 6; see further Klinck, *Conscience, Equity and the Court of Chancery* (n 3) 34–36. The idea dates back to Aristotle: see Aristotle, *Nicomachean Ethics* (R Crisp ed, 2nd edn, CUP 2018) xix, III.I, 1110a–b, p 37; III.1, 1111a, p 39; and III.5, 1113b–1114a, p 46.

[5] G Rosen, 'Culpability and Ignorance' in *Proceedings of the Aristotelian Society*, New Series, vol 103 (OUP 2003) 61; G Rosen, 'Skepticism About Moral Responsibility' (2004) 18 Phil. Perspect. 295; H Smith, 'The Subjective Moral Duty to Inform Oneself Before Acting' (2014) 125 Ethics 11, 13. See further J Gardner, 'Some Rule of Law Anxieties About Strict Liability in Private Law' in L Austin and D Klimchuk (eds), *Private Law and the Rule of Law* (OUP 2014) 207, 218–19.

[6] Klinck, *Conscience, Equity and the Court of Chancery* (n 3) 34; see further Drakopolou, 'Equity, Conscience and the Art of Judgment' (n 3) 352.

[7] M Macnair, 'Equity and Conscience' (2007) 27 OJLS 659.

[8] L Knafla, 'Conscience in the English Common Law Tradition' (1976) UTLJ 1; N Doe, *Fundamental Authority in Late Medieval English Law* (CUP 1990), Ch 6; D Seipp, 'Trust and Conscience in the Early Common Law' in F Cranmer, M Hill, C Kenny, and R Sandberg (eds), *The Confluence of Law and Religion: Reflections on the Work of Norman Doe* (CUP 2016).

[9] Klinck, *Conscience, Equity and the Court of Chancery* (n 3); R Hedlund, 'The Theological Foundations of Equity's Conscience' (2015) 4 OJLS 119 (hereafter Hedlund, 'The Theological Foundations of Equity's Conscience'); H Coing, 'English Equity and the *Denunciatio Evangelica* of the Canon Law' (1955) 71 LQR 223; FT Roughley, 'The Development of the Conscience of Equity' in JT Gleeson, JA Watson, and RCA Higgins (eds), *Historical Foundations of Australian Law* (The Federation Press 2013); R Havelock, 'The Evolution of Equitable "Conscience"' (2014) 8 J Eq 128.

early modern periods. Although initially, this idea of conscience was explicitly rooted in divine law,[10] over time it came to be grounded in the law itself,[11] especially in equity.

As equity became systematised through the doctrine of precedent, judges such as Lord Nottingham began to delineate more clearly the boundaries between matters of private conscience, which were purely moral questions for the individual, and matters of conscience, which were justiciable in equity.[12] Two features of Lord Nottingham's idea of justiciable conscience[13] are relevant for present purposes. First, the difference between internal and external acts was significant. Equity would not intervene in respect of a matter that was internal to the defendant and unknowable to the court, and the making of an internal resolution to hold an asset on trust was not justiciable.[14] Secondly, matters of conscience that were justiciable did not include the enforcement of virtues such as generosity.[15] Outside the context of fiduciary relationships, equity allowed parties to engage in self-interested bargaining and was unlikely to interfere to assist volunteers.[16]

The ideas of conscience and unconscionability are still frequently invoked in judicial reasoning, both in equity[17] and at common law.[18] However, as the courts are at pains to emphasise, these ideas are context-dependent[19] and, consistently with the late scholastic idea of conscience,[20] the courts purport to apply objective principles and standards which are embedded in equitable doctrine.[21]

[10] W Holdsworth, 'The Early History of Equity' (1914–1915) 13 Mich L Rev 293, 294–95.

[11] In large part due to the work of St German, whose theory of conscience closely followed the Thomist model. See T Plucknett and J Barton (eds), *'Introduction' to St German's Doctor and Student* (Selden Society 1974) xxvi; Klinck, *Conscience, Equity and the Court of Chancery* (n 3) 54, 89.

[12] See, eg, *Coke v Fountaine* (1676) 3 Swanst 585, 600, 36 ER 984 (hereafter *Coke v Fountaine*); M Macnair, '*Coke v Fountaine* (1676)' in C Mitchell and P Mitchell (eds), *Landmark Cases in Equity* (Hart 2012) 57 (hereafter Macnair, '*Coke v Fountaine*').

[13] D Klinck, 'Lord Nottingham and the Conscience of Equity' (2006) 67 J Hist Ideas 123, 127 (hereafter Klinck, 'Lord Nottingham and the Conscience of Equity').

[14] ibid 129.

[15] ibid 141.

[16] Klinck, *Conscience, Equity and the Court of Chancery* (n 3) 51, 250. See, eg, *The Earl of Oxford's Case in Chancery* (1615) 1 Ch Rep 1, 5; 21 ER 485, 486.

[17] eg *Westdeutsche Landesbank Girozentrale v Islington LBC* [1996] 1 AC 669, 705 (Lord Browne-Wilkinson) (hereafter *Westdeutsche*) (trust obligations); *Akers v Samba Group* [2017] UKSC 6, [2017] AC 424, [89] (Lord Sumption) (hereafter *Akers v Samba*) (equitable proprietary claim); *BCCI (Overseas) Ltd v Akindele* [1991] Ch 437 (CA), 455 (Nourse LJ) (hereafter *BCCI v Akindele*); *Byers v Samba Financial Group* [2021] EWHC 60 (Ch), [109] (Fancourt J) (knowing receipt).

[18] eg *Pakistan International Airline Corporation v Times Travel (UK) Ltd* [2021] UKSC 40, [2021] 3 WLR 727 (hereafter *Pakistan v Times Travel*) (lawful act duress); *Tinkler v Revenue Commissioners* [2021] UKSC 39, [2021] 3 WLR 697, [88] (Lord Briggs JSC) (estoppel by convention).

[19] *Pakistan v Times Travel* (n 18) [23] (Lord Hodge).

[20] Hedlund, 'The Theological Foundations of Equity's Conscience' (n 9).

[21] See, eg, *Allcard v Skinner* (1887) 35 Ch D 145 (CA), 190 (Bowen LJ) (undue influence); *Thor Navigation v Ingosstrakh Insurance Co Ltd* [2005] EWHC 19 (Comm), [2005] 1 CLC 12, [57] (Gloster J) (rectification); *Pitt v Holt* [2013] UKSC 26, [2013] 2 AC 108, [125]–[126] (Lord Walker) (mistaken voluntary dispositions); *Kakavas v Crown Melbourne Ltd* [2013] HCA 25, (2013) 298 ALR 35, [16] (unconscionable dealing); *Commonwealth v Verwayen* (1990) 170 CLR 394, 441 (Deane J) (promissory estoppel); *Tanwar Enterprises Pty Ltd v Cauchi* (2003) 217 CLR 313, [20] (Gleeson, McHugh, Gummow, Hayne and Heydon JJ) and [84] (Kirby J).

C. Conscience and Trustees' Duties

There is a close connection between the idea of conscience and trustees' duties, which were initially regarded as moral duties, binding only in honour and conscience.[22] Over time, equity came to regard these moral duties as justiciable, and the idea of conscience is still relevant to their incidence. It is said that 'the equitable jurisdiction to enforce trusts depends upon the conscience of the holder of the legal interest being affected' by knowledge of the relevant facts.[23] And further '[E]quity operates on the conscience of the owner of a legal interest': in the case of an express trust his conscience 'requires him to carry out the purposes for which the property was vested in him'.[24]

Here, we can see the idea of conscience as applied knowledge at work. Unless the putative trustee's conscience is affected by knowledge (so that she can work out what she *ought* to do with the assets), it is unreasonable to treat her conscience as *bound* by any enforceable duty in respect of the assets to which equity will give effect.[25] Thus, knowledge of the relevant facts has moral relevance and is a necessary precondition to the recognition and enforcement of trustees' duties.

Sometimes, factual knowledge coupled with possession of the trust assets is sufficient to trigger a custodial duty. Take, for example, the way in which equity treats third-party recipients of assets transferred in breach of trust. If, while a recipient has the assets in her possession her conscience is affected by knowledge,[26] eg because she knows[27] or (perhaps) has reason to know[28] that they were transferred in breach of trust, equity regards her as subject to a custodial duty, which means that she cannot deal with the assets other than for the benefit of the beneficiary (B): she must restore them or, failing that, make good their value.[29] In principle, it is arguable that an intended express

[22] A Simpson, *A History of the Land Law* (2nd edn, Clarendon 1986) 173–76. See further R Helmholz, 'The Early Enforcement of Uses' (1979) 79 Colum L Rev 1503; R Helmholz, *The Oxford History of the Laws of England*, vol 1 (J Baker ed) (OUP 2004) 422–23.

[23] *Westdeutsche* (n 17) 705.

[24] ibid. For similar comments, see *Akers v Samba* (n 17) [89] (Lord Sumption); *Investec v Glenalla* [2018] UKPC 7, [2018] 2 WLR 1465, [228] (Lord Mance).

[25] There is some debate about whether both the personal *and* the proprietary aspects of a trust depend on the state of the legal owner's conscience. In *Westdeutsche* (n 17), Lord Browne-Wilkinson (at 705, 707–08, and 714) and Lord Goff (at 709) seemed to take the view that they do. For the view that a split between legal and equitable title may arise without the legal owner's knowledge, see, eg, *Hardoon v Belilios* [1901] AC 118 (HL), 123 (Lord Lindley); *Allan v Rea Bros Trustees Ltd* [2002] EWCA Civ 85, 4 ITELR 627, [45]–[46] (Walker LJ); P Birks, 'Trusts Raised to Reverse Unjust Enrichment: The Westdeutsche Case' (1996) 4 RLR 3, 12; P Millett, 'Restitution and Constructive Trusts' (1998) 114 LQR 399, 403–05; S Worthington, 'The Proprietary Consequences of Rescission' (2002) 10 RLR 28, 50.

[26] *BCCI v Akindele* (n 17) 455 (Nourse LJ); *Independent Trustee Services Ltd v GP Noble Trustees Ltd* [2012] EWCA Civ 195, [2013] Ch 91, [75]–[78] (Lloyd LJ) (hereafter *ITS v Noble*).

[27] *Arthur v A-G of Turks and Caicos* [2012] UKPC 30, [33] (Sir Terence Etherton).

[28] *Papadimitriou v Crédit Agricole Corpn and Investment Bank* [2015] UKPC 13, [2015] 1 WLR 4264 [33] (Lord Sumption) (obiter). In principle, one's conscience may be affected not only by what she knows but also by what she ought to know: S Agnew, 'The Meaning and Significance of Conscience in Private Law' (2018) 77 CLJ 479, 489.

[29] *Relfo v Varsani* [2012] EWHC 2168 (Ch), [78] (Sales J); *Byers v Saudi National Bank* [2022] EWCA Civ 43, [2022] 4 WLR 22. See also C Mitchell and S Watterson, 'Remedies for Knowing Receipt' in C Mitchell (ed), *Constructive and Resulting Trusts* (Hart 2010).

trustee, T should be subject to a similar duty if specific assets have vested in her and she knows that S intends her to hold them *qua* trustee.[30]

However, in the case of an express trust by transfer acceptance by T is required before she will be bound by its terms and the full range of duties which it imposes.[31] Acceptance may be express.[32] It may also be inferred from the taking of some steps to deal with the assets in connection with the administration of the trust or acts of ownership,[33] but actions which are not referable to the character of the trustee will not suffice.[34] Where T has notice of the trust but does nothing for a long period, the better view is that acceptance should not be inferred from her inaction.[35] In that situation, it makes more sense to infer an intention not to undertake a duty than an intention to undertake it and breach it through neglect.[36]

It follows that an intentional assumption of responsibility by T towards B in respect of the trust assets is required to bind her conscience with the full panoply of administrative, dispositive, and fiduciary[37] duties imposed by an express trust. The fact that her intention may be inferred from her actions suggests that intention is judged objectively. This echoes Lord Nottingham's emphasis on external acts as an important feature of justiciable conscience. Nevertheless, the idea of conscience as applied knowledge is still implicitly relevant. T must know the terms of the trust, and if she acts in such a way as would convey to others that she accepts them, she *ought* to know that B (and possibly others) may rely on her actions as a manifestation of her intention to undertake the relevant duties. Thus, it is not unreasonable for equity to treat her conscience as bound by the assumption of responsibility and impose the equitable duties of trusteeship.

[30] See S Agnew, 'What We Talk About When We Talk About Conscience' (unpublished PhD thesis, LSE 2015) 71–72; YK Liew and C Mitchell, 'The Creation of Express Trusts' (2017) 11 J Eq 133 (hereafter Liew and Mitchell, 'The Creation of Express Trusts'). See further *Conyngham v Conyngham* (1750) 1 Ves Sen 221, 28 ER 506 and *Conyngham v Conyngham* (1750) 1 Ves Sen 522, 523, 27 ER 1181. cf *Mackay v Wesley* [2020] EWHC 3400, [25] (v) (hereafter *Mackay v Wesley*).

[31] *Robinson v Pett* (1734) 3 P Wms 249, 24 ER 1049; *Re Reynolds: Official Assignee v Wilson* [2008] NZCA 122, (2007–2008) 10 ITELR 1064, [118] (Robertson J) (hereafter *Re Reynolds*); *Mackay v Wesley* (n 30) [25] (v).

[32] This does not depend on receipt of the trust property by the intended trustee: *Ong v Ping* [2015] EWHC 1742 (Ch) [98]; *Mackay v Wesley* (n 30), [25] (iv)(a) (Meade J).

[33] See, eg, *White v Barton* (1854) 18 Beav 192, 52 ER 76.

[34] See, eg, *Evans v John* (1841) 4 Beav 35, 49 ER 250; *Stacey v Elph* (1833) 1 MY & K 195, 39 ER 655 (hereafter *Stacey v Elph*).

[35] *Re Clout and Frewer's Contract* [1924] 2 Ch 230 (hereafter *Re Clout and Frewer's Contract*); *Noble v Meymott* (1865) 14 Beav 471, 51 ER 367; *Jago v Jago* (1893) 68 LT 654. cf *Doe D Chidgey v Harris* (1847) 16 M & W 517, 153 ER 1294, where acceptance was inferred from inaction.

[36] P Matthews, C Mitchell, J Harris, and S Agnew, *Underhill and Hayton: Law of Trusts and Trustees* (20th edn, LexisNexis 2022) [37.8] (hereafter Matthews and others, *Underhill and Hayton: Law of Trusts*); L Tucker, N Le Poidevin, and J Brightwell, *Lewin on Trusts* (20th edn, Sweet & Maxwell 2020) [13-026] (hereafter Tucker and others, *Lewin on Trusts*).

[37] The prevailing view is that an active assumption of responsibility is necessary to trigger fiduciary obligations: see, eg, *Sheikh Al Nehayan v Kent* [2018] EWHC 333 (Comm), [2018] 1 CLC 216, [159] (Leggatt LJ); *Lehtimaki v Cooper* [2020] UKSC 33, [2022] AC 155, [48] (Lady Arden). cf S Worthington, 'Exposing Third-Party Liability in Equity' in PS Davies and J Penner (eds), *Equity, Trusts and Commerce* (Hart 2017).

III. The Settlor's Conscience—Self-Declared Trusts

The idea of an assumption of responsibility is also crucial to the way in which S' conscience is bound by the obligations of express trusteeship. S's external acts are key: if, interpreted objectively, they manifest an unequivocal and final intention to hold specific assets *for* B, S's conscience will be bound despite any inconsistent internal intention on her part. This is justifiable because S ought to know that others may rely on her actions and there is value in upholding the conventional effect of performative utterances and equivalent actions.

A. Self-Declarations of Trusts as Performative Utterances

Like an order, a promise, or a warning, a declaration is what linguistic philosophers refer to as a performative utterance, ie an act of speaking or writing[38] where 'the uttering of the [words] is, or is a part of, the doing of the action'.[39] As Austin explains, performative utterances 'have a certain (conventional) force',[40] as long as the utterance purports to invoke an accepted conventional procedure, the persons and circumstances are appropriate, and the procedure is executed properly. For example, the convention is that if I say 'I do' in a marriage ceremony, I perform the act of marrying. However, I cannot marry if I am already married.[41] Where the procedure 'is designed for use by persons having certain thoughts or feelings', if the participants do not *in fact* have those thoughts or feelings, the act may still be effective but the attendant insincerity amounts to an abuse of the procedure.[42] Thus, if I say 'I promise' but I do not intend to keep that promise, I *have* promised but the conventional force of the procedure of promising is undermined by my insincerity.

The conventional force of performative utterances is well recognised, and certain types of performative utterances may ground moral duties. For example, if I make a promise to you, I have intentionally invoked 'a convention whose function it is to give grounds—moral grounds—for another to expect the promised performance', and this is true irrespective of why we treat promises as binding.[43] The idea of conscience as applied knowledge is linked to the conventional (normative) force of performative utterances. For promises to be effective, people must be able to rely on them, and so one of the reasons my conscience is affected when I make a promise is because I *ought* to know

[38] JL Austin, *How to Do Things with Words* (JO Urmson and M Sbisá eds, 2nd edn, OUP 1976) 57 (hereafter Austin, *How to Do Things with Words*).
[39] ibid 6.
[40] ibid 109, 116–17.
[41] ibid 15–16.
[42] ibid 14–16; JL Austin, 'Performative Utterances' in JO Urmson and GJ Warnock (eds), *Philosophical Papers* (3rd edn, OUP 1979) 237–40.
[43] C Fried, *Contract as Promise* (2nd edn, OUP 2015) 16–17.

that you may legitimately expect me to perform my promise. But it is the deliberate act, the making of the promise, which generates the duty that binds my conscience. And of course, the law sets the conditions for the legal recognition and enforcement of that duty. For a promise to be legally binding, the speech act itself is not enough: it must be contained in a deed or consideration must be provided.

An explicit oral or written self-declaration of trust is also a performative utterance. The saying of the words gives immediate effect to the content of the declaration, which is constitutive of the trust itself.[44] Before the early nineteenth century, the courts would not give effect to a self-declaration of trust absent consideration.[45] Lord Eldon's decision in *Ex p Pye*[46] marked a recognition by the courts that a sufficiently clear expression of will by the settlor would suffice to create a trust absent consideration. Simply by declaring herself trustee, S could exercise a power to confer an equitable interest in the trust assets on the intended beneficiary *and* undertake the obligations of trusteeship. Subsequently, in *Ellison v Ellison*,[47] Lord Eldon (*obiter*) drew a strict line between a promise to create a trust, which would be ineffective unless supported by consideration,[48] and a completely constituted trust, which, although gratuitous, would be effective.[49] This was, effectively, the modern iteration of the principle that equity will not assist a volunteer.[50]

Why do the common law and equity treat performative utterances such as promises and self-declarations of trust as binding? One answer to this is that they are socially valuable forms of voluntary undertakings, which allow us to impose duties on ourselves as a means of creating special bonds with other people.[51] Self-declarations of trust are valuable in a second way too; they allow us as property owners to exercise our powers of disposition in a particular manner, and thereby enhance our autonomy in utilising our assets to achieve our goals.[52] This autonomy-enhancing feature may help to explain why gratuitous self-declarations of trust became enforceable.[53]

[44] J Mee, 'Presumed Resulting Trusts, Intention and Declaration' [2014] CLJ 86, 109; S Agnew and S Douglas, 'Self-Declarations of Trust' (2019) 135 LQR 67 (hereafter Agnew and Douglas, 'Self-Declarations of Trust').

[45] AWB Simpson, *A History of the Common Law of Contract* (OUP 1975) 373–74.

[46] *Ex p Pye* (1811) 18 Ves Jun 140, 149–50, 34 ER 271, 274 (Lord Eldon LC).

[47] *Ellison v Ellison* (1802) 6 Ves Jun 656, 31 ER 1243 (hereafter *Ellison v Ellison*). See also *Pulvertoft v Pulvertoft* (1811) 18 Ves Jun 84, 34 ER 249 (hereafter *Pulvertoft v Pulvertoft*).

[48] *Ellison v Ellison* (n 47) 662, citing *Colman v Sarrel* (1789) 1 Ves JR 50, 30 ER 225 (hereafter *Colman v Sarrel*).

[49] See further *Pulvertoft v Pulvertoft* (n 47); *Ex p Pye* (n 46); *Kekewich v Manning* (1851) 3 De GM & G 176, 188, 42 ER 519 (Knight-Bruce LJ) (hereafter *Kekewich v Manning*).

[50] M Macnair, 'Equity and Volunteers' [1988] LS 172, 173–74 (hereafter Macnair, 'Equity and Volunteers').

[51] As explained by J Raz, 'Promises and Obligations' in P Hacker (ed) *Law, Morality and Society, Essays in Honour of HLA Hart* (1977) 211, 224–28; J Raz, 'Promises in Morality and Law' (1982) 95 Harv L Rev 916. See also Agnew and Douglas, 'Self-Declarations of Trust' (n 44) 85–86. Of course, there may be other reasons why contracts and trusts are valuable too: see, eg, J Hudson and C Mitchell, 'Justificanda' in this book.

[52] See YK Liew, 'Trusts: Modern Taxonomy and Autonomy' (2021) 35 TLI 27; see further C Webb, *Reason and Restitution* (OUP 2017) 70–73.

[53] Note that this change occurred as the will theory was in the ascendancy: Agnew and Douglas (n 44) 85.

B. Self-Declarations of Trust and Conscience

There has not been much judicial discussion of the link between self-declared trusts and S's conscience, but two cases are instructive. In *Commissioner of Stamp Duties (Queensland) v Jolliffe*,[54] Mr Jolliffe had a bank account in his own name. The bank's regulations provided that a depositor could not hold a second account other than as trustee. Mr Jolliffe opened a second account and declared that he did so as trustee for his wife. He did so without any intention of making a gift to his wife and solely for the purpose of procuring interest on the money for himself. The Commissioner of Stamp Duties assessed Mr Jolliffe, as administrator of his wife's estate, for tax, and it included in the assessment the money withdrawn by him from the account in his wife's name. The majority held that as Mr Jolliffe never really intended to create a trust, no trust in his wife's favour was created (despite the express declaration). Thus, the money did not form part of her estate and was not liable to tax.[55]

Isaacs J dissented on the ground that Mr Jolliffe had explicitly declared himself a trustee[56] and no evidence of his secret, undisclosed, intention was admissible to contradict that. He held that in light of Lord Nottingham's judgment in *Coke v Fountaine*[57] the court looks for a 'declaration' of trust. If there is one, that is conclusive; if there is not, 'it examines the evidence to see whether such a "declaration" should be presumed'[58] (or, more precisely, inferred from circumstantial evidence).[59] Isaacs J continued:

> And the basic principle … is that equity operates on the conscience. While it enforces a conscientious duty, it is not hasty in assuming it. It would be morally improper to fasten on a man's conscience the obligation of a trust of his property for another, where he has not undertaken it. It is just as improper morally to permit a man who has openly undertaken a trust to escape his conscientious obligation by reason merely of a secret mental reservation not to fulfil what he has openly undertaken. An open declaration of trust is therefore an expression of intention that is final and beyond recall. Other acts and conduct have to be examined to see how far they are its equivalent, because the declaration of a trust, except where statute intervenes, is not necessarily formal. These considerations, in my opinion, are at the root of *Cook v Fountain* and of later decisions.

[54] *Commissioner of Stamp Duties (Queensland) v Jolliffe* [1920] 128 CLR 178 (HCA) (hereafter *Commissioners of Stamp Duties v Jolliffe*).

[55] The decision has since been overruled, and the dissenting judgment of Isaacs J preferred, in *Byrnes v Kendle* [2011] HCA 26, (2011) 243 CLR 253 (hereafter *Byrnes v Kendle*).

[56] *Commissioners of Stamp Duties v Jolliffe* (n 54) 190.

[57] *Coke v Fountaine* (n 12) 591, 36 ER 984, 987.

[58] *Commissioners of Stamp Duties v Jolliffe* (n 54) 187.

[59] This seems to have been what Lord Nottingham meant when he referred to trusts arising 'by presumption': see Macnair, '*Coke v Fountaine*' (n 12) 58.

In *Choithram v Pagarani*,[60] Mr Pagarani, on his death bed, surrounded by his family and trusted advisors, 'in the most solemn circumstances' and 'in one composite transaction', executed a trust deed in favour of a charitable foundation (in which he was named as one of the trustees) and declared that he was giving his assets (comprising shares in certain companies) to the foundation. Shortly thereafter, the other trustees executed the deed but the foundation was not finally registered as the new owner of the shares until after Mr Pagarani had died. Those entitled under Mr Pagarani's will argued that the gift to the foundation was imperfect. The Privy Council rejected this argument. It gave the words 'I give to the foundation' a benevolent construction and treated them as indicating a gift to the trustees of the foundation to be held on the terms of the trust. Because Mr Pagarani was a trustee of the foundation, this could be construed to a gift to himself *qua* trustee, ie a valid self-declaration of trust.[61]

Lord Browne-Wilkinson emphasised[62] that it did not matter whether Mr Pagarani had declared himself to be sole trustee or one of several trustees for a donee or purpose: in both cases, 'his conscience is affected and it would be unconscionable and contrary to the principles of equity to allow such a donor to resile from his gift'. If Mr Pagarani had survived and tried to change his mind, he could not have validly denied that he was a trustee 'in light of all the steps that he had taken to assert that position and to assert his trusteeship'.[63] He would also have been bound to transfer the trust assets into the names of all the trustees.

These judgments tell us several things about the connection between conscience and self-declarations of trust. First, a self-declaration of trust grounds equitable duties which bind S's conscience. Secondly, as Isaacs J pointed out in *Jolliffe*, for S's conscience to be bound by the obligations of a trustee it is not enough that S merely *intends* to assume them: S must *act* in such a way as to *undertake* them, and she does so by manifesting her intention in the form of a declaration or its equivalent. Thirdly, the open nature of the declaration is important. This is consistent with a key feature of Lord Nottingham's idea of justiciable conscience: equity will not take cognisance of a private unexpressed intention to create a trust,[64] and so S's intention to assume the obligations of a trustee must be externally manifested.[65] Fourthly, both judgments emphasise the fact that an explicit self-declaration of trust is a final manifestation of intention beyond recall, 'a complete transaction'[66] from which it would be unconscionable for S to resile.

[60] *T Choithram International SA v Pagarani* [2001] 1 WLR 1 (hereafter *Choithram v Pagarani*).

[61] This construction of TCP's words is controversial. Contrast C Rickett, 'Completely Constituting an Inter Vivos Trust: Property Rules?' [2001] Conv 515, 519 (hereafter Rickett, 'Completely Constituting an Inter Vivos Trust') with M Smith and N Leslie, *The Law of Assignment* (3rd edn, Sweet & Maxwell 2018) [11.128] (hereafter Smith and Leslie, *The Law of Assignment*).

[62] *Choithram v Pagarani* (n 60) 12.

[63] ibid.

[64] *Coke v Fountaine* (n 12) 591, 36 ER 984, 987; *Re Vandervell's Trusts (No 2)* [1974] Ch 269 (CA), 294; *Bellis v Challinor* [2015] EWCA Civ 59, [2016] WTLR 43 [59] (Briggs LJ) (hereafter *Bellis v Challinor*).

[65] See further *In re Kayford Ltd (In Liquidation)* [1975] 1 WLR 279, 282, [1975] 1 All ER 604, 607; *Twinsectra v Yardley* [2002] 2 AC 164, [71]. There is no requirement of contemporaneous communication by S to B: *Benbow v Townsend* (1833) 1 My & K 506, 510, 39 ER 772; *Wheatley v Purr* (1837) 1 Keen 551, 48 ER 419 (hereafter *Wheatley v Purr*); *Middleton v Pollock* (1876) 2 ChD 104 (CA). But the failure by S to communicate a trust raises a strong inference that she did not intend to create one: *Re Cozens* [1913] 2 Ch 478, 486.

[66] *M'Fadden v Jenkyns* (1842) 1 Hare 458, 462; 66 ER 1112.

As Isaacs J explained in *Jolliffe*, when construing S's intentions, the courts have regard to the meaning revealed by what she said and did[67] (rather than what she thought) at the time the trust is alleged to have arisen.[68] It follows that if a *reasonable* person would interpret S's words and actions as amounting to an undertaking to act as a trustee for B, then S's conscience will be bound by a trust obligation *even if* S holds an undisclosed and inconsistent internal intention.[69]

This objective approach to interpreting S's intention is consistent with the nature of the declaration as a speech act. Recall Austin's suggestion that if a performative utterance is made by a person who holds an inconsistent internal intention, the act is performed, albeit insincerely and in a way which constitutes an abuse of the conventional procedure. Equity addresses this type of abuse through the sham doctrine.[70] Thus, S is usually not permitted to argue that a written self-declaration is a sham to resist a claim for breach of trust,[71] recover the property from B for her own benefit or disadvantage an innocent third party (such as a creditor of S).[72] Equally, the risk of abuse is addressed by permitting *third parties* to plead that a written self-declaration is a sham,[73] eg where S uses it to give the false impression that a trust has been created in order to defeat legitimate claims against her.[74]

The objective approach is also consistent with the need for the rules governing the validity of trusts to work in such a way that anyone who has an interest in understanding how an asset is held (eg a putative beneficiary, third-party recipients, or S's creditors)[75] can tell at any given moment whether the asset is held by S for someone else's benefit or not. Were this not possible, the reliability and utility of the trust as an institution would be undermined. For these reasons, it follows that if S has externally manifested her intention to create a trust through an explicit self-declaration, she ought to know that others will rely on it and it is not unreasonable to treat her conscience as bound by the duties of trusteeship.

[67] *Byrnes v Kendle* (n 55) [26], [53].

[68] *Bellis v Challinor* (n 64) [58] (Briggs LJ); *National Stadium Project (Grenada) Corporation v NH International (Caribbean) Ltd* [2020] UKPC 25, [39] (hereafter *National Stadium Project (Grenada)*).

[69] For similar remarks in relation to gifts, see *Shalson v Russo* [2003] EWHC 1637 (Ch), [2005] Ch 281, [190] (Rimer J).

[70] However, if a genuine mistake was made in the recording of the terms of the trust, there is no insincerity in the performance of the act, and therefore no abuse on S's part in seeking to have the trust deed rectified.

[71] As in *Byrnes v Kendle* (n 55).

[72] *Carman v Yates* [2004] EWHC 3448 (Ch), [2005] BPIR 476, [219]; *National Westminster Bank Plc v Jones* [2001] 1 BCLC 98, [60]; *Re the Esteem Settlement* [2003] JLR 188, 221 (hereafter *Re the Esteem Settlement*); *Re Reynolds* (n 31) [109]. cf *Painter v Hutchison* [2007] EWHC 758 (Ch), where S was permitted to set aside as a sham a self-declaration of trust over her family home in favour of a bank as trustee of another settlement which the defendant had established. However, it is material that *none* of the parties—least of all, the bank or the defendant—had intended the trust to take effect on its terms and S's purpose was not to conceal assets from innocent third parties.

[73] cf D Coshott, 'The Sham Doctrine and Intention: Addressing the Bilateral Nature of Sham Trusts' (2022) 138 LQR 114.

[74] See, eg, *Midland Bank v Wyatt* [1995] 1 FLR 697, where a written self-declaration of trust by Mr Wyatt was successfully challenged as a sham.

[75] cf B McFarlane and S Douglas, 'Sham Trusts' in H Conway and R Hickey (eds), *Modern Studies in Property Law, Volume 9* (Hart 2017) 244–45, who suggest that the question of the identity of the reasonable addressee of a declaration of trust is unresolved.

C. From Performative Utterances to Manifestations of Intention

Even in the absence of a single performative utterance, the courts may be prepared to find that S has declared herself trustee by words and/or acts which they regard as *equivalent* to a declaration. The key question is whether 'the expressions actually used do convey in the circumstances in which they are used that the person using them considers himself a trustee or adopts that character'.[76] The word 'trust' need not be used: all that is necessary is that S must intend by her words and actions[77] to divest herself of the beneficial enjoyment of specific assets in favour of B,[78] by obligating herself to hold them for B.[79] Although this might be described as a composite intention,[80] the courts do not necessarily require an express assumption of an obligation by S: a sufficiently clear intention to deprive herself of the beneficial interest in the assets is likely to suffice.[81]

For example, in *Vandenberg v Palmer*[82] Mr Vandenberg directed his bankers to transfer £1,000 from his tea account and invest it in East India Company bills for his children. This was sufficient to constitute him a trustee of the fund for his children. In reaching this conclusion the court had regard to subsequent correspondence with his bankers in which he said the money belonged to his children and he had appropriated it to them. Although Mr Vandenberg had retained control over the fund, he had done so *qua* trustee and there were no acts by S which suggested that he retained dominion over the fund for his own benefit.[83]

Much more recently, in *Paul v Constance*[84] Mr Constance's repeated use of the phrase, 'this money is as much yours as it is mine', to his life partner in respect of money held in a bank account, amounted to an express self-declaration of trust. Scarman LJ held that although it was 'not easy to pin-point a specific moment of declaration', the use of the words by Mr Constance, when understood in their domestic context and in light of his unsophisticated character, 'conveyed clearly a present declaration that the existing fund was as much [his partner's] as his own'.[85] Bridge LJ put it slightly differently. In his view, by using the words 'according to the proper meaning and in the context in which [they] were spoken', Mr Constance had done something which was equivalent to a self-declaration.[86]

[76] *Jones v Lock* (1865–1866) LR 1 Ch 25, 28; *Commissioners of Stamp Duties v Jolliffe* (n 54) 188 (Isaacs J).

[77] An intention to create a trust by executing a document in the future will not suffice: *Bayley v Boulcott* (1828) 4 Russ 346, 38 ER 385; *Yusuf v Yusuf* [2019] EWHC 90 (Ch).

[78] *Bentley v Mackay* (1851) 15 Beav 12, 51 ER 440.

[79] F Maitland, *Equity, a Course of Lectures* (A Chaytor and W Whittaker eds, CUP 1936) 72. See further *Dipple v Corles* (1853) 11 Hare 183, 186, 68 ER 1239 (Page-Wood VC); *Lyell v Kennedy, Kennedy v Lyell* (1889) 14 App Cas 437 (HL), 457 (Lord Selborne); *Shah v Shah* [2010] EWCA Civ 1408, [2011] WTLR 519; *Hilton v Cosnier* [2018] EWHC 2728 (Ch).

[80] Agnew and Douglas, *Self-Declarations of Trust* (n 44) 79–82.

[81] *Deslauriers v Guardian Asset Management Ltd* [2017] UKPC 34, [2018] 2 All ER (Comm) 596, [41]–[42].

[82] *Vandenberg v Palmer* (1858) 4 K & J 204, 70 ER 85 (hereafter *Vandenberg v Palmer*).

[83] cf *Smith v Warde* (1845) 15 Sim 56, 60 ER 537, where S clearly retained dominion over the relevant fund and received dividends for his own benefit until he died.

[84] *Paul v Constance* [1977] 1 WLR 527 (hereafter *Paul v Constance*).

[85] ibid 532.

[86] ibid (Bridge LJ). See further *Rowe v Prance* [1999] 2 FLR 787.

Thus, words and acts which manifest a sufficiently clear and final intention that B should benefit from property retained in S's name will suffice to bind S's conscience with the duties of trusteeship. The question is whether S's words and acts are so clear that her continued retention of legal title is consistent only with the explanation that she has chosen to hold the assets *for* B. This depends very much on context. While the cases above show that the courts are relaxed about inferring such an intention from S's words and acts in a domestic context, recent cases[87] suggest that they are slower to do so a commercial context, where certainty as to the parties' rights and obligations is crucial.

Thus, S becomes an express trustee in a similar way to T in the context of a trust by transfer. In both cases, it is a positive assumption of responsibility towards B which triggers the full range of duties,[88] but it is also true that when T or S decides to act, she *ought* to know that others may rely on her actions, and this is one of the reasons why it is not unreasonable to treat her conscience as bound.

IV. The Settlor's Conscience—Trusts by Transfer

In the context of trusts by transfer, S's intention is not to become an express trustee herself. Nevertheless, there are circumstances in which equity will impose a constructive trust which binds S's conscience with a minimal custodial duty to hold the assets for B's benefit.[89] These trusts are usually temporary, and they are deployed to address problems which arise in the creation of an express trust, eg due to incomplete constitution or disclaimer. The reasons why S's conscience is bound are explored below.

A. Incompletely Constituted Trusts and the Rule in *Re Rose*

A trust by transfer is constituted once S has declared the trusts on which T is to hold the assets *and* successfully vests title to them in T. In the case of registered land and shares not within the CREST system this involves the acts of a third party, as T must be registered as the new owner in the Land Register or on the company's share register.[90] In *Milroy v Lord*[91] Mr Milroy purported to assign some bank shares to Mr Lord to hold on trust for the benefit of his daughter. He did so by executing a voluntary deed, but this was ineffective to assign the shares which were transferable only by entry in the books of the bank. As there was more that Mr Milroy could have done to complete the transfer of the shares, the express trust was not properly constituted.[92] The court held that an

[87] See, eg, *National Stadium Project (Grenada)* (n 68).

[88] There can be no argument that S's knowledge that she holds an unexpressed intention to create a trust generates a custodial duty. cf the position of T: see the text to note 30.

[89] Either directly or through a constructive trust in favour of T: see the text to notes 116–117 below.

[90] Companies Act 2006, s 771; Stock Transfer Act 1963, s 1.

[91] *Milroy v Lord* (1862) 4 De GF & J 264, 45 ER 1185 (hereafter *Milroy v Lord*); *Richards v Delbridge* (1874) LR 18 Eq 11, 15 (Sir George Jessel MR).

[92] *Milroy v Lord* (n 91) 273 (Knight-Bruce LJ).

ineffective transfer of title could not be rescued by re-classifying it as a self-declaration of trust, as equity would not assist a volunteer and there was no evidence that S intended to assume the obligations of trusteeship himself.

The stringency of the rule in *Milroy v Lord* is tempered by the rule in *Re Rose*.[93] In *Rose v IRC*,[94] Mr Rose attempted to make two transfers of shares: the first as a gift to his wife, and the second to trustees to hold upon the trusts of a settlement for his wife and son. He handed validly executed share transfer forms and the relevant share certificates for both transfers to the company secretary (who was also one of the intended trustees) for the purpose of registration but died before his wife and the trustees could be registered as the new owners. The Court of Appeal found the transfers were valid when Mr Rose handed over the transfer forms and share certificates.[95] At that point, he had 'done all in his power to divest himself of and to transfer to the transferees the whole of his right, title and interest, legal and equitable, in the shares in question', and his actions were sufficient to give the transferees the right to be placed on the register as the new owners of the shares, subject to the directors' power to refuse registration.[96]

Jenkins LJ emphasised that it was 'impossible to suppose' that Mr Rose could have successfully brought an action to recall the transfers and prevent the directors from registering the transferees as the new owners of the shares.[97] In his view, the transfers were transfers of 'the whole of the deceased's title, both legal and equitable, in the shares', subject to registration by the company.[98] Pending registration, Mr Rose 'had no beneficial interest left whatever ... having parted in fact with the whole of his beneficial interest, he could not, in my view, assert any beneficial title by virtue of his position as registered holder'.[99] Therefore, Mr Rose 'was in the position of a trustee of the legal title in the shares for the transferees', and had a dividend been paid to him during that period, he would have had to account for it to the transferees on the basis that the gift was complete in equity.[100]

The rule in *Re Rose* has been the subject of criticism on the basis that its rationale is difficult to identify, there is no obvious reason why equity should bypass the common law rules on the transfer of property,[101] and it is doubtful that a transferor in Mr Rose's position subjectively intends to assume the obligations of a trustee let alone relinquish any dividends which may be declared in his favour between the date of transfer and the

[93] So named after *Re Rose* [1949] Ch 78; *Rose v IRC* [1952] Ch 499 (hereafter *Rose v IRC*). For an earlier iteration of the principle, see *Fortescue v Barnett* (1834) 3 My & K 36, 43, 40 ER 14; Macnair, 'Equity and Volunteers' (n 50) 185.

[94] *Rose v IRC* (n 93).

[95] In *Pennington v Waine (No 1)* [2002] EWCA Civ 227, [2002] 1 WLR 2075 (CA), [65] (hereafter *Pennington v Waine*), the majority took this to be the ratio of the case.

[96] *Rose v IRC* (n 93) 515 (Jenkins LJ). Lord Evershed's judgment is not quite as clear as to the precise date: Smith and Leslie, *The Law of Assignment* (n 61) [11.151].

[97] *Rose v IRC* (n 93) 515.

[98] ibid 517.

[99] ibid 518.

[100] ibid.

[101] B McFarlane and C Mitchell, *Hayton and Mitchell: Text, Cases and Materials on the Law of Trusts and Equitable Remedies* (14th edn, Sweet & Maxwell 2015) 52 (hereafter McFarlane and Mitchell, *Hayton and Mitchell*).

date of registration.[102] There is also uncertainty as to the type of trust which arises, for whom, and whether it is temporary or permanent.

Nevertheless, it may be possible to discern a rationale for the rule by analogy with self-declared trusts. In that context, we saw that an explicit self-declaration of trust *or* a sufficiently clear manifestation of an intention to confer the beneficial interest in an asset (which S retains) on B will suffice to create a trust and bind S's conscience with the duties of trusteeship.[103] It might be said that the rule in *Re Rose* works similarly. Once Mr Rose had done all that *he* needed to do to complete the transfer of legal title to the transferees, he had fully manifested his present intention (objectively construed) to confer the beneficial enjoyment of the shares on the intended donee and beneficiaries. Jenkins LJ emphasised that Mr Rose had put the transferees in a position to get in the legal title and that as far as *duty* is concerned, it is *beneficial* ownership that matters and the location of the legal estate is neither here nor there.[104] It might therefore be said that Mr Rose's actions counted as a present manifestation of intention to benefit B that was 'final and beyond recall', and this counted as an assumption of responsibility sufficient to bind his conscience in equity.[105]

There are questions as to whether the analogy with self-declared trusts offers a sufficiently secure basis for the rule in *Re Rose*. It is one thing to analogise from an explicit declaration of trust by S to acts by S which demonstrate a similarly unequivocal intention to *hold* her assets *for* B. It is more difficult to infer an assumption of responsibility by *S* towards B in respect of the assets where S's actions demonstrate an intention to *transfer* those assets to *T* to hold for B, particularly given that in some cases there was more that S could have done to manifest that intention.[106]

However, if it is true that most donors would regard a gift of shares as having been made once they have put the transferee in a position to register themselves as the new owner,[107] then perhaps S ought to know that once she has done this, others will rely on her actions as a manifestation of an intention immediately to confer the beneficial enjoyment of the assets on B. If that is right, it may be reasonable to treat S's conscience as bound by a custodial duty not to deal with the assets other than for B's benefit, at least pending the registration of T as the new legal owner.

It may be argued further that by ensuring that 'the perfection of a gift in equity, or the complete constitution of a trust, must depend solely on the act and will of the donor or settlor',[108] the rule promotes

[102] See J Edelman, 'Two Fundamental Questions for the Law of Trusts' (2013) 129 LQR 66, 78–79 (hereafter Edelman, 'Two Fundamental Questions').

[103] See, eg, *Vandenberg v Palmer* (n 82) and *Paul v Constance* (n 84).

[104] *Rose v IRC* (n 93) 518.

[105] cf Tucker and others, *Lewin on Trusts* (n 36) [3-039], which suggests there is no reason for S's conscience to be affected.

[106] See, eg, *Mascall v Mascall* (1985) 50 P & CR 119 (hereafter *Mascall v Mascall*), where the claimant was held to have done everything in his power 'in the ordinary way of registered property' to transfer land to his son by executing the transfer and handing it and the land certificate to his son, even though he could have asked the Land Registry to register the transfer and had not done so. See further Smith and Leslie, *The Law of Assignment* (n 61) [11.164]–[11.167], who are of the view that the rule in *Re Rose* offers 'spurious certainty'.

[107] As argued by P Luxton, 'In Search of Perfection: The *Re Rose* Rationale' [2012] Conv 70, 74 (hereafter Luxton, 'In Search of Perfection').

[108] ibid 173.

autonomy.[109] While it is true of course that equity will not force someone to make a gift 'which in the mode of making it he has left imperfect',[110] that rationale 'cannot justify continued refusal to recognise any interest in the donee after the point when the donor has done all that is necessary to be done on his part to complete the gift'.[111] Once S has put it in T's power to perfect his own title,[112] it is arguable that S's *locus poenitentiae* has expired, so she may no longer resile from the transfer.[113] Furthermore, T does not need equity's assistance to perfect the gift.[114]

Re Rose itself is silent as to the nature of the trust which arises. In imperfect gift cases, the donor has no intention to create a trust at all, so any trust that arises must be a constructive trust.[115] It is difficult to see why that should change simply because S tries to create an express trust instead of a gift. If S has put it within T's power to get in the legal title, then her conscience is affected, but as S explicitly intends *T* to be the express trustee, it would be inappropriate to impose all the trust obligations on S. It is more plausible to say that a bare constructive trust arises to prevent S from resiling unconscionably from her actions.[116]

In the case of an incompletely constituted trust, S would hold the assets on constructive trust *either* for B as the intended beneficiary under the express trust[117] *or* for T as the intended transferee of the legal title, with T holding the equitable interest in the shares for B on the terms of the express trust pending registration as legal owner.[118] It may be that the difference does not matter.[119] On the second analysis, once T is registered as legal owner of the shares, the legal and equitable title merge in T, the constructive trust falls away and the express trust stands alone. The advantage of this construction is that it treats the express trust as complete from the date on which the transfer is regarded as effective in equity.

The trust that arises should be treated as temporary pending registration of the transferee as legal owner.[120] What would happen if the transferee were to refuse to register himself as legal owner within a reasonable period? It is submitted that the answer must lie in the law on disclaimer of gifts and trusts. For example, were a donee to refuse or

[109] For similar views, see: YK Liew, *Rationalising Constructive Trusts* (Hart 2017) 208–11; YK Liew, 'Justifying Anglo-American Trusts Law' (2021) 12 Wm & Mary Bus L Rev 685, 722–23; M Freeman and Z Pullar, 'Equity: Now Assisting Volunteers? A Case Comment on *Khan v Mahmood*' [2021] EWHC 597 (Ch)' (hereafter Freeman and Pullar, 'Equity: Now Assisting Volunteers?').

[110] *Antrobus v Smith* (1805) 12 Ves Jr 39, 46, 33 ER 16.

[111] *Corin v Patton* [1990] HCA 12, (1990) 92 ALR 1, 13 (Mason CJ and McHugh J) (hereafter *Corin v Patton*).

[112] cf *Milroy v Lord* (n 91), as explained by the court in *Mascall v Mascall* (n 106). See also *Re Fry* [1946] Ch 312, as explained by Jenkins J in *Rose v IRC* (n 93) 89.

[113] *Corin v Patton* (n 111).

[114] *Mascall v Mascall* (n 106) (Browne-Wilkinson LJ); Luxton, 'In Search of Perfection' (n 107) 72; Freeman and Pullar, 'Equity: Now Assisting Volunteers?' (n 109) 144.

[115] PS Davies and G Virgo, *Equity and Trusts: Text, Cases and Materials* (3rd edn, OUP 2019) 154.

[116] J Garton, 'The Role of the Trust Mechanism in the Rule in *Re Rose*' [2003] Conv 364, 374–75.

[117] B McFarlane and C Mitchell, *Hayton and Mitchell* (n 101) 51; Matthews and others, *Underhill and Hayton: Law of Trusts and Trustees* (n 36) [11.41].

[118] J McGhee QC and S Elliott (eds), *Snell's Equity* (34th edn, Sweet & Maxwell 2020) [22-048].

[119] Tucker and others, *Lewin on Trusts* (n 36) [3-038].

[120] *Rose v IRC* (n 93) 511 (Lord Evershed); P Matthews, 'Constitution of Disclaimed Trusts Inter Vivos' [1981] Conv 141, 148 (hereafter Matthews, 'Constitution of Disclaimed Trusts'); L Katz, 'Pathways to Legal Rights' in D Klimchuk, I Samet, and HE Smith (eds), *Philosophical Foundations of the Law of Equity* (OUP 2020) 182; Freeman and Pullar, 'Equity: Now Assisting Volunteers?' (n 109) 44.

fail to register herself as the legal owner of shares within a reasonable period of time, it is submitted that a court would be sympathetic to an argument by the donor that she should not be subject to a court-imposed custodial duty indefinitely, and the donee should be put to her election as to acceptance or disclaimer. In the case of an incompletely constituted trust, if T has already accepted the office of trusteeship, he would be in breach of his duty to get in legal title to the trust assets. If T has not accepted the trust, his refusal may amount to an act inconsistent with acceptance, which counts as disclaimer.[121] This would usually result in the revesting of the legal title to any assets in S via a resulting trust, and she would then hold the assets on trust for B pending the appointment of a new trustee.[122]

B. Beyond the Rule in *Re Rose*

The courts have recently held that it would be unconscionable for a donor of a gift to resile from the gift even where she has *not* done everything that is necessary for her to do to complete the transfer of legal title to the donee. In *Pennington v Waine (No 1)*,[123] Ada Crampton decided to give 400 of her shares in a company to her nephew, Harold, who was the company secretary. She told him this and indicated that she wished him to become a director of the company. Ada instructed Mr Pennington, a partner in the company's firm of auditors to prepare a share transfer form for her, which she signed and returned to him. He then placed it in the company's file in his office and wrote to Harold to inform him of the gift, told him this required no action on his part and asked him to complete a statutorily prescribed form of consent to act as a director. Harold did this and Ada countersigned it. Mr Pennington retained the share transfer form. Subsequently, Ada died, leaving a will which did not mention the shares.

Although the requirements of the rule in *Re Rose* had not been met, a majority of the Court of Appeal held that the question whether an apparently incomplete gift should be treated as completely constituted could be answered by reference to the principle that a donor will not be permitted to change her mind if it would be unconscionable for her to do so.[124] Ada had done enough to make it 'unconscionable, in the eyes of equity, vis-à-vis [Harold]' for her to change her mind.[125] The key facts that led to this conclusion were that Ada had clearly intended to make the gift and did so of her own free will, Mr Pennington (as Ada's agent) had told Harold that he need take no action, and Harold had consented to become a director of the company. Arden LJ took the view

[121] *Stacey v Elph* (n 34). Failing that, a long period of inaction on T's part would suffice: see the text to notes 35–36.

[122] See Liew and Mitchell, 'The Creation of Express Trusts' (n 30).

[123] *Pennington v Waine* (n 95).

[124] ibid [64]. In reaching this conclusion, at [59] Arden LJ relied on the discussion of unconscionability in *Choithram v Pagarani* (n 60). Note, however, that the discussion in that case concerned the effects of a successful self-declaration of trust by Mr Pagarani. Although it appears nowhere in Lord Browne-Wilkinson's judgment, Arden LJ thought that the obligation on Mr Pagarani to transfer the assets to the other trustees was imposed by constructive trust, a view shared by Rickett, 'Completely Constituting an Inter Vivos Trust' (n 61).

[125] *Pennington v Waine* (n 95) [64].

that delivery of the share transfer form before Ada's death was unnecessary to perfect the gift in equity, and a constructive trust arose in Harold's favour when he signed the consent form.[126]

The decision in *Pennington* has been much criticised, not least for the lack of specificity as to what will trigger a finding that it would be unconscionable for the donor to resile from the gift.[127] Clearly, Ada's actions did not manifest a present intention to confer the beneficial enjoyment of the shares on Harold that was final and beyond recall, as she had not done all that it was necessary *for her* to do to complete the transfer.

Nevertheless, in *Curtis v Pulbrook*, Briggs J suggested that the outcome in *Pennington* might be justified on the basis that 'some detrimental reliance by the donee upon an apparent although ineffective gift may so bind the conscience of the donor to justify the imposition of a constructive trust'.[128] When Harold signed the consent form he became a director of the company pending acquisition of the relevant share qualification,[129] and perhaps he could be said to have acted to his detriment by assuming the obligations of a director in reliance on the assurance that there was nothing more for him to do.

It may therefore be possible to identify a conscience-based rationale for *Pennington* by analogy with common intention constructive trusts and/or proprietary estoppel. A common intention constructive trust may arise where there is an express understanding between two people, A and B, that B has (or will have) an interest in an asset owned by A (usually the family home),[130] and B reasonably relies to her detriment on that understanding.[131] Although historically common intention constructive trusts have been driven by policy considerations which are specific to the family home context,[132] the courts have recently recognised that they may arise in a commercial context.[133] Under the doctrine of proprietary estoppel, it may be unconscionable for A to resile (without more) from an assurance made by her to B that B will get an interest in A's asset (usually but not necessarily land),[134] where B has reasonably relied on that promise to her detriment. If so, the court has a discretion as to how best to remedy the unconscionability.[135]

[126] ibid.

[127] See, eg, M Halliwell, 'Perfecting Imperfect Gifts and Trusts: Have We Reached the End of the Chancellor's Foot?' [2003] Conv 192; Edelman, 'Two Fundamental Questions' (n 102) 79; P Luxton, 'In Search of Perfection' (n 107); R Havelock, 'Conscience and Unconscionability in Modern Equity' (2015) 9 J Eq 1; YK Liew, '"Unconscionability" and the Case Against Lumping: Three Case Studies' (2021) 27 T & T 118, 128ff (hereafter Liew, '"Unconscionability" and the Case Against Lumping').

[128] *Curtis v Pulbrook* [2011] EWHC 167 (Ch) [43] (Briggs J). Interestingly, here Briggs J made no reference to Arden LJ's discussion of *Choithram* at all and instead interpreted her mention of a constructive trust as turning on detrimental reliance.

[129] *Pennington v Waine* (n 95) [7].

[130] *Lloyds Bank Plc v Rosset* [1991] 1 AC 107, 132 (Lord Bridge).

[131] Detrimental reliance is still required in sole ownership cases: *O'Neill v Holland* [2020] EWCA Civ 1583, [2021] 2 FLR 1016, [27]–[37], [62] (Henderson LJ) (hereafter *O'Neill v Holland*).

[132] *Crossco No. 4 Unlimited v Jolan* Ltd [2012] 2 All ER 757 [85] (Etherton LJ).

[133] See, eg, *Marr v Collie* [2017] UKPC 17, [2018] AC 631; *Kahrmann v Harrison-Morgan* [2019] EWCA Civ 2094.

[134] For the application to other assets, see, eg, *Fisher v Brooker* [2009] UKHL 4, [2009] 1 WLR 1764 (copyright); *Optis Cellular Technology LLC v Apple Retail UK Ltd* [2021] EWHC 1739 (Pat) (patent infringement); *LA Micro Group (UK) Ltd v LA Micro Group Inc* [2022] EWHC 1304 (Ch) (claims to beneficial ownership of shares).

[135] *Thorner v Major* [2009] UKHL 18, [2009] 1 WLR 776 (hereafter *Thorner v Major*); *Guest v Guest* [2022] UKSC 27 (hereafter *Guest v Guest*).

On either analogy, in a case like *Pennington*, where a donor tells a donee that she is making a gift of shares to her and assures her that there is nothing further she needs to do, the donor has reason to know that the donee might rely on what the donor has said.[136] Even though the donor has not done all that it is necessary for her to do to effect the transfer, it is not unreasonable to treat her as having assumed responsibility towards the donee in respect of the effect of her assurance. This, combined with proof of the requisite detrimental reliance by the donee, would make it unconscionable for the donor to resile from the assurance without more.

However, questions arise as to the way in which such a conscience-based rationale works. What is the nature of the responsibility which the donor can be taken to have assumed? Is it a responsibility merely to prevent the donee from suffering harm if she relies on the assurance? If so, from the date of the assurance the donor's conscience may be regarded as bound by an equitable duty to take reasonable steps to prevent the donee from suffering reliance-based loss but no more.[137] Alternatively, does the donor assume a moral responsibility to make good on the assurance, which becomes justiciable in equity upon proof of detrimental reliance by the donee? If so, from the date of detrimental reliance the donor's conscience may be regarded as bound by an equitable custodial duty in respect of the asset, such that she may no longer resile from the gift, which is now complete in equity. The decision in *Pennington* and Briggs J's comments in *Zeital v Kaye* indicate that the courts tend towards the latter view. This contrasts with the approach taken in proprietary estoppel cases, where the enforcement of the assurance is not inevitable.[138] The difference may turn on the nature of the question being asked. In *Pennington*-type cases, the question is whether and, if so, when the donor ceased to hold her right to the shares for her own benefit and began to hold it for the benefit of the donee. In proprietary estoppel cases, the question is how best to remedy any injustice between the parties that may have arisen from B's detrimental reliance on A's assurance in relation to property rights held by A. In any event, for the reasons given in relation to the rule in *Re Rose*, there are good reasons for saying that any trust that is imposed in a *Pennington*-type case should be temporary pending registration of the donee as legal owner.[139]

[136] Especially if the donee can show that she reasonably understood that the donor intended the assurance/express understanding to be capable of being relied on by the donee. This is a requirement in proprietary estoppel cases: see *Thorner v Major* (n 135) [5] (Lord Hoffmann), and it would make sense to require it in the *Pennington* scenario too. I am grateful to Jessica Hudson for reminding me of this point.

[137] For the view that the remedy for proprietary estoppel should do no more than is necessary to prevent detriment, see Lord Leggatt JSC's minority judgment in *Guest v Guest* (n 135) [190], [255], [261] (with whom Lord Stephens JSC agreed). For similar views, see: I Samet, 'The Morality of Proprietary Estoppel' in JM Penner and H Smith (eds), *The Philosophical Foundations of Property Law* (OUP 2013); B McFarlane, *Proprietary Estoppel* (2nd edn, Sweet & Maxwell 2020) [7.37]; I Samet, *Equity: Conscience Goes to Market* (OUP 2018), Ch 2; B McFarlane, 'Equitable Estoppel as a Cause of Action: Neither One Thing Nor One Other' in A Dyson, J Goudkamp, and F Wilmot-Smith (eds), *Defences in Contract* (Hart 2017) 373.

[138] See eg *Guest v Guest* (n 135) [8], [74]–[75] where Lord Briggs JSC (with whom Lady Rose JSC and Lady Arden JSC agreed) held that the assumption is that the best way to remedy any unconscionability is to hold A to her assurance. However, if A can show that enforcing the promise would be out of all proportion to the detriment suffered by B, the court may exercise its discretion to limit the extent of the remedy: [76].

[139] cf *Hurst v Crampton Bros Ltd* [2002] EWHC 1375 (Ch), [2003] 1 BCLC 304, a further chapter in the *Pennington* saga, where another shareholder in the company successfully claimed that the purported transfer of shares from Ada to Harold had breached a pre-emption clause in the articles. Jacob J remarked that Harold

What ought to count as detriment for these purposes? Should it include any conduct which leaves the donee worse off than she would otherwise be, or should it be limited to conduct in which the donee could not reasonably be expected to have engaged unless she was to have an interest in the subject-matter of the gift?[140] Any detriment suffered by Harold in *Pennington* was slight, when compared with the type of substantial detriment often seen in proprietary estoppel cases (eg opportunities forgone over many years) and common intention constructive trust cases (eg financial contributions to the parties' joint household). If a gift is to be perfected on the basis of detrimental reliance, there are good reasons for saying that the detriment should be more than minimal, and the donee must prove that it resulted from her reliance on the assurance. In the case of an incompletely constituted trust, three parties—S, T, and B—are involved, and so additional questions arise. To whom must S make the assurance that there is nothing more T needs to do to complete the transfer, and whose detrimental reliance counts for these purposes? These questions require careful consideration by the courts.

Recent cases such as *Khan v Mahmood*[141] demonstrate that the inherent ambiguities in the *Pennington* doctrine allow the courts to arrogate to themselves an even broader discretion to perfect imperfect gifts in the name of unconscionability.[142] A house was jointly owned by a nephew and his elderly uncle (who lived in it). They held the beneficial interest as tenants in common in equal shares. The nephew had been charged with fraud for having failed to declare his interest in the house when claiming housing benefit. He purported to transfer legal title to the house into his uncle's sole name gratuitously. The transfer was ineffective as he failed to name his uncle as one of the transferors, pay the registration fee or pass on the TR1 form for registration (although he did show the form to his uncle). Later the nephew sought a declaration that he was entitled to a 50 per cent share in the house and succeeded. The uncle successfully appealed on the basis that *inter alia* equity should perfect the imperfect gift of the house to him.

The court considered *Pennington* and held that despite the absence of detrimental reliance by the uncle, it was unconscionable for the nephew to resile from the transfer. In the view of the judge, 'unconscionability ... focuses more on the conduct of the donor, whereas reliance focuses more on the conduct of the donee in respect to the donor's gift'.[143] The whole exercise was designed to help the nephew defend the fraud claim and, although he intended to divest himself of his interest, he also intended to seek payment from his uncle later, but the uncle believed that the property was now his alone. This was sufficient to justify perfecting the gift.

had never registered himself as legal owner of the shares for fear of breaching the clause, but in fact it had been breached anyway by Ada's actions. The case does not stand as authority for the proposition that the trust that arises in a *Pennington* scenario is necessarily permanent. See further the text to notes 120–122.

[140] As is often required in the common intention constructive trust context: *Grant v Edwards* [1986] Ch 639, 649–50 (Nourse LJ). cf *O'Neill v Holland* (n 131).

[141] *Khan v Mahmood* [2021] EWHC 597 (Ch) (hereafter *Khan v Mahmood*). See also *Nospehnpetsj Ltd (in liq) v Watersheds Capital Partners Ltd* [2020] EWHC 1938 (Ch) as discussed by Liew, '"Unconscionability" and the Case Against Lumping' (n 127) 130 and A Morris, 'No Longer Waning: *Pennington* Revived? (2021) 35 TLI 50, 54.

[142] See Freeman and Pullar, 'Equity: Now Assisting Volunteers?' (n 109) 146.

[143] *Khan v Mahmood* (n 141) [44].

The decision on this ground is problematic as it suggests that equity may assist a volunteer to perfect a gift even if the donor's acts do not demonstrate an unequivocal intention to transfer legal title to the donee and there is no detrimental reliance by the donee. In these circumstances, it is difficult to identify a clear reason why the donor's conscience should be bound by a custodial duty towards the donee other than because he had behaved shabbily, which arguably should not be enough.

Ultimately, cases like *Pennington* and *Khan* show that the courts are keen to offer more protection to intended donees (and beneficiaries) than the rule in *Re Rose* affords. However, such protection must be offered on a principled basis. A conscience-based approach, according to which a constructive trust arises in response to detrimental reliance, is plausible, but the parameters of such a doctrine must be carefully worked out and clearly articulated.

C. Relationship with Promises to Assign and to Create Trusts

It remains to consider whether and, if so, how the rule in *Re Rose* and the *Pennington* doctrine may be reconciled with the fact that a voluntary promise by S to B that she will create a trust over specific assets for B is unenforceable, even if contained in a deed.[144] The provision of consideration[145] is said to affect or bind S's conscience,[146] and it is necessary to convert what would otherwise be a purely moral duty to honour the promise to grant B a property right into a binding equitable duty to do so.[147] Authority also suggests that where S voluntarily covenants with *T* that she will transfer assets to T to hold on trust for B, T will usually be directed not to enforce the covenant unless there was a fully constituted trust of the benefit of the covenant itself (rather than the underlying assets) for B.[148]

It may be possible to square the rule in *Re Rose* with these principles. Macnair argues convincingly that the rule that a voluntary covenant is not enforceable in equity is weakly supported by authority and principle.[149] In any event, where S makes a promise that she will assign a chose in action to B or transfer assets into trust for her, S has simply undertaken to exercise her power to create a trust of those assets *in the future*. The parties necessarily anticipate that S will have to take further steps to perform the promise.[150] Thus, it makes sense to regard S as having a *locus poenitentiae* during which

144 *Colman v Sarrel* (n 48); *Ellison v Ellison* (n 47); *Kekewich v Manning* (n 49).

145 This includes marriage consideration: *Pullan v Koe* [1913] 1 Ch 9.

146 See *Re Burton's Settlements* [1955] Ch 82, 103 (Upjohn J); *Re Cook's Settlement Trusts* [1965] Ch 902, 909 (argument) (trusts); *Re Ellenborough* [1903] 1 Ch 697, 700 (Buckley J); *Tailby v Official Receiver* (1888) 13 App Cas 523 (HL) 543, 546 (Lord Macnaghten); *Re McArdle* [1951] 1 Ch 669, 677 (Jenkins LJ) (assignment).

147 Which is anticipated by the imposition of an immediate constructive trust in accordance with the doctrine *Walsh v Lonsdale* (1882) 21 Ch D 9 (CA); *Lysaght v Edwards* (1876) 2 Ch D 499, 509–10 (Jessel MR). A detailed discussion of this doctrine is beyond the scope of this chapter.

148 *Re Pryce* [1917] 1 Ch 234; *Re Kay's Settlement* [1939] Ch 329; *Re Cook's Settlement Trusts* [1965] Ch 902. As B is not a party to the covenant, she is unlikely to be able to enforce the covenant unless she comes within marriage consideration or can avail of the Contracts (Rights of Third Parties) Act 1999. The latter seems unlikely: Matthews and others, *Underhill and Hayton: Law of Trusts and Trustees* (n 36) [11.120].

149 Macnair, 'Equity and Volunteers' (n 50) 187.

150 cf ibid 184.

she may change her mind, unless B has provided consideration. By contrast, in a *Re Rose* scenario, S has done all that it is necessary for *her* to do to make a gift or create a trust *now*, and she has put it exclusively within the power of the donee or T to get in the legal title to the assets, which may be sufficient to bring her *locus poenitentiae* to an end.

We have seen that under the *Pennington* doctrine, a combination of S's clear (though imperfectly manifested) intention to benefit B, an assurance by S (to T, or possibly B) that there is nothing more for her to do to complete the transfer, and detrimental reliance (by T, or possibly B) may also be sufficient to bring S's *locus poenitentiae* to an end and bind her conscience with a custodial duty. If that is right, then the *Pennington* doctrine can also be differentiated on this basis.

D. Disclaimer

S's conscience also becomes relevant when T disclaims a trust by transfer. Generally, the legal estate to the trust property is thought to vest in T pending acceptance or disclaimer.[151] If T ultimately disclaims the office, she also disclaims the legal estate,[152] but in these circumstances the courts will not allow B's beneficial interest under the trust to fail. In *Mallott v Wilson*[153] S created a voluntary settlement of land to the use of T upon certain trusts. The settlement contained no power of revocation. The following year, T executed a deed of disclaimer and S also purported to put an end to the settlement and create a second settlement that dealt with the land in a different way. Byrne J held that the settlement had been duly constituted and it was not destroyed by the fact that T had disclaimed. Instead, 'the settlor himself held in trust ... It is really imposing the trust on the legal owner in whom by operation of law the estate is revested after the creation of the trust'.[154] Therefore, it was not open to S to bring the first settlement to an end or create a second settlement which was inconsistent with it.

Matthews[155] has criticised the decision in *Mallott* on the basis once a gift is disclaimed, it is treated as never having come into existence in the first place, and the same should apply in the case of voluntary settlements. The legal estate should be treated as never having passed from S to T, and so S was entitled to create the second settlement. Matthews' analysis has been cited with approval and *Mallott* has been doubted.[156] Nevertheless, as Mitchell and Liew argue,[157] there are good reasons for disputing it, not least because if B's equitable property rights could be extinguished by T's later disclaimer, this would give T undesirable power vis-à-vis B, and the approach in *Mallott* is consistent with the principle that equity will not permit a trust to fail if a trustee dies

[151] *Smith v Wheeler* (1671) 1 Lew 279, 86 ER 88; *Siggers v Evans* (1855) 5 E & B 367, 119 ER 518; *Re Arbib & Class's Contract* [1891] 1 Ch 601 (CA).
[152] *Re Birchall* (1889) 40 Ch D 436.
[153] *Mallott v Wilson* [1903] Ch 494 (hereafter *Mallott v Wilson*).
[154] ibid 502–03 (Byrne J).
[155] Matthews, 'Constitution of Disclaimed Trusts Inter Vivos' (n 120).
[156] See *Re the Esteem Settlement* (n 72) 219 (Birt DB); *Mackay v Wesley* (n 30) [25] (Meade J).
[157] Liew and Mitchell, 'The Creation of Express Trusts' (n 30).

or becomes incapable, but will appoint a new trustee if necessary to give effect to the trust.[158]

Irrespective of whether the legal title is treated as never having left S (as Matthews suggests) or as having revested in her upon re-transfer by the disclaiming trustee (as Mitchell and Liew argue), generally there is nothing to prevent equity from imposing a constructive trust on S. This constructive trust may be justified by analogy with the autonomy-based justification for the rule in *Re Rose* (to the extent that this is accepted).[159] On this analysis, the fact that S did all that it was necessary for her to do to transfer the assets to T is sufficient to bind her conscience with a custodial duty. Therefore, she may not deal with the assets other than for B's benefit, pending the appointment of a new trustee to administer the assets in accordance with the terms of the original express trust.[160]

If the express trust is void ab initio, B can be treated as having had a continuous beneficial interest in the property from the date on which S had done all she could to transfer the legal title to T. However, if the legal title vests in T initially and then revests in S on disclaimer, the constructive trust only arises at this later date. There is no need for it before then because before disclaimer, T's retention of legal title with knowledge that it is not for her benefit means that her conscience is bound by a minimal custodial duty,[161] and once T reconveys the property to S, S's conscience is already affected for the reasons described above.

Thus, equity will rescue an express trust that would otherwise fail due to incomplete constitution or disclaimer by binding S's conscience with a custodial duty in respect of the assets where through her actions she has manifested an unequivocal and final intention to divest herself of the beneficial enjoyment of the assets in favour of B. Here, it may be possible to draw an analogy (albeit imperfect) with self-declared trusts, such that S can be taken to have assumed responsibility in respect of the assets in favour of B, albeit temporarily.

It may also be possible to rescue an incompletely constituted trust where, although S has imperfectly manifested the intention to divest herself of the beneficial enjoyment of the asset in favour of B, she has made an assurance (to T, or possibly B) that there is nothing more that T needs to do to complete the transfer and the addressee has relied on it to his detriment. Here, it is more difficult to infer an assumption of responsibility by S towards T or B in respect of the assets themselves, but the addressee's detrimental reliance provides an additional reason why S's conscience may be bound.

In all cases, S's actions are what cause her conscience to be bound by the duty, but the idea of conscience as applied knowledge helps us to test whether it is reasonable for the relevant duty to be imposed on S in all the circumstances.

158 See, eg, *Dodkin v Brunt* (1868) LR 6 Eq 580 (Ch); *Re Smirthwaite's Trusts* (1870–1871) LR 11 Eq 251 (Ch).

159 Liew and Mitchell, 'The Creation of Express Trusts' (n 30). Tucker and others, *Lewin on Trusts* (n 36) [13-019] suggest that because the trust was constituted, once title revests in S, she must hold on the terms of the original settlement, but this is not inevitable.

160 cf Matthews, 'Constitution of Disclaimed Trusts' (n 120) 146, who suggests this would fatally undermine the rule in *Milroy v Lord*.

161 Liew and Mitchell, 'The Creation of Express Trusts' (n 30).

V. Conclusion

This chapter has demonstrated and explained the significance of the settlor's conscience in the context of express trusts. The analysis also reveals that the courts are engaged in a balancing act. On the one hand, they seek give effect to S's dispositive autonomy while protecting her from the premature imposition of equitable duties. Equally, they try to uphold the conventional force of performative utterances and external acts that manifest a sufficiently clear dispositive intention by S, with a view to protecting those who rely on them. The gradual relaxation of the rule in *Milroy v Lord* is a striking example of how the courts' focus has shifted towards the latter goal. It remains to be seen whether the right balance has been struck. And as this chapter has shown, the use of the language of unconscionability as a justification for the courts' conclusions often raises more questions than it answers.

4

Trusts, Estates, and Personhood

*Simon Douglas**

The conventional view of the trust is that it has no legal personality. As Lord Hodge said in *Investec Trust (Guernsey) Ltd v Glenalla Properties Ltd*, 'A trust is not a legal person. Its assets are vested in trustees, who are the only entities capable of assuming legal rights and liabilities in relation to the trust'.[1] While this statement is undoubtedly correct, we often speak of the trust as if it were a legal person. Judgments and scholarly writings are replete with references to trusts having suffered a 'loss', become 'insolvent', or been burdened with 'liabilities'. Trusts, like companies, are usually named and registered[2], need to make their own tax returns,[3] and will have their own accounts prepared. While Lord Hodge was correct to say that the trust lacks legal personality, the statement needs some unpacking. This chapter will argue that trusts share a common feature with legal persons in that they have an 'estate'. A focus on the trust's estate will explain the apparent similarities between trusts and legal persons, and shed light upon some peculiar features of the trust institution.

I. Explaining the Trust

Much ink has been spilt on attempting to define the trust. The protean structure of the institution, and its application to a wide range of contexts, makes it difficult to pin down. I do not propose to give an overview of the different accounts that scholars have offered over the years. Instead, I wish to point out a feature present in most accounts of the trust. Whether a theory focuses on the 'proprietary nature' of the beneficiary's interest, or upon the obligations pertaining between the trustee and beneficiary, most accounts of the trust implicitly rely upon what we commonly call 'Hohfeldian' jural relations.

Hohfeld famously showed that terms such as 'right' and 'duty' often denoted a complex set of jural relations. His work sought to articulate these relations by distinguishing

* I am grateful to Jessica Hudson, Ben McFarlane, Andreas Televantos, Paul Millar, Alec Morris, Sinead Agnew, Charles Mitchell, Mitch Cleaver, and all the participants at the KCL Philosophical Foundations of Trust Law Conference (August 2021) for their helpful comments on this paper.

[1] [2019] AC 271, [2018] UKPC 7 at [59(i)].

[2] The Trusts Registration Service is maintained under the Money Laundering and Terrorist Financing (Amendment) Regulations 2019 (2019 No 1511).

[3] Most express trusts are separate taxable entities for both Inheritance Tax and Capital Gains Tax purposes. See, for instance, the case of *Swires v Renton* [1991] STC 490.

Simon Douglas, *Trusts, Estates, and Personhood* In: *Philosophical Foundations of the Law of Express Trusts*. Edited by: Simone Degeling, Jessica Hudson, and Irit Samet, Oxford University Press. © Simon Douglas 2023. DOI: 10.1093/oso/9780192844934.003.0005

between 'claim-rights' and 'privileges', as well as 'powers' and 'immunities'. Hohfeld's scheme is predicated on the assumption that jural relations are relationships between two or more people. A claim-right or privilege could not exist in the abstract, but is always something held by one person (A) against another person (B). As Hohfeld stated: 'To say that all rights, or claims, must be against *persons* is, of course, simply another way of asserting that all *duties* must be predicated of persons.'[4] To take a simple example, if a person, A, has a right to payment of a sum of money, this can only be a genuine 'claim-right' if there is another person, B, with a corresponding duty to pay A. Conversely, B can only be under a genuine duty if the duty is owed to a particular person, ie A. The Hohfeldian scheme does not permit legal rights or duties to be held or owed in the abstract; they must always be directed towards another person.

While accounts of the trust are many and varied, they tend to share a basic Hohfeldian methodology. What I mean by this is that most accounts attempt to explain the trust by articulating the jural relations between the relevant parties. Take Maitland's preferred definition of the beneficiary's interest:

> *Cestui que trust* has rights enforceable against any person who has undertaken the trust, against all who claim through or under him as volunteers (heirs, devisees, personal restoratives, donees) against creditors, and against those who acquire the thing with notice actual or constructive of the trust.[5]

This account is Hohfeldian in the sense that the beneficiary's interest is articulated through their jural relations with others. Maitland does not describe the beneficiary as having a right in a thing, but as having 'rights enforceable against' particular people, namely, the trustee and those deriving title from the trustee; equally, the trustee's duty is owed to someone, the beneficiary. For Maitland, the essence of the trust lies in this jural relationship between the beneficiary and trustee, and one can describe the trust by articulating this relationship. Scholars who, in contrast to Maitland, have emphasised the proprietary nature of the trust also tend to describe the institution in relational terms. An example is Nolan's argument that:

> The beneficiary has, at root, a primary, negative, right to exclude non-beneficiaries from the enjoyment of trust assets. Infringement of this primary right will generate secondary rights, subject to applicable defences . . .[6]

[4] WN Hohfeld, 'Fundamental Legal Conceptions as Applied in Judicial Reasoning' (1916) 26 YLJ 710, 722f. This passage is highlighted in Visa Kurki's illuminating work on legal personhood: V Kurki, *A Theory of Legal Personhood* (OUP 2019), 60.

[5] F W Maitland, *Equity: A Course of Lectures* (repr, CUP 2011) 115. Maitland's lectures obviously pre-date Hohfeld's work. However, I am not claiming that the notion of a jural relation began with Hohfeld. The concept had clear antecedents in work that Maitland was familiar with.

[6] R Nolan, 'Equitable Property' (2006) 122 LQR 232, 251.

Although Nolan's definition does not focus on the relationship between the trustees and the beneficiary,[7] it still relies on Hohfeldian concepts. The beneficiary's right is not an abstract concept, but is a relationship with another person, namely, a third-party recipient of trust property. To say that a beneficiary's right is 'proprietary' is simply to emphasise a different jural relationship.[8]

While the conclusions reached by these scholars differ, their methodologies are broadly the same, as each attempts to explain the trust through a description of the right-duty relations between the relevant parties. These theories are therefore predicated on the same assumption as Hohfeld's work, that is that the trust exists as a jural relation between persons. It must follow that a trust cannot exist as a legal entity if the parties, particularly the beneficiary, are not extant. After all, if there is no beneficiary, then there is no person to whom a trustee's (or third party's) legal duties are owed. While different approaches have been adopted in certain offshore jurisdictions, English and Welsh law has never developed the notion that a trustee owes duties to a settlor of a trust.[9] The trustee's duties are directed to the beneficiary to the extent that it becomes difficult to explain a trust without an extant beneficiary. Lionel Smith makes this point in his critique of massively discretionary trusts, where he states that a beneficiary is the object of:

> ... an obligation with respect to the benefit of the property held in trust. It is because of that obligation that we can say that the property is held in trust; ... And this is why, outside of trusts for charitable purposes, there is no trust unless there is a beneficiary: to say that the trustee owes an obligation with respect to the benefit of the property is to say that someone is owed that obligation.[10]

If the core of the trust is the jural relation between the beneficiary and trustee (and certain third parties), then Smith must be correct. Just as a contract could not exist without at least one person holding rights against another, how could a trust exist unless there is a beneficiary holding rights against the trustee (and third parties)?

It is not the purpose of this chapter to critique the views of Maitland, Nolan, or any other scholar who has proffered a relational account of the trust. The beneficiary clearly does have legal relations with the trustee and (to some extent) with third parties, so

[7] The relationship between the trustee and the beneficiary in the focus of R Nolan, 'Invoking the Administrative Jurisdiction: The Enforcement of Modern Trust Structures' in P Davies and J Penner (eds), *Equity, Trusts and Commerce* (Hart 2017).

[8] The difficulties in applying Hohfeld's jural relations to conventional property rights is explored in S Douglas and B McFarlane, 'Defining Property Rights' in J Penner & H Smith (eds), *Philosophical Foundations of Property Law* (OUP 2013).

[9] There is, for instance, no authority for the view that trustees are under a duty to disclose information to a settlor. Moreover, in many cases the settlor is deceased, such as in the common case of trusts settled by will. For an example of an offshore jurisdiction which gives settlors rights to information, see Trusts (Guernsey) Law 2007, s 26(1).

[10] L Smith, 'Trust and Patrimony' in R Vaslan (ed), *Trusts and Patrimonies* (EUP 2015) 44. See also P Parkinson, 'Reconceptualising the Express Trust' (2002) 61 CLJ 657, 663; and P Matthews, 'From Obligation to Property, and Back Again? The Future of the Non-Charitable Purpose Trust' in D Hayton (ed), *Extending the Boundaries of Trusts and Similar Ring-Fenced Funds* (Kluwer Law International 2002), 203.

these accounts must be partially correct, at the very least. The only point I would like to make is that a relational account of the trust will always be an incomplete one. The reason for this is that the party holding the right/power, the beneficiary, is often non-existent and yet, contrary to Smith's view, this does not cause the trust to fail. It necessarily follows that a trust must be more than just a web of jural relations between the relevant parties.

That a trust can exist without a beneficiary is a point acknowledged by most scholars writing on this topic in respect of charitable trusts, where there is no beneficiary and enforcement is dependent upon Crown's position as *parens patriae*. Yet charitable trusts are not exceptional in this respect. Trustees of fixed trusts that exist for the benefit of a settlor's 'issue and remoter descendants' can find that there is no living beneficiary at the time of the trust's creation.[11] Take a simple case of a trust established under A's will for the benefit 'of the first child of B to attain 21 years of age'. When the trust comes into existence on A's death, B may have no children, and none may be born for several years. Yet that does not prevent the existence of the trust.[12] Indeed, under the Perpetuities and Accumulations Act 2009, it would be entirely possible for a settlor to direct that income be accumulated for 125 years, and for the trustees to then pay out to any great-grandchildren (or their descendants) then living. If the settlor has no great-grandchildren at the time the trust is made then there is no potential beneficiary at the outset of the trust; in fact, there may not be any potential beneficiaries born for another forty or fifty years. Trust lawyers have sometimes said of these cases that the beneficial interest is 'in suspense' or is a mere 'floating right'.[13] While I have no objection to these descriptions, my only point is that they make little sense in Hohfeldian terms. If a 'trust' does not have legal personality, but is nothing more than the aggregate of jural relations between a beneficiary and trustee (and some third parties), then any period of time in which there is no beneficiary must be fatal to the existence of the trust; simply saying that the trust is 'in suspense' does not explain away this problem.[14]

Where there are no extant beneficiaries, one might still be able to salvage the Hohfeldian account of the trust by focusing on the settlor. The argument would be as follows: if a trust is established for a class of beneficiaries, and the class has no members (because, for instance, the beneficiaries are all unborn), then the trustees will hold the fund upon a resulting trust for the settlor. On this account, the resulting trust ensures

[11] The most famous example of this was *Thelluson v Woodford* (1817) 1 Ves Jr 440, where the interests did not vest for over a century.

[12] The only limitation is that the interest must vest, if at all, within the perpetuity period, which was traditionally a life in being plus twenty-one years (hence the common contingency that the child attain twenty-one years of age). See Law Commission, *Rules against Perpetuities and Excessive Accumulations Report* (LC251 1998) [4.9] and *Re Flavel's Will Trust* [1969] 1 WLR 444.

[13] See, for example, C Davis, 'Floating Rights' [2002] CLJ 423. The issue is also discussed in relation to a beneficiaries interest in an unadministered estate in C Mitchell, '*Commissioner of Stamp Duties (Queensland) v Livingston* (1964): Rights of Estate Beneficiaries and Trust Beneficiaries Compared' in B Sloan (ed), *Landmark Cases in Succession Law* (Hart 2019).

[14] Similar problems attend discretionary trusts where the totality of the trustee's duties appears to have no corresponding right vested in any beneficiaries in these cases. For discussion see J Hudson, 'Mere and Other Discretionary Objects in Australia' in Y Liew and M Harding (eds), *Asia-Pacific Trusts Law: Theory and Practice in Context* (Hart 2021), 29–30.

that there is no 'beneficial gap' and that there is no point where the trustees have undirected duties. While this may seem an appealing argument, my view is that it is not convincing. Take, for instance, the above example of a trust to accumulate for 125 years. In this case, a resulting trust does not arise immediately to plug the 'beneficial gap', but only when the potential class of beneficiaries has completely failed, which may not happen until the very end of the term. Until this happens, it is difficult to see how any duties could be owed to the settlor.[15]

The better view is that trusts can, and do, exist without extant beneficiaries. Indeed, the example of the charitable trust shows that this has never been a problem for the law. Scholars commonly sideline charitable trusts as *sui generis*, quasi-public institutions.[16] This belies the fact that a charitable trustee's duties and powers are largely indistinguishable from those of a normal trustee. If charitable trusts belong to the core of trusts, not the periphery, then it should be accepted that there is nothing conceptually problematic with the notion of a trust without a beneficiary.

What I have tried to show in this section is that any relational account of the trust will necessarily be an incomplete explanation of the trust. After all, if a trust is no more than a right-duty relationship between the beneficiary and trustee, then how can it exist for any period of time when the right-holder is missing? This forces us to the conclusion that a trust must be more than a mere aggregate of jural relations between the beneficiary and trustee (and third parties). The challenge is to locate some other characteristic of the trust, which allows it to exist independently of these parties. I would suggest that this can be found in the concept of the trust 'estate'.

II. Estates and Personhood

A. Persons

As the 'estate' is, first and foremost, an incident of personhood, it will be helpful to start with a brief account of 'personhood'. A 'person', for legal purposes, denotes an entity capable of holding rights or being the subject of duties.[17] A natural person can become a registered proprietor of land,[18] commit a tort, assume a contractual duty, or do any number of other acts that have legal consequences for them. When we speak of property rights, contractual rights, or similar legal relations, we assume that there is a person who is the object or subject of the right. It is this attribute of natural persons—the

[15] The 'resulting trust' explanation would struggle to explain self-declared trusts. If a settlor, A, self-declares that they shall henceforth hold their shares in a company upon trust to accumulate for 125 years, a resulting trust analysis would entail A being both the sole beneficiary and sole trustee, which would destroy the trust.

[16] For example, J Langbein, 'The Contractarian Basis of the Law of Trusts' (1995) 105 Yale LJ 625, 631.

[17] Visa Kurki describes this as the 'orthodox' view of personhood: V Kurki, *A Theory of Legal Personhood* (OUP 2019), 4. Kurki is critical of this definition, pointing out that, among other things, children cannot generally be the subject of a legal duty yet are considered 'persons' in legal contexts. See also N MacCormick, *Institutions of Law: An Essay in Legal Theory* (OUP 2007), ch 5; and T Liau, 'Privity, Rights, Standing and the Road Not Taken' (2021) 41 OJLS 803.

[18] Land Registration Act 2002, s 3(2).

ability to enter legal relations—that is shared by 'juristic' or 'legal' persons. A company can enter a contract,[19] commit a tort,[20] and hold property rights like a natural person can. For some this is the very reason that the law permits groups of natural persons to incorporate and create separate legal entities.[21]

The law has afforded the status of personhood to groups incorporated under the Companies Acts and Limited Liability Partnership legislation,[22] bodies granted a Royal Charter,[23] and bodies created by private Acts of Parliament.[24] Groups, associations, and other things outside of this list lack the ability to hold rights or bear duties.[25] This is often seen in procedural issues in litigation. As a general partnership does not have legal personality, the general rule is that individual partners should be named as claimants or defendants, rather than the name of the partnership.[26] More outlandishly, an attempt by a claimant to join her two dogs to a long-running claim against her bank was struck out as 'void' in *Moosun v HSBC Bank PLC*,[27] with Snowden J saying that he did not see how a dog could 'be liable for any orders made against it'.[28] In *Bumper Development Corp v Commissioner of Police of the Metropolis*,[29] Purchas LJ stated the general position that a religious building could not be made party to proceedings given that 'on one view [it] is little more than a pile of stones'.[30] Without legal personality, such things are unable to enter legal relations and therefore can take no part in litigation.

B. Estates

As persons can both hold rights and become the subject of duties, they naturally become 'containers' for assets and liabilities. Each person can become the locus of rights which have a pecuniary value (their assets) as well as duties to pay or perform for

[19] The Joint Stock Companies Act 1844, s 25, sets out the powers and privileges obtained by the registration of a company, which include 'the Purpose of suing and being sued, and of taking and enjoying the Property and Effects of the said Company'. The general principle is now found in Companies Act 2006, s 16(3), and the specific powers of a company to enter legal relations in ss 39–52.

[20] *Stone & Rolls Ltd v Moore Stephens* [2009] UKHL 39.

[21] G Deisner, 'The Juristic Person' (1908) 57 U of Penn LR 131, 137.

[22] Limited Liability Partnerships Act 2000, s 1(2) provides: 'A limited liability partnership is a body corporate (with legal personality separate from that of its members) ... '

[23] A full list of bodies created this way is provided at https://privycouncil.independent.gov.uk/royal-charters/list-of-charters-granted/.

[24] The list is sometimes criticised as being a short one, in contrast to other legal systems that have conferred legal personality on a far wider range of entities. See Salmond, *Jurisprudence* (12th edn, Sweet and Maxwell 1966), 306–08.

[25] *Investec Trust (Guernsey) Ltd v Glenalla Properties Ltd* [2019] AC 271, [59(ii)]; *Von Hellfeld v E Rechnitzer and Mayer Frères & Co* [1914] 1 Ch 748, 754.

[26] *Oxnard Financing S.A. v Rahn* [1998] 1 WLR 1465. This is subject to a specific exception in the Civil Procedure Rules 1998, PD 7A, para 4.1(3). Outside of this exception, the White Book states the general rule is that 'members of the partnership or body of persons must sue or be sued as individuals and the full names of each person by or whom the proceedings are taken should appear in the title of the proceedings ...' B Fontaine and others, *The White Book* (Sweet & Maxwell 2021) [19.1.2].

[27] [2015] EWHC 3308. See also S Wise, 'Legal Personhood and the Nonhuman Rights Project' (2010) 17 Animal L Rev 1.

[28] ibid [10].

[29] [1991] 1 WLR 1362.

[30] ibid at 1371. In the case the court permitted the religious temple to join the proceedings under private international law principles, as it had legal personality in its own jurisdiction.

another (their liabilities). The aggregate of these two things is called a 'patrimony' in civil law systems. As Lionel Smith explains, a person's patrimony:

> ... must be capable of containing both assets (pecuniary rights) and liabilities. The assets are available to answer to the liabilities, and in this way the general principle that a person can have only one patrimony serves in part to support the principle that it should not generally be possible to shield assets from creditors.[31]

I would suggest that the common law has the same concept, although we typically refer to it as an 'estate'.[32]

A person's estate is the totality of their pecuniary rights and liabilities, effectively the person's net value.[33] We see courts referring to a person's estate at certain pinch-points, where it becomes necessary to assess a person's ability to discharge their debts. The obvious example is bankruptcy. The insolvency legislation requires the bankrupt's 'estate' to be administered by a trustee,[34] and makes detailed provision for ascertaining the bankrupt's assets and liabilities. Once the estate is ascertained, and the bankrupt's net value determined, the trustee then uses it to meet the bankrupt's liabilities, effectively executing the bankrupt's estate. A similar stock-taking occurs when a person dies and their estate vests in their personal representative.[35] The personal representative's first duty is to determine the deceased person's net value and collect it in.[36] Once this is done the estate is then administered by using those assets to meet the deceased person's liabilities, following which the remainder can be distributed to the beneficiaries of the estate. Ascertaining the estate is also essential for inheritance tax purposes, as the deceased's net worth determines how much tax is payable.[37] Divorce is another snapshot in a person's life where the size of their assets and liabilities needs to be ascertained, so as to determine the appropriate financial order. If the Revenue were to introduce an annual wealth tax, the concept of an 'estate' would be well known to all, as we would each need to take stock of our net value on an annual basis.[38] In each of these cases, the definition of 'estate' differs in small details, but in essence it is the same. It is the aggregate of a person's pecuniary rights and liabilities. Rights of a personal nature, that do

[31] L Smith, 'Trust and Patrimony' in R Vaslan (ed), *Trusts and Patrimonies* (EUP 2015), 44–45. See also Gretton, 'Ownership and its Objects' (2007) 71(4) RabelsZ 802, 831–32.

[32] G Gretton, 'Trusts without Equity' (2000) 49 ICLQ 599, 609.

[33] This definition of 'estate' is that used in the Inheritance Tax Act 1984, s 5.

[34] Insolvency Act 1986, s 306(2). Section 436 of the Insolvency Act 1986 defines the bankrupt's property as 'money, goods, things in action, land and every description of property wherever situated and also obligations and every description of interest whether present or future or vested or contingent, arising out of, or incidental to, property'. As a definition of 'property' this might be thought to be too wide. However, the purpose of the section is to define a person's estate, which includes any rights with a pecuniary value including, for instance, a trade secret (*Re Keene* [1922] 2 Ch 475) or intellectual property (*Performing Right Society Ltd v Rowland* [1997] 3 All ER 336).

[35] Administration of Estates Act 1925, s 1(1); Law Reform (Miscellaneous Provisions) Act 1934, s 1(1).

[36] Administration of Estates Act 1925, s 25(a).

[37] Inheritance Tax Act 1984, s 4(1).

[38] See Advani, Chamberlain and Summers, 'A Wealth Tax for the UK' (2020), ch 5 (accessed at https://www.wealthandpolicy.com/wp/WealthTaxFinalReport.pdf).

not easily translate into an economic value, are outside of the estate, as they cannot be used to satisfy the person's liabilities.[39]

The utility of the 'estate' as an analytical tool is that it treats a person's assets and liabilities as belonging to a legally distinct pool. This has both internal and external aspects:

(1) The *internal aspect* of an estate is that *all* of a person's assets are available to meet *each* of their liabilities. For instance, if A borrows a sum of money from a mortgage provider (B) in order to purchase land, all of A's assets will be available to meet the debt to B. Should A go bankrupt, then in addition to the land, any cash savings or investments that A has will be available to meet the liability to B. In other words, the debt to B is not hypothecated to the land. As Hansmann, Kraakman, and Squire point out, it is an elementary principle that when a person assumes a contractual liability, 'modern law in effect inserts a default term by which an individual pledges all his personal property to bond his performance'.[40]

(2) The *external aspect* of an estate is that one person's assets *ought not to be* available to meet the liabilities in *another person's* estate. The famous case of *Salomon v A Salomon & Co* is an example of this.[41] Mr Salomon made and sold leather boots through a company, A Salomon & Co Ltd, of which he owned all but a small number of shares. When the company went insolvent, its creditors argued that it was a mere alias of Mr Salomon, and therefore he should indemnify the creditors for the company's debts. In a celebrated decision the House of Lords rejected the argument, with each of the Law Lords emphasising the separate legal personalities of Mr Salomon and the company. As Lord Macnaghten stated: 'The company is at law a different person altogether from the subscribers to the memorandum. . . .'[42] Because the company was a different person to Mr Salomon, they each had distinct estates and the liabilities belonging to A Salomon & Co Ltd's estate could not be enforced against Mr Salomon's assets. Equally, Mr Salomon's creditors had no recourse against the company's assets.[43]

While most estates display these characteristics most of the time, exceptions can be found, where liabilities in one person's estate can leak into another person's estate. This can occur for policy reasons, such as where a person has deliberately established a separate legal entity in order to shield assets from creditors. In other cases, it occurs more

[39] For example, a right to bring a tort claim for defamation does not pass to a trustee in bankruptcy nor a personal representative of a deceased: *Re Wilson* (1878) 8 ch D 364; *Wilson v United Counties Bank Ltd* [1920] AC 102. Similarly, rights under a contract of agency (*Friend v Young* [1897] 2 Ch 421) or apprenticeship (*Baxter v Burfield* (1747) 1 Bott PL (6th edn) 696) will not form part of a person's estate, and nor do rights to financial maintenance on divorce (*Barder v Caluori* [1988] AC 20) or death (*Roberts v Fresco* [2017] EWHC 283). Rights to sue for infringement of an ECHR right are also considered personal and will not form part of an estate: *Ringeisen v Austria*, Case 2614/65, 1 EHRR 455, 504, 513.

[40] H Hansmann, R Kraakman and R Squire, 'Law and the Rise of the Firm' (2005) 119 HLR 1335, 1337.

[41] [1897] AC 22.

[42] ibid 51.

[43] H Hansmann, R Kraakman and R Squire, 'Law and the Rise of the Firm' (2005) 119 HLR 1335 argue that the rise of the firm was due to the need to protect the company's assets from its shareholders' creditors, not the other way around.

by accident than design. An example is the general partnership, where the partnership's assets are primarily responsible for meeting the partnership's liabilities.[44] However, if the partnership's assets are insufficient, the individual partners' assets stand as surety for the liabilities.[45] Hansmann, Kraakman, and Squire make this point in their account of the growth of the legal firm. Some estates, or 'entities', are strong, in the sense that its creditors can never look beyond that entity's assets to enforce their debts. Others, like the partnership, are 'weak', in that it is sometimes possible to look to another's assets to satisfy the liabilities. We will return to this point below because, as we will see, a trust is like a partnership in that its estate is a weak one.

C. Estates Without Persons

The existence of an estate is apparent whenever liabilities are limited to a distinct pool of assets. This happens naturally with persons. As Gretton says, 'If one recognises personality one must recognise patrimony: personality implies patrimony'.[46] Yet the existence of a person is not necessary for the existence of an estate, and legally distinct pools of assets and liabilities can exist without being attached to a person. Two examples of this are the general partnership and the estate of a deceased person. I will illustrate this with the latter, as the estate of a deceased person offers a useful analogy for the trust.

As explained above, on the death of a person both their assets and liabilities vest in their personal representative.[47] If the deceased had a will naming an executor, then this vesting occurs immediately on death;[48] in other cases, where it is necessary to appoint an administrator, the vesting occurs upon the grant of letters of administration.[49] Although the deceased's estate vests in the personal representative, there is not a merger with the personal representative's own estate; the deceased's estate continues to exist as an entirely separate entity. This is apparent when one considers what happens to a deceased's assets and liabilities:

(1) Assets: Starting with the deceased's assets, legal title to these will vest in the personal representative. It is commonly stated that the personal representative is an owner of the deceased's assets in the fullest sense, not a mere bare trustee. In *Marshall v Kerr*,[50] Lord Templeman approved the following formulation: 'the entire ownership of the property comprised in the estate of the deceased person which remains unadministered is in the deceased's legal representative for the

[44] As Lord Lindley said: '[T]he leading principle of administration is, if possible, to pay the debts of the firm (joint debts) out of the assets of the firm (joint estate), and the private debts of each partner (separate debts) out of his own private property (separate estate): in other words, to make each estate pay its own creditors': *Re Elton* (1796) 3 Ves Jr 238.

[45] Partnership Act 1890, s 12. See also *Investment and Advisory Service Ltd v Gray* [1990] BCLC 38.

[46] G Gretton, 'Trusts without Equity' (2000) 49 ICLQ 599, 617.

[47] Law Reform (Miscellaneous Provisions) Act 1934, s 1(1).

[48] *Wooley v Clark* (1822) 5 B & A 744.

[49] *Chetty v Chetty* [1916] 1 AC 603.

[50] [1995] 1 AC 148, 157.

purpose of administration without any differentiation between legal and equitable interests...'[51] Notwithstanding this statement, it is clear that the deceased's assets form no part of the personal representative's estate as they are not available to meet the personal representative's own liabilities. As Grose J said in *Farr v Newman*:

> [W]hy may not the executor devise the testator's goods? Why may not his administrator take them? Why are they not forfeited to the Crown on the attainder? Why are they not liable to be seized under a commission of bankrupt against the executor? The answer and reason is, I think, obvious. It is because they are not his goods ... [52]

If the deceased's assets are not available to meet the personal representative's liabilities, then it necessarily follows that they are not in the personal representative's estate. As Lord Kenyon CJ said in the same case, 'in general there is a distinction between those goods which an executor has in his own right, and those which he has as executor ... '[53]

If the assets are not in the personal representative's estate, then it might be assumed that they belong to the beneficiaries of the estate. Such an assumption would be wrong. During administration of the estate the assets are not available to meet the beneficiaries' liabilities.[54] If a beneficiary goes bankrupt, their trustee in bankruptcy has no right to call for possession of any of the deceased's assets so that they may be used to discharge the beneficiary's liabilities.[55] As the deceased's assets do not fall into the estates of either the personal representative or the beneficiaries, it must follow that they remain in their own separate estate.

(2) Liabilities: Turning to the deceased's liabilities, it is again apparent that these do not form part of the estate of the beneficiaries or the personal representative, even though, in the case of the representative, they are under a duty to discharge such liabilities.[56] The evidence for this is that assets in the personal representative's own estate are not available to meet the deceased's liabilities. In *Buchan's Case*,[57]

[51] See also *Chappell v Sommers & Brake (a Firm)* [2004] Ch 19, [20] and *Commissioner of Stamp Duties (Queensland) v Livingston* [1965] AC 694.

[52] (1792) 4 TR 621, 629. See also *Howard v Jemmett* (1763) 3 Burrow 1368, 97 ER 878 and *Re Morgan* (1881) 18 Ch D 93.

[53] ibid 648.

[54] The period of administration continues until it becomes possible to ascertain the residue of the estate: *Cochrane's Executors v Commissioners of Inland Revenue* [1974] STC 335. At this point the personal representative becomes a bare trustee for the beneficiaries of the estate.

[55] *Williams v Holland* [1965] 1 WLR 739. The only right that the beneficiary has during administration, which clearly does form part of their estate, is a right against the personal representative for the due administration of the estate: *Barnardo's Home v IRC* [1921] 2 AC 1 and *Commissioner of Stamp Duties (Queensland) v Livingston* [1965] AC 694. This forms part of the beneficiary's estate, and may be valuable in its own right as it ensures payment of any legacy or share of the residue on completion of administration. See also C Mitchell, '*Commissioner of Stamp Duties (Queensland) v Livingston* (1964): Rights of Estate Beneficiaries and Trust Beneficiaries Compared' in B Sloan (ed), *Landmark Cases in Succession Law* (Hart 2019).

[56] Law Reform (Miscellaneous Provisions) Act 1934, s 1(1).

[57] (1879) 4 App Cas 547. See also *New Zealand Gold Extraction Co (Newberry-Vautin Process) v Peacock* [1894] 1 QB 622. A personal representative will become fully liable if they have the shares registered in their own name: *Re Duff's Executor's Case* (1886) 32 ch D 301.

the deceased's estate included shares in the City of Glasgow Bank, which made the estate liable to significant calls following the bank's insolvency. The assets in the deceased's estate were insufficient to satisfy these liabilities. The deceased's executor successfully argued that his own assets were safe from execution as they belonged to his personal estate. As such, where a person dies insolvent, their personal representative does not indemnify the deceased's creditors against the shortfall in the value of the estate.[58]

The only assets that are available to meet the deceased person's liabilities are the deceased's assets. It follows that they form part of a legally distinct pool that is entirely separate from the estates of the personal representative and beneficiaries. The deceased's estate, therefore, is an example of an estate without legal personality.[59] The way that the law accommodates this is by permitting another person, the personal representative, to act as a 'proxy' or 'representative' for the estate.

III. The Trust's Estate

A. Introduction

To summarise the position so far, an estate is a legally distinct pool of assets and liabilities that has both an *internal aspect* (where *all* of the assets in the estate are available to meet *each* of its liabilities) and an *external aspect* (where *assets in one estate* are not (usually) available to meet the *liabilities in another's estate*). It was also noted that some estates, while displaying these core features, can 'leak', whereby a person closely connected with the estate stands as a surety for its liabilities. An example of this is a partnership. Whereas the partnership's liabilities are payable from the partnership's assets, once the partnership's assets have been exhausted creditors can pursue the individual partners.[60] As such, the individual partners effectively stand as sureties for the partnership's liabilities. In this section, we will see that a trust shares these features. In particular, a trust has both assets and liabilities that form a legally distinct pool separate from the estates of the trustee and beneficiary. However, like a partnership, it is a weak estate, as the trustee often stands as a surety for the trust's liabilities. This is most likely a result of the fact that the trust estate has been developed without the benefit of a distinct legal personality.

[58] *Dowse v* Coxe (1825) 3 Bing 20; *Powell v Graham* (1817) 7 Taunt 581. The only potential liability of the representative is that which can arise where they pay the deceased's debts in the wrong order, or distribute to beneficiaries before discharging debts. However, in such cases the liability arises from the representative's own act of *devastavit* by wrongful depletion of the estate. However, the position appears to be different in respect of liabilities personally incurred by the personal representative during the course of administration.

[59] Lionel Smith reaches this conclusion in L Smith, 'Scottish Trusts in the Common Law' (2013) 17 Edin LR 283 and in 'Trust and Patrimony' in R Vaslan (ed), *Trusts and Patrimonies* (EUP 2015).

[60] Partnership Act 1890, s 44(a).

B. Trust Assets

Starting with the trust's assets, I would suggest that in most express trusts, trust assets form no part of the personal estates of the trustee and beneficiary. While the trustee is the legal owner of the trust's assets, those assets are not available to meet the trustee's liabilities. Assets held upon trust are not included in a trustee's estate for the purpose of computing their inheritance tax.[61] They are not available to a trustee's general creditors on bankruptcy,[62] nor are they taken into account when ascertaining the trustee's 'resources' when imposing a financial remedy for divorce.

As the trust assets are not in a trustee's estate, one might assume that they belong to the beneficiary's estate. This is sometimes expressed as the idea that the trust 'splits' ownership, with the trustee owning at law and the beneficiary 'owing in equity'.[63] Yet to form part of the beneficiary's estate, the trust assets must be available to meet the beneficiary's liabilities. This will depend upon the nature of the trust.

A convenient starting point is a trust without extant beneficiaries. As discussed above, in addition to charitable trusts and the exceptional cases of private purpose trusts,[64] fixed trusts can have no extant beneficiaries. A trust established under A's will for the benefit 'of the first child of B to attain 21 years of age' may have no beneficiaries if B has no children at the time of A's death. Where a trust has no living beneficiaries then it obviously follows that the trust assets cannot fall into a beneficiary's estate. Another example is a discretionary trust, where there are beneficiaries, yet it is equally clear that the trust assets form no part of their estates. This was confirmed in a series of tax cases in the 1960s, where the Revenue sought to establish that trust assets should be included in a beneficiary's estate on their death for Estate Duty purposes. This was rejected in *Gartside v IRC*,[65] where Lord Wilberforce said that a beneficiary's interest in a discretionary trust 'may be a right, with some degree of concreteness or solidity, one which attracts the protection of a court of equity, yet it may still lack the necessary quality of definable extent which must exist before it can be taxed'.[66] If a beneficiary of a discretionary trust goes bankrupt, none of the trust assets will vest in the trustee in bankruptcy or be available to the beneficiary's creditors.[67] For similar reasons, when

[61] Inheritance Tax Act 1984, s 5(1) defines a person's estate as 'the aggregate of all the property to which he is beneficially entitled'. See *Anand v IRC* [1997] STC (SCD) 58.

[62] Insolvency Act 1986, s 283(3)(a). See also *Carter Holt Harvey Woodproducts Australia Pty Ltd v Commonwealth* [2019] HCA 20, [27].

[63] For example, M Amos, 'The Common Law and the Civil Law in the British Commonwealth of Nations' (1936–37) 50 HLR 1249, 1264: 'trust property has two contemporaneous owners'.

[64] For example, *Re Denley's Trust Deed* [1969] 1 Ch 373. The absence of a beneficiary in private purpose trusts is the very reason why they prove so controversial, with Harman J describing them as 'troublesome, anomalous and aberrant': *Re Endacott* [1960] Ch 232, 250.

[65] [1968] AC 553.

[66] ibid 618. The same position now applies under the Inheritance Tax Act 1984, as interests in discretionary trusts are not taxed as part of a deceased person's estate, but under a separate charging regime contained in ss 58–63.

[67] Such an interest is not within the definition of an 'estate' in s 436 of the Act, as the interest is not a 'present or future or vested or contingent' interest in the capital. Furthermore, s 436 has to be read in conjunction with s 283(1)(a) which provides that 'property belonging to or vested in the bankrupt at the commencement of the bankruptcy' will vest in the trustee. As the capital in a discretionary trust is not 'vested' in the beneficiary until an appointment is made to them, it falls outside the scope of s 283(1)(a).

assessing a person's resources for the purposes of a financial remedy on divorce, the courts tend to disregard a beneficiary's interest in a discretionary trust.[68] It is clear that assets in a discretionary trust are not available to meet a beneficiary's liabilities.

Turning to fixed trusts with successive and contingent interests, again it is usually the case that the trust assets form no part of the beneficiary's estate. Take the example of a trust which provides that 'the income is to be paid to A for life and, after A's death, the fund shall be held for such of A's children then living in equal shares absolutely'. The trust assets are obviously not part of A's estate, as A's interest is limited to their income. But what of A's children? The difficulty is that until A dies it is not clear if any of them will satisfy the contingency of surviving A, meaning that it is uncertain whether the assets will vest in them. For this reason, if any of A's children become bankrupt, their trustee in bankruptcy cannot call for the conveyance of the trust property to discharge the bankrupt beneficiary's liabilities.[69] Of course, the beneficiary's contingent interest will form part of their estate,[70] and this will have its own value (depending upon the chance of it vesting) which can be realised for the benefit of the creditors by selling it. However, the contingent interest does not, of itself, allow the trustee in bankruptcy to access the trust assets until the contingency is satisfied.

Once the contingency is satisfied—eg where one of A's children (B) survives A—then B's interest in the trust fund will become vested absolutely and in possession. At this point the trust assets do fall into B's estate, as B is entitled to call for the transfer of the trust asset under the rule in *Saunders v Vautier*.[71] B's trustee in bankruptcy would be able to do the same should B become bankrupt. In this way the trust assets can be used to meet B's liabilities. What this shows is that assets only form part of the beneficiary's estate when the interest vests absolutely in possession in the beneficiary,[72] as in the final example of B. It is interesting to note that when this occurs the relevant legislation often treats the trust as coming to an end, even though the trustee continues to hold a bare legal title.[73] Bare trusts are often considered to be no more than mere nomineeship.[74] This may be tied to the fact that the trust assets have fallen into the beneficiary's estate at this point.

If trust assets do not form part of the trustee's estate, and do not (apart from the case of the beneficiary with an absolute vested interest in possession) fall into the beneficiary's estate, then this raises the question of whose estate they belong to. One

[68] The courts will only take the discretionary trust into account if it was established to reduce wealth, or there is an expectation and probability that appointments will be made to the beneficiary: *Howard v Howard* [1945] P 1; *Charman v Charman (No 4)* [2007] 1 FLR 1246. For commentary see C Mitchell, 'Judicious encouragement or judicial bullying?' [2017] Conv 287. I'm grateful to Irit Samet for the reference.

[69] The same applies if A were to die, as the assets would not form part of their estate: *Coutts & Co v IRC* [1953] AC 267.

[70] 'Estate' in s 436 of the Insolvency Act 1986 is expressly defined as meaning 'present or future or vested or contingent'.

[71] *Saunders v Vautier* [1841] EWHC J82, (1841) 4 Beav 115.

[72] Approaches to reversionary interests differ. For instance, a reversionary interest is considered as being outside a person's estate for Inheritance Tax purposes (Inheritance Act 1984, s 47), yet in the estate for bankruptcy purposes.

[73] This is assumption made in the Inheritance Tax legislation: Inheritance Act 1984, s 43.

[74] Inheritance Tax Act 1984, s 43; Taxation of Capital Gains Act, s 60. Similar arguments are made in respect of constructive trusts in W Swadling, 'The Fiction of the Constructive Trust' (2011) 64 CLP 399.

option is to say that they belong to no one, or that the interest is in 'suspense' pending the vesting.[75] Yet it cannot be correct to say that trust assets do not belong to anyone, otherwise they would not be available to meet any liabilities. As trust assets (as will be shown below) are available to meet liabilities, they must belong to an estate.

C. Trust Liabilities

Trust liabilities are those liabilities incurred by the trustee in the administration of the trust,[76] or which are incidental to the holding of trust assets. Common examples include contractual duties to pay professional advisors to the trust, such as accountants and lawyers. Where the trust fund includes shares, there is a liability to a call on the shares should the company become bankrupt; if the trust fund includes let land, then the trustee has the normal liabilities of a landlord to a tenant.

Because a trust lacks legal personality, it has no capacity to incur contractual liabilities with a third party directly. The liability, therefore, is incurred by the trustee who contracts with the third party. The personal liability of the trustee puts them in a difficult position as they take the risk of being sued by a third party. To protect themselves, the trustees have an indemnity against the trust assets to be reimbursed for their expenses. In this way external liabilities are filtered through the trustee's indemnity to the trust assets. Difficulties can arise where a trustee has incurred liability to a third party, but the assets in the trust fund are insufficient to indemnify the trustee. The question then is whether the trustee's liability to the third party ought to be limited to the value of the trust assets. The House of Lords held that they were not so limited in the case of *Muir v City of Glasgow Bank*,[77] one of several claims that arose from the spectacular collapse of the City of Glasgow Bank in 1878. As was common at the time, the shareholders of the bank had unlimited liability and most were made bankrupt following calls from the bank's creditors. In *Muir* the shares were held by trustees who argued that their liability to the bank's creditors ought to be limited to the extent of the trust assets they held. The House of Lords rejected the argument and held that the trustees were personally liable to the full extent. The House expressed sympathy for their position, with Lord Cairns commenting that they '. . . have become subject to loss or ruin by entering, for the advantage of others, into a partnership attended with risks of which they probably were forgetful or which they did not fully realize'.[78] However, the outcome followed naturally from the fact that 'a trustee acts as a principal (not as an agent) in connection with the administration of his trust and so will incur personal liabilities to third parties not limited only to the value of his trust assets'.[79]

[75] This is how the beneficial interest in a deceased person's estate is explained in *Commissioner of Stamp Duties (Queensland) v Livingston* [1965] AC 694.

[76] Trustee Act 2000, s 31(1) provides that the trustee's indemnity only arises in respect of expenses 'properly incurred by him when acting on behalf of the trust'.

[77] (1879) 4 App Cas 337.

[78] ibid 363.

[79] *ATC (Cayman) Ltd v Rothschild Trust Cayman Ltd* (2011) 14 ITELR 523, [57] (Smellie CJ).

Muir shows that liabilities incurred when dealing with third parties are personal to the trustee, and assets from the trustee's personal estate will be available to the trust creditors. The trust creditors can gain indirect access to the trust's assets, as they can be subrogated to the trustee's indemnity against the trust fund.[80] Smith argues that 'this does not mean that the trust forms a patrimony; quite the opposite, since clearly trust creditors do have access to personal assets of the trustee . . . .'[81] For Smith, the fact that liabilities to third parties form part of the trustee's personal estate is the decisive point which shows that the trust does not have an estate or 'patrimony', as (according to Smith) it means that trusts can hold rights but not be the subject of liabilities. While this line of argument is a compelling one, in my view it overlooks the significance of the trustee's indemnity.

The trustee's indemnity is now on a statutory footing although it long existed at common law.[82] It can be viewed as two connected rights. First, where the trustee has expended their own funds in discharging a third-party liability, they have a right to be reimbursed for their expenses.[83] Second, the trustee has a right to be 'exonerated', and require trust assets be used to discharge the third-party liability directly.[84] Additional rights, such as the right to retain or realise assets, exist as an incident to these two rights. The aggregate of these various rights and powers constitute the trustee's right of indemnity. The existence of this right of indemnity effectively creates two levels of liability: when the trustee incurs a liability to a third party there is, in turn, a liability incurred to the trustee. The trust's estate hoves into view when one focuses on this secondary liability to indemnify the trustee.

Who, it might be asked, does this liability to indemnify the trustee belong to? Put differently, who is under a duty to ensure that the trustee is not out of pocket? The liability is not that of the settlor of the trust, unless an express undertaking is given to that effect.[85] Nor is it a liability of any of the beneficiaries unless the trust has been terminated and the assets appointed out.[86] While the trust is in existence, the only assets available to reimburse or exonerate the trustees are those of the trust itself.[87] It is for this reason that the indemnity is often referred to as a 'charge' upon the trust fund, or a 'proprietary interest' in the same.[88] It shows that a specific pool of assets—the trust's assets—are available to meet this liability to the trustees. Where the trustee has title to the goods, it may seem odd to refer to it as a charge upon the fund, as the trustee could be viewed as

[80] This indirect method is dependent upon the strength of the indemnity. If the trustee has lost their indemnity because they are in breach, then the creditor cannot rely upon it: *Re Johnson* (1880) 15 ch D 548.

[81] L Smith, 'Trust and Patrimony' in R Vaslan (ed), *Trust and Patrimonies* (EUP 2015), 50.

[82] Trustee Act 2000, s 31. This merely re-enacted the statutory indemnity under the Trustee Act 1925, which was in turn based upon a common law rule. See *Re Grimthorpe* [1958] Ch 615, 623.

[83] *Re Exhall Coal Co* (1866) 35 Beav 449. This power is now on a statutory footing under the Trustee Act 2000, s 31(1)(a).

[84] *Re Blundell* (1888) 40 ch D 370; Trustee Act 2000, s 31(1)(b).

[85] Tucker and others (eds), *Lewin on Trusts* (20th edn, Sweet & Maxwell 2020) [19–61]. Some cases have suggested that the indemnity is founded upon a contract between the trustee and settlor, eg *Re Spurling's Will Trust* [1966] 1 WLR 980, 984. However, this does not translate to a liability for the settlor to reimburse an out-of-pocket trustee.

[86] *Hardoon v Belilios* [1901] AC 118.

[87] A Olikainen, 'Creditors' claims against trustees and trust funds' (2018) 24 Trusts & Trustees 177, 192.

[88] *Jones v Mather* [1902] 1 KB 1, 6.

simply exercising their powers as owner to take assets from the trust account and move them to their personal account. However, where the trustee does not have title and possession, the language of a charge or property is more useful. For instance, if a trustee retires and assets vest in the new trustees, the retired trustee appears to remain entitled to an indemnity.

The liability to reimburse or exonerate a trustee behaves just like any other liability in a person's estate. First, we can see the *internal aspect* of an estate, as *all* of the trust's assets are available to meet *each* of the liabilities to the trustee. For instance, if a trust fund consists of land, shares, and cash, and a trustee incurs expenses in maintaining the land, their power to be reimbursed is not limited to the land. Any asset in the fund can be used to reimburse the trustee, meaning that the shares could be sold or the cash savings utilised.[89] The liabilities, therefore, presuppose that they belong to the same pool as the trust's assets. Second, we can see the *external aspect* of an estate, as *assets belonging to one trust's estate* are not (usually) available to meet the *liabilities in another's estate*. In *Fraser v Murdoch*,[90] the trustees had exercised their power to divide the trust fund into two separate settlements, effectively creating two distinct estates. This meant that liabilities in one settlement could not be set against assets in the other. This will be the case even if there are two trusts with the same set of trustees and beneficiaries.[91] An example is *White v Williams*,[92] where trustees had acquired three buildings as places of worship, but had incurred significant expenses in relation to one of the buildings and sought to exercise the indemnity against another. Although the buildings were owned by the same trustees and held for the same charitable purpose, it was found that the intention was to establish three separate trusts. This meant that the costs of repairing one could not be set against the value of any of the other buildings, as they were assets belonging to separate estates.

As a final point, it is helpful to return to Lionel Smith's line of argument, which focuses on the fact that third-party liabilities belong to the trustee, not the trust. This section has sought to show that this does not prevent the trust from having an estate, as there is a separate set of liabilities—the liability to reimburse or exonerate a trustee—that does belong to the trust. Yet Smith's point remains an important one, as it means that a trustee effectively acts as a surety for the trust's liabilities: when a trust's assets are insufficient to meet liabilities, there is always the option of proceeding against assets in the trustee's personal estate. The significance of this point is that the trust's estate is a weak one, as its liabilities 'leak' into the trustee's personal estate. In this sense the closest analogy to the trust's estate is that of a common partnership, where individual partners also stand as sureties for the partnership's liabilities. One suspects that in both cases this has arisen as the 'estate' has been developed without the benefit of a distinct legal personality.[93]

[89] *Hardoon v Belilios* [1901] AC 118, 123; *Roome v Edwards* [1982] AC 279.
[90] (1881) 6 App Cas 855.
[91] *Price v Loaden* (1856) 21 Beav 508.
[92] [2011] EWHC 494.
[93] An interesting comparison is with liabilities attached to a deceased person's estate. There appears to be a distinction between liabilities incurred before the deceased's death, for which the personal representative has no

D. Conclusion

Drawing the threads together, the following propositions can be stated:

(1) Until a beneficiary acquires an absolute vested interest in trust property, the trust's assets do not form part of their estate, and nor do they form part of the trustee's estate.
(2) While it would be possible to conceive of the trust assets as being 'ownerless', in the sense that they belong to the estate of no-one, this would also mean that trust assets are not available to meet any liabilities.
(3) Trust assets are available to meet liabilities, specifically the liability to reimburse or exonerate the trustee.
(4) As such, the trust has both asset and liabilities, which exist in a legally distinct pool (the 'trust's estate').
(5) The trust's estate is a weak one, as the trustee stands as a surety should the trust's assets be insufficient to meet its liabilities.

IV. Further Matters

A. Demarcating Trusts

In this final section, I will consider some of the implications of the thesis developed in this chapter. The first is the difficulty faced in demarcating a trust's estate. How does one separate one trust's estate from another's, especially where the two trusts share the same set of trustees and, in some cases, the same set of beneficiaries.[94] With a company, the act of naming and registering the company serves to separate it, and its estate, from other legal entities. Without legal personality, demarcating one trust from another becomes more difficult.[95]

When the courts have considered this issue their approach has been to defer to the settlor by asking whether they intended to create one or more settlements. An example is the case of *Rysaffe Trustee Co (CI) Ltd v Commissioners of Inland Revenue*,[96]

personal liability, and those incurred after death, for which the personal representative is liable but with an indemnity against the estate: *Owen v Delamere* (1872) LR 15 Eq 134, 138. As the estate lacks legal personality, it is perhaps unsurprising that its liabilities can leak into its representative's personal estate. I am grateful to Jessica Hudson for this point.

[94] This was the issue in *Roome v Edwards* [1982] AC 279, where it was held that there was a single trust, notwithstanding that there were two sets of trustees and beneficiaries holding different assets.
[95] The Scottish Law Commission considered making trusts legal persons, possibly for this reason: Scottish Law Commission, *Discussion Paper on the Nature and Constitution of Trusts* (Scot Law Com DP 133, 2006) para [2.29]–[2.46].
[96] [2002] EWHC 1114.

where a settlor was found to have established five separate settlements on the same day, each with the same trustees and beneficiaries. The intention to create different settlements was apparent from the fact that each settlement had been named ('Settlement 1', 'Settlement 2', etc.) and had its own (albeit identical with the others) trust document. The court held that each trust was a separate entity with its own tax liabilities and reporting requirements. The act of labelling the trust, like the naming of a company, appears to be significant.[97] Where the intention of the settlor is less express the courts look to other factors as evidence of intention. These indicia are noted by Lord Wilberforce in *Roome v Edwards*:

> There are a number of obvious indicia which may help to show whether a settlement, or a settlement separate from another settlement, exists. One might expect to find separate and defined property; separate trusts; and separate trustees. One might also expect to find a separate disposition bringing the separate settlement into existence. These indicia may be helpful, but they are not decisive.[98]

Labelling trusts as distinct entities is a common practice, now encouraged by registration requirements for trusts.[99] By labelling a settlement, the settlor makes clear that it is a distinct asset pool containing its own liabilities.

B. The Beneficiary Principle

One of the aims of this chapter has been to locate a feature in the trust which could explain how it can subsist without extant beneficiaries. The 'estate' provides this, as it allows us to see the trust as a legally distinct pool of assets and liabilities which can exist independently of the parties to a trust. One of the criticisms that might be levelled at this argument is that it is contrary to the 'beneficiary principle'. The beneficiary principle was explained by Viscount Simonds in *Leahy v Attorney General of New South Wales*[100] in the following passage:

> A gift can be made to persons (including a corporation) but it cannot be made to a purpose or to an object: so also, a trust may be created for the benefit of persons as *cestuis que trust* but not for a purpose or object unless the purpose or object be charitable. For a purpose or object cannot sue . . . [101]

[97] 'Distinct in law, the patrimonies should also be kept distinct in practice by proper labelling and accounting. The assets of one patrimony cannot normally be transferred to the other, and if an asset is sold from one patrimony, the proceeds of the sale are paid into the same patrimony, each patrimony thus operating its own real subrogation': K Reid, 'Patrimony not Equity: The Trust in Scotland' in R Vaslan, *Trusts and Patrimonies* (EUP 2015), 116–17.

[98] [1982] AC 279, 292–93.

[99] Most express trusts now need to be registered under the Trusts Registration Service: Money Laundering and Terrorist Financing (Amendment) Regulations 2019 (2019 No. 1511).

[100] [1959] AC 457.

[101] ibid 478–79. See also *Re Endacott* [1960] Ch 232, 246.

If a trust estate can be created and subsist without a beneficiary able to enforce it, the argument might be made that it is contrary to this beneficiary principle.

The strength of this criticism depends upon how one interprets the beneficiary principle. The principle might be understood as a version of the 'relational' view of trusts, discussed in the first section of this chapter, where the trust exists solely as a right-duty (or power-liability) relation between the beneficiary and trustee (or third party). This Hohfeldian view of the trust treats it as something like a contract, where it is no more than a web of legal relations between various parties. If this interpretation of the beneficiary principle is correct, then the thesis developed in this chapter is clearly inconsistent with it. However, other parts of trust law would also contradict such a principle. As explained above, it is not just the exceptional trusts for the maintenance of tombstones and pets that are difficult to explain; standard fixed trusts for unborn beneficiaries become problematic, as do discretionary trusts where the vague nature of the beneficiary's interest is difficult to define. Moreover, this version of the beneficiary principle encourages the view that charitable trusts are fundamentally different from other trusts, which belies their shared characteristics.

An alternative view of the beneficiary principle is that it is a shorthand for various policy arguments against the recognition of private purpose trusts. This may be the better interpretation of *Morice v Bishop of Durham*, where Grant MR said that a trust cannot exist if it is 'too indefinite to be executed' by the court.[102] Under this view, there is no danger of the 'trust estate' leading to a proliferation of private purpose trusts. While such trusts would be technically possible, the uncertainty and perpetuity issues that would attend such trusts make it undesirable to give effect to them.

C. Role of the Trustee

Viewing the trust as an estate without legal personality may also affect how we think about the role of the trustee. In the case of a deceased person's estate, the lack of legal personality is dealt with by the appointment of a person, the personal representative, who acts 'in the stead'[103] of the deceased person. As their name indicates, their role is to 'represent' the estate by administering its assets and liabilities.[104] The job of a representative is defined by its powers and discretions, with a particular focus on the representative's motives; it is far more than a mere set of duties owed to a defined beneficiary.

If the trust has an estate, then the trustee also takes on the role of a representative. Conceiving of the trustee in this way may explain certain features of their role. First, it helps explain why trustees are completely interchangeable, with the court having

[102] (1804) 9 Ves J 399, 404, 32 ER 656, 658.

[103] This term was used by Henry Swinbourne in '*A briefe treatise of Testaments and last Wills*' (1590), pt 4, s 2, pl 2.

[104] The label 'personal representative' was used to distinguish the executor from the 'real representative' (ie the deceased's heir) who inherited the land. Now that both land and personal chattels vest in the personal representative, the 'personal' label is superfluous: Learmonth and others (eds), *Williams, Mortimer and Sunnucks on Executors, Administrators and Probate* (21st edn, Thomson Reuters 2018), [1-08].

extensive powers to remove a trustee and appoint a new person in their place.[105] As Gretton says, 'Imagine a debtor who, if he is dissatisfied with his creditor, may ask the court for a better one. That is the trust'.[106] What may be unthinkable for a contract is commonplace for the trust. The reason for this is that the trustee is primarily a proxy for the trust estate, and that role may easily be filled by another person (or even the court); by contrast, the role of a contractual debtor cannot so easily be swapped with another person. Second, viewing the trustee as a representative would explain why various trust rules coincide with equivalent rules found in the law of personal representatives, powers of attorney, deputies, and other representative roles. For instance, the test for the removal of a trustee is precisely the same as the test for the removal of a personal representative,[107] and similar to that for the removal of a power of attorney and deputy for property and affairs.[108] In none of these cases is it necessary to show that the representative is in breach of their duty or has caused loss to the estate. Rather, the question is always whether their continuation would be in the best interests of the estate. Third, conceiving of the trustee as a representative would also explain the close connection between the court and the trustee.[109] The trustee can apply to court for the guidance on the interpretation of the trust deed,[110] upon the use of their powers, for the court's blessing for a momentous decision,[111] and can even surrender discretion to the court entirely.[112] No equivalent powers exist for a party to a contract or a tortfeasor; in such cases, any application to court is likely to be contentious. By contrast, personal representatives, attorneys, deputies, and other representatives enjoy the same close connection with the court, and can generally apply for guidance or blessing.[113]

D. Equitable Remedies

A final context in which it may be useful to focus on the trust's estate is that of remedies for breach of trust. A curious feature of equitable remedies is that, where a claim is successful, the amount that a trustee (or third party) is ordered to pay is often far greater than the value of the beneficiary's interest. An example is a beneficiary of a discretionary trust who sues the trustee for misappropriating trust property. Notwithstanding that the beneficiary has no vested interest in the trust fund, the trustee will be compelled to repay the full amount. In *Joel v Mills*, Page Wood VC explained:

[105] Trustee Act 1925, s 41. A trust deed may contain express provisions for the removal of a trustee by the settlor or beneficiary. Where there is a trust of land, there is a statutory power of the beneficiaries to remove a trustee: Trusts of Land and Appointment of Trustees Act 1996, s 19.
[106] G Gretton, 'Trusts without Equity' (2000) 49 ICLQ 599, 606.
[107] *Letterstedt v Broers* (1884) 9 App Cas 371.
[108] *Re AB (Revocation of an enduring power of attorney)* [2014] EWCOP 12.
[109] See generally: D Clarry, *The Supervisory Jurisdiction Over Trust Administration* (OUP 2018).
[110] Civil Procedure Rules 1998, pt 64, r 64.2(a).
[111] *Public Trustee v Cooper* [2001] WTLR 901.
[112] Civil Procedure Rules 1998, pt 64, r 64.2(b).
[113] For discussion of this point, and the notion of trusteeship as an 'office', see K Reid, 'Patrimony not Equity: The Trust in Scotland' in R Vaslan, *Trusts and Patrimonies* (EUP 2015).

> If it were a power to appoint among such of the next of kin of A. as B. should choose, anyone of the next of kin of A. would be entitled to file a bill to have the fund secured, although the trustees might afterwards disappoint him, and say, you shall not have a share until an appointment had been actually made under the power. Anyone of the class of possible appointees would have a right to file such a bill.[114]

A beneficiary of a discretionary trust may be able to show that the trustee has committed a breach of trust, but as they have no more than a right to be considered for an appointment it is impossible for them to show that they have suffered any loss. What standing, then, does the beneficiary have to insist that the sum be re-paid? Moreover, to whom is the sum 'repaid', as the trustee need only transfer funds from their personal account to their trustee account?[115] The remedy bears little resemblance to the equivalent claim for damages for breach of contract.

When these rules are reconsidered in light of the trust's estate, the outcome makes more sense. In the above example of a discretionary trust, the loss is not suffered by the beneficiary but by the trust estate itself; the assets in the estate are depleted by the trustee's wrongdoing. Furthermore, the direction to the trustee to repay the trust monies no longer looks like an accounting exercise where funds are moved from one account to another. In taking money from the trustee's personal account to be paid into their trust account, assets are moving from the trustee's personal estate to the trust's estate. The claim by the beneficiary, therefore, is not to recoup their loss, but to recoup the loss suffered by the trust's estate.[116] It is not surprising that references to the 'trust's estate' are commonplace in claims for breach of trust. An example is *Target Holdings v Redferns*, where Lord Browne-Wilkinson said:

> Accordingly, in the case of a breach of such a trust involving the wrongful paying away of trust assets, the liability of the trustee is to restore to the trust fund, often called '*the trust estate*', what ought to have been there. … The equitable rules of compensation for breach of trust have been largely developed in relation to such traditional trusts, where the only way in which all the beneficiaries' rights can be protected is to restore to the trust fund what ought to be there. In such a case the basic rule is that a trustee in breach of trust must restore or pay to the *trust estate* either the assets which have been lost to the estate by reason of the breach or compensation for such loss.[117]

A similar analysis can be applied to claims by beneficiaries against third parties, such as a tracing claim against a recipient of trust property. Where a trustee disposes of trust

[114] (1857) 3 Kay and Johnson 458, 474; 69 ER 1189, 1196–97.

[115] The trustee may, of course, be removed for their wrongdoing, in which case they would need to pay the funds to the new trustee. However, that is not necessarily the case (eg *Patel v Brent LBC (No 2)* [2003] EWHC 3081), in which case the 'compensation' is paid by moving funds from one account to another.

[116] See *Patel v Brent LBC (No 2)* [2003] EWHC 3081, [32], where the court said: 'In the case of a conventional trust, with successive or concurrent interests, any one beneficiary may sue in respect of a breach of trust, but that beneficiary is not alone entitled to the fruits of the action.'

[117] [1996] AC 421, 434 (emphasis added).

property, a third party can trace it into a third party's hands notwithstanding that they do not have an absolute vested interest in the property.[118] The purpose of the claim is to secure the return of the asset to the trust estate, and in this sense the beneficiary represents the estate in such a claim. As Lord Templeman said in a similar context in *Hayim v Citybank NA*, the role of the beneficiary when suing a third party is 'to protect the *trust estate* or to protect the interests of the beneficiary in the trust estate'.[119] A focus on the trust's estate prevents an equitable remedy from being more than the sum of its parts, as beneficiaries are not suing to vindicate their own interests but to recover losses suffered by the estate.

[118] See Tucker and others (eds), *Lewin on Trusts* (20th edn, Sweet & Maxwell 2020) [41-72–41-73] and [44-36].

[119] [1987] AC 730, 748 (emphasis added). See also *Parker-Tweedale v Dunbar Bank Plc* [1991] Ch 12, 19 and *Commissioner of Stamp Duties (Queensland) v Livingston* [1965] AC 694.

5

Historical Conceptions of the Express Trust, *c* 1600–1900

David Foster[*]

I. Introduction

In a volume on the philosophical foundations of the express trust, it may be salutary to consider the role which historical conceptions of the trust have played in shaping modern legal thought. In the late sixteenth century, the trust was conceived as a 'confidence annexed in privity'. This definition promoted a highly personal conception of the trust which emphasised the reposing of trust in an identified individual and the binding of their conscience to perform the trust. Such a personal conception tended towards some significant limitations on the enforceability of the trust but, as the trust concept evolved over the course of the seventeenth century, many of these limitations began to fade from the case law. Increasingly the trust came to be conceived as attaching not merely to the trustee's conscience, but to the trust property itself. This shift in emphasis from 'confidence' to 'property' had a number of consequences for the creation, administration, and enforceability of trusts, but also encouraged a reconceptualisation of the trust in explicitly proprietary terms. By the late 1820s indeed, John Austin could conceive of trusts as giving rise to proprietary rights which he described as 'rights *in rem*'. By the 1880s, Austin's adoption of the civilian terminology of rights *in rem* triggered responses from scholars who considered the beneficiary's right to be better characterised as a right *in personam*. There followed the famous debates in the school of analytical jurisprudence which, by the early twentieth century, had produced a raft of essays explaining the nature of the beneficiary's right as either '*in rem*' or '*in personam*' in nature. Since then, this language has seeped into the collective legal conscious and has become the orthodox way to describe equitable rights.[1]

* The author is grateful to Mitchell Cleaver, Astron Douglas, Julius Grower, Neil Jones, Michael Lobban, Charles Mitchell, Judith Skillen, Andreas Televantos, Ian Williams, and the editors for their comments on earlier drafts.

[1] *Sinclair v Brougham* [1914] AC 398, 418 (Haldane LC); *Re Diplock* [1947] Ch 716, 787 (Wynn-Parry J); *Re Diplock* [1948] Ch 465, 475–76 (Greene MR); *Shiloh Spinners v Harding* [1973] AC 691, 721 (Lord Wilberforce); *Webb v Webb* [1992] ILPr 374, [13] (Scott LJ), [16] (Nourse LJ); *Webb v Webb* (C–294/92) [1994] QB 696, [34]–[54] (AG Darmon); *Tinsley v Milligan* [1994] 1 AC 340, 371 (Lord Browne-Wilkinson); *Westdeutsche Landesbank Girozentrale v Islington BC* [1996] AC 669, 711 (Lord Browne-Wilkinson); *Akers v Samba* [2017] AC 424, 461 (Lord Sumption).

David Foster, *Historical Conceptions of the Express Trust, c 1600–1900* In: *Philosophical Foundations of the Law of Express Trusts*. Edited by: Simone Degeling, Jessica Hudson, and Irit Samet, Oxford University Press. © David Foster 2023.
DOI: 10.1093/oso/9780192844934.003.0006

In spite of the ubiquity of the *in rem/in personam* distinction, few modern writers have stopped to consider why technical procedural terms lifted from classical Roman law should be apt descriptors of such a quintessentially common law concept as the trust. Fewer still have considered the continuing significance of the historical conception of the trust which both pre-dated and existed alongside the Austinian analytical models. Ultimately, the debate over the proper classification of the beneficiary's rights as either *in rem* or *in personam* remained inconclusive precisely because these civilian tags did not map neatly onto the privity-based, historical conception of the trust which was reflected in the case law and the treatise literature. After all, what would come to be described as variously the *in rem* or *in personam* aspects of the beneficiary's right had themselves been determined according to the historical conception of the trust as annexed in privity. Thus, that which the school of analytical jurisprudence regarded as a source of intense speculation was readily intelligible to historians of equity. This chapter will consider each conception in turn, paying regard to their origins and significance in the history and philosophy of the express trust.

II. The Historical Conception of the Trust

The privity-based conception of the trust had deep roots, stretching back to the sixteenth century,[2] and owing much to the medieval use.[3] In Coke's report of *Chudleigh's case* (1594), we find the following definition:

> A use is a trust or confidence reposed in some other, which is not issuing out of the land, but as a thing collateral, annexed in privity to the estate of the land, and to the person touching the land, *scilicet*, that *cestuy que use* shall take the profit, and that the terre-tenant shall make an estate according to his direction. So as *cestuy que use* had neither *jus neque in re, neque ad rem*, but only a confidence and trust, for which he had no remedy by the common law, but his remedy was only by *subpoena* in Chancery.[4]

This definition of the use/trust was a *locus classicus*. At its heart lay two key elements which would be foundational for later writers: 'confidence' and 'privity'. These two ideas combined to produce a highly personal conception of the trust which emphasised the reposal of trust in an identified person and which was enforceable only against a narrow class of individuals who were deemed 'privy' to the confidence. Over the course

[2] *Delamere v Barnard* (1567) 1 Plow 346, 352; *Chudleigh's case* (1594) 1 Co Rep 120a, 121b; *Witham v Waterhouse* (1596) Cro Eliz 466; *Sir Moyle Finch's Case* (1600) 4 Co Inst 85; *R v Holland* (1648) Style 20 and 40; *Pawlett v AG* (1667) Hardres 465, 469; H Finch (later Lord Nottingham), *Prolegomena* (written c 1670) in DEC Yale (ed), *Lord Nottingham's 'Manual of Chancery Practice' and 'Prolegomena of Chancery and Equity'* (CUP 1965), c 12, s 5, c 14, s 1 (hereafter Yale (ed), *Prolegomena*); *Burgess v Wheate* (1759) 1 Wm Bl 123, 162.

[3] DEC Yale, *Nottingham's Chancery Cases*, vol ii (1961–62) 79 Selden Society 87–91 (hereafter Yale (ed), *Nottingham's Chancery Cases*, vol ii).

[4] *Chudleigh's case* (1594) 1 Co Rep 120a, 121b. Similar sentiments are attributed in Popham's report to Ewens, Owen, Bateman, and Fenner JJ (Poph 70, 71–72). This definition originated in *Delamere v Barnard* (1567) 1 Plow 346, 352.

of the seventeenth and eighteenth centuries, many of the more restrictive aspects of these ideas were discarded and a more proprietary conception of the trust was allowed to take root. The following sections illustrate how this shift from the personal to the proprietary conception took place in the case law and treatise literature of the period.

A. Confidence

'Confidence'—sometimes referred to as 'privity in person'—[5] referred to the act of entrusting another person to carry out the trust. The reposal of trust and confidence was essential because it burdened the trustee's conscience and grounded the beneficiary's right to enforcement.[6] The need to repose confidence in an identifiable person naturally emphasised the personal relationship between the parties to the trust but had some peculiar consequences for the creation and enforceability of express trusts—many of which did not survive into the modern law—including: a refusal to recognise corporate trusteeship; limitations on enforceability by third-party beneficiaries; and restrictions on equity's supervisory jurisdiction over trusts. As each of these aspects of confidence were discarded from the case law, the conceptual focus shifted from 'confidence reposed' to the trust property itself and encouraged more explicitly proprietary conceptions of the trust. By the end of our period indeed, trusts were conceived not as mere personal confidences reposed in another, but as vesting equitable rights in the trust property which could not be impugned for lack of an express reposal of trust in an identified trustee.

The rule against corporate trustees stemmed from the idea that corporations were not natural persons in whom confidence could be reposed. In *Chudleigh's case* (1594), it was said that 'a confidence cannot be in land, or other dead thing . . . nor a corporation, because it is a dead body, although it consist of natural persons: and in this dead body a confidence cannot be put, but in bodies natural'.[7] The focus on the confidence reposed in the trustee served to underline the importance of the personal relationship between the parties, but limited capacity for trusteeship to *natural* persons only.[8] Understandably, this aspect of confidence was found inconvenient and was abandoned in the later seventeenth and eighteenth centuries as courts recognised the possibility of both corporate[9] and royal

[5] C Butler (ed), *An Essay on the learning of Contingent Remainders and Executory Devises* (7th edn, J Butterworth 1820) 290, n (h); T Lewin, *A Practical Treatise on the Law of Trusts and Trustees* (A Maxwell 1837) 19 (hereafter Lewin, *Trusts and Trustees*).

[6] NG Jones, 'Trusts in England after the Statute of Uses: A View from the 16th Century', in R Helmholz and R Zimmermann (eds), *Itinera Fiduciae* (Duncker & Humblot 1998) 173, 193–95 (hereafter Jones, 'Trusts in England'); NG Jones, 'Aspects of Privity in England: Equity to 1680' in EJH Schrage (ed), *Ius Quaesitum Tertio* (Duncker & Humblot 2008) 135, 170–72 (hereafter Jones, 'Aspects of Privity').

[7] Poph 70, 71–72. See also 1 Co Rep 120a, 127a, and *Anon* (1598x1603) 117 Selden Society 290, no 119–23.

[8] Although Jones, 'Trusts in England' (n 6) 194, n 131, observes that there was seemingly no objection to corporations acting as trustees of charitable trusts in the sixteenth century. Notably, infants were also considered to have the capacity for trusteeship: *Ridgway v Forth* (1590) 117 Selden Society 247, no 119.

[9] *Sterling v Wilford* (1676/77) 79 Selden Society 447. See copious authorities listed by J Willis, *A Practical Treatise on the Duties and Responsibilities of Trustees* (R Pheney, S Sweet, and Stevens & Sons 1827) 32, n 11.

trusteeship.[10] By the eighteenth century, a trustee's lack of capacity would not bar the creation of an express trust. Such decisions tended to downplay the significance of confidence in the creation of express trusts.[11]

The requirement of confidence also affected the rights of third-party beneficiaries under a trust (ie beneficiaries who were not themselves settlors). In 1564, Weston J had observed that one 'cannot have any trust or confidence in those whom he does not know'[12] and this sentiment was repeated by Egerton LK in the 1590s.[13] But this conception of confidence operated to render trusts readily defeasible by the settlor. In *Yelverton v Yelverton* (1599), for example, Egerton held that:

> it is no breach of trust if any man of his own accord, minding to do good to another, do put one in trust with assurance and the party trusted do redeliver it at the request of him which did trust him without the privity of him to whom the good was meant, for the party to whom the good was meant did not trust him, but the party which did mean to do good.[14]

Where a third-party beneficiary was unaware of the trust, therefore, the trustee would not be liable for breach where he reconveyed the trust property at the request of the settlor.[15] It was the settlor who had reposed confidence in the trustee, not the beneficiary. For this reason, the trust was revocable at the settlor's election and it was no breach for the trustee to comply.

The rule was otherwise where the third-party beneficiary had provided consideration.[16] Where consideration had passed from the beneficiary, a trustee who made a reconveyance would be liable for breach. In *Pye v George* (1710),[17] for example, it was held that trustees to preserve contingent remainders who joined in a conveyance to bar the remainder before a son was born were guilty of a breach of trust. Although unborn at the time of the breach and incapable of reposing confidence in the trustee, the son was within the marriage consideration of the parties to the settlement and had thus provided the consideration necessary to ground a claim for breach. The recognition of liability to an unborn beneficiary was necessary to ensure the efficacy of the trust to preserve contingent remainders, but also served to detract from the requirement of a personal confidence reposed by the beneficiary in the trustee. Rather, where the

[10] *Earl of Kildare v Eustace* (1686) 1 Vern 438, 439 (Trevor MR); *Penn v Lord Baltimore* (1750) 1 Ves Sen 444, 453 (Hardwicke LC).

[11] Yale (ed), *Nottingham's Chancery Cases*, vol ii (n 3) 90–91.

[12] *Anon* (1564) Moo KB 61 (translated from Law French). See NG Jones, 'Wills, Trusts and Trusting from the Statute of Uses to Lord Nottingham' (2010) 31 JLH 273, 291 (hereafter Jones, 'Wills, Trusts and Trusting').

[13] Jones, 'Trusts in England' (n 6) 194.

[14] 117 Selden Society 270, no 118–[308].

[15] Jones, 'Trusts in England' (n 6) 194.

[16] JL Barton, 'The Medieval Use' (1965) 81 LQR 562, 570–72; TFT Plucknett and JL Barton (eds), *St German's Doctor and Student* (1974) 91 Selden Society xliii; AWB Simpson, *A History of the Common Law of Contract* (Clarendon 1975) 337–44; S Anderson, 'Trusts and Trustees' in W Cornish and others (eds), *Oxford History of the Laws of England*, vol xii (OUP 2010) 252–68.

[17] 2 Salk 680; 1 P Wms 128; Prec Ch 308; (1712) 7 Bro PC 221. Followed in *Mansell v Mansell* (1732) Cas t Talb 252; 2 P Wms 678.

beneficiary had provided consideration, they could be regarded as having purchased an interest under the trust which could not be readily destroyed by the settlor and trustee acting in concert.

Where the beneficiary was a mere volunteer, however, equity retained a discretion to order trustees to join conveyances to destroy contingent remainders.[18] The case law thus suggested that, even by the eighteenth century, the beneficiary's right remained somewhat ephemeral.[19] It was only in the early nineteenth century that the link between consideration and the defeasibility of the beneficiary's right was effectively broken. In *Ellison v Ellison* (1802),[20] Eldon LC held that, where the trust was completely constituted, the beneficiary's equitable interest could be enforced in chancery regardless of whether consideration had passed from the beneficiary or not. Thereafter, consideration would only be necessary where the trust was incompletely constituted.[21] Trusts could now be conceived as vesting rights to the trust property in the beneficiary which were not defeasible either for lack of confidence reposed or lack of consideration moving from the beneficiary. This shift from confidence to consideration and then to constitution served to emphasise the beneficiary's equitable interest in the trust property and to diminish the role of confidence as an organising principle in the creation and enforcement of express trusts.

The final consequence of the language of confidence in the sixteenth century was to limit equity's supervisory jurisdiction in the event of a failure by those in whom trust had been reposed. In *Bonefant v Greinfeld* (1586),[22] for example, the testator had devised land to four executors with instructions to sell, but one executor refused to act. Coke argued that the remaining executors could not sell because 'it is a speciall trust, and a joynt trust, and shall never survive: for perhaps, the devisor who is dead, reposed more confidence in him who refused, than in the others'. By the middle of the seventeenth century though, it came to be accepted that trusts bound the land, not merely the consciences of those in whom trust had been reposed. In the event of failure of the testamentary trustees, equity would instead imply a trust on the testator's heir.[23] In *Gwilliams v Rowel* (1661),[24] the testator had left his property on a trust to sell but, on the death of one of the trustees, the surviving trustee and the testator's heir were ordered to sell the property because 'the lands were tied with a trust, which will survive in equity'. *Gwilliams* suggested that the trust was moving beyond the *dictum* in *Chudleigh's case* (1594), that 'a confidence cannot be in land'.[25] Nevertheless, chancery practice remained unsettled in this period. In *Pitt v Pelham* (1667–69),[26] the testator purported to devise lands upon trust but failed to name a trustee. When the testator died, the lands

[18] *Tipping v Piggot* (1711) Gilb Rep 34; *Basset v Clapham* (1717) 1 P Wms 358.

[19] MRT Macnair, 'The Conceptual Basis of Trusts in the Later 17th and 18th Centuries' in R Helmholz and R Zimmermann (eds), *Itinera Fiduciae* (n 6) 224 (hereafter Macnair, 'Conceptual Basis').

[20] 6 Ves Jr 656, 662.

[21] MRT Macnair, 'Equity and Volunteers' (1988) 8 LS 172, 181–82.

[22] Godb 77.

[23] *Locton v Locton* (1637/8) 2 Freem 136.

[24] Hardres 204.

[25] Poph 70, 71–72.

[26] 1 Ch Cas 176; 1 Ch Rep 283; 2 Freem 134; Yale (ed), *Prolegomena* (n 2) c 13, s 3.

instead descended to the heir. The will was held void at law and Bridgman LK decreed there was 'no cause or colour to make good the same in equity'.[27] Although eventually reversed on appeal to the House of Lords,[28] Bridgman's decision demonstrated that, even by the later seventeenth century, a failure to identify the person in whom trust was reposed could be fatal to the creation of an express trust.[29]

As with the other inconveniences arising from the requirement of personal confidence, this aspect of trusteeship faded by the later seventeenth century. In the 1670s, Nottingham would readily imply a trust on the heir on the grounds that 'a trust is fixed upon the land',[30] and in *Eales v England* (1702–04),[31] it was held that a trust of a legacy would not lapse where the trustee predeceased the testator. In *Bennet v Davis* (1725),[32] the testator devised lands to his daughter upon a trust for her separate use but failed to nominate a trustee. By analogy with the testamentary cases, Jekyll MR decreed that the daughter's bankrupt husband held the property as trustee for his wife. Around this time, we also see a rising practice of judicial exercise of trust powers in the event of default by the trustee.[33] Such expansions of the supervisory jurisdiction were ultimately viewed by later writers as the origin of the maxim that 'a trust shall not fail for want of a trustee'[34] and demonstrated how far the need to repose trust and confidence had receded from the case law. In none of these cases had the testator actually reposed trust in the court, or the court-appointed trustee. Instead, as Charles Butler noted in 1794, 'the relief is administered by considering the land in whatever person vested, as bound by the trust'.[35] The cases thus demonstrated a shift from confidence reposed in the trustee to the equities attaching to the subject matter of the trust. The concern for the court was not that trust had been reposed in a particular person, but that the case involved trust property and ought to be administered according to the terms of the trust.

These developments demonstrated that the sixteenth century language of 'reposing trust and confidence' could no longer adequately describe the basis upon which modern trusts were enforced. By the late seventeenth century, we find the early institutional writers on equity grappling with the evolving nature of the trust and struggling to create new models to explain the nature of the beneficiary's right. There was a notable reliance on civilian analogies when explaining the nature of the trust,[36] although the precise

[27] 1 Ch Rep 283, 288.

[28] (1669–70) 1 Lev 304; Rep t Jones 25.

[29] See Lord Mansfield's discussion of *Pitt v Pelham* in *Burgess v Wheate* (1759) 1 Bl Wm 123, 159–60, as an example of the ephemeral nature of the trust prior to Nottingham's chancellorship.

[30] *Stutville v Rossell* (1674) 79 Selden Society 49, no 86. See also Yale (ed), *Nottingham's Chancery Cases*, vol ii (n 3) 106–08, and Jones, 'Wills, Trusts and Trusting' (n 12) 290–92.

[31] (1702) Prec Ch 200; (1704) 2 Vern 466.

[32] 2 P Wms 316.

[33] *Moseley v Moseley* (1673) Rep t Finch 53; *Clarke v Turner* (1694) 2 Freem 198; *Warburton v Warburton* (1701) 2 Vern 420; (1702) 4 Bro PC 1; *Harding v Glyn* (1739) 1 Atk 469. These decisions were canvassed by Lord Wilberforce in his seminal speech on judicial execution of trust powers in *McPhail v Doulton* [1971] AC 424, 451–52.

[34] Lewin, *Trusts and Trustees* (n 5) 572–73; G Spence, *Equitable Jurisdiction*, vol i (V Stevens, R Stevens and GS Norton 1846) 500–01 (hereafter Spence, *Equitable Jurisdiction*, vol i).

[35] F Hargrave and C Butler (eds), *Notes on Lord Coke's First Institute or Commentary upon Littleton*, vol iii (E and R Brooke 1794) 113a, n 2.

[36] DJ Ibbetson, 'Natural Law and Common Law' (2001) 5 Edin LR 4, 13–14; IS Williams, 'The Tudor Genesis of Edward Coke's Immemorial Common Law' (2012) 43 Sixteenth Century Journal 103, 120–21. An early example

analogy chosen would depend on the author's conception of the trust as either obligational or proprietary. In his *Prolegomena* (*c* 1670), Nottingham had emphasised the proprietary nature of the beneficiary's right, defining the trust as 'an equitable interest in the land'[37] and, thereafter, explained that '[s]uch kinds of trusts in the Civil Law are called *fideicommissa*'.[38] Jeffrey Gilbert (*c* 1700), on the other hand, seemed to favour an analogy with the *usufruct*.[39] Both analogies were designed to buttress the conception of the beneficiary's right as an equitable interest in land;[40] the right of beneficiary did not arise from any contract or agreement with the trustee, but because the trust invested the beneficiary with a property right. By contrast, the author of *A Treatise of Equity* (1737)—attributed to Henry Ballow—adopted the more radical explanation of the trust as a type of contract (specifically, *depositum*).[41] For Ballow, equity's enforcement of trusts was merely an instance of specific performance of a contractual obligation;[42] the trustee's duty and the beneficiary's right emerged from agreement and were, therefore, personal in nature. It is notable, however, that as his analysis progressed Ballow quickly abandoned this analogy and returned to the language of confidence found in *Chudleigh's case*.[43]

Ultimately, Ballow's contractual analysis found few supporters[44] and, by the dawn of the nineteenth century, we find a pivot back to more proprietary conceptions in the treatise literature—this time with a marked focus on the trust property itself as the basis for the beneficiary's rights and the trustee's duties. In 1813, Francis Sanders wrote that 'all the questions concerning the capacity of persons to stand seised to a use are avoided in the case of modern trusts; as the courts of equity fasten the trust upon the estate, and not upon the person'.[45] Similarly, in his notes to the 1826 edition of Coke's *Reports*,[46] John Henry Thomas remarked that 'the courts of equity now hold, that a trust shall never fail on account of the disability or non-appointment of the trustee, because the trust, if properly created, will fasten upon and attach to the land'.[47] In 1837, Thomas Lewin was careful to downplay the role of confidence in his account of the trust, observing that a trust 'is a *confidence*; not necessarily a confidence *expressly* reposed by one party in

was Francis Bacon's analogy with the *fideicommissum*: see F Bacon, *Reading on the Statute of Uses* (M Wallbancke and L Chapman 1642) 7 and 15–16 (hereafter Bacon, *Reading*).

37 Yale (ed), *Prolegomena* (n 2) c 12, s 5.

38 ibid c 12, s 8. See also c 14, ss 15–18 and W Blackstone, *Commentaries on the Laws of England*, vol ii (Clarendon 1766) 327–29.

39 J Gilbert, *Law of Uses and Trusts* (E Nutt, R Nutt, and R Gosling 1734) 3 (hereafter Gilbert, *Uses and Trusts*). cf usufruct analogy in *Re Henry de Vere* (1625) W Jones 96, 127 (Dodderidge *in arguendo*).

40 For the limitations of these analogies, see Macnair, 'Conceptual Basis' (n 19) 213–16.

41 [H Ballow], *A Treatise of Equity* (E Nutt, R Nutt, and R Gosling 1737) bk 2, c 1, s 1 (hereafter [Ballow], *Treatise of Equity*). This analysis had some limited support in the case law (*Lord Hollis' case* (1674) 2 Vent 345; 1 Eq Cas Abr 380, in which money lent for a purpose was referred to as 'a *depositum* and a trust' for the lender).

42 Macnair, 'Conceptual Basis' (n 19) 216–18.

43 [Ballow], *Treatise of Equity* (n 41) bk 2, c 1, s 2. See Jones, 'Aspects of Privity' (n 6) 162–64.

44 cf W Blackstone, *Commentaries on the Laws of England*, vol iii (Clarendon 1768) 432.

45 *An Essay on the Nature and Laws of Uses and Trusts* (3rd edn, W Walker 1813) 34. See also Spence, *Equitable Jurisdiction*, vol i (n 34) 500–01.

46 JH Thomas and JF Fraser (eds), *Reports of Sir Edward Coke* (J Butterworth 1826), 13 parts in six volumes. This edition was reproduced in the *English Reports*.

47 76 ER 270, 292, n E2 (*Chudleigh's case* (1594) 1 Co Rep 120a, 127a).

another, for it may be raised by implication of law; nor need the trustee of the estate *actually* be capable of confidence, for the capacity itself may be supplied by legal fiction, as where the administration of the trust is committed to a body corporate'.[48] These ideas were subsequently combined by George Spence in the first volume of his highly influential treatise, *The Equitable Jurisdiction of the Court of Chancery* (1846):

> a body corporate might be compelled to execute a trust, thus abolishing the rule that there must be a *person* in whom the confidence is placed … The trust, in fact, was treated as if it were fastened on the estate rather than the person; and a trust was never allowed to fail for want of a trustee, whether the trustee named died, or was an improper or incapable person. When trustees refused to act, it was considered that the trust devolved upon the court.[49]

By the nineteenth century, the notion of confidence had become dislocated from the trust and the attendant case law was relied upon by institutional writers to emphasise a more proprietary conception of the trust. Neither the trustee's capacity to be trusteed, nor the beneficiary's capacity to trust, was an objection to the enforceability of a trust and, in dubious cases, the court could exercise its supervisory jurisdiction to ensure the efficacy of the trust instrument. Even in the absence of an express entrusting between beneficiary and trustee, the trust could be enforced because it gave rise to rights which were now understood to enure in the trust *res*.

B. Privity

The second aspect of the early modern definition of a trust was the doctrine of privity. Privity governed the 'continuation' of the confidence and allowed the trust to be enforced by and against those who were not the original parties to the trust.[50] The rules of privity provided that the beneficiary's right could only be enforced against, and claimed by, those whose rights were derived from an act of the parties to the trust (eg by grant or assignment). By contrast, those whose rights arose by operation of law (eg the lord by escheat, the disseisor, or the judgment creditor) were outwith the privity and could neither claim the benefit of the trust, nor could they be bound by it. The doctrine of privity thus governed the contours of the trust's exigibility and enforceability, but also affected how the trust was conceptualised, first as a type of *chose* in action and subsequently as attaching to the trustee's estate in the trust *res*. These shifts in the understanding of privity reflected the same slow proprietisation of the trust outlined in the preceding section.

[48] Lewin, *Trusts and Trustees* (n 5) 15. Emphasis in original.

[49] Spence, *Equitable Jurisdiction*, vol i (n 34) 500–01.

[50] *Chudleigh's case* (1594) Poph 70, 71 ('confidence shall bind but in privity'). Fenner J (*c* 1594) said that privity was 'nothing else but a continuance of the confidence without interruption … ' (Bacon, *Reading* (n 36) 8–9).

Privity had governed the medieval use and was, originally, an exceptionally strict doctrine. In the mid-fifteenth century, it had been said that the chancery *subpoena* was only available against the feoffee personally and did not extend to the feoffee's heir[51] or the feoffee's assignee.[52] Around the same time, it was also held that the use could not be enforced other than by the *cestui que use*.[53] The central idea was that the confidence reposed in the feoffee was personal and incapable of being enforced by or against one who was not a party to the use.[54] Charles Butler explained the effects of this doctrine in the following terms:

> between the feoffee and *cestuy que use*, there was a confidence in the person and privity in estate ... But this was only between the feoffee and *cestuy que use*. To all other persons the feoffee was as much the real owner of the fee, as if he did not hold it to the use of another. *He* performed the feudal duties; *his* wife was entitled to dower; *his* infant heir was in wardship to the lord; and, upon *his* attainder, the estate was forfeited.[55]

In effect, therefore, privity rendered the trust property immune to the liabilities of the *cestui que use*, and liable to those of the feoffee. This strict formulation of the doctrine of privity had inconvenient consequences for the enforceability of the use—particularly where the feoffee died—but, in the mid-to-late fifteenth century, exceptions were carved out to permit enforcement of the use against the feoffee's heir[56] and the feoffee's assignee.[57]

This partially relaxed doctrine of privity was subsequently transposed from the use into the trust and helped to structure the rules of the trust in its formative period (*c* 1536–1600). There was, however, a significant debate about the nature of privity in the later sixteenth century which produced some instability in the case law. In the mid-1590s, 'privity' was understood ambiguously as meaning either 'privity of contract' or 'privity of estate'. It was the latter version of the doctrine which would make a lasting impact on the trust, but, for a period in the 1590s, the trust was being analogised to *choses* in action and, by extension, was thought to be governed by privity of contract.[58] On this view, the beneficiary's right was merely a right to the chancery *subpoena* to enforce the trust (rather than an interest in the trust property itself). In *Witham's case* (1596), for example, a trust of a lease was described as 'a thing in privity, and in the nature of an action, for which no remedy was but by writ of *subpoena* ... for the trust runneth in privity'.[59] In *Sir Moyle Finch's case* (1600),[60] this analogy was carried further

[51] YB 8 Edw IV, f 5b, pl 1. See also YB Pas 22 Edw IV, f 6, pl 18 (Hussey CJ).

[52] *Anon* (1453) Fitz Abr tit *Subpoena*, pl 19.

[53] YB 5 Edw IV, f 7b, pl 18 (*subpoena* could not be brought by lord claiming by escheat upon the *cestui que use's* attainder of felony).

[54] RW Turner, *Equity of Redemption* (CUP 1931) 43 (hereafter Turner, *Equity of Redemption*).

[55] C Butler (ed), *The First Part of the Institutes of the Laws of the Realm or, A Commentary upon Littleton*, vol ii (19th edn, J & WT Clarke 1833) 271b, n 1; emphasis in original.

[56] *Dod v Chyttynden* (1502) 116 Selden Society 395, 396 (Vavasour J).

[57] YB 5 Edw IV, f 7b, pl 16 (enforcement against purchaser with notice).

[58] MRT Macnair, 'Development of Uses and Trusts: Contract or Property and European Influences' (2015) 66 Studi Urbinati A—Scienze giuridiche, politiche ed economiche 305, 315–18 (hereafter Macnair, 'Development of Uses and Trusts').

[59] 4 Co Inst 87.

[60] 4 Co Inst 85.

with the resolution that a trust was unassignable 'because it was a matter in privity between them, and was in the nature of a *chose* in action, for [the beneficiary] had no power of the land, but only to seek remedy by *subpoena*'.[61] This highly personal conception of the trust was short-lived; indeed, it seems to have been doubted even at the time it was being crafted.[62] By the mid-seventeenth century, any doubt as to the assignability of the trust had been dispelled and the analogy with the *chose* in action was roundly rejected.[63] By this stage, the trust was clearly more than an unassignable *chose*, but its precise classification remained a matter of speculation.[64]

By contrast, the 'privity of estate' approach endured rather longer than the 'privity of contract' theory and continued to inform conceptions of the trust until the middle of the nineteenth century. The language of privity of estate suggested that the enforceability of trusts was being explained by analogy to the running of real covenants.[65] Such an analogy strongly implied a more proprietary conception of the trust was taking root.[66] The core idea was that the trust attached to the estate vested in the trustee and would bind the trustee's successors in title, such as those claiming by grant or assignment. Where, for example, the trustee assigned the trust estate to a volunteer, the volunteer claimed the *same estate* as the trustee—or, in the technical language of the time, they claimed *per* the trustee—and would take subject to the rights of the beneficiary. Privity of estate came to end, however, when one entered the land by virtue of an estate arising by operation of law, which was not derived from an act of the trustee. Such legal right-holders were not privy to the trustee's estate and were said to enter the land 'in the *post*'. Where the trustee was disseised of the trust lands, for example, the disseisor took the lands free of the beneficiary's rights (even where they had prior notice of the trust's existence).[67] The disseisor was not bound by the trust because they did not claim the same estate as the trustee. Instead, the disseisor claimed a new estate (known as a 'tortious fee') to which the trust was not annexed and thus lacked the privity of estate required to be bound by the beneficiary's rights. The same was true of the lord by escheat; where the trustee died intestate and without heirs, the trustee's estate came to an end and the land went to the lord discharged of the trust.[68] Privity of estate thus explained

[61] ibid

[62] Bacon, *Reading* (n 36) 13. Macnair, 'Development of Uses and Trusts' (n 58) 317–18, views Bacon's analysis as 'not stating the dominant position, but arguing against it' in order to 'demonstrate legal skill by contrarianism'. cf NG Jones, 'The Trust Beneficiary's Interest before *R v Holland* (1648)', in ADE Lewis, P Brand and P Mitchell (eds), *Law in the City: Proceedings of the Seventeenth British Legal History Conference, London, 2005* (Four Courts 2007) 95, 111–16, suggesting that the late sixteenth century chancery did not see a difficulty in accepting assignments or devises of beneficial interests.

[63] *R v Holland* (1648) Style 20, 21 (Rolle J).

[64] Macnair, 'Conceptual Basis' (n 19) 216–18.

[65] ibid 228. The language of privity of estate ('*per*' and '*post*') appears in connection with the use/trust in *Chudleigh's case* (1594) 1 Co Rep 120a, 122a, and also in *Spencer's case* (1583) 5 Co Rep 16a, 17a–17b, on the running of real covenants.

[66] *Hopkins v Hodylo* (1591) 117 Selden Society 193, no 118: 'There is a difference between a trust and a promise concerning land, because the one goes annexed to the land and will bind the heir whereas the other is collateral to the land and will not bind the heir'. Approved by Peryam CB at *Anon* (*c* 1594) 117 Selden Society 248, no 123.

[67] *Lord Compton's case* (1587) 3 Leo 196; *Chudleigh's case* (1594) 1 Co Rep 120a, 122a; *Sir Moyle Finch's case* (1600) 4 Co Inst 85; Gilbert, *Uses and Trusts* (n 39) 168–69; Lewin, *Trusts and Trustees* (n 5) 13, 124; G Spence, *Equitable Jurisdiction*, vol ii (V Stevens, R Stevens and GS Norton 1849) 196 (hereafter Spence, *Equitable Jurisdiction*, vol ii).

[68] *Wickes' case* (1609) Lane 54.

why certain classes of legal right-holders might take free of the trust. In this way, the doctrine placed clear limitations on the enforceability of the beneficiary's rights against third parties and thus represented an obstacle to the further proprietisation of the trust.

When discussing privity of estate, the trust was sometimes contrasted with rights annexed to the possession of the land.[69] A right annexed to the possession of the land was capable of binding any subsequent holder of the land (whether claiming in the *post* or otherwise). By the later seventeenth century, it had been recognised that certain equitable rights were capable of binding the possession of the land. In 1667, Sir Matthew Hale CB said that the equity of redemption could bind in the *post*, but explained this rule in contradistinction to the trust:

> There is a diversity betwixt a trust and a power of redemption; for a trust is created by the contract of the party, and he may direct it as he pleaseth ... and therefore they only are bound by it, who come *in* in privity of estate....But a power of redemption is an equitable right inherent in the land, and binds all persons in the *post*, or otherwise.[70]

It was clear, therefore, that certain equitable rights could inhere in the land such that they might bind all takers in the *post*, but this step seems never to have been decisively taken with the trust. Throughout our period, the position regarding the enforcement of trusts against the Crown in the *post* remained deeply unclear,[71] although there were suggestions that the equity side of the exchequer might grant relief in such cases[72] and that the chancery ought to take similar steps against other parties claiming in the *post* (such as the lord by escheat).[73]

Notwithstanding any agitation for further proprietisation, the trust seems to have remained unenforceable against the disseisor and the lord by escheat. In 1811, Edward Sugden wrote that:

> At this day everyone is bound by a trust who obtains the estate without a valuable consideration, or even for a valuable consideration if with notice, unless perhaps the lord by escheat. But persons claiming the legal estate by an actual disseisin, without collusion with the trustee, will not be bound by the trust. Therefore, if I oust A., who is a trustee for B., and a claim is not made in due time, A. will be barred, and his *cestui que* trust with him, although I had notice of the trust.[74]

[69] *Chudleigh's case* (1594) 1 Co Rep 120a, 122a.

[70] *Pawlett v AG* (1667) Hardres 465, 469; Yale (ed), *Prolegomena* (n 2) c 12, s 12. See also *Roscarrick v Barton* (1672) 1 Ch Cas 17; Yale (ed), *Prolegomena* (n 2) c 21, ss 22–23.

[71] *Burgess v Wheate* (1759) 1 Eden 177, 225 (Henley LK): 'Whether this remedy has since been settled in the Exchequer, where alone it can, I really do not know: but I hope it is so settled'.

[72] *Scounden v Hawley* (1689) Comb 172; *Reeve v AG* (1741) 2 Atk 223.

[73] *Geary v Bearcroft* (1665) Carter 57, 67; *Eales v England* (1702) Prec Ch 200, 202; *Burgess v Wheate* (1759) 1 Bl Wm 123, 165–66.

[74] EB Sugden (ed), *Gilbert on Uses and Trusts* (3rd edn, W Reed and P Phelan 1811) 429, n 6. This passage was relied upon unsuccessfully by counsel in *Re Nisbet and Potts' Contract* [1906] 1 Ch 386, 391, 394–95, when arguing that a restrictive covenant should only bind if the defendant derived possession from the covenantor.

By the nineteenth century, the trust had clearly gained a proprietary hue through its association with privity of estate, but this self-same association prevented the enforcement of a trust against the disseisor or the lord by escheat. While the trust never quite became an interest annexed to the possession of the trust property, the limitations of privity were rolled back in other respects which brought a more proprietary conception brought to the fore. To better explain these developments, it is helpful at this stage to separate the contexts in which these changes took place.

1. Exigibility

According to the doctrine of privity, the trust property would be liable for legal demands made against the trustee, but immune to those made against the beneficiary.[75] The trust property was regarded as forming part of the trustee's estate; it was liable to execution for the trustee's debts, to forfeiture for the trustee's treason, to the dower of the trustee's widow, and to escheat upon the trustee's felony or death intestate and without heirs.[76] The rights of the trustee's legal demandants arose by operation of law and hence were not bound by the trust.[77] By equal logic, the trust property did not form part of the beneficiary's estate and was, initially, exempt from the legal demands of the beneficiary's judgment creditors, surviving spouse, and the Crown claiming by forfeiture or escheat for the acts of the beneficiary.[78] The beneficiary's legal demandants were thus barred from claiming the trust assets; they did not claim in the *per*, and so were not entitled to claim the benefit of the trust. Over time, however, these restrictions were loosened and, as a by-product of these developments, the trust came to be cast in more proprietary terms.

In the middle decades of the seventeenth century, the trust was increasingly subjected to liability to the Crown for the acts of the beneficiary.[79] Under section 10 of the Statute of Frauds, the beneficial interest was made liable to execution for the beneficiary's judgment debts.[80] Meanwhile, Nottingham LC led the way in strengthening the trust's protection against the trustee's legal demandants.[81] In *Medley v Martin* (1673),[82] Nottingham (then Finch LK) held that the beneficiary could be relieved

[75] For excruciating detail on this subject, see DA Foster, *Legal Demands Against the Beneficial Interest under a Trust, c 1590–1759* (2020) Queen Mary, University of London (unpublished PhD thesis).

[76] *R v Boys* (1568) 3 Dyer 283b (forfeiture for trustee's alienage); *Pimb's case* (1585) Moo KB 196 (forfeiture for trustee's treason); *Wickes' case* (1609) Lane 54 (forfeiture for trustee's treason); *Nash v Preston* (1630) Cro Car 190 (liability to mortgagee's dowress; the case was thought to apply equally to the trustee's dowress in *Noel v Jevon* (1678) 2 Freem 43).

[77] *Gervys v Cooke* (1522) 119 Selden Society 108, 117 (Broke J), 118 (Pollard J); *Chudleigh's case* (1594) 1 Co Rep 120a, 122a. It should be noted that there was some debate in the seventeenth century as to who precisely was regarded as privy to the trust: W Sheppard, *A Touchstone of Common Assurances* (W Lee, M Walbancke, D Pakeman, and G Bedell 1648) 503; *Pawlett v AG* (1667) Hardres 465, 467–68 (Hale CB).

[78] *Kemp v Lady Reresby* (1626) Toth 99 (dowress); *Bennet v Box* (1665) 1 Ch Cas 11; 2 Freem 184 (judgment creditor); *AG v Sands* (1669) Hardres 488 (Crown by escheat for felony); *Burgess v Wheate* (1759) 1 Eden 177; 1 Bl Wm 123 (Crown by escheat for want of heirs).

[79] *AG v Bindloes* (1628) 118 Selden Society 556 (liability to execution for Crown debts); *R v Holland* (1648) Aleyn 14; Style 20, 40, 75, 84, 90, 94 (liability to forfeiture for alienage); *AG v Fitzjames* (1672) Lincoln's Inn MS Misc 500, f 197v, British Library Add MS 36,197, f 394, 398 (liability to forfeiture for outlawry).

[80] 29 Car II, c 3.

[81] Although see too the earlier decisions in *Cholmeley v Cave* (1623) TNA WARD 9/539, f 77 (relief against the trustee's judgment creditor) and *Stephens v Baily* (1665) 1 Nels 106 (relief against special occupant).

[82] Rep t Finch 63.

against the claims of trustee's judgment creditors, and in *Tassel v Hare* (1675),[83] the beneficiary was similarly relieved against the trustee's widow claiming dower.[84] This line of cases was reaffirmed in the early eighteenth century[85] and began to suggest that, in certain contexts, the trust could indeed be enforced against those claiming an estate arising by operation of law.[86] Between the seventeenth and nineteenth centuries, there was a concerted effort by both parliament and the courts to subject trust assets to the liabilities of the beneficiary, while simultaneously shielding them from those of the trustee.[87] The result was a partial reversal of the precepts of privity and naturally tended to undermine any conception of the trust which depended upon privity as its organising concept.

One of the most significant attacks on privity in this context had been launched in the mid-eighteenth century by Lord Mansfield. In *Burgess v Wheate* (1759), Mansfield opined that 'the old law of uses does not conclude trusts now... that part of the old law of uses, which did not allow any relief to be given for or against estates in the *post*, does not now bind by its authority in the case of trusts'.[88] Mansfield's *dictum* was repeated by successive treatise writers, including Cruise (1804),[89] Willis (1827),[90] and Jeremy (1828).[91] Each relied expressly upon Mansfield's opinion in *Burgess* as a basis for suggesting that the doctrine of privity no longer applied to the trust. Significant as Mansfield's opinion was, it did not gain universal endorsement. In *Burgess v Wheate* itself, Henley LK largely rejected Mansfield's view, and in his *Jurisconsult Exercitationes* (1811), Francis Hargrave remarked that: 'I must confess the more I consider the argument his Lordship [Mansfield] so eloquently delivered in that case, the more I am convinced, that the doctrine he endeavoured to establish is irreconcilable, both with the principles of our law, and with the current authorities.'[92] The suspicion of Mansfield's opinion was shared by Thomas Lewin[93] and George Spence[94]—both of whom continued to rely on a modified version of the doctrine of privity in their accounts of the trust.

Lewin recognised that many of the technical aspects of privity had been steadily abandoned by successive chancellors—particularly regarding the demands which could be levied upon trust assets.[95] By the nineteenth century, the surviving spouse

[83] 73 Selden Society 230, case 339.

[84] Affirmed in: *Noel v Jevon* (1678) 2 Freem 43; *Norman v Woodfall* (1680) 79 Selden Society 835, case 1046; *Bevant v Pope* (1681) 2 Freem 71, 79 Selden Society 890, case 1121.

[85] *Finch v Winchelsea* (1715) 1 P Wms 277; *ex p Chion* (1721) Lincoln's Inn MS Misc 384, f 243; 3 P Wms 186, n 2; *Bennet v Davis* (1725) 2 P Wms 316.

[86] cf *Morrice v Bank of England* (1736) Cas T Talb 217, 220, in which Talbot LC suggested that where the legal demandant had already taken possession of the land, equity would be powerless to assist.

[87] Dower Act 1833 (3&4 Will IV, c 105), s 2; Escheat Act 1834 (4&5 Will IV, c 23), s 2; Judgments Act 1838 (1&2 Vict, c 110), s 13; Trustee Act 1850 (13&14 Vict, c 60), s 46; Bankruptcy Act 1869 (32&33 Vict, c 71), s 15; Forfeiture Act 1870 (33&34 Vict, c 23), s 1.

[88] 1 Bl Wm 123, 155.

[89] W Cruise, *A Digest of the Laws of England respecting Real Property*, vol i (J Butterworth 1804) 492.

[90] J Willis, *A Practical Treatise on the Duties and Responsibilities of Trustees* (R Pheney, S Sweet, and Stevens & Sons 1827) 109, n 99, citing Cruise's treatise and Lord Mansfield in *Burgess*.

[91] G Jeremy, *A Treatise on the Equity Jurisdiction of the High Court of Chancery* (J & WT Clarke 1828) 20.

[92] F Hargrave, *Jurisconsult Exercitationes*, vol i (J Butterworth 1811) ch xv, 383, 388.

[93] Lewin, *Trusts and Trustees* (n 5) 15–20, 476–97, 498–571.

[94] G Spence, *Equitable Jurisdiction*, vol ii (n 67) 196.

[95] *Trusts and Trustees* (n 5) 11.

and judgment creditors of the trustee and beneficiary, though claiming by operation of law, were respectively bound by and could claim the benefit of the trust. For this reason, Lewin retained the doctrine of privity in his account of the trust but in an altered form:

> A trust is *annexed in privity to the estate*, that is, must stand or fall with the interest of the person by whom the trust is created ... And if the trustee die and leave no heir, the lord who takes by escheat is not privy to the estate upon which the trust was ingrafted, and therefore will not be bound by it, but will hold beneficially. And upon the same principle, if the trustee be disseised, the tortious fee is adverse to that impressed with the trust, and therefore the equitable owner cannot sue the disseisor in Chancery, but must bring an action against him in the name of the trustee.
>
> During the system of uses, and also while trusts were in their infancy, the notion of privity of estate was not extended to tenant[s] by the curtesy, or in dower, or by *elegit*, or in fact to any person claiming by operation of law, though through the trustee; but in this respect the landmarks have since been carried forward, and at the present day a trust follows the estate into the hands of everyone claiming under the trustee, whether in the *per* or in the *post*. A lord by escheat and a disseisor are the only persons not bound: the lord, because he claims by title paramount; a disseisor, because his possession is adverse.[96]

Lewin explained that those who claimed derivatively from the trustee or beneficiary could be bound by or take advantage of the trust. The beneficiary's judgment creditors claimed by operation of law but were entitled to the trust property because they claimed the benefit of the trust 'through' the beneficiary. The trustee's judgment creditors also entered by operation of law but were bound by the trust because they claimed 'through' the trustee and could only claim the (limited) estate to which the trustee was entitled. By contrast, neither the disseisor nor the lord by escheat claimed through the trustee. The lord claimed by a title paramount—a precedent estate in the land which came into possession on the death of the legal owner—to which the trust was not annexed. The disseisor meanwhile claimed a tortious fee, arising by adverse possession; it was a new estate, distinct from that of the trustee, and again was not bound by the trust. For Lewin, therefore, the exigibility of the trust no longer depended on whether the defendant entered in the *per* by act of the parties, or in the *post* by operation of law. Rather, exigibility was determined by whether the legal demandant's title was in some way derived from the trustee or beneficiary. So long as the recipient of trust property derived their claim from the trustee, they could be said to be privy to the trust and, hence, capable of being bound by it. Lewin's analysis was a significant marker in the development of the trust and demonstrated the extent to which the doctrine of privity had been altered over time. The importance of these developments for the proprietisation of the trust was explicitly remarked upon by Spence, who wrote that:

[96] ibid 18–19.

> the subtle distinctions which formerly attended the nature of privity of estate were gradually discarded; and tenant in dower, tenant by the curtesy, and tenant by statute merchant were held bound by the trust. The trust, in fact, was treated as if it were fastened on the estate rather than the person.[97]

By the middle of the nineteenth century, therefore, the rules on exigibility had contributed significantly to the reification of the trust by strengthening the enforceability of the beneficiary's right against non-privies, as well as subjecting the trust assets to liability for the beneficiary's acts.

2. Enforceability against privies

Where the trustee, in breach of trust, conveyed the land to a volunteer, the beneficiary could enforce the trust against the volunteer because the volunteer's title was derived from the trustee (ie the volunteer was bound because she claimed *per* the trustee and was privy to the trust).[98] Privity explained the liability of the volunteer, but where the trustee's successor in title had given consideration, privity did not conclude the matter. When dealing with a purchaser, the doctrine of privity overlapped with the doctrine of notice. In Coke's report of *Chudleigh's case* (1594), it was said that:

> If the feoffee to a use, upon good consideration, infeoffeth another who hath no notice, here is privity in estate, but there is no confidence in the person, either expressed or implied, and therefore the use is gone: but if a feoffment be made without consideration to one who hath no notice, there is privity in estate, and the law implies notice, and therefore the use remains, but not as a thing annexed to the land, but to the privity of the estate.[99]

From this statement, we can see that all assignees were privy to the trust and thus *capable* of being bound, but that the enforceability of the beneficiary's right might also depend on notice. Where the assignee was a volunteer, no actual or presumed notice was required; the mere fact of privity itself was sufficient grounds to imply notice.[100] Where the assignee was a purchaser, however, the beneficiary could only enforce her right where the purchaser took with notice of the trust.[101] It is important to reiterate,

[97] Spence, *Equitable Jurisdiction*, vol i (n 34) 500–01.

[98] *Gervys v Cooke* (1522) 119 Selden Society 108; *Chudleigh's case* (1594) 1 Co Rep 120a, 122b; Pop 70, 71–72; *Cole v Moore* (1607) Moo KB 806; *Pye v George* (1710) 2 Salk 680; *Mansell v Mansell* (1732) 2 P Wms 678; *Burgess v Wheate* (1759) 1 Eden 177, 251.

[99] 1 Co Rep 120a, 122b. See also Pop 70, 71. These rules had been previously mapped out in: *Anon* (1453) Fitz. Abr., tit. *subp.*, pl 19; *Gervys v Cooke* (1522) 119 Selden Society 108; *Delamere v Barnard* (1567) 1 Plow 346, 351. See also D Fox, 'Purchase for Value Without Notice', in PS Davies, S Douglas and J Goudkamp (eds), *Defences in Equity* (Hart 2018) 53, 57–62.

[100] Yale (ed), *Prolegomena* (n 2) c 14, s 1, c 15, s 1; Gilbert, *Uses and Trusts* (n 39) 167–68; [Ballow], *Treatise of Equity* (n 41) 68; F Sanders, An *Essay on the Nature and Laws of Uses and Trusts* (E and R Brooke 1791) 87; Lewin, *Trusts and Trustees* (n 5) 205. For a modern treatment making significant use of the historical case law, see P Ridge, 'Third Party Volunteers and Undue Influence' (2014) 130 LQR 112, 113–16, discussing the 'strict liability' of the volunteer in the context of rescission for undue influence.

[101] In *Gervys v Cooke* (1522) 119 Selden Society 108, 117, Broke J explained that 'if he has notice, he is *particeps criminis*'. This same reasoning appears in [Ballow], *Treatise of Equity* (n 41) 69.

however, that the doctrine of notice was only relevant in cases of grant or assignment; the lord by escheat and the disseisor could not be bound by the trust regardless whether they had notice or not.[102]

The doctrine of privity was, therefore, the means by which the trustee's successors in title might be bound by the trust. As the lynchpin to explaining third-party enforceability, privity was a key element of the proprietary conception of the trust. Nevertheless, as the language of privity faded from the rules on exigibility, we see a similar decline in privity-based accounts of the enforceability of trusts against assignees. By the mid-nineteenth century, greater emphasis was placed on the derivative title analysis found in Lewin,[103] but without mention of the doctrine of privity. By basing the enforceability of the trust on derivative title, mid-to-late nineteenth century treatises tended towards a *nemo dat*-type explanation; the assignee was bound because the trustee had merely transferred their own limited rights in the trust *res*. In 1845, for example, James Hill explained that 'the party, in whom the property has become vested, will be bound by the trust to the same extent, as the trustee from whom he took'.[104] While, in 1879, Henry Godefroi stated that 'the grantee, though he have no notice of the trust, stands in place of the grantors, and is liable to the trust in the same manner as the trustees were liable to it, and the property may be followed by the *cestui que trust*'.[105] Arthur Underhill took a more explicitly proprietary line in 1878, remarking that '[i]f an alienee is a volunteer, then the estate will remain burdened with the trust, whether he had notice of the trust or not; for a volunteer has no equity as against a true owner'.[106] On this view, trusts were understood to bind the property—not the person—and any person into whose hands the property fell would be liable to the trust (excepting the disseisor and the lord by escheat). Such analyses take us beyond the more narrow concepts of 'privity of person' and 'privity of estate' and suggest the emergence of more pronounced proprietary notions in later nineteenth century conceptions of the trust.[107]

III. The Analytical Conceptions of the Trust

In the preceding sections, I have canvassed some of the mechanisms by which the trust was converted from an obligation in confidence into an equitable interest annexed to trustee's estate. We have seen that these developments encouraged the view among both judges and treatise writers that the trust had been substantially reified by the first decades of the nineteenth century. These developments form the doctrinal backdrop to the

[102] See authorities listed in note 67.
[103] See quoted text on p 123.
[104] J Hill, *A Practical Treatise on the Law Relating to Trustees* (Stevens & Norton 1845) 147.
[105] H Godefroi, *A Digest of the Principles of the Law of Trusts and Trustees* (Stevens & Sons 1879) 295.
[106] A Underhill, *A Concise Manual of the Law Relating to Private Trusts and Trustees* (Butterworths 1878) 194 (hereafter Underhill, *Concise Manual*).
[107] It may be that this change in emphasis from 'privity' to 'derivative title' encouraged a move from the 'engrafting principle' (see, eg, Lewin, *Trusts and Trustees* (n 5) 18) to the 'carving out principle' found in later writings (see, eg, B Green, 'Grey, Oughtred and Vandervell—A Contextual Reappraisal' (1984) 47 MLR 385, 387).

early analytical conceptions of the trust in this period. Given the extent to which the trust was conceived and described in proprietary terms, it is unsurprising to find the founder of the school of analytical jurisprudence—John Austin—reflecting this proprietary conception in his jurisprudential writing. As we shall see, however, this was an issue over which successive members of analytical school would vacillate, producing what WN Hohfeld called a 'striking divergence of opinion' in the analytical conceptions of the trust.[108]

A. Austin and the Early Analytical Conceptions of the Trust

In his *Lectures on Jurisprudence* (delivered 1829–33, published posthumously in 1863), John Austin endeavoured to explain the distinction between rights *in rem* and rights *in personam* in English law generally.[109] Despite its civilian flavour, this language of 'rights' *in rem* and 'rights' *in personam* was decidedly un-Roman; the Roman jurists had only used the terms *in rem* and *in personam* to describe *actiones*, rather than substantive rights.[110] Austin himself seemed to recognise their novelty when applied to the common law, remarking that 'I adopt them without hesitation, though at the risk of offending your ears'.[111] Nevertheless, in the course of lecture XIV, Austin gave a definition of rights *in rem* and rights *in personam* which would prove immensely influential for later writers:

> The phrase *in rem* denotes the *compass*, and not the *subject* of the right. It denotes that the right in question avails against persons generally; and *not* that the right in question is a right over a *thing* … The phrase *in personam* is an elliptical or abridged expression for 'in personam certam sive determinatum.' Like the phrase *in rem*, it denotes the *compass* of the right. It denotes that the right avails *exclusively* against a *determinate* person, or against *determinate* persons.[112]

Unfortunately, Austin's health did not permit him to continue with his project and he was unable to consider the English trust *in extenso*, but we are left with an intriguing glimpse into his views on the subject. When discussing the right of a purchaser under a specifically enforceable contract for sale of land, Austin remarked that:

[108] WN Hohfeld, 'Some Fundamental Legal Conceptions as Applied in Judicial Reasoning' (1913) 23 Yale LJ 16, 19.

[109] J Austin, *Lectures on Jurisprudence or the Philosophy of Positive Law* (1st edn, J Murray 1863) (hereafter Austin, *Lectures on Jurisprudence*). An outline of the lectures was appended to J Austin, *The Province of Jurisprudence Determined* (J Murray 1832), in which Austin discussed the *in rem/in personam* distinction: see appendix, xxv–xli.

[110] Discussions of *iura in rem* and *in personam* originated with the medieval canonists: B Tierney, *The Idea of Natural Rights* (WB Eerdmans 2001) 18–19, 283–84.

[111] Austin, *Lectures on Jurisprudence*, vol ii (n 109) 32. Although the phrase was used by King LC in *Anon* (1729) 2 Eq Cas Abr 108 and by Plumer MR in *Dearle v Hall* (1828) 3 Russ 1, 24.

[112] ibid 32.

> By the provisions of that part of the English law which is called equity, a contract to sell at once vests *jus in rem* or ownership in the buyer, and the seller has only *jus in re alienâ*. But according to the conflicting provisions of that part of the English system called peculiarly *law*, a sale and purchase without certain formalities merely gives *jus ad rem*, or a right to receive the ownership, not ownership itself: and for this reason a contract to sell, though in equity it confers ownership, is yet an imperfect conveyance, in consequence of the conflicting pretensions of law.[113]

Austin thus seemed to regard the equity to specific performance (and, by extension, the beneficial interest under a vendor-purchaser constructive trust) as an equitable right *in rem*. While Austin's work was important in the field of analytical jurisprudence, there is little evidence to suggest that his writings had an immediate effect on the way in which equitable rights were being conceptualised more generally.[114] Following Austin's death, there is certainly no suggestion in the law reports that the *in rem/in personam* distinction became commonplace; indeed, we find few references to 'rights *in rem*' in the law reports at all until the very late nineteenth century.[115]

In the latter half of the nineteenth century, however, there was a shift in how the trust was being conceptualised by the new treatise writers of the period. A particular problem posed by Lewin and Spence's reliance on the doctrine of privity of estate as an organising principle for the trust was its non-application to trusts of personalty. Lewin had stated that 'trusts of chattels ... were conducted upon the same principles, *mutatis mutandis*, as were trusts of freeholds; the right to sue a *subpoena* turned equally on privity'.[116] But, in an era where trusts of personalty were increasingly common,[117] an estates-based theory of trusts was ill-suited; after all, the doctrine of estates did not apply to personalty at common law.[118] Lewin himself gave little consideration to the point, but the problem of trusts of personalty would provide ballast to his detractors. In 1878, Arthur Underhill took issue with Lewin's account of the trust, remarking that:

> Mr Lewin adopts Lord Coke's definition of a use ... This definition would seem applicable to real estate only, and certainly not to trusts of choses in action, the equities attaching to which are, generally speaking, not merely collateral.[119]

For Underhill, therefore, trusts could not be explained as annexed to the trustee's estate in the subject matter of the trust. Nor were they merely obligations personal to the trustee ('not merely collateral'). By the late nineteenth century, the new treatise

113 R Campbell (ed), *Lectures on Jurisprudence or the Philosophy of Positive Law*, vol i (5th edn, J Murray 1885) 377. This section was not present in the first edition of 1863, but can be found in the third edition in 1869: see vol i, 388.

114 cf *ex p Pollard* (1840) Mont & Ch 239, 250 (Cottenham LC).

115 See, eg, *Allen v Flood* [1898] AC 1, 34 (Cave J).

116 Lewin, *Trusts and Trustees* (n 5) 5, citing *Witham v Waterhouse* (1596) 4 Co Int 87.

117 S Stebbings, *The Private Trustee in Victorian England* (CUP 2001) 6–8.

118 J Williams, *Principles of the Law of Real Property* (S Sweet 1845) 5.

119 Underhill, *Concise Manual* (n 106) 1, n (a).

writers—Snell (1868), Underhill (1878), and Godefroi (1879)—rarely made reference to privity of estate and the historical conception of the trust began to slip from view.[120] In its place, there emerged a tendency to discuss the trust simply in terms of 'equitable ownership' and to refer to the beneficiary as the 'true owner' of the trust property.[121] This notion of equitable ownership was somewhat undertheorised, but the language was convenient. By removing focus from the requirement of privity of estate, the late nineteenth century treatise writers could more easily accommodate trusts of personalty within their general schemes, while retaining a proprietary conception of the trust as a whole.

At precisely the same time, the *in rem/in personam* distinction was increasingly being applied to equitable rights by academic commentators. With the publication of successive editions of Austin's *Lectures on Jurisprudence* in the 1860s and 1870s, the language of rights *in rem* and *in personam* had become commonplace in English jurisprudence and Austin's followers dutifully carried his project further. Crucially, however, the early adopters of this civilian language tended, when analysing equitable rights, to classify the right of the beneficiary as a right *in personam* (*contra* Austin). In 1880, Thomas Erskine Holland's *The Elements of Jurisprudence* contained an unapologetically civilian discussion of the classification of rights.[122] In his discussion of equitable rights, Holland specifically referred to the beneficiary under a trust as having a right *in personam* against the trustee—apparently on the basis of an analogy with the Roman *fideicommissum*, but the point was not otherwise developed.[123] Holland's view was shared by CC Langdell and JB Ames and, subsequently, given its classic form by FW Maitland in his lectures on equity delivered in 1906. The collective aim of Langdell, Ames, and Maitland was to place trusts within Austin's definition of a right *in personam* (ie a right enforceable against determinate persons, rather than persons generally). They sought to support their view by, variously: (i) demonstrating that equity was incapable of producing rights *in rem*; (ii) denigrating the concept of 'equitable ownership' and the idea of the beneficiary as 'true owner'; and (iii) providing a list of those definite persons against whom the trust could be enforced. Through this work, they produced a powerful case for the *in personam* theory of the trust.

[120] Although the doctrine of privity of estate was discussed briefly in OW Holmes Jr, *The Common Law* (Macmillan 1882) 399, 407–09.

[121] Underhill, *Concise Manual* (n 106) 194; J Adams, *The Doctrine of Equity* (T&JW Johnson 1890) xxxvii; JW Salmond, *The First Principles of Jurisprudence* (Stevens & Haynes 1893) 278. Lewin, *Trusts and Trustees* (n 5) 18–19, had also used the phrase, albeit in the course of his privity-based analysis. The language of 'equitable ownership' appeared in the reports in the mid-eighteenth century (see, eg, *Hawkins v Chappel* (1739) 1 Atk 621, 624), but became increasingly common during the nineteenth century.

[122] TE Holland, *The Elements of Jurisprudence* (Clarendon 1880) 107–09.

[123] ibid 168.

B. Langdell, Ames, and Maitland

Langdell derived his *in personam* conception of the trust at least in part from the maxim *aequitas agit in personam*. Historically, this maxim merely described aspects of equitable procedure, and was not concerned with the classification of substantive equitable rights.[124] Langdell, however, viewed the maxim as foundational for understanding the equitable jurisdiction as whole; if equity acted solely *in personam*, he reasoned, then equity was only capable of producing rights *in personam*. In his treatise on pleading in equity, for example, Langdell observed:

> It is only by a figure of speech that a person who has not the legal title to property can be said to be the equitable owner of it. What is called equitable ownership or equitable title or an equitable estate is in truth only a personal claim against the real owner; for equity has no jurisdiction *in rem*, and cannot, therefore, confer a true ownership, except by its power over the person with whom the ownership resides, i.e., by compelling him to convey.[125]

According to Langdell, equity operated *in personam* by making decrees against the defendant's person and could make no decrees *in rem* against the defendant's property directly. Langdell thus reasoned that the beneficiary's right was merely enforceable by a decree against the trustee's person, not against the trust *res* itself, and as such could only be categorised as a personal right against the trustee (ie a right *in personam*). Indeed, it was key to Langdell's understanding of equity that there could be no equitable rights *in rem* at all. As evidence for this assertion, Langdell laid particular stress on the immunity of the *bona fide* purchaser to the beneficiary's claim. In 1887, he wrote:

> if equitable rights were rights *in rem*, they would follow the *res* into the hands of a purchaser for value and without notice; a result which would not only be intolerable to those for whose benefit equity exists, but would be especially abhorrent to equity itself. Upon the whole, it may be said that equity could not create rights *in rem* if it would, and that it would not if it could.[126]

For Langdell, the touchstone of a right *in rem* was its capacity to bind the purchaser for value without notice; the beneficial interest did not bind the *bona fide* purchaser, hence it could not be a right *in rem*. Such a strict definition of rights *in rem* necessarily excluded the trust but it was overbroad; Ames and Maitland each observed that, even at common law, the rights of the legal owner could be barred (for example) by a purchaser in market

[124] Yale (ed), *Prolegomena* (n 2) 16–45.

[125] CC Langdell, *Summary of Equity Pleading* (CW Sever 1877) 90 (hereafter Langdell, *Summary*).

[126] CC Langdell, 'A Brief Survey of the Equitable Jurisdiction' (1887) 1(2) HLR 55, 60. See also earlier statements in Langdell, *Summary* (n 125) 90.

overt.[127] In this regard, Langdell's *in personam* account of the trust was not particularly successful, but his discussion of the maxim *aequitas agit in personam* would prove influential for his successors.

Langdell's influence was particularly marked in the work of James Barr Ames. Ames too was sceptical of equity's ability to produce rights *in rem*[128] and referred to the maxim *aequitas agit in personam* as 'the key to the mastery of equity'.[129] Like Langdell, Ames also appealed to the basic nature of equity in support of his *in personam* conception of the trust. For Ames, the purpose of equity was to complement—but never to contradict—the principles of the common law. The common law acted *in rem*, whereas equity acted *in personam* and could not set up rules in opposition to the common law position.[130] Applying this understanding of equity to the trust, Ames asserted that the common law regarded the trustee as the 'owner' of the trust property, invested with rights *in rem*. To view the beneficiary as the 'owner' and to classify the beneficiary's right as a right *in rem*, therefore, would be for equity to contradict the position at law. As Ames explained in 1887:

> A *cestui que trust* is frequently spoken of as an equitable owner of the land. This, though a convenient form of expression, is clearly inaccurate. The trustee is the owner of the land, and, of course, two persons with adverse interests cannot be owners of the same thing.[131]

To avoid such a conflict with the common law rules, Ames argued that the beneficiary had a mere personal right against the trustee:

> What the *cestui que trust* really owns is the obligation of the trustee; for an obligation is as truly the subject-matter of property as any physical *res*. The most striking difference between property in a thing and property in an obligation is in the mode of enjoyment. The owner of a house or a horse enjoys the fruits of ownership without the aid of any other person. The only way in which the owner of an obligation can realize his ownership is by compelling its performance by the obligor. Hence, in the one case, the owner is said to have a right *in rem*, and, in the other, a right *in personam*.[132]

Ames' theory provided a neat solution to the problem of conflicting rules of law and equity, but it was not without difficulties. According to Ames, a right *in rem* included

[127] JB Ames, *Lectures on Legal History* (HUP 1913) 76 (hereafter Ames, *Lectures*); JW Brunyate (ed), *Equity: A Course of Lectures by FW Maitland* (CUP 1936) 139–40 (hereafter Brunyate (ed), *Equity*). See also RP Pound, 'Review' (1912–13) 26 Harv LR 462, 463 (hereafter Pound, 'Review').

[128] JB Ames, *A Selection of Cases on the Law of Trusts*, vol i (2nd edn, HLRPA 1893) 244; Ames, *Lectures* (n 127) 76.

[129] Ames, *Lectures* (n 127) 233.

[130] ibid 76. This view was later approved in CC Langdell, 'Classification of Rights and Wrongs, Part II' (1900) 13 HLR 659, 673, and Brunyate (ed), *Equity* (n 127) 17–19. Ames' 'no conflict' theory of equity was seemingly calculated to counter Austin's original account of equitable rights *in rem* as 'conflicting' with the 'pretentions of law' (see text quoted at note 113).

[131] JB Ames, 'Purchaser for Value without Notice' (1887) 1 HLR 1, 9.

[132] ibid 9–10.

the right to the enjoyment, income, or fruits of the *res*, whereas the beneficiary merely had a right under a trust to compel the trustee to transfer the fruits of the trust property.[133] This explanation of the beneficiary's right came close to the sixteenth century *chose* in action approach in emphasising the beneficiary's right to compel performance by means of the chancery *subpoena*. In that regard, however, it tended to overlook the other contexts in which the trust had been reified in the intervening centuries. In other words, Ames' analytical theory failed to account for historical change and could not explain the slow reification of the trust from the time of Coke to the present day.

The classic statement of the *in personam* theory belongs to FW Maitland in his lectures on equity (first published 1909, revised 1936).[134] In these lectures, Maitland borrowed much from Langdell and Ames, but combined them into a more subtle and arguably more successful thesis. Maitland's starting point was an immediate rejection of Austin's *in rem* account of the trust, quipping that 'as a piece of speculative jurisprudence this seems to me nonsense, while as an exposition of our English rules, I think it not merely nonsensical but mischievous'.[135] For Maitland, the beneficiary could not be regarded as having a right *in rem* because, following Langdell, he considered equity incapable of creating rights *in rem*.[136] To do so, Maitland believed, would be to create two conflicting notions of ownership—one at law, the other in equity—and which would result in 'utter anarchy'.[137] Instead, he explained, equity acted merely *in personam*, as a gloss upon the law, and could not contradict common law rules;[138] as such, the beneficiary could not be regarded as 'owner'[139] and the beneficial interest could not be a right *in rem*.[140] Having synthesised the work of Langdell and Ames, Maitland could assert that the beneficiary's right was very clearly a right *in personam*:

> equitable estates and interests are not *jura in rem*. For reasons that we shall perceive by and by, they have come to look very like *jura in rem*; but just for this very reason it is the more necessary for us to observe that they are essentially *jura in personam*, not rights against the world at large, but rights against certain persons.[141]

The great strength of Maitland's analysis, however, was his sensitivity to the currents of legal change; while he regarded the beneficiary's right as a right *in personam*, he recognised the need to explain how, over time, the trust had come to 'look very like' a right *in*

133 This emphasis on enjoyment and possession as the hallmark of a right *in rem* was roundly criticised by WN Hohfeld, 'Fundamental Legal Conceptions as Applied in Judicial Reasoning' (1917) 26 Yale LJ 710, 754–57 (hereafter Hohfeld, 'Fundamental Legal Conceptions').

134 Brunyate (ed), *Equity* (n 127) lecture IX.

135 ibid 106. cf WG Hart's observation that Austin's tentative remarks on the nature of the trust 'hardly deserves ... the violent criticism to which it has been subjected by Professor Maitland': WG Hart, 'The Place of Trust in Jurisprudence' (1912) 28 LQR 290, 291, n 1.

136 Brunyate (ed), *Equity* (n 127) 31; Maitland, *Collected Papers*, vol iii (CUP 1911) 350, n 1, quoting Langdell (hereafter Maitland, *Collected Papers*).

137 Brunyate (ed), *Equity* (n 127) 17, 107.

138 ibid 17–19.

139 ibid 17–18, 106–07.

140 ibid 107.

141 ibid 107.

rem. This sensitivity to history was, in turn, reflected in his approach to the Austinian terminology itself, which was more nuanced than that of his predecessors.

While Maitland made extensive use of the Austinian terminology, it must be recalled that his lectures were intended for an undergraduate audience and that, elsewhere in his work, he had admitted the limitations of this language. In 'Trust and Corporation' (written in 1904), for example, Maitland had expressed misgivings as to the wisdom of pigeonholing the beneficial interest according to civilian categories:

> it seems to me, the Trust could hardly have been evolved among a people who had clearly formulated the distinction between a right *in personam* and a right *in rem*, and had made that distinction one of the main outlines of their legal system ... For my own part if a foreign friend asked me to tell him in one word whether the right of the English *Destinatär* (the person for whom property is held in trust) is *dinglich* or *obligatorisch*, I should be inclined to say: "No, I cannot do that. If I said *dinglich*, that would be untrue. If I said *obligatorisch*, I should suggest what is false. In ultimate analysis the right may be *obligatorisch*; but for many practical purposes of great importance it has been treated as though it were *dinglich*".[142]

Maitland's caution in adopting the Austinian classification ultimately led him to embark on a historical analysis of the means by which the beneficiary's rights had evolved from an equitable obligation in the sixteenth century to something 'analogous to true proprietary rights' by the early twentieth century.[143] Through this historical analysis, and while maintaining focus upon the *in personam* theory, Maitland could account for the various ways in which the beneficial interest had been reified over time.

From the time of Coke, Maitland tells us, 'the use or trust was originally regarded as an obligation, in point of fact a contract though not usually so called'.[144] For Maitland, therefore, the source of the trustee's duty and the beneficiary's correlative right was the trustee's agreement to be bound. By emphasising the agreement of the trustee, Maitland could cast the trust in obligational terms:

> the Law of Trusts (formerly Uses) begins with this, a person who has undertaken a trust is bound to fulfil it. We have no difficulty in finding a ground for this—the trustee, the feoffee to uses, is bound because he has bound himself. This is the original notion. The right of the *cestui que trust* is the benefit of an obligation. This is how Coke understood the matter. 'An use is a trust or confidence reposed in some other ... '[145]

[142] Maitland, *Collected Papers* (n 136) 325–26.
[143] Brunyate (ed), *Equity* (n 127) 110.
[144] ibid 110. Maitland emphasised the importance of agreement in trusts elsewhere in his lectures: see 28–30, 54–55. cf AW Scott, 'The Nature of the Rights of the Cestui Que Trust' (1917) 17 Col LR 269, 269–71 (hereafter Scott, 'Rights of the Cestui'), who was at pains to distinguish trust from contract.
[145] ibid 111–12, citing Co Litt 272b.

Thereafter, however, Maitland set out the steps by which the trust had come to look like a right in *rem*, namely: (i) enforceability against the trustee; (ii) enforceability against those 'who come to the lands or goods by inheritance or succession' who 'may be regarded as sustaining wholly or partially the *persona* of the original trustee' (including the trustee's heir, executor, administrator, and dowress); (iii) enforceability against the trustee's creditors; (iv) enforceability against the trustee's donee without valuable consideration 'who came to the thing through or under the trustee as a volunteer ... even though he had no notice of the trust'; (v) enforceability against the purchaser with actual notice; and (vi) enforceability against purchasers with constructive notice.[146] The cumulative effect of these developments was, according to Maitland, that the trust began to appear 'real'. In spite of the extent to which the beneficial interest had been reified, Maitland was quick to emphasise that the trust had remained unenforceable against the *bona fide* purchaser, the lord by escheat, and the disseisor.[147]

Maitland had thus shown how, in the period *c* 1600–1900, the trust had grown from an equitable obligation, arising from agreement, into something akin to a property right. This partial reification of the trust had, however, created problems of classification which he now endeavoured to solve. According to Maitland, the nature of the trust could, in the final analysis, be formulated in one of two ways. Either the beneficiary's right was enforceable *in personam*, against specific classes of persons (ie the trustee's heirs, devisees, personal representatives, donees, creditors, etc.) or it was enforceable *in rem* against an indeterminate class (with the exception of the *bona fide* purchaser, the lord by escheat, and the disseisor).[148] Maitland preferred the first formulation on the grounds that 'it puts us at what is historically the right point of view—the benefit of an obligation has been so treated that it has come to look rather like a true proprietary right'.[149] The proprietary dimension had indeed been developed over time, such that the beneficiary's right was enforceable against a larger class of persons than (eg) a simple contract debt. Nevertheless, Maitland asserted that this process of reification had produced rights which were merely 'analogous to true proprietary rights'[150] and only 'misleadingly like *iura in rem*'.[151] For Maitland, the trust had, from its inception, been an equitable obligation and equitable obligations could *never* acquire the status of a right *in rem* for the simple reason that equity was incapable of creating such rights. To do otherwise would produce contradiction and anarchy in the relations between law and equity.

[146] Brunyate (ed), *Equity* (n 127) 112–14.

[147] ibid 115–16.

[148] For Maitland (*contra* Langdell), unenforceability against a *bona fide* purchaser was not in itself sufficient to determine the nature of the trust: 'I do not for one moment think that it should be part of our conception of a right *in rem*, that the person who has that right can never be deprived of it save by his own act' (Brunyate (ed), *Equity* (n 127) 139).

[149] Brunyate (ed), *Equity* (n 127) 110.

[150] ibid 110.

[151] ibid 112.

C. Post-Maitland

Maitland's analysis had much to recommend it; it proceeded upon clear, logical lines and purported to explain the changing nature of the trust over time. A major weakness of the theory, however, was its reliance on the maxim *aequitas agit in personam*. In 1915, Walter Wheeler Cook observed two key criticisms of Maitland's use of the maxim:

> a word or two may be said concerning the statements so often made that all equitable rights are rights *in personam*; that they had to be such because of the fact that equity acts only *in personam* ... [I]t seems that two things may be said: first, that the premise is untrue; second, that even if the premise were true, the conclusion would not follow ... [A] better example of a simple *non sequitur* could hardly be asked for ... [152]

The first criticism noted by Cook was historical in nature; as a matter of legal history, the maxim had only ever described certain aspects of equitable procedure and that it was not the 'key' to equity that Ames had considered it.[153] While it was true that, under the writ of *subpoena*, the chancery could only act upon the person of the defendant (ie *in personam*), the *subpoena* was not the only writ used in chancery.[154] By the early seventeenth century, the chancery had developed an *in rem* jurisdiction through the writs of assistance and sequestration; these writs commanded the sheriff to seize the defendant's property directly in satisfaction of the plaintiff's claim.[155] As a description of equitable procedure, therefore, the maxim failed to capture how equity had evolved beyond purely personal modes of enforcement.

The second of Cook's criticisms was analytic in nature; any historical inaccuracies aside, Maitland's use of the maxim failed to distinguish the substantive right from the procedure for its enforcement.[156] Proceedings *in personam* could, and often did, vindicate rights *in rem*. It was, therefore, specious to reason from a form of procedure to the nature of a substantive right. WN Hohfeld provided a simple example to illustrate the point:

> Suppose ... that A is owner of Blackacre, and that B drives his automobile over A's lawn and shrubbery. A's primary right *in rem* is thereby violated, and a secondary right *in personam* arises in favour of A against B ... It will thus be seen that, *even in the law*

[152] WW Cook, 'The Powers of Courts of Equity, Part II' (1915) 15 Col LR 106, 139 (hereafter Cook, 'Powers Part II').

[153] RMP Willoughby, *The Distinctions and Anomalies arising out of the Equitable Doctrine of the Legal Estate* (CUP 1912) 88–92; CA Huston, *The Enforcement of Decrees in Equity* (HUP 1915) 135–36 (hereafter Huston, *Enforcement*); WW Cook, 'The Powers of Courts of Equity, Part I' (1915) 15 Col LR 37, 39 (hereafter Cook, 'Powers Part I'); Cook, 'Powers Part II' (n 152) 139–41; Hohfeld, 'Fundamental Legal Conceptions' (n 133) 764, n 108.

[154] *Penn v Lord Baltimore* (1750) 1 Ves Sen 444, 454 (Hardwicke LC); Yale (ed), *Prolegomena* (n 2) 16–45.

[155] Langdell, *Summary* (n 125) xxiv had noted the existence of these writs but sought to downplay their significance. For criticism of Langdell's analysis, see Cook, 'Powers Part II' (n 152) 110–15.

[156] Cook, 'Powers Part I' (n 153) 39, 52–54; Huston, *Enforcement* (n 153) 136–44; Hohfeld, 'Fundamental Legal Conceptions' (n 133) 714–16, 757–66.

> *courts* the vindication of primary rights *in rem* may, according to circumstances be by proceedings *in personam* . . . [157]

Hohfeld thus concluded that:

> the intrinsic nature of substantive primary rights—whether they be rights *in rem* or rights *in personam*—is not dependent on the character of the proceedings by which they may be vindicated.[158]

This reasoning was particularly important in the context of foreign trusts, where the *situs* of the trust *res* was outside the jurisdiction of the court (and no *in rem* proceedings were, therefore, possible). While the enforcement of foreign trusts necessarily took effect by means of a decree *in personam* for the defendant to perform the trust,[159] the enforcement procedure by itself was an insufficient basis on which to classify the beneficiary's right as either *in rem* or *in personam*.[160] It thus appeared that Langdell and Maitland had erected their *in personam* conception of the trust on a misunderstanding of the meaning of the maxim. In the field of procedure, equity did not act solely *in personam* and, even where it did, the procedure could not determine the underlying nature of the beneficiary's right.

With the first pillar of the *in personam* conception under threat, Maitland's general account of equity—as a gloss which could not contradict the basic precepts of the law—also came under pressure. In 1913, Hohfeld argued that:

> there is . . . a very marked and constantly recurring conflict between legal and equitable rules relating to various jural relations; and whenever such conflict occurs, the equitable rule is, in the last analysis, paramount and determinative. Or, putting the matter another way, the so-called legal rule in every such case has, *to that extent*, only an apparent validity and operation as a matter of *genuine* law.[161]

For Hohfeld, it was a basic characteristic of equity to contradict the law and he considered trusts an example of such conflict. At law, the beneficiary had no right to the trust *res* whatsoever, but in equity she could control the rights of the legal owner.[162] Looking past the law-equity division and focusing on the 'ultimate jural realties'[163] between the trustee and beneficiary, Hohfeld saw a conflict between the rules which was resolved in favour of the beneficiary:

157 Hohfeld, 'Fundamental Legal Conceptions' (n 133) 760–62. Emphasis original.
158 ibid 766.
159 *Penn v Lord Baltimore* (1750) 1 Ves Sen 444, 447 (Hardwicke LC); *ex p Pollard* (1840) Mont & Ch 239, 250 (Cottenham LC); *Ewing v Orr Ewing (No 1)* (1883) 9 App Cas 34, 40 (Selbourne LC).
160 JH Beale, 'Equitable Interests in Foreign Property' (1907) 20 HLR 382, 386; Huston, *Enforcement* (n 153) 138; Cook, 'Powers Part II' (n 152) 128–29; Scott, 'Rights of the Cestui' (n 144) 287–89. cf HF Stone, 'The Nature of the Rights of the Cestui Que Trust' (1917) 17 Col LR 467, 497–98.
161 WN Hohfeld, 'The Relations Between Equity and Law' (1913) 11 Mich LR 537, 544. Emphasis original.
162 ibid 555. See also Hohfeld, 'Fundamental Legal Conceptions' (n 133) 767–70.
163 Hohfeld, 'Fundamental Legal Conceptions' (n 133) 770.

> the interest of a *cestui que trust* constitutes a complex aggregate of exclusively equitable rights, privileges, powers, and immunities, (some of these being *in rem*. . . .and some of them *in personam* . . .); [and] . . . in order to appreciate clearly the exact nature of all these jural elements it is necessary to consider definitively the 'conflict' of the 'legal' and 'equitable' relations involved and to discover the net residuum derived from a 'fusion' of law and equity.[164]

Far from equity respecting the law, Hohfeld conceived of equity in cases of conflict as 'repealing' the law *pro tanto*.[165] This self-avowedly fusionist attack on Maitland would engender its own debates on the nature of equity, but, for our purposes, Hohfeld's arguments showed that Maitland's 'no conflict' view of equity remained contentious ground.

With the primary bases of Maitland's theory subject to criticism, later treatments turned to the final element of Maitland's account of the trust: the contention that the beneficiary's right was good only against a determinate class of persons and thus lay within Austin's definition of a right *in personam*. Maitland himself had admitted that the beneficiary's right *might* be explained as 'enforceable against all save a *bona fide* purchaser'[166] but had rejected this formulation on the grounds that equity could not create rights *in rem* and that, to do so, would conflict with the rules at law. Now that these reasons for rejecting the *in rem* conception of the trust had been shown wanting, it was possible to argue that the beneficiary's right was enforceable against an indeterminate class (ie *in rem*). A typical example of this argument is found in CA Huston's, *The Enforcement of Decrees in Equity* (1915):

> the essence of a right *in rem* is not that it is good against all the world, including even a *bona fide* purchaser for value. It is sufficient if it is good generally against an indefinite number, as distinguished from those available only against sufficient persons.[167]

For Huston, the beneficiary's right might not have been enforceable against the *bona fide* purchaser, the disseisor, or the lord by escheat, but it was nevertheless a right *in rem* by virtue of its enforceability against the trustee's successors in title (which, in his view, amounted to an indeterminate class).[168] In a review of Huston's book, Hohfeld wrote of his 'hearty agreement with the author's main position'[169] and offered some further refinements to Huston's *in rem* account:

> Such comparatively few persons as actually know of a particular trust are under actual, or present, equitable duties not to accept conveyance of the legal title from the trustee . . . But how about the vast majority of persons, who, of course, have no present

[164] ibid 767.
[165] ibid 767.
[166] Brunyate (ed), *Equity* (n 127) 115.
[167] Huston, *Enforcement* (n 153) 126. See also Pound, 'Review' (n 127) 463. Pound had supervised Huston's doctoral thesis, so some consonance in their views is perhaps unsurprising.
[168] Huston, *Enforcement* (n 153) 87–114.
[169] WN Hohfeld, 'Review' (1915) 25 Yale LJ 166, 168.

knowledge or notice of the trust?... Perhaps, as a mere matter of legal terms and sufficient communication of ideas, it would suffice to say that the *cestui* has actual, or present, rights *in rem* against such persons, *to wit*, that they should not *knowingly* accept conveyance from the trustee ... If, however, it should be objected that, under a more strict use of terms, the *cestui* has actual, or present, rights only against those having actual knowledge or notice, that technical difficulty could be met by explaining that, as against innocent parties, the *cestui* has, at the very least, very important 'possibilities' *in rem*,—that is, 'potential, or inchoate rights' *in rem*.[170]

Huston and Hohfeld thus demonstrated that a shift in emphasis, from specific persons bound by the trust (the heir, the judgment creditor, etc.) to those exempted from liability (the *bona fide* purchaser, the disseisor, etc.), could support an *in rem* conception of the trust. Conceivably, the trust property could come into the hands of anyone in the world and they would be bound unless they fell within the class of individuals who were immune to liability. In this sense, therefore, the potential class of individuals who might be bound by the trust was indeterminate and, as such, the beneficiary's right was deserving of the description 'right *in rem*'.[171]

IV. Conclusion

In subsequent decades, the debate within the analytical school over the precise classification of the trust rumbled on, the inconclusive nature of the debate merely serving to further embed the Austinian language in popular legal usage. The analytical debates themselves did much to lay the foundations for modern approaches to classification and taxation of trusts, as well as the enforcement of foreign trusts.[172] For the legal historian, however, the continued use of the Austinian terminology to describe equitable rights remained controversial. By substituting the language of rights *in personam* and *in rem* for the language of confidence and privity, analytical models of the trust were denuded of the very ideas which had explained the trust's development over time. It was this loss of the historical conception of the trust that later scholars would criticise. The most vociferous critic of the Austinian categories was undoubtedly RW Turner. In

170 ibid 168–69. See also Hohfeld, 'Fundamental Legal Conceptions' (n 133) 764–66.

171 cf HF Stone, 'The Nature of the Rights of the Cestui Que Trust' (1917) 17 Col LR 467, 469–73, who deprecated attempts to widen the definition of rights *in rem* such that it 'might ultimately embrace the whole field of law and thereby make [the] classification worthless'.

172 See, for example, HG Hanbury, 'The Field of Modern Equity' (1929) 45 LQR 196, 197–201; DMW Waters, 'The Nature of the Trust Beneficiary's Interest' (1967) 45 Can Bar Rev 219, especially 223–26; RP Meagher, WMC Gummow, and JRF Lehane, *Equity: Doctrines and Remedies* (3rd edn, Butterworths 1992) 96–100; RC Nolan, 'Equitable Property' (2006) 122 LQR 232; B McFarlane and R Stevens, 'The Nature of Equitable Property' (2010) 4 JoE 1; JE Penner, 'The (True) Nature of a Beneficiary's Equitable Proprietary Interest under a Trust' (2014) 27 Can JLJ 473; EC Zaccaria, 'The Nature of the Beneficiary's Right Under a Trust: Proprietary Right, Purely Personal Right or Right Against a Right?' (2019) 135 LQR 460; S Agnew and B McFarlane, 'The Nature of Trusts and the Conflict of Laws' (2021) 137 LQR 405.

a passage later approved by Kitto J in *Livingston v Cmmr of Stamp Duties (Queensland)* (1960),[173] Turner wrote that:

> The classification of the Austinian School ... does not seem to rest on any true historical basis, but is rather an attempt to explain seventeenth and eighteenth-century legal phenomena in terms of nineteenth-century doctrine. The School's jurisprudential juggling with an arbitrary classification of its own making has not produced anything which might be considered creative or explanatory ... [T]he whole matter is a piece of juristic skittles of little or no importance.[174]

While this summation of the Austinian School's contribution to legal science is perhaps not wholly accurate (or fair), Turner's words capture well the dissatisfaction of the legal historian when reading analytical treatments of the trust. When doctrinal writers in the Austinian tradition purported to describe the features of the modern trust, they did so without an understanding of the ideas which underpinned the precedents and maxims on which they relied. In this way, the analytical school had become untethered from the very case law which it purported to explain.

Notwithstanding Turner's misgivings, the classification of equitable rights as either rights *in rem* or rights *in personam* has continued on an ascendant path. Having recently been endorsed in the Supreme Court—there concluding that '[a]n equitable interest possesses the essential hallmark of any right *in rem*'[175]—the Austinian analytical project now holds a strong claim to orthodoxy. By contrast, the historical conception of the trust has receded ever further from the legal consciousness. Over the preceding century, the matter has received little attention from historians of equity who, perhaps understandably, have avoided analytical jurisprudence to at least the same extent that legal philosophers have eschewed legal history.[176] The effect of this disciplinary monism, however, has been to rob the modern lawyer of a guide to the three centuries of legal debate which preceded the modern orthodoxy, and which have determined the content of much of our law of trusts. It is hoped that this chapter has gone some little way towards bridging this gap in the historiography and jurisprudence of the express trust.

173 107 CLR 411, 449.

174 Turner, *Equity of Redemption* (n 54) 149–50. Turner's views were, in turn, echoed by DEC Yale: see DEC Yale (ed), *Epieikeia: A Dialogue on Equity in Three Parts by Edward Hake* (Yale 1953) xv, n 6; Yale (ed), *Prolegomena* (n 2) 18.

175 *Akers v Samba* (n 1) 461 (Lord Sumption).

176 For a discussion of ahistoricism in analytical jurisprudence, see MJW Lobban, 'Legal Theory and Legal History: Prospects for Dialogue' in M Del Mar and MJW Lobban (eds), *Law in Theory and History: New Essays on a Neglected Dialogue* (Hart 2016).

6

Express Trust: The Dark Horse of the Liberal Property Regime

Hanoch Dagan and Irit Samet[*]

I. Introduction

The trust is standing at a crossroad. From a complex form of ownership that was little noticed by the general public, it has become (in)famous as one of the favourite tools used by super-rich people in order to escape their duties to society and individuals.[1] This is, of course, not the whole story. As we demonstrate in this chapter, in modern economies the trust is being widely used as an indispensable vehicle for achieving many worthy and socially beneficial purposes. Examples abound, from vast pension funds through charities and even the management of consumer-oriented class actions.[2] But the bad publicity and the real danger which recent development of new trust forms pose to the reputation of trust mean that, as friends of the trust, we must take stock.[3] It is time to ask whether the trust can (still) be justified as a form of ownership in a modern democratic society.[4]

In this chapter we argue that the answer is a resounding 'yes'—the trust fulfils a crucial role in the fabric of the ideal property system, and as such it should be nurtured,

* Thanks to Greg Alexander, Ruth Chang, Simone Degeling, Jonathan Gingerich, Jessica Hudson, Matt Kramer, Mark Lunney, Paul Miller, Yifat Naftali, Aruna Nair, James Penner, Tom Sinclair, and participants at the King's Private Law Forum, the Philosophical Foundations of Trust Law Workshop, and the UK Analytical Legal and Political Philosophy Conference for their helpful comments.

1 See for instance 'The Paradise Papers'—a special investigation by *The Guardian* and 95 media partners worldwide into a leak of 13.4 million files from two offshore service providers and 19 tax havens' company registries which found that many of the schemes relied on the trust structure (https://www.theguardian.com/news/series/paradise-papers); BBC Panorama exposed how wealthy business people used trusts and other tricks to keep hold of their wealth, while those they owe money to are left with nothing: https://www.bbc.co.uk/programmes/b09m5wdd.

2 See detailed examples in Part III, and S Degeling, 'Administrators as Trustees of Australian Class Action Settlements' in this book.

3 Indeed, using trust to escape uncomfortable legal rules of all sorts is nothing new: as Baker explains, '[a]nother unworthy purpose of the uses, noted in 1370, was to place land beyond the reach of creditors' (John H Baker, *An Introduction to English Legal History* (3rd edn, Butterworths 1990) 284). The abuse of trust has, however, significantly picked up in recent decades, and so has the public backlash against it. See, for example, Andres Knobel, *Trusts: Weapons of Mass Injustice?* (Tax Justice Network 2017); Keynote by Justice Richard Snowden, 'The Use and Abuse of Trusts and Other Wealth Management Devices' 31 Trust Law Int 99. As this is not a historical inquiry, we do not attempt to assess the legitimacy of past uses of trust. The question we are interested in is whether the trust can be justified *now* and what boundaries this justification imposes on its use.

4 We explain why the trust is a form of ownership for the beneficiaries as well, and not only for the trustee in Hanoch Dagan and Irit Samet, 'The Beneficiary's Ownership Rights in the Trust Res in a Liberal Property Regime' (2023) 86 MLR 701.

Hanoch Dagan and Irit Samet, *Express Trust: The Dark Horse of the Liberal Property Regime* In: *Philosophical Foundations of the Law of Express Trusts*. Edited by: Simone Degeling, Jessica Hudson, and Irit Samet, Oxford University Press.
 DOI: 10.1093/oso/9780192844934.003.0007

but also, trimmed where it grew beyond its proper normative borders. In a nutshell, if property law is to fulfil its potential to be a truly liberal regime that acts to enhance people's autonomy, it must feature trusts, or other legal devices that allow owners to tailor property rights that serve their individual plans, as long as they do not externalise the costs to third parties. Further, we explain how promotion of the autonomy ideal—understood much more robustly than only an increased number of options—sets limits on the contours of the trust, and thereby serves as a tool for assessing the different facets of modern trust law.[5] We therefore conclude that taking autonomy as the justifying principle of the trust can (re)establish it as an honourable member of a modern legal system. More precisely, our thesis explains (a) how including the device of trust in the law boosts the liberal credentials of a legal system, and (b) why notorious uses of the trust must be treated as *ultra vires* the trust as they undermine the autonomy-based justification on which its legitimacy is founded.[6]

Our starting point is the liberal conception of property. Private property is justified as an empowering institution which enables people to define and pursue their own goals; to self-determine. In a liberal polity, the commitment to individual autonomy, which must dominate property's justification, also shapes its constitution and thus grounds its most fundamental legal contours. The concept of autonomy serves to justify and at the same time limit the power of private owners: their authority should not go beyond property's autonomy-enhancing service and it must not include powers that allows them to disrespect other people's self-determination. Accordingly, a genuinely liberal property law refines its rules so that the private authority property instantiates is indeed circumscribed by this autonomy-enhancing telos; and it proactively facilitates diverse ways for people's self-determination, either on their own or with others.

This means that liberal property law must be structurally pluralist; that is, it must offer an inventory of diverse property types which facilitate a plethora of forms that covers all major spheres of human action and interaction. The trust, we argue, plays a crucial role in this inventory as its open-endedness allows law to offer a wide range of ways—much wider than what a simple inventory of only state-designed property types would have allowed—to both settlors and beneficiaries to enjoy property. But the express trust would not be an autonomy-enhancing device had it not also paid due attention to the autonomy-based limitations just noted, which are part and parcel of this ideal.

In developing the trust, the courts of equity struggled to strike a fine balance between the need for stability and clarity with regards to property rights, as expressed by the *numerus clausus* requirement and the protection it extends to the interests of non-owners, and the need to offer owners some freedom from pre-designed forms of

[5] Mark J Bennett and Adam Hofri-Winogradow, 'Against Subversion, a Contribution to the Normative Theory of Trust Law' (2021) 41 OJLS 692, which misrepresents the autonomy-based theory of trusts.

[6] This term is typically associated with the limited legal capacity of some legal persons, but we use it deliberately here in order to convey the proposition that once the trust is interpreted in line with our theory, settlors and their lawyers would no longer be able to use that legal device in this way. (Consider, by (crude) analogy, the claim that, properly interpreted, trading in body parts is *ultra vires* (liberal) contract, since it abuses the very normative foundation on which contract's legitimacy is founded.)

property-holding. Consideration towards the legitimate interests of third parties is, crucially, not an external constraint that limits an unbounded freedom that is called for by the value of autonomy, but rather, as noted, an internal limitation of what securing autonomy entails. Thus, the analysis of trust as standing, normatively speaking, on foundations of autonomy can help us understand which uses of trust breach their own justificatory limits and hence cannot be considered as instances of a legitimate trust: when the parties attempt to use a trust to achieve goals that go beyond the trust's inherent limits as an autonomy-enhancing property type, this is abuse that must fall through as *ultra vires*.

Indeed, as a legal institution that is justified by reference to its autonomy-enhancing service, the trust must be interpreted and (where necessary) reformed in light of this foundational telos. Thus, an important part of our task is to examine what implications might an analysis of trust as a proud member of liberal property have on the way we approach some thorny issues in this intricate field of law. We do not claim that such an analysis can resolve all the difficult puzzles that engage trust lawyers and scholars. But, unlike some scholars of trust law,[7] we do argue that understanding the trust as serving a role in the liberal picture of property ownership sheds light on the way the trust should operate given this role.[8]

More specifically, the implications of our account are of two sorts. First, in the context of registered land, studied in Part III, examining the trust vis-à-vis its liberal mission as a residual property type for private arrangements shows that granting owners the option to create a trust over their property is important but may not be sufficient in a genuinely liberal property regime; some reform of the registration rules is called for as well. The second set of implications, addressed in Part IV, is broader. If our account is to escape the risk of apologising for, or even legitimising, prevailing practices in which trusts have become a key instrument for shielding people from their legal obligations, we must show that—when it is properly interpreted—the trust is not amenable to such abuses. Hence, we discuss some rather significant reforms that reinterpreting the trust as liberal property's missing piece requires.

But before we can discuss these implications, we must briefly sketch (in Part II) the liberal theory of property that guides us and then (in Part III) explore in more detail the unique role liberal property theory assigns to the express trust.

II. A Liberal Property Regime

Free individuals are entitled to plot their own course through life—to have some measure of self-determination. Autonomy requires appropriate mental abilities. It also

[7] See James Penner, 'An Untheory of the Law of Trusts, or Some Notes Towards Understanding the Structure of Trusts Law Doctrine' 63 CLP 653.

[8] The remaining indeterminacy is a feature, rather than a bug, of theories like ours which aspire to apply across time and place. Theories of this type must leave room not just for local adjustments based on social, cultural, and economic circumstances, but also for democratic prescriptions.

necessitates a measure of independence. But autonomy is not guaranteed by merely a structure of negative rights.[9] As Joseph Raz famously argued, autonomy is also dependent upon both material conditions and a sufficiently heterogeneous inventory of alternatives.[10] This lesson explains why in a liberal polity people are entitled to a system of law *supportive* of their ability to shape a life they can view as their own, rather than merely one that respects their capacity for uncoerced choice.

An important part of this task is assigned to public law: the most basic preconditions of personal self-determination are undoubtedly health, education, and means of subsistence. Nonetheless, private law also plays an irreducible role in empowering people. Private law's distinct responsibility is in forming and sustaining the variety of frameworks necessary for our ability to lead our chosen conception of life. Property law, more specifically, has a distinctive role in this fundamental obligation of the law.[11] Elsewhere, one of us develops a theory of liberal property and shows how this autonomy-enhancing telos is crucial to both ensuring property's legitimacy and elucidating property law's core features.[12] Here we focus on the aspects of this theory that are particularly pertinent to our account of the place of express trusts in a liberal scheme of property.[13]

A. Autonomy-Enhancing Property

Property both empowers people and disables them, enhances their self-determination while also rendering them vulnerable. Appreciating both property's autonomy-enhancing service and the vulnerabilities it generates is key to the three guiding principles—the three pillars—of a liberal theory of property.

Property is conducive to people's self-determination because self-determination is an intertemporal achievement, consisting of planning and carrying out projects, which requires a temporal horizon of action. Property follows suit by conferring upon people some measure of private authority over resources: a normative power to determine what others may or may not do with the resource. This authority over things (both

[9] HLA Hart, 'Between Utility and Rights' (1979) 79 Colum L Rev 828, 836.

[10] Joseph Raz, *The Morality of Freedom* (OUP 1986) 372, 398.

[11] As the text below clarifies, property's service to our autonomy is distinctive from what public law—say a public regime that secures stuff for us to use—can do because property's normative signature involves the private authority we have over resources. And, as is clarified elsewhere, while there are some continuities between property and contract (law's two major power-conferring instruments), their autonomy-enhancing potentials are not fully interchangeable. See Hanoch Dagan, *A Liberal Theory of Property* (CUP 2021) 25–26.

[12] Dagan (n 11). As the text implies and the following paragraphs briefly explain, because the burden of justifying the private authority property law authorises and coercively enforces is awesome, property law can nonetheless be justified if, but only if, its architecture follows its (implicit) autonomy-enhancing telos.

[13] In this chapter, we do not have the space, nor do we see the necessity, to define the trust in precise terms. We do not dispute Hudson and Mitchell's argument in this volume that a successful justification must rely on a good understanding of the law. See J Hudson and C Mitchell, 'Justificanda' in this volume. But we believe that while the justification process can, and should, start off with a consensual or even intuitive conception of the justificanda (of the kind they suggest at section III B i of their chapter), it must remain open to revisitation in a Rawlsian spirit of reflective equilibrium. We therefore explicate the way in which undisputed rules of the law of trust reflect our theory, and set its boundaries. Later on (and in other pieces of work) we talk about the way in which the theory we suggest here can, in turn, help us to formulate a position on controversial aspects of the trust.

tangible and intangible) dramatically affects people's ability to plan and carry out—on their own or with the cooperation of others—meaningful projects.

Liberal law further augments property's autonomy-enhancing potential because it constitutes a *variety* of stable frameworks of interpersonal cooperation, as different property types support divergent forms of interpersonal relationships from which people can choose. Thus, properly configured, property law functions as an empowering device for self-authorship, enabling people to act upon their own goals and values, their objectives, and their life plans. By conferring on individuals the power to invoke various property types that facilitate differing life plans, a liberal property law makes a crucial contribution to people's ability to realise the right to self-authorship.

Alas, indispensable as it is, this autonomy-enhancing service is also the source of property's daunting legitimacy challenge. By proactively empowering owners, property law generates new normative powers, which imply new liabilities on others. Since the law of property renders non-owners vulnerable to such powers, it must be justified in principle to the subjects of the powers it creates. Without good justification, the demand (or even expectation) that non-owners defer to owners' authority regarding what to do with an object seems arbitrary and unjust.

In a liberal order, property law is justified in vesting private authority in owners insofar as this is critical to people's self-determination, which the state is obligated to facilitate, and everyone must respect. Non-owners are justifiably subjected to the powers of property because people's foundational right of reciprocal respect for self-determination implies that these instruments of self-determination deserve respect from others.

This means, however, that the legitimacy of any given property system hangs on its performance as to property's autonomy-enhancing telos. A genuinely liberal property law proactively augments people's opportunities for both individual and collective self-determination, while carefully restricting their opportunities for interpersonal domination. This is why—unlike property *simpliciter*—the notion of private authority cannot exhaust the idea of *liberal* property.

To be justified, property's empowerment potential must not be limited to a few; it must be available for the many. This requirement implies that in a liberal polity, property law must rely on a robust background regime, which should guarantee everyone the material, social, and intellectual preconditions of self-authorship. Such a regime is particularly necessary because property's justificatory challenge is not limited to the moment of its creation. Rather, it continuously resurfaces, partly due to certain features of property—notably accession—which imply that property leads to more property and thus tends to generate greater inequality and vulnerability. Because one can suspect that the marginal autonomy-enhancement of each additional unit of property is likely to be diminishing, a liberal property law imposes the costs of the ongoing maintenance of the background regime necessary for property's legitimacy on those who are particularly well-off. The duty of the well-off to cover these costs is justified both by their

(Rawlsian[14]) duty to support just institutions and as a precondition to the legitimacy of their own property rights.

A genuinely liberal law, however, is not contented with such a general background (public law) regime. The freestanding significance of property to self-determination implies that a liberal law properly-called also shapes its property regime in accordance with property's autonomy-enhancing telos. This is why a liberal property system must not instantiate only one form of property. In order to foster autonomy-enhancing pluralism, it offers a *variety* of frameworks for both individual and communal self-determination from which prospective owners (and other right-holders) can choose. A liberal property law is also always, as noted, attentive to the concerns of non-owners. This is why it must ensure that no private authority can be claimed that is in excess of what is required for owners' self-determination. Moreover, since owners' legitimate claims are premised on the maxim of reciprocal respect for self-determination, their authority must be consistent with the self-determination of others.

These short comments point out to the three pillars of liberal property, the features that distinguish it from property *simpliciter*: carefully delineated private authority, structural pluralism, and relational justice.

(1) liberal property carefully circumscribes owners' private authority so that it is adjusted to its contribution to self-determination;
(2) it includes a structurally pluralist inventory of property types to offer people real choice; and
(3) it complies with the prescriptions of relational justice to ensure that ownership does not offend the maxim of reciprocal respect for self-determination on which property's legitimacy is grounded.[15]

Because liberal property's second pillar is key to the unique autonomy-enhancing function of the express trust, the following discussion focuses on structural pluralism. We revisit, however, liberal property's first and third pillars later on in the chapter, since these commitments are key to justifying some of the existing limitations of the trust, to explaining why the illicit uses of the trust should be analysed as corruptions of this property type, and to point out to further necessary reforms.

B. Structural Pluralism

Property manifests itself in law in a nuanced, contextualised, and multifaceted fashion. The profound heterogeneity of property types causes difficulties for monistic theories that look for *the* structural core of property, most notably the many variants of the

[14] John Rawls, *A Theory of Justice* (HUP 1971) 293–94.

[15] The notion of 'relational justice' in the liberal theory of property is close to, but nonetheless importantly distinct from, the relational egalitarianism of Elizabeth Anderson or Samuel Scheffler. See Hanoch Dagan and Avihay Dorfman, 'Justice in Private: Beyond the Rawlsian Framework' (2018) 36 L & Phil 171, 182–86.

Blackstonian school, in which property stands for 'sole and despotic dominion'.[16] These theories tend to present one property type—the fee simple—as the core or the default of our understanding of property, while suppressing other property types as mere variations on a common theme, or marginalising them as peripheral exceptions to this one solid core.

For liberal property, by contrast, this multiplicity is a virtue rather than a concern since it ensures an inventory of alternatives from which people can choose.[17] Property law *should* be heterogeneous because there are many ways in which property can support people's self-determination, either on their own or, quite often, with others. The internal life of property is accordingly structured through sophisticated governance mechanisms that facilitate various forms of interpersonal relationships, which would not be possible without an enabling legal infrastructure.

Instead of overemphasising the common denominator of these diverse types, liberal property celebrates the pluralistic architecture of property law and its many options. It conceptualises these types as default frameworks of interpersonal interaction regarding various resources. This understanding implies that these property types need to be properly standardised and their interpretation and evaluation should, by and large, look to their specific 'local' animating principles. (Think, for example, of the different DNAs of condos, co-ops, joint tenancies, leaseholds, and for that matter the fee simple absolute.)

At its best, this plurality of types enables property law to offer varying balances between the different intrinsic and instrumental values that property can serve—independence, personhood, community, and utility—in diverse social settings and with respect to a variety of resources. Each of these property types constitutes a distinctive framework of private authority; each offers its own recipe for some temporally extended control that people can have over a resource, either as individuals or as members of a community of owners. When the law's menu of property types is sufficiently rich for each major sphere of human action, it offers people a range of meaningful choices for resource governance and co-governance that supports self-determination.

The obligation of the liberal state to facilitate meaningful choices in important spheres of life implies a duty to facilitate people's autonomy by ensuring this *intra-sphere multiplicity*, namely, to actively shape for each major category of human action and interaction distinct property types that function as *partial functional substitutes*. This duty is not limited to satisfying demand for more types, as it may be in utility-based accounts. Rather, property plays a crucial role in delivering on the liberal promise of self-determination. Property types need to be substitutes because choice is not enhanced with alternatives that are orthogonal to each other; and their substitutability should not be too complete because types that are too similar also do not offer meaningful choice. Thus, the state can betray its autonomy-enhancing mission not only by having bad or

[16] 2 Bl Comm 1765-69 *2.
[17] For an extended analysis on which this section draws, see Dagan (n 11) at ch 4.

too much property law. The absence of law, or an attempt to limit property's heterogeneity, will have the same effect.

Some liberal friends of the dominion conception of property accept the normative significance of pluralism, but insist that it need not affect the law. Law in this view can—and, for some, should—largely adhere to the monistic conception of property as sole and despotic dominion. To be sure, no one seriously thinks that property always entails unqualified dominion. But for some theorists, property's architecture is one of a clear core, in which property is defined by owners' right to exclude (or its cognates), and some possible exceptions (eg easements) situated at property's periphery. Pluralism, in this view, does not require more than a few basic forms as long as individuals can use their freedom of contract and further tailor their interpersonal arrangements so that they best serve their own purposes.[18]

Alas, such a hands-off approach to property law would have failed to deliver on property's autonomy-enhancing promise. To see why the rich diversity of property arrangements that pluralism requires will not spontaneously emerge without the active support of viable legal institutions (or law-like social conventions), we need to appreciate the insights of both lawyer-economists and critical scholars.

Economic analysis of private law investigates its incentive effects, and forcefully demonstrates how many of our existing practices rely on legal devices which serve to overcome numerous types of transaction costs: information costs (symmetric and asymmetric), bilateral monopolies, cognitive biases, and heightened risks of opportunistic behaviour that generate endemic vulnerabilities in most cooperative interpersonal interactions.

Merely enforcing the parties' expressed intentions would not be sufficient to overcome these inherent impediments of such endeavours. If many (most?) of the property law types currently offered (let alone the further types an even more autonomy-friendly law would develop) are to become or remain viable alternatives, law must provide the background reassurances tailored to the specific category of interaction at hand, which are necessary for its success. Even where parties are guided by their own social norms, law often plays an important role in providing them background safeguards, a safety net for a rainy day that can help establish trust in their routine interactions.

Moreover, law's effects are not only material. Because private law tends to blend quietly into the backdrop of our lives, its categories play a crucial role in structuring our daily interactions. Thus, alongside these material effects, many of our conventions—including many social practices we take for granted as the options we currently have (think of a condo or a corporation)—become available to us only due to cultural conventions that often, especially in modern times, are legally constructed.

Hence, if these notions were not legally coined, people would not only have to consider the transaction costs of constructing these arrangements from scratch but they would also face 'obstacles of the imagination' just coming up with the options in the

[18] Robert Nozick, *Anarchy, State, and Utopia* (Basic Books 1974) 150–57, 159–64, 167–72, 329; Thomas W Merrill, 'Property as Modularity' (2012) 125 Harv L Rev Forum 151, 157–58.

first place. Indeed, the property types established by law play an important cultural role. Like other social conventions, they serve a crucial function in consolidating people's expectations and in expressing the animating principles of the categories of interpersonal relationships they participate in constructing.

Both the material and the cultural functions of private law imply that freedom of contract, though significant, cannot possibly replace active legal facilitation if the liberal state's obligation to enhance autonomy by fostering diversity and multiplicity of property forms is taken seriously. Lack of active legal support is often tantamount to undermining—maybe even obliterating—many cooperative forms of interpersonal relationships and thus people's ability to seek their own conception of the good.

Thus, what explains and justifies liberal property's structural pluralism is the way it provides a set of viable frameworks—of property types—from which people can choose. Property law offers a variety of forms which are all heavily relying on enabling legal infrastructure; co-ops, common-interest communities, joint tenancies, and leaseholds are only some examples of the existing inventory of land-ownership. Nothing short of the robust legal edifice of structural pluralism will do if property law is to be guided by the autonomy-enhancing telos.

C. Residual Category

Securing a multiplicity of property types is not an add-on feature of liberal property. Rather, for a property regime which takes its liberal telos and legitimacy challenge seriously, this multiplicity is essential. Structural pluralism, in other words, is a fundamental design principle of a genuinely liberal property law. For each major category of human action and interaction, liberal property must instantiate and support a sufficiently diverse repertoire of property types, each governed by a distinct animating principle, meaning a different value or balance of values.

A rich variety of state-designed frameworks is a necessary feature of both liberal property and liberal contract.[19] If properly constituted, it is likely to facilitate the self-determination of most people. But even if perfected along these lines, private law would still fall short of its liberal promise. In a liberal society, people should be able to create their own idiosyncratic frameworks of interpersonal interactions and not merely pick and choose from state-designed frameworks. The practical significance of this option is surely impacted by the quality and diversity of these frameworks (and it may further vary across resources). But its normative significance is not similarly contingent. If (but only if) people comply with private law's *grundnorm* of respect for each other's self-determination, a genuinely liberal law should support parties' ability to reject its default frameworks—even if its property law offers a properly diverse repertoire of

[19] For liberal contract, see Hanoch Dagan and Michael A Heller, *The Choice Theory of Contracts* (CUP 2017); Hanoch Dagan and Michael Heller, 'Choice Theory: A Restatement' in Hanoch Dagan, Benjamin Zipursky (eds), *Research Handbook on Private Law Theory* (Edward Elgar 2020) 112.

property types—and tailor their arrangements according to their particular needs and circumstances.

Accordingly, an autonomy-enhancing private law should offer, wherever feasible,[20] a residual category allowing autonomous individuals to 'invent' their own private forms of interaction. Contract law complies with this requirement. It has long discarded a system that only recognised 'nominate' contracts.[21] Although the familiar contract types probably fit the needs of most contractors, both common law and civil law systems (in which the distinction between nominate and innominate contracts still persists) properly allow, and indeed support, freestanding bargains that do not fit into these conventional categories. Property law, by contrast, fails to offer a salient and vibrant residual category of private arrangements, at least in systems that uphold the prevailing understanding of the *numerus clausus* principle.

To clarify: property's autonomy-enhancing telos fully justifies the *numerus clausus* as a principle of standardisation. Law's list of property types is commendable because it facilitates stable categories of state-supported property types by standardising their incidents. For law to consolidate people's expectations in compliance with the prescriptions of structural pluralism (as well as those of the rule of law[22]), it must recognise a necessarily limited number of categories of relationships and resources. But the conventional understanding of the *numerus clausus* principle goes further. It stands for the proposition that 'property rights exist [only] in a fixed number of forms', so that private arrangements can enjoy the status of property *only if* they are pigeonholed into the delimited menu of the state-designed property forms.[23] This additional, normalising[24] dimension of the *numerus clausus* principle is, we argue, unjustified.

Liberal property, to be sure, does not require law to adopt a *numerus apertus* (open list) principle, allowing 'fancy rights' to be registered or recorded on par with law's standardised types and thus require every third party to further inquiries.[25] What is

[20] The qualified language is not coincidental. As the previous paragraph clarifies, while there is always a principled gap between law's menu of state-shaped property type and the liberal ideal of property, its practical significance—and thus its urgency—admittedly depends on the specific legal system's performance of designing such a menu in line with liberal property's prescriptions. This means that absence of a residual category does not necessarily render a property regime illiberal; its normalising effects can be mitigated if the state-designed inventory fully complies with the prescription of intra-sphere multiplicity, and if it includes—as liberal property theory further prescribes—minoritarian or utopian property types: Dagan (n 11) 78, 107, 109.

[21] Reinhardt Zimmerman, The Law of Obligations: Roman Foundations of the Civil Tradition (OUP 1990) 534–35.

[22] Dagan (n 11) 159–73.

[23] Thomas W Merrill and Henry E Smith, 'Optimal Standardization in the Law of Property: The Numerus Clausus Principle' (2000) 110 Yale LJ 1, 3; Law of Property Act 1925, ss 1, 4(1). English courts worried lest unrestricted freedom for estate owners to invent proprietary rights would 'impress upon their lands and tenements a peculiar character, which should follow them into all hands, however remote' (*Keppell v Bailey* (1834) 2 My & K 517 at 536, 39 ER 1042 at 1049 per Lord Brougham LC); *Ackroyd v Smith* (1850) 10 CB 164 at 188, 138 ER 68 at 77–78 per Cresswell J; *Camden LBC v Shortlife Community Housing Ltd* (1992) 90 LGR 358 at 373 per Millett J; *Lloyd v Dugdale* [2002] 2 P & CR 13 at [52(4)] per Sir Christopher Slade.

[24] cf Jürgen Habermas, Between Facts and Norms: Contributions to a Discourse Theory of Law and Democracy (MIT Print 1996) 413, 416.

[25] Ben McFarlane, 'The Numerus Clausus Principle and Covenants Relating to Land' in Susan Bright (ed), *Modern Studies in Property Law*, vol 6 (Hart 2011); Michael Weir, 'Pushing the Envelope of Proprietary Interests: The Nadir of the Numerus Clausus Principle?' (2015) 39 Melbourne University L Rev 651; Yun-chien Chang & Henry E Smith, 'The Numerus Clausus Principle, Property Customs, and the Emergence of New Property Forms' (2015) 100 Iowa L Rev 2275, 2287–88.

needed instead is that, like contract law, property law would also include *one* residual category for private arrangements in addition to the state-shaped property types. Such a category would flag to third parties that the property at hand is subject to an unconventional arrangement and provide effective notice as to its content. Moreover, both the risks of possible misunderstandings due to its idiosyncrasy or ambiguity, as well as the costs of administering such a residual property type, should be allocated to the parties to such an arrangement rather than to third parties.

We by no means deny that property law is justified in proscribing idiosyncratic arrangements insofar as they entail negative external effects, both social (eg segregation) and economic (eg fragmentation), or impinge on individual rights (either those of the parties themselves or of third parties). But these concerns are (or at least should be) addressed even respecting state-shaped property types. They can, and should, similarly limit the ability of people to tailor their property arrangements in accordance with the way they prefer to shape their interpersonal relationships. (This proposition is the starting point of our discussion in Part IV.) But they do not establish an a priori obstacle to such private orderings.

Hence, the significance to people's autonomy of opening up such a residual category for freestanding forms of interaction requires a liberal polity to reconsider the hostility of *numerus clausus* toward tailor-made property rights. But wouldn't designing such a category and making it sufficiently salient and vibrant be too costly? Conventional wisdom suggests that it would; given the communication costs such idiosyncrasies impose on third parties—who need to determine the attributes of property rights in order to avoid violating them or to acquire them from present owners—the ability to create these rights comes, in this view, at too high a price.[26] We do not belittle this concern, but nonetheless think that, as with any efficiency analysis, the answer to this question is contingent on the facts and likely to change from one context to another.

Commentators focus in this context on both the verification costs that such an additional property type imposes on third parties and the processing costs of such novelties by the relevant recording office.[27] But one should be more specific here. Evaluating the significance of this concern requires an assessment of the *marginal* verification and processing costs as well as the costs of the pertinent technologies that can facilitate such a reform on the one hand and the possible benefits its reform may yield on the other. This empirical inquiry, which needs to be closely tailored to the particular features of the existing system and devise a way to compare monetary costs with benefits to autonomy, is well beyond the scope of this chapter. But two quick observations suggest that a summary dismissal of the autonomy-based plea for a residual property type on grounds of excessive information costs would be imprudent, at least insofar as English law is concerned.

[26] Merrill and Smith (n 23) 26–34.

[27] See respectively Henry Hansmann and Reinier Kraakman, 'Property, Contract, and Verification: The Numerus Clausus Problem and the Divisibility of Rights' (2002) 31 J L Studies 373, 374–75, 380–84, 416–17, 419; Merrill and Smith (n 23) 33, 43–45.

First, the marginal cost of such a reform seems quite limited given the open-endedness of one tool that is already available for tailoring property rights, namely the restrictive covenant, which entails rather significant verification costs.[28] Second, unlike most American jurisdictions, England applies a registration (rather than merely recordation) system,[29] which is thus much more amenable to such a reform. Indeed, there are registration systems which allow such entries and, as one observer notes, 'the[ir] economy has not collapsed and legal certainty and third-party protection [there] remain assured'.[30]

These systems, such as the Spanish one, typically employ professionals—notably notaries and legally-trained registrars—as gatekeepers, who ensure that the property right at hand does not fall within an existing type, that it is clearly defined and sufficiently detailed, and that it does not impose external costs.[31] While transfer of property rights in England does not require a notary seal, a process of professional assessment of the viability of newly designed property rights can be easily established. A specialist desk in the land registry that would be in charge of reviewing applications for registration of 'fancy' rights, or a requirement of independent professional review of such cases, would ensure that only rights that do not create externalities for third parties and comply with the requirements of liberal property discussed in Part IV would be registered.

We do not make any strong claim about one-on-one application of the Spanish model to the English system. The volatile nature of legal transplants would render this kind of claim presumptuous.[32] But the principle stands: every system must find a way to allow property dark horses as long as they do not trample the rights of third parties.

[28] See McFarlane (n 25) 317–26; Chris Bevan, 'The Doctrine of Benefit and Burden: Reforming the Law of Covenants and the Numerus Clausus Problem' (2018) 77 CLJ 72. One difference between 'fancy' rights like easements or covenants and the trust is the price the buyer pays if she does not find out about them in time, or misinterprets what they imply. Whereas in the former she has to learn to live with the interest that encumbers her land, in the case of trust she has to give it up if it was transferred to her in breach of trust. However, this difference loses much of its edge if we take note of the following points: (a) a misunderstood burden on the land can have a serious adverse effect on the buyer's enjoyment, and/or on its value; (b) the effects of misunderstood trust terms can be mitigated by requiring guarantee from the trustees or the settlors or beneficiaries (depending who is eager to get the sale going) or by purchasing an insurance (indeed of the kind that is widely available to cover the risk posed by unclear covenants); and (c) as long as the buyer understands the risk (and since land conveyancing usually involves legal professionals, they will alert the buyer to the situation), it should be her choice whether to take it. The point of autonomy enhancement is to open up valuable options, not perfect ones.

[29] On the American predicament, see Nadav Shoked, 'Who Needs Adverse Possession?' (2021) 89 Fordham L Rev 2639, 2665–68.

[30] Bram Akkermans, *The Principle of Numerus Clausus in European Property Law* (2nd edn, Intersentia 2014) 553. For similar argument in the Australian context see Brendan Edgeworth, 'The Numerus Clausus Principle in Contemporary Australian Property Law' (2006) 32 Monash University L Rev 387.

[31] Christoph U Schmid & Christian Hertel, 'Real Property Law and Procedure in the European Union: General Report' (2005) 15, 50, 53, https://www.eui.eu/Documents/DepartmentsCentres/Law/ResearchTeaching/ResearchThemes/EuropeanPrivateLaw/RealPropertyProject/GeneralReport.pdf; Isabel V González Pacanowska and Carlos Manuel Díez Soto, 'National Report on the Transfer of Movables in Spain' in Wolfgang Faber and Brigitta Lurger (eds), *National Reports on the Transfer of Movables in Europe: Sweden, Norway and Denmark, Finland Spain* (2011) 393, 429–31; Javier Gómez Gálligo, 'The Property Registry' (ELRA, 23 April 2010) <http://www.elra.eu>, accessed 23 September 2020.

[32] Gunther Teubner, 'Legal Irritants: Good Faith in British Law or How Unifying Law Ends up in New Divergencies' 61 MLR 11.

III. The Dark Horse

When the trust features on the law books it typically functions as a vehicle for realising the state's duty to facilitate the creation of such unorthodox forms of property. In English law, which we focus on here, the trust indeed fulfils this role in two ways: first, due to its *structure*, namely, the split between beneficial and legal interest, the trust is a platform of an almost infinitive flexibility in tailoring property-holding and gifting. Second, given the fairly strict *numerus clausus* that informs the land registration system, the trust functions as a substitute, albeit imperfect (at least on its own), for an open-ended category of registrable property forms. Historically, the need to break through the rigid stricture of medieval land law gave rise to the invention of the split interest device. But, like other legal devices, the trust has now taken a life of its own and its contribution to the autonomy of property holders has gone well beyond a key to the stocks of state-sponsored property types (be they medieval or modern). In what follows, we begin with some observations regarding the contribution to autonomy which is facilitated by the structure of the trust, and then turn to a more extensive discussion of the way in which the trust stands for the open-ended registration category, which is a more innovative and controversial claim we make here.

A. Established Autonomy-Enhancing Uses

It is, we think, beyond controversy that the trust *can* play a highly positive role in a modern economy, as it facilitates numerous types of transactions and modes of holdings that could not materialise by combining the standard building blocks of property.[33] There are a number of familiar ways in which the trust participates in the state autonomy-enhancing mission.[34] The trust can boost autonomy by alleviating beneficiaries of the need to invest the time that is required to manage their wealth (and learning how to do so);[35] and specific forms of trusts, governed by specific sets of rules, likewise perform significant autonomy-enhancing roles, such as securing employees' retirement via pension funds or facilitating options for acting altruistically via

[33] See examples in D Schenkel Kent, 'Trust Law and the Title-Split: A Beneficial Perspective' 78 U MKC L Rev 181, 181, 183, 196.

[34] One might think that trust's contribution to autonomy is not unique as similar enhancement of owners' range of options can be achieved by other means. However, as Henry Hansmann and Ugo Mattei show, in civilian systems, which lack the common law trust, people who enter an arrangement in which they transfer their property to someone else to manage are in materially inferior position in comparison with settlors of trust. For example, it is impractical for them to defend the property against the manager's insolvency by using contracts. Instead, these transferors seek to insure themselves against the risk of trustee bankruptcy by employing only large and stable institutions, such as banks, to manage the property. This restriction on the identity of the manager severely limits the range of options that are available for settlors, and in particular it rules out individuals who know the parties personally and understand their wishes and needs: Henry Hansmann and Ugo Mattei, 'The Functions of Trust Law: A Comparative Legal and Economic Analysis' (1998) 73 NYULR 434, 438.

[35] Hanoch Dagan and Sharon Hannes, 'Managing Our Money: The Law of Financial Fiduciaries as a Private Law Institution' in Andrew Gold and Paul Miller (eds), *Philosophical Foundations of Fiduciary Law* (OUP 2014) 91.

charitable trusts.[36] Moreover, trusts open a wide range of possibilities for the acquisition, investment, and disposal of property for commercial purposes. Original or unconventional ideas on how to run one's business or assets, which cannot be carried out by using the ordinary framework of shares in a limited company, may well be realisable within a structure of trust.

Take, for example, the syndicated loan, which plays a major role in financing the capital markets of Europe by providing an important source of large-scale lending.[37] The syndicated loan is a fundraising scheme in which a security trustee coalesces a group of lenders to provide loans on the same terms and conditions under a single contract to satisfy the funding needs of clients. A trustee holds the various security interests created on trust for the various creditors, who can change, as required, along the life of the loan. This trust structure empowers: it enables small players to take part in big security deals that would otherwise be beyond their reach by precluding the need to grant security separately to all creditors which would have been costly and possibly even impractical.[38]

In other cases, structuring property rights as trusts can significantly reduce information and other transaction costs that are associated with ordinary forms of property, thereby enlarging the range of viable options for realising one's property rights. One example is the 'land pool' that is mostly used by small farmers who wish to develop their land by transforming its use from farming to housing.[39] Converting the use of large-scale tracts of green field is often seriously complicated by multiple ownerships. The land pool devise enables multiple owners to co-operate in order to obtain planning permission and ultimately sell the entire lot to a developer: small owners (whose number can be in the hundreds) transfer their landholdings into a common trust, which owns the entire site and in which they each become beneficial owner in proportion to their original acreage or value; when any part or all of the trust's land is sold, they receive their due share of the proceeds. This trust structure allows small farmers to follow a

[36] As the text implies, the trust's autonomy-enhancing telos does not imply that other values, such as solicitude of the needs of others or cooperation and coordination, are insignificant. It only means that they are—as they should in a properly liberal property regime—recognised as constitutive or instrumental values; they are valuable, in other words, due to their contribution to people's autonomy, to which law is ultimately committed. See Dagan (n 11) 46–58.

[37] In 2017 alone, €720 billion was raised across all of Europe according to the European Commission (EC) (EU loan syndication on competition and its impact in credit markets European Commission report, available in https://ec.europa.eu/competition/publications/reports/kd0419330enn.pdf).

[38] The Crest Depository Interest (CDI) can serve as another example for an 'out of the box' use of the trust. The CDI is a UK financial security that represents a stock traded on a stock exchange outside the UK. The underlying shares are held on trust for the owners of the CDI. Since international shares cannot be settled directly in CREST, without a CDI it is not possible to deal and settle in GBP in the same way as UK shares. See more at https://the-international-investor.com/investment-faq/crest-depository-interest-cdi. For more examples, see Hayton & Mitchell, *Commentary & Cases on the Law of Trusts & Equitable Remedies* (Sweet & Maxwell, 2010) 1-62-1-84; David Hayton 'The Trust as the Modern Vehicle for Investment and Estate Planning in Common Law and Civil Law Countries' available on https://ccj.org/wp-content/uploads/2021/03/Remarks-by-Mr-Justice-David-Hayton-at-the-CALCA-Conference-in-St-Maarten_20161027.pdf.

[39] Or woodlands; see report by Rewilding Britain on the great advantages to the environment and society by such move away from farming, available in https://www.rewildingbritain.org.uk/. On a parallel structure in the United States, and the way it can be used to promote environmental reforms see Jessica Grannis, 'Community-Driven Climate Solutions: How Public-Private Partnerships with Land Trusts Can Advance Climate Action' 44 Wm & Mary Envtl L & Pol'y Rev 701.

life-changing decision to convert their land to be used for a far more socially beneficial activity like tree planting or house building without falling prey to prohibitive transaction costs. As in our previous example, the trust device assists small- and medium-sized entities to flourish, thus demonstrating its great 'levelling up' potential.

The trust can only function as the organising framework for these and other worthwhile schemes due to the almost boundless elasticity in the instructions settlors can give to trustees on how to manage and distribute the property. But the autonomy-enhancing potential of the trust can be further realised by using the number of ways open to settlors who wish to retain some power over the settled property after the trust is up and running. One important component of this added layer of empowerment is the duty of trustees of a discretionary trust to consult with the settlor before making significant exercise of their allocation powers.[40] Settlors may further augment their control by composing a 'letter of wishes' and/or appointing a 'protector' to the trust.

Thus, a settlor who wishes to extend her control over the management of the trust can use a letter of wishes and inform the trustees of considerations that ought to be taken into account when exercising their discretionary powers of allocation, investment, or administration.[41] A letter of wishes is not binding on the trustees, but they have to take it into account, and where professional trustees are concerned, their reputation is dependent on the satisfaction level of their clients, which is likely to be in the red if their wishes are ignored.[42] In turn, by appointing a protector—who can be the settlor herself or any individual (or company)—the settlor can restructure the power relations within the trust. The protector can be vested with the power to veto, scrutinise, and police the trustees' decisions to distribute the property or invest it in a certain way, with the power to replace the trustees or to change the law governing the trust by appointing foreign trustees.[43] Both the 'letter of wishes' and the 'protector' devices can be (and are) abused;[44] but when properly used, they can raise a positive contribution to the potential of trust to achieve its liberal telos.

These and other trust arrangements, which expand the horizons of the way property rights can be used, allocated, created, and terminated, support our claim that the trust goes a long way to satisfy the liberal state's obligation to provide the citizens the opportunity to structure their property-holding and gifting in ways that suits their individual agendas. But there is also, as noted, a second function the trust serves—one that at times is also the path to its role as the home for well-established trust types: the express trust is the vehicle for creating an individual story for one's property within the strictures of English land registration regime.

[40] *Abacus Trusts Co v Barr* [2003] Ch 409 at [23]–[25].

[41] For more details on the way this device can be used, see Stephen Moverley Smith and Andrew Holden, 'Letters of Wishes and the Ongoing Role of the Settlor' 20 T&T 712.

[42] As Hoffmann J (as he then was) explains in *Re TR Technology Investment Trust plc* [1988] BCLC 256: 'The business of providing offshore financial services requires a reputation for probity, efficiency and discretion in executing such trusts in accordance with the confidential wishes of clients' (at 264).

[43] The 'protector' function gives rise to complicated issues that are way beyond our interests here. See, for example, Paul B Miller, 'Regularizing the Trust Protector' 103 Iowa L Rev 2097; Donovan Waters, 'The Protector: New Wine in Old Bottles?' in AJ Oakley (ed), *Trends in Contemporary Trust Law* (Clarendon Press 1996).

[44] Examples can be found in Bennet and Hofri-Winogradow (n 5). For a preview, see below Part IV.A.

B. The Missing Piece in Liberal Property Rights Jigsaw

Recall the liberal case for a residual property type. While the *numerus clausus* rule is a necessary framework for property rights, liberal property calls for a more nuanced approach: an exception should be made for those whose life story cannot be told by using the typeset provided by the state. And while concerns of information costs should not be dismissed lightly, an autonomy-enhancing property law should strive to ensure that they do not frustrate people's ability to opt out of state-favoured forms. A registration reform in England along the lines noted above may well be the first best way of securing this goal. In the meantime, however, we explore whether the express trust can function as a (close?) second-best.

As a 'form of property of ever-increasing importance because of its adaptability and convenience in effecting complicated forms of settlements',[45] the trust seems to be a good candidate for the task. There are, to be sure, other property types which are adjustable, but the trust is *qualitatively* more open-ended. Unlike all other property types, trusts' open-endedness is their defining signature. This does not mean, of course, that the trust is structureless. Quite the contrary: trusts have certain fixed elements, notably fiduciary administration, ascertainable beneficiaries or charitable purposes, and a *res* that is the subject matter of the trust. But this structure allows exactly the kind of flexibility in terms of uses and allocation of rights and powers that various complicated arrangements require.

Indeed, as the previous section demonstrated, under the broad category of the trust one can easily trace established 'trust types', each with its own local DNA. But can the broad category of trust also serve as a freestanding property type, open to autonomy-enhancing tailor-made engineering which is not similarly mediated by any pre-existing DNA? Can, and indeed does, the traditional express trust go beyond these familiar types and serve as the residual category of property which is a necessary component in a truly liberal system? Note that the way in which the trust itself is fairly rigidly structured, with 'core' requirements that must be fulfilled, does not in itself undermine its autonomy-enhancing potential; on the contrary, the regimented relationship between settlor, trustee, and beneficiary serve as a scaffolding on which great variety of property types can be constructed. We start by highlighting the extent to which the trust satisfies the duty of the liberal state to allow people to create property rights that exceed the state-shaped categories. We then turn to consider the ways in which existing trust law seems to fall short of the ideal residual category.

1. Properly open-ended

The Law of Property Act 1925 ('LPA') sets out in section 1 a short list of the legal estates that one can create over land, with equitable interests mirroring the legal ones where

[45] Charles Mitchell, *Hayton and Mitchell: Text, Cases and Materials on the Law of Trusts and Equitable Remedies* (14th edn, Sweet & Maxwell 2015) 3-002, 64.

formality requirements have not been duly complied with. And while English judges do not resort to the language of *numerus clausus*, they do follow the rule that unless a right can be categorised under one of the subsections, in accordance with the way they were interpreted by the courts, it cannot be proprietary.[46] Yet, when the settlor formulates the rights under a properly constructed trust (as determined by the rules of the jurisdiction), she is bounded almost exclusively by the limits of her creativity.

The LPA sets no limitation on the way the beneficiary can benefit from the property, on the way the benefit is allocated between various beneficiaries, or on the duration of their enjoyment.[47] This feature is not coincidental. It captures the legacy of the trust as a formalities-crunching device, which underlies its pathway throughout history. The medieval predecessor of the trust ('use') was designed to enable property owners to tailor rights to their property in a way that would suit their needs when these were not catered for by the highly restrictive property law of that time. For example, until 1540 it was not possible to leave land upon death to anyone but the owner's legal heir. A trust circumvented this harsh restriction of the owners' power to make decisions about his land.[48] Similarly, a father who wanted to provide some financial independence to his married daughter could not do so by giving her a gift, as the doctrine of coverture transferred the rights to her husband. The trust, through the family settlement, enabled parents to provide for their daughters before this notorious doctrine was abolished in the middle of the nineteenth century.[49]

Our theory, which grounds the trust on liberal property's autonomy-enhancing telos, explains why this use of the trust is categorically different than illegitimate uses (then and now) although both evade the legal rules of their time. The reason for us is straightforward: owners who chose the trust to bypass morally abhorrent limitation on the available forms of property-holding were not abusing the trust. Quite the contrary, the trust they created was used in order to ameliorate the illegitimate autonomy-reducing features of a property regime that failed to abide by the requirements of relational justice.

But the authorities were naturally deeply displeased. A cat and mouse battle between freedom-seeking owners and a centralist government raged for centuries, and ended in a (temporary) defeat for the former under the reign of Henry VIII: the Statute of Uses 1535 effectively abolished the use by providing that the *cestui que use* (equivalent to

[46] See, for example, how a right to be 'protected from the weather' was not recognised an easement in *Phipps v Pears* [1964] EWCA Civ 3, [1965] 1 QB 76, since '[t]here is no such easement known to the law' (at 83). See also *Berrisford v Mexfield* [2011] UKSC 52, where the Supreme Court used the common law in a highly dubious way in order to avoid a clear injustice that would have resulted from a straightforward application of the principle that a lease must have a term. A much simpler solution would have been to arrange the relationship between the parties around a trust.

[47] Though there are rules to stop trusts in England & Wales from existing for an excessive time. See the Perpetuities and Accumulations Act 2009 (and the Perpetuities and Accumulations Act 1964 for instruments taking effect before 6 April 2010).

[48] On the way the use increased the owner's freedom of alienation see JL Barton, 'The Medieval Use' (1965) 81 LQR 562.

[49] See Alecia Simmonds, 'Courtship, Coverture and Marital Cruelty: Historicising Intimate Violence in the Civil Courts' 45 AFemLJ 131 (the author is critical of the way this form of protection was reserved for the well-to-do, a concern we share: see below section III B 3 (a)). For further examples of the advantages of settling property on trust in this period see Baker (n 3) ch 14.

the beneficiary in a modern trust) is to be treated as the legal owner of land. The creativity of owners was condemned by the preamble as 'divers and sundry imaginations, subtle inventions and practices … craftily made to secret uses … sometimes by signs and tokens'. The highly unpopular statute, which gave rise to spectacular legal sophistry aimed to circumvent it and en-route gave rise to the law of modern trust, was finally abolished in 1925.[50]

The urgency felt by owners to find a structure of rights that would best suit the specific needs of their family or business pushed many of them to choose to settle their property on trust.[51] For the flexibility offered by trust is hard to compete with.[52] Under a trust one can, for example, create a testamentary fixed trust for her surviving spouse for life, with the remainder divided in shares of 20 per cent/50 per cent/30 per cent for life among children A, B, and C, with remainder to their children in equal part, subject to the power of her spouse to appoint capital in his absolute discretion if their medical condition requires extra expenses, with the discretion vesting in the trustees upon his death (subject to perpetuity period). Creating the same structure by using the ordinary bricks of property rights would be either impossible or fiendishly complicated.[53] In the previous section we saw some examples of innovative and creative uses of the trust that exemplify trust law's claim as one of the best tools for working on DIY (to distinguish from off-the-shelf) property structures.

However, some central aspects of English trust law may cast doubt on the notion that the trust supplies an out-of-the-box property type that gets us close enough to the liberal ideal of autonomy-enhancement. When we examine this question in the following subsections we focus on the beneficiary's dependence on the trustee as well as her exposure to trustee wrongdoing and third parties' claims and the limitations on her ability to protect her interest in the trusts of land. From this perspective, we ask whether these limitations on the property right it embodies preclude the trust from serving the liberal property regime in the way we envisage.

2. The challenge of dependence

As we have just seen, depending on the settlor's and beneficiary appetite for investing time and resources in managing the property, a trust can be designed to reflect a measure of reliance on the trustee that suits their needs.[54]

[50] Frederic William Maitland, *Equity: A Course of Lectures* (2nd edn, CUP 1936) 34.

[51] For the reasons that motivated the creation of trusts in the sixteenth and seventeenth centuries after the demise of feudalism see Baker (n 3) 330–1.

[52] See, eg, Matthew Harding, 'An Argument for Limited Fission' in John CP Goldberg and others (eds), *Equity and Law: Fusion and Fission* (CUP 2020) 374, 382–3.

[53] At least following the abolition of interests like life estates, and estates in reversion in the post-1925 legislation. The significant culling of estate types in the new Act attest to the fact that common law did a poor job in facilitating the flexibility that the trust was (and is) so nimble in supplying.

[54] Despite Lord Sales' statement that 'trusts can be created (and often are created) by the unilateral act of the settlor without any involvement on the part of the beneficiaries' (*Pleshakov v Sky Stream Corp* [2021] UKPC 15 [47]), as Mitchell and Hudson show, in trust creation the settlor is dependent on at least one beneficiary and one trustee who do not decline to take the post, as well as on compliance with the common law rules on transferring ownership in the particular *res* (unless it's a self-declaratory trust). This is, of course, another way in which the settlor is dependent on others to fulfil her wishes, but we think this limitation is clearly justified and we therefore continue to examine the effect of the rules that apply post-creation on the settlor's autonomy (J Hudson and C Mitchell, 'Justificanda' in this book). On the way in which beneficiaries and trustees can come together to create new rights

Alas, from the perspective of the beneficiary, property rights under trust seem to lack an important element of the self-determination that is enjoyed as a matter of course by owners of ordinary property rights; for the beneficiary cannot sue (directly) third parties who damaged the property, stole it, or trespassed onto it. The way in which the beneficiary's rights are recognised only in equity, whereas the property-protecting torts operate in law, means that these tortfeasors cannot be sued by the beneficiary; only the trustee has a claim against him, for only he is recognised in law as the owner of the trust property.[55] This dependency on the trustee for preserving the beneficiary's rights in the pursuit of legal remedies against tortfeasors and trespassers is therefore not an accidental feature of English trust law; it is inherent in the formal structure of the beneficiary's right. The beneficiary can of course sue the trustee for a breach of trust if he declines to pursue charges against a tortfeasor, as his refusal would (presumably) go against the interests of the beneficiary.[56] But a direct action against those who harm or trespass on the property is beyond her reach.

This pitfall, if left unaddressed, not only jeopardises the beneficiary's material benefit but it also implies that the trust form fails to deliver the right to civil recourse, which is a fundamental feature of property in a liberal polity.[57] Luckily, the courts devised a roundabout way to mitigate the real-life consequences of this ingrained feature of the trust structure: if a trustee refuses to use the power to sue, the beneficiary can resort to the so-called '*Vandepitte* procedure', which allows her to sue a trespasser or tortfeasor as long as she joins the trustee as a party to the proceedings.[58]

The *Vandepitte* procedure is often portrayed in case law and commentaries as a pragmatic solution to what would otherwise be a cumbersome process in which the beneficiary first has to sue the trustee to force her to sue the trespasser/tortfeasor (or ask for her replacement if she remains incalcitrant). But if the trust is to fill its role in the system of a liberal property regime, the availability of civil recourse against third parties who undermine the integrity of ownership is much more than a procedural shortcut. Far from being a mere pragmatic solution, it is a brilliant device that retains the important distinction between legal and equitable rights (without which no trust can exist), while addressing the need to empower the beneficiary to protect his right vis-à-vis third parties (without which the trust cannot function as an out-of-the-box

under the trust (even contrary to the settlor's wishes) see Ying Khai Liew and Charles Mitchell, 'Beneficiaries' Consent to Trustees' Unauthorised Acts' in Paul Davies, Simon Douglas and James Goudkamp (eds), *Defences in Equity* (Hart 2018).

[55] *Leigh and Sillavan Ltd v Aliakmon Shipping Company Ltd (The Aliakmon)* [1986] AC 785, at 812; *Mcc Proceeds Inc v Lehman Brothers International (Europe)* [1997] EWCA Civ 3068. If the beneficiary is in possession, she can sue for conversion, but then she will be claiming on the basis of her own possessory right (*Healy v Healy* [1915] 1 KB 938).

[56] *Barbados Trust Co Ltd v Bank of Zambia* [2007] EWCA Civ 148. On the trustee's duty to safeguard trust assets, see James Glister and James Lee, *Hanbury and Martin Modern Equity* (21st edn, Sweet & Maxwell 2018) 19-002-003.

[57] See generally: John CP Goldberg & Benjamin C Zipursky, *Recognizing Wrongs* (HUP 2020) 25–178.

[58] *Roberts v Gill & Co & Anor* [2011] 1 AC 240, [62]; *Vandepitte v Preferred Accident Insurance Corp of New York* [1933] AC 70; *The Albazero* [1977] AC 774; see generally: Glister and Lee (n 56) 19-003 and sources cited there. For a critical review of the beneficiary's recourse to sue the third party, see Andrew Tettenborn, 'Trust Property and Conversion: An Equitable Confusion' (1996) 55 CLJ 36.

property type). The *Vandepitte* procedure is therefore a necessary part—indeed a core feature—of the package of rights which beneficiaries under a trust should enjoy.[59] Its basis in trust law is much more robust than the way it is usually portrayed. Dependence on the kindness of strangers, or even their willingness to perform their legal duties, for realising one's property rights lends severe blow to these rights. The courts of equity (once again) saved the day.

Less can be done, however, for people who potentially stand to benefit from discretionary trusts. They may legitimately feel that by relying on the trustee's discretion on whether and how much to appoint to them, the trust relationship reduces them to supplicants and undermines their autonomy. In that particular trust arrangement, the autonomy of settlors to structure the gift in a way that suits the story they want to write for the property, may indeed come at the expense of the beneficiary's sense of autonomy. But, at the end of the day, the beneficiary can choose to walk away from the arrangement and the gift, and build his life independently of it. In contrast to the discriminatory conditions for gifts which we discuss below, in ordinary discretionary trusts the settlor is using the power that is given to any owner to decide who should benefit from the property. The trust adds some strings to this particular bow by allowing the settlor to replace her discretion with that of a (hopefully) knowledgeable third party, and indeed stretch it into the future (over the perpetuity period). But the beneficiary, like everyone else in English law, has no right to receive a gift in or after the settlor's life. Inasmuch as they feel that waiting and relying on the trustee's discretion is degrading to their sense of autonomy, they can leave it behind. That said, the way in which the discretionary trust may encourage a life of dependency, especially where the settlor herself cultivated the expectation and/or need as part of their relationship with the beneficiary, is indeed problematic from the point of view of autonomy.[60] Examining the precise way in which dependency undermines autonomy—and considering possibilities of reconstruction or reform that would remedy this defect—is beyond the boundaries of this chapter. (Below, just before our concluding remarks, we nonetheless offer some rudimentary thoughts.)

In the next section we will come across a particularly stubborn dent in the trust as a form of property, one that is likewise rooted in the split between the management of assets and ownership, but in which the conflict with the interests of third parties could not be resolved as elegantly. Before we get there, however, we should briefly address the

[59] Proponents of the 'Right against Right' analysis of the beneficiary's rights believe that the beneficiary's inability to directly sue the trustee attests to the non-proprietary nature of their rights (Ben McFarlane and Rob Stevens, 'The Nature of Equitable Property' (2010) 4 J Eq 1; Lionel Smith, 'Trusts and Patrimony' in Remus Valsan (ed), *Trusts and Patrimonies* (Edinburgh University Press 2015)). However, if they are happy to go along with viewing the trust as a non-property solution to the liberal requirement to supply out-of-the-box category, they can endorse the *Vandepitte* procedure as a welcome solution that expresses this role for the trust, while still retaining the conceptual difference owners who have rights in the property and beneficiaries who only have rights against their trustees.

[60] Equity, of course, deals with legitimate expectations to inherit that are created by the owner's representation that led to detrimental reliance via the doctrine of estoppel (*Thorner v Major* [2009] UKHL 18). We explain why beneficiaries of discretionary trust should still be considered as owners of the trustee property in H Dagan and I Samet, 'The Beneficiary's Ownership Rights in the Trust Res in a Liberal Property Regime' (2023) 86 Mod Law Rev 701.

mirror image of the deficiency in the beneficiary's independence, namely, the settlor's standing to enforce the trust. The settlor's lack of power to enforce the arrangement she envisaged for her property (unless she is also a beneficiary) is subject of a lively debate in trust theory.[61] It is another aspect of the law to which our theory makes a difference. For the way in which settlors do not have an automatic right to enforce the trust—which corresponds with the way the fiduciary duties of the trustee are owed to the beneficiary and not the settlor—reduces the efficacy with which the trust device can serve as a tool for implementing idiosyncratic agenda for one's property.[62]

In principle, placing the trustee under fiduciary duties and the duty to account for any deviation from the settlor's plan as it is stated in the trust terms should resolve this agency problem. However, this barrier to trustees' abuse of their position is likely to underperform in reality for a few reasons. First, the beneficiaries' interest may not align with the settlor's agenda, and in such cases, they can authorise conflicts of interest, endorse breaches, or fail to sue for them. Moreover, there is a good chance that the beneficiaries are less than the rational and educated principals the settlor can rely on to endorse her plans for benefiting them, otherwise she would have just transferred the property to them in the first place. And even beyond the question of motivation, beneficiaries who lack financial acumen and sophistication are unable to monitor the trustees' action in a satisfactory manner.[63]

Writers on the settlor's right of standing (or lack thereof) and the practical solutions that have been developed to cope with the problematics of this state of affairs take different approaches to the question.[64] The argument we make here about the normative underpinnings of the trust, while unable by itself to resolve the intricate question of the settlor's standing, adds weight to the 'empower the settlor' side of the scales. A law that grants the settlor the standing to enforce the terms of trust which embody her vision for the property is conducive for facilitating the potential of the trust to serve as an autonomy-enhancing property type. Once the normative DNA of the trust is thought of as a discharge of duty to diversify the categories of property, arguments against granting standing to the settlor must be heavy if they are to hold water, heavier than they would need to be to win against arguments from concept, doctrine, or efficiency alone.

3. The challenge of exposure

People's ability to count on the stability of their rights stands, as we've seen, at the core of property's service to their functioning as planning agents who can set up long-term

[61] See *Re Astor's ST* [1952] Ch 534 at 542. Once the trust is settled, the settlor drops out of the picture and cannot enforce it.

[62] Only an express provision in the trust instrument that allows the settlor to remove trustees, revoke the trust, etc., can grant the settlor the power to intervene to enforce it. *Re Flavell, Murray v Flavell* (1883) 25 Ch D 89 at 102–03; *Standing v Bowring* (1885) 31 Ch D 282.

[63] See discussion in Robert Sitkoff, 'An Agency Costs Theory of Trust Law' (2004) 89 Cornell L Rev 621, 643–46.

[64] For law and economics perspectives, see ibid 668; John T Gaubatz, 'Grantor Enforcement of Trusts: Standing in One Private Law Setting' (1984) NCL Rev 905; and Stewart Sterk, 'Trust Protectors, Agency Costs, and Fiduciary Duty' (2006) 27 Cardozo L Rev 2761, 2771. For doctrinal perspectives, see David J Hayton, 'Developing the Obligation Characteristic of the Trust' (2001) 117 LQR 96, 106; and Michael Houston, '*Estate of Wall v Commissioner*: An Answer to the Problem of Settlor Standing in Trust Law' (2005) 99 Northwestern University L Rev 1723.

projects and life goals. In a dynamic civil society, this stability cannot—and indeed must not—be boundless; owners' Rawlsian duty to support just institutions justifies, as shown elsewhere, *some* susceptibility to the power of state authorities to revise the content of their property rights.[65] Our focus here is different: we zoom in on the exposure of the beneficiary's right to derogations either due to its vulnerability to the transgressions of a rogue trustee (or his creditors) or to claims of third parties who may acquire title to the property against her will. This vulnerability entails, of course, instability of the settlor's agenda for his property. If plans for property that do not fall within state-sponsored categories can only be realised by converting it to an unsteady right, the state does not fulfil its duty to supply a route for unconventional property forms. We will argue that in spite of the exposure that is integral to the transfer of legal title to the trustee, the protection awarded to the beneficiary's right and the settlor's plans provides them with the level of stability that a liberal property regime requires in the circumstances.

(a) Rogue trustees

The courts of equity have always been acutely aware of the inbuilt vulnerabilities of hands-off beneficiaries and settlors. The opportunities to embezzle the trust fund, they realised, imply that the trust can only be viable if the trust property is duly protected. Indeed, the safeguards they developed drove Maitland to call the beneficiary a 'lucky being, the spoilt child of English jurisprudence'.[66] For these, as the next paragraph shows, go beyond anything an ordinary owner can dream of getting in common law.

For starters, equity is generous with the personal claims against trustees, including gain-based remedies and (in some jurisdictions) exemplary damages.[67] Furthermore, in contrast with the ordinary tort of conversion, where the owner can only claim damages from whoever converted her property to his own use, equity offers the beneficiary an enhanced proprietary remedy if they can identify the trust property among the trustee's assets.[68] If the beneficiary can follow the very asset that formed part of the trust subject matter or trace its value into a new asset, she will get it *in specie* regardless of the trustee's solvency. Moreover, if the trustee mixed her own assets with those of the trust, any uncertainty as to the contribution each made to the mixture is determined against the trustee.[69] And when tracing into substitution is possible, the beneficiary is free to pick and choose between different rules that address evidential uncertainty in order to reach the best result for herself.[70] Insofar as these rules focus on

[65] See Dagan (n 11) ch 8.

[66] Frederic Maitland, 'Trust and Corporation' (1904) 32 Grünhut's Zeitschrift für das Privat- and Öffentliche Recht 1, 21.

[67] On remedies against trustee in breach see Glister and Lee (n 56) 24-001-24-028; Samuel L Bray, 'Punitive Damages against Trustees?' in D Gordon Smith and Andrew S Gold (eds), *Research Handbook on Fiduciary Law* (Edward Elgar 2018).

[68] *Foskett v McKeown* [2001] 1 AC 102, 127–28.

[69] *Infabrics Ltd v Jaytex Ltd* [1985] FSR 75.

[70] See Charles Mitchell and David J Hayton, *Hayton and Mitchell: Commentary and Cases on the Law of Trusts and Equitable Remedies* (13th edn, Sweet & Maxwell 2010)13–17.

the rights of the beneficiary vis-à-vis the rogue trustee, which is our focus here, they are commendable.[71]

However, even these extraordinary measures are not foolproof, as once the trust asset (or its traced value) is destroyed or dissipated, the beneficiary is left with a (likely worthless) personal claim against the trustee. A wary settlor may consider appointing herself either as a sole trustee or as a co-trustee, and thus eliminate this risk or at least greatly reduce it; or she might place the trustee under strict duties to consult with, and provide information to, the settlor and/or the beneficiaries. But at the end of the day, the risks at hand—not only of betrayal but also of incompetence—are, at least to an extent, a function of the resources a settlor is willing and able to put into the management of the trust. Hiring a professional, skilful, and reputable trustee comes, however, with a price tag that may well place it outside the reach of the less well-off. This unfortunately means that when the only out-of-the-box form of property is trust, it is easier for the well-to-do to realise their autonomy through property rights they have.

(b) Third parties

The risk of losing property rights as a result of interaction with third parties—innocent or blameworthy—is common to all forms of property rights. What is unique, and on its face disturbing, for the trust context is that the right of the beneficiary is inherently weaker than a fully-fledged ownership: being based in equity, the rights of beneficiaries cannot win the upper hand against good faith purchasers of the trust property.

According to the 'equity's darling' rule, if a bona fide purchaser gives value to the trustee in return for his legal title to the trust property, she gets a clean title to the property even where the transfer was made in breach of trust.[72] The beneficiary can of course sue the trustee for breach of trust and require that he accounts for whatever consideration was paid for the trust property (or adopt the investment); but the property itself and the right to sue the transferee for conversion is lost to her. For in common law, the trustee passed good title to the third party, and equity will not intervene to change the parties' rights unless unconscionability is involved.[73] Below (subsection c) we explain how, in England, the beneficiary's situation is even worse if the subject matter of the trust is registered land. Does this inferiority of the trust in relation to the conventional types of property render it unsuitable to serve as the 'out of the box' category that a liberal system must supply? We think that it probably does not, both because of the way this disadvantage is 'set off' elsewhere, and—even more fundamentally—because equity's darling rule nicely follows the tenets of liberal property.

To start with, equity's protection of the beneficiary from the risk posed by third parties who are not deemed 'darlings' greatly exceeds what is on offer by applicable rules to

[71] The language of the text is intentionally careful. The justifiability of some of these rules is much less obvious insofar as third parties are concerned. See Hanoch Dagan, 'Restitution in Bankruptcy: Why All Involuntary Creditors Be Preferred' (2004) 78 Am Bankr LJ 247.

[72] See further: Aruna Nair and Irit Samet, 'What Can "Equity's Darling" Tell Us About Equity?' in D Klimchuk, I Samet and HE Smith (eds), *Philosophical Foundations of the Law of Equity* (OUP 2019).

[73] ibid pt 3, s 2.

owners of ordinary property. On balance, it is hard to say that 'beneficiaries are significantly less well-protected from the risk that third parties take good title over their property' since, in important respects, equity does a *better* job at protecting the beneficiary's right than does the common law with respect to ordinary property rights. A prime example is the way in which a beneficiary who is able to identify the original trust asset or its value in the hands of third parties (who did not pay consideration, or had, or should have had, notice of the trust), can follow or trace it into their hands and claim that they hold it for her on constructive trust.[74] Unlike legal owners, beneficiaries enjoy a proprietary remedy which not only allows them to put their hands on the property itself, but also grants them a status of 'secured creditor' if the third party goes bankrupt. Thus, while the rules of tracing and following that apply to innocent third parties are not as generous as those that apply to wrongdoers, equity still affords the beneficial owner a defence that is clearly superior to the personal claim which is available in common law to legal owners whose property was stolen.[75]

The elevated protection awarded by equity is historically rooted in the *in rem* nature of its remedies, and not necessarily in a wish to reinstate the autonomy-enhancing status of the trust by adding more weight to the 'protection for beneficiaries' rights' side of the scale. But for our purposes the result is what matters: in a significant number of cases, equity assists the settlors and beneficiaries to realise their plans for the property in a way ordinary owners can only dream of. At the bottom line, the trust creates a title which, like all other titles, is sensitive to other people's claims in some cases, and resistant to them in others.

Furthermore—and we now turn to our more principled answer—it would be wrong to deem the trust second best to the liberal property ideal due to the bona-fide-purchaser rule, because this rule is fully justified not only from the viewpoint of equity, but also from the perspective of liberal property itself. To see why, recall that for liberal property, commitment to relational justice is not an exogenous imposition. Quite the contrary, relational justice is part and parcel of liberal property's *raison d'être*. A liberal account of property, as noted, grounds owners' claim of legitimate private authority in people's interpersonal obligation of *reciprocal* respect for self-determination. This necessarily means that owners are also subject to this maxim in applying their authority vis-à-vis others, which is why relational justice is liberal property's third pillar.[76] And because respect for others' self-determination is hollow without *some* attention to their predicament, relational justice is not limited to a negative duty of non-interference that is the correlative of others' right to independence.

[74] For example, *Williams v Central Bank of Nigeria* [2014] UKSC 10; [2014] AC 1189, at [31]. The advantages of the proprietary remedy are noted by Lewison LJ in *FHR European Ventures LLP v Mankarious* [2013] EWCA Civ 17; [2014] Ch 1, at [14], including tracing as in *Foskett v McKeown* [2001] 1 AC 102 (HL).

[75] There is a discretionary remedy similar to specific performance in common law (Torts (Interference with Goods) Act 1977, s 3), but 'that remedy will rarely be available' unless the claimant can show that the good at hand is unique: Nick Curwen, 'The Remedy in Conversion: Confusing Property and Obligation' (2006) 26 Leg Stud 570, 573.

[76] Dagan (n 11) ch 5, on which the next three paragraphs draws. On relational justice more generally, see Hanoch Dagan & Avihay Dorfman, 'Just Relationships' (2016) 116 Colum L Rev 1395.

Implementing relational justice in property law is a complex task, which requires carefully to follow HLA Hart's advice that we distinguish 'between the gravity of the different restrictions on different specific liberties and their importance for the conduct of a meaningful life'.[77] One important entailment of this guideline is that liberal property's relational justice need not, and indeed does not, overwhelm the ability of owners to self-determine (this would have been self-defeating). Accordingly, the affirmative duties and burdens it imposes on owners and other property rights-holders are quite modest.

One such category involves rules that require owners to take some responsibility for guiding non-owners in the fulfilment of their duty to respect the owners' property rights. The obligation to accommodate non-owners' self-determination justifies along these lines the doctrines of consent, mistake, and proprietary estoppel, as well as burdens arising from registration or recordation law. All these doctrines and rules prescribe modest responsibilities to give notice to non-owners in order to mitigate their possible mistakes while interacting—by way of physical entrance or through legal transactions—with owners' property rights.[78] The equity's darling rule squarely falls within this category of doctrines. If beneficiaries do not make known to third parties of their private arrangement with the legal owner (their trustee), they cannot externalise the costs of this arrangement on such third parties.[79] Since they do not incur the burden of publicisation, they justifiably bear both the risk and the potential cost of the possible 'conflict between innocents' that may come about.

(c) *Registered land*

But is this answer fully satisfying? After all, even if a settlor is willing, indeed happy, to incur the costs of publicisation in order to secure full protection against the risk of third parties gaining good title to the trust property, she cannot do so if the subject matter of the trust is land. When it comes to ownership of land, English law severely limits the ability of the settlor and beneficiary to protect their vision for, and right to, the settled property by means of registration. The registration system, which was introduced to English law in 1925, includes as one of its three foundation principles the 'curtain principle' according to which 'references to trusts should be kept off the register'. Consequently, the register records the ownership of the legal estate, but not the beneficial interests that encumber them, and the registrar is not affected with notice of a trust.[80]

Moreover, purchasers of interest in registered land are allowed to assume, regardless of their actual state of knowledge, that the registered owners, ie the trustees, have unlimited power to dispose of the estate, free from any limitation contained in the terms

[77] HLA Hart, 'Between Utility and Rights' (1979) 79 Columbia L Rev 828, at 835.

[78] Equity is particularly keen on this point. See Irit Samet, 'Proprietary Estoppel and Responsibility for Omissions' (2015) 78 MLR 85.

[79] For an analysis of trust in terms of cost externalisation and 'common pool' problem, see Kent (n 33), pts IV and V.

[80] Land Registration Act 2002, s 78.

of trust on the validity of such disposition. And so, generally, as long as two legal owners convey the interest to the purchaser, she gets good title and need not worry about satisfying the conditions of the 'equity's darling' principle.[81] The only protection the beneficial interest can enjoy is in the form of 'restriction' on transactions that are contrary to the terms of the trust—but the interest does not gain priority over an interest bought in defiance of the restriction; all that is needed in order to satisfy the registrar that the terms of the trust were complied with is a statement by the trustee that this is indeed the case.[82] Thus, bad intentions or negligence of the trustee are enough to frustrate the beneficiary's interest in the property and the settlor's plans for it, regardless of the buyer's state of mind. This means that rights under trust form an important part of this infamous class of 'property rights that can neither be registered nor recorded... [and whose] validity is [therefore] not guaranteed, and they cannot have their priority protected by being recorded'.[83]

The injury to the beneficiary's property right is somewhat mitigated by it being transformed to a different proprietary right: in what Martin Dixon calls the 'statutory magic' of overreaching, the beneficiary's right which was 'swept off' of the land is attached to the purchase money;[84] once the purchase money is paid, the money becomes subject to the trust in lieu of the land, which has now moved out of the trust and into the hands of the purchaser (or become subject to a charge). To be sure, the requirement that two trustees should be party to the conveyance if overreaching is to happen helps to prevent 'a feckless, reckless or malevolent sole trustee from compromising the transient proprietary interests of the equitable co-owners'.[85] Alas, as the case law readily reveals, it offers only a partial protection to the beneficiaries.[86] For, as Dixon observes, '[e]ven if capital money has been paid, the beneficiaries are in practice ... very likely to receive nothing because the trustees will have spent the ... [purchase] money'.[87] The bottom line is that

[81] The standard 'Form A restriction' on transaction in trust subject to trust provides that capital money must be paid to two trustees or a trust corporation, for which the trustees who register the land or the beneficiaries can apply.

[82] See Form B, Schedule 4 of the Land Registration Rules 2003; a 'Form N restriction' which requires the consent of the *beneficiaries* will not normally be allowed (see more details in HM Land Registry 'Practice guide 19: notices, restrictions and the protection of third-party interests in the register', available at https://www.gov.uk/government/publications/notices-restrictions-and-the-protection-of-third-party-interests-in-the-register/practice-guide-19-notices-restrictions-and-the-protection-of-third-party-interests-in-the-register. Beneficiaries can also apply for a restriction in Form II which ensures that they be notified of the disposition, thereby giving them the opportunity of pursuing the proceeds of sale. But the mechanism of notice (which gives *priority* to the interest subject to the notice) cannot be used with respect of interest under trust (LRA 2002, ss 32, 33).

[83] Law Commission, Consultation Paper No 227: Updating the Land Registration Act 2002, s 2.32.

[84] Martin Dixon, *Modern Land Law* (Taylor & Francis 2018), 2.9.

[85] Martin Dixon, 'Reaching up for the Box in the Attic' Conv 165, 166.

[86] See, for example, *Birmingham Midshires Mortgage Services Limited v Sabherwal* [2000] 80 P&CR 256; *London Building Society v Flegg* [1988] 1 AC 54.

[87] Dixon (n 85) 166. In *State Bank of India v Sood* [1997] 2 WLR 421 it was decided that if the payment to the legal owner (ie the trustee) was in the form of a valid mortgage executed to secure future lending so that no capital money was transferred at the time when the property was charged, the beneficiary's interest will be overreached *even if only one trustee was party to the transaction.* This looks like a further serious blow to the meagre protection of the two-trustees requirement. However, as Dixon explains, in reality, since in these cases at least the trustee cannot take the money and disappear (or lose it to creditors in bankruptcy), the beneficiary's situation is improved, so that *Sood* does not place the beneficiaries in any worse position in practice than *Flegg*.

when it comes to registered land, the trust as a type of property right is clearly inferior to other estates which can enjoy the strong protection of the public register.

If the way in which the state discharges its duty to make available a miscellaneous property type is by making available the mechanism of the trust, there must be powerful justification(s) behind such serious limitation on the way settlors and beneficiaries can ensure that third parties do not knowingly interfere with their plans for the property. Are the reasons that have been offered in support of the deficient protection that interests under trust of land enjoy indeed strong enough? In *London Building Society v Flegg*—in which the beneficiaries' right was overreached in spite of the fact that they actually lived in the house—the House of Lords explained: '[o]ne of the main objects of the legislation of 1925 was to effect a compromise between on the one hand the interests of the public in securing that land held in trust is freely marketable and, on the other hand, the interests of the beneficiaries in preserving their rights under the trust'.[88] The concern that allowing the registration of interests under trust would clutter the register and undermine the goal of enhancing the marketability of land is repeated by leading textbooks and commentators with few, if any, critical comments on its viability.[89] In its report from 2018, the Law Commission opined that 'the existing mechanisms are sufficient to protect beneficial interests under trusts', and moreover that 'because of the curtain principle, further protection would be inappropriate'; and anyway, they thought, examining the viability of the curtain principle was beyond the Commission's remit.[90]

The Commission was not blind to the difficulties that are raised by the current form of the curtain principle, and the consultation paper recognises the way in which '[t]he treatment of beneficial interests under the Act... reflects an ongoing debate about the correct balance to strike between the rights of purchasers and mortgagees on the one hand, and beneficiaries on the other'.[91] The Commission rightly sensed that the 'debate raises broad questions of social policy that ultimately touch on the appropriate balance the law strikes between property as a "home" and as a financial investment for homeowners to realise', and that as a result '[t]he treatment of beneficial interests in the LRA 2002 sits within a much wider matrix of considerations of how the law balances the desire of home owners to secure their interest in the home, with the interests of purchasers and of those (such as mortgage lenders) with a financial interest in the property'. But the members nevertheless decided that it would be inappropriate 'to interfere with long-established assumptions' of the LRA 2002.[92]

[88] [1988] 1 AC 54, 73–74, per Lord Templeman.

[89] See for instance Emma Lees, *The Principles of Land Law* (OUP 2020) 89; Elizabeth Cooke, *The New Law of Land Registration* (Bloomsbury 2003) 32.

[90] Law Commission, *Updating the Land Registration Act 2002: Report* (2018) 10.89; see Law Commission, *Updating the Land Registration Act 2002: Consultation Paper* (2016) 1.20: '[o]verreaching is a general principle, which applies to personal property as well as land and to unregistered as well as registered land. It is governed primarily by provisions in the Law of Property Act 1925. We therefore concluded that its operation did not fall within our current review'.

[91] Law Commission, *Updating the Land Registration Act 2002: Consultation Paper* (2016) 1.21.

[92] ibid. The Law Commission did however go some way further to secure interests under the trusts when it recommended that a holder of a derivative interest under a trust (ie sub beneficiary) would also be entitled to lodge a caution against first registration if the beneficiaries have failed to do so: 4.84–4.85.

These are indeed complicated issues, which we cannot hope to resolve here, but a few observations may be in order. We agree that the Registrar should not be required to examine whether a dealing constitutes a breach of trust. However, it is unclear to us whether it is indeed impossible to afford more protection to beneficiaries who are willing to undertake the burden of publicisation[93] without deteriorating registration into recordation.[94] We believe that this chapter's argument about the normative foundations of the trust adds an important factor that ought to be considered when the issue of protecting beneficiaries' interests and settlors' plans in registered land finally does get the attention it deserves: the current law weighs upon the ability of the trust to function as the miscellaneous category, and hence (at least unless an alternative is introduced) it hinders the aspiration of English property law to be worthy of the label 'liberal'.

IV. The Path to Rehabilitation

We opened this chapter with sympathy for the concerns which animate the sharp critique of trust as a vehicle for absconding from one's duties—towards creditors, estranged spouses, third parties who trade on the basis of a façade of wealth created by the trust, and the community at large. We concluded, however, that, rather than throwing the baby with the bathwater, a liberal property regime should seek to preserve the express trust and further its functioning as an autonomy-enhancing property type. But lest this chapter ends up as an exercise of apology and legitimation, we must emphasise that in fine-tuning the doctrine in line with the liberal telos we ascribe to the trust, the law should be particularly vigilant to ensure that trust doctrine is not amenable to uses that offend the very justification which underwrites its legitimacy. While we cannot fully explore the implications of this prescription in this chapter, it is imperative that we point out to the two main directions of its reform, which is—we should reemphasise—critical to its liberal credentials.

The fact that both reforms rely on limitations inherent in the trust's own animating principle is institutionally significant. It suggests that the burden of facing up to these (and similar) abuses of the trust lies not only with legislatures. As the most traditional carriers of our private law, the courts share the responsibility for maintaining the integrity of its institutions. Thus, judges can—and dare we say should—participate in shepherding the development of trust law to remove mistakes and eccentricities and preserve 'whatever is pure and sound and fine'.[95]

[93] As an aside, we note that there is an important public interest in increasing transparency of landownership as it can help crack down on tax fraud and money laundering, and it would be interesting in this respect to follow British Columbia's Land Owner Transparency Act of 2019, which passed the first reading. See Bill 19, Land Owner Transparency Act, 2019, 4th Session, 41st Parliament, 2019. See also Ministry of Finance, *Land Owner Transparency Act White Paper: Draft Legislation with Annotations* (2018).

[94] It is not surprising that in the United States, where most states offer only recordation, some states permit—and a few require—the recording of trust declarations. See George G. Bogert and Amy Morris Hess, *The Law of Trusts and Trustees* (rev 2nd edn, Thomson Returers 1977) § 149.

[95] Benjamin N. Cardozo, *The Nature of the Judicial Process* (Yale University Press 1921) 179.

A. Delineating Trusts' Private Authority

In response to harsh criticism of the way trust law is manipulated to undermine distributive and relational justice, the state can, and at times does, intervene and modify aspects of trust law as well as of other neighbouring areas to mitigate the potential for harm.[96] It is not our intention here to review these measures or offer new ones.[97] Our account can contribute to these efforts by showing that their *justification* need not rely only on concerns of public policy external to trust law. This internal point of view is premised on the very foundations of liberal property, which is justified, as we repeatedly emphasise, by reference to—and to the extent of—its support of people's self-determination.

We have already invoked this premise, which implies that liberal property types must comply with their autonomy-enhancing telos, when we accounted for the effect of equity's darling rule on the trust. A similar analysis underpins familiar limitations on the settlor's freedom to determine the content or the form of the beneficiaries' entitlement, such as the perpetuity and *Saunders* rules, which are justified by reference to the autonomy of other parties, either existing or down the line;[98] it is also the background for a most powerful critique of certain abusive uses of trust law, which we cannot fully address here, dealing with improperly shielding resources from people's creditors. One prominent example is the US spendthrift trust that is designed to prevent creditors of a bankrupt beneficiary from satisfying their debt by recourse to the trust property she enjoyed. As John Chipman Gray maintained in his well-known (and justified) critique of spendthrift trusts (sadly common in the United States), the law should not allow people to 'have an estate to live on, but not an estate to pay his debts with'; owners, in other words, should not 'have the benefits of wealth without the responsibilities'.[99] For our purposes of explaining why liberal property offers internal critique of the disturbing tax abuse practices that are currently on the policymaking agenda, it is enough to add a few words on liberal property's first pillar as well as on the background precondition to property's legitimacy.

Liberal property's first pillar, as noted, is that the private authority which any given property type establishes should be carefully adjusted to its potential contribution to owners' self-determination. This maxim is particularly pertinent to commercial property types: where ownership is justified by its *indirect* contribution to people's

[96] See examples in HMRC, *The Taxation of Trusts: A Review', Consultation Document* (2018); and HMRC, *No Safe Havens* (2019). This effort by the British government is surely (also) a response to *The Guardian's* special investigation dubbed the 'Paradise Papers' (https://www.theguardian.com/news/2017/nov/05/what-are-the-paradise-papers-and-what-do-they-tell-us).

[97] We offer an analysis of the way in which Liberal property regime can tackle such abuses, with reference to detailed examples in H Dagan and I Samet-Porat, 'What is Wrong with Massively Discretionary Trusts' (2022) 138 LQR 129.

[98] See a few examples in Liew, 'Justifying Anglo-American Trusts Law' 12 William & Mary Business L Rev 685, s 3:1.

[99] John Chipman Gray, *Restraints on the Alienation of Property* (2nd edn, Kessinger 1895) 242–43. See also Carla Spivack, 'Democracy and Trust' (2017) 42 ACTEC Law Journal 339.

self-determination (as it is regarding commercial property), the private authority property instantiates should be strictly circumscribed in line with its instrumental role.[100] This conclusion is even more straightforwardly relevant here, since the use of the trust for tax abuse purposes cannot plausibly be justified by reference to owners' self-determination. We cannot here attempt to draw the line between legitimate and illegitimate tax planning. The idea that trusts used for aggressive tax planning are frowned upon is now well-established and our theory can offer a rich normative explanation on why this is so.[101]

Property's background condition of legitimacy is likewise crucial for our purposes. As noted, the legitimacy of the property rights of the well-off relies on and indeed depends upon their contribution to a viable background regime that guarantees everyone the material, social, and intellectual preconditions of self-authorship. This again points to a property-related reason for condemning the way trusts perversely turned into a tax-abuse instrument, a means that, rather than serving people's autonomy, subverts their compliance with their duties as owners.

These practices thus undermine the very autonomy-enhancing ideal on which the trust's legitimacy relies. Therefore, friends of the trust who celebrate its contribution to people's self-determination cannot but object to these practices and work to eradicate or transform them. Accordingly, legal reforms for abolishing or curtailing these abuses should not be understood as impositions on or limits of trust law. Instead, these are means for pushing the trust to live up to its own *raison d'être* as a liberal property type; measures of *perfecting* the trust's laudable autonomy-enhancing telos.

Thus, in a separate article,[102] we critique along these lines the way in which law and legal scholarship tackle one of the most important (fairly) recent developments in this area of law: the 'massively discretionary trust' (MDT), also known as 'black hole trusts'.[103] In an MDT, trustees' discretion is stretched to the limit (or beyond) as they are given absolute discretion to appoint property to almost anyone in the world, while the people who are really intended to benefit from the trust (eg the settlor's children) are not named as beneficiaries in the trust instrument.[104] Along with the practice of forming MDTs, we find a flourishing industry of drafting instruments that are designed to (at least) pressurise the trustee to submit the absolute discretion she is given on paper to the wishes of the settlor, who thereby retains much, if not all, power over the settled property. The 'letter of wishes', for example, is a popular device with settlors of MDTs, as it allows the settlor 'to indicate in a confidential manner matters which he would like a trustee to take into account'.[105]

[100] Dagan (n 11) ch 3.
[101] See Lord Walker in *Futter v HMRC* [2013] UKSC 26, [135].
[102] Dagan and Samet (n 97).
[103] Term coined in Lionel Smith, 'Massively Discretionary Trusts' (2017) 25 T&T 397.
[104] A good description of the structure is provided by Hoffmann J in *Re TR Technology Investment Trust plc* [1988] BCLC 256 at 623–24.
[105] Terence Tan Zhong Wei, 'The Irreducible Core Content of Modern Trust Law' (2009) 15 T&T 477, 489.

Why would a settlor choose to create an MDT rather than an ordinary discretionary trust? One reason, as private client lawyers like to put it, is harnessing 'tax efficiencies'.[106] A more significant advantage of structuring one's trust as an MDT may come from the way it enables the 'ghost beneficiaries' to enjoy the many advantages of property that is available to satisfy their wishes, without the duty to submit this property to paying their debts.

As we show there, although the three familiar responses to the destabilising effect of MDTs—the 'conceptual', the 'doctrinal', and the 'public policy' critique, as we call them—do important work in tackling the challenges that MDTs pose for friends of the trust, their power is limited. The consensus among judges and many impartial academic commentators that these are abusive devices is, however, supported by (what we call) an 'internal-normative' reason. The MDT is rightly condemned because it blatantly disregards liberal property's first, and most fundamental, pillar as well as, by extension, its third pillar of relational justice. Settling property on an MDT is not a legitimate move within the open category of property, because it accedes the powers which this property type—like any other types within a genuinely liberal property regime—lends legitimacy to. If we indeed manage to show that, our analysis of the role of trust as fulfilling the state duty to provide an out-of-the-box property type is an essential buttress for a robust response to this particular abuse of the trust institution.

Indeed, reinterpreting the trust as an important building block of a liberal property law can shed light on hazy corners of trust law, excavate the foundations of the debates that surround them, and thereby help to resolve the disputes to which they give rise. In the next section, we explore a very different area of trust law in which, unlike the MDTs, the water has been choppy for over a century. Yet, again, legitimising the trust as part of our commitment to a liberal telos strongly tilts the scales in favour of one solution—a solution that was favoured by many judges who lacked the theoretical foundation that underlies it, and hence did not feel confident enough to adopt it.

B. Relational Justice and Discriminatory Trusts

Sir Adolph Tuck gained some fame among trust law students by creating a trust the benefit of which can only be enjoyed by a descendent 'of the Jewish faith'. To qualify, the descendent can only take an 'approved wife', defined in the settlement as a woman 'of Jewish blood by one or both of her parents and who has been brought up in and has never departed from and at the date of her marriage continues to worship according to the Jewish faith'.[107] In attaching this condition to the settlement, Tuck joined a long line of donors who set the terms for allocating the largess they settled on a trust in

[106] Sunil Gadhia, Konrad Rodgers and Joe-han Ho, 'Sham Trusts' (2016) 22 T&T 464, 464. Where the assets or the trust itself are in the UK, tax benefits for discretionary trusts have largely evaporated when the Income Tax Act 2007 stipulated that trustees must pay income tax at the highest rate for any income from the trust assets (See pt 9 Special rules about settlements and trustees).

[107] Re Tuck's Settlement Trusts [1976] 1 All ER 545.

a discriminatory fashion. In this section we explore the way in which our analytical framework sheds light on the way forward with respect to the thorny issue of discriminatory patterns for appointing trust property.

Discrimination against potential beneficiaries on the basis of religion, race, or ethnicity—including trusts that were created many years ago, but are now coming to fruition—is, unfortunately, far from rare.[108] Common law jurisdictions have struggled to offer solutions that would adequately account for the different values that are at play in such scenarios.[109] Take the English case: public disapproval of discriminatory practices is crystal clear; the Equality Act 2010 is described by the British government as aiming to protect people 'in the workplace and in wider society' from discrimination on the background of age, gender reassignment, being married or in a civil partnership, being pregnant or on maternity leave, disability, race including colour, nationality, ethnic or national origin, religion or belief, sex or sexual orientation' ('protected groups').[110] The law explicitly applies in a wide range of social contexts: at work, in education, when using public services, when buying or renting property or engaging in consumer transactions, as well as insofar as members or guests of a private club or association are concerned. The act allows charitable trusts to discriminate *in favour* of members of protected groups, but explicitly disallows discrimination against them.[111]

We are interested, however, in private trusts, ie trusts where the potential pool of beneficiaries is limited to individuals who are usually identified by their close relationship with the testator. And when it comes to such private trusts, the strong message of the Equality Act seems to be facing a wall: the owner's freedom to leave their property to whomever they choose, so the argument goes, includes the right to settle property in a discriminatory manner, and a trust can therefore be used as a vehicle to fulfil the testator's wishes in this, as in (almost) every other regard. The tension between these propositions and our strongly held anti-discrimination commitments resulted in a case law that is marred with uncertainty and lack of transparency as judges endeavoured to utilise technicalities to achieve a resolution that alluded their best efforts.

When discriminatory conditions in trusts showed up in their docket, courts have apparently felt too uncomfortable to enforce them, but not confident enough to strike them down outright; hence, such conditions have suspiciously often failed on the basis of uncertainty of objects. Thus, rather than voiding discriminatory conditions by

[108] See Rex J Ahdar, *Religious Freedom in the Liberal State* (OUP 2013) who concludes from the large number of reported decision that 'this was a matter who preoccupied many Victorians when they contemplated their own mortality' (129). For more modern cases see for example *Re Donn's Will Trusts* [1943] 2 All ER 564; *Re Selby's Will Trust* [1966] 1 WLR 43; *Re Abrahams' Will Trusts* [1969] 1 ch 463.

[109] Many Canadian cases are discussed in Jonas-Sebastien Beaudry and Aruna Nair, 'Property and the Freedom to Discriminate: Markets, Gifts, and the Scope of Anti-Discrimination Norms' in Sue Farran, Russell Hewitson and Adam Ramshaw (eds), *Modern Studies in Property Law vol 11* (Hart 2021). Australian cases can be found in Matthew Harding, 'Some Arguments against Discriminatory Gifts and Trusts' (2011) 31 OJLS 303, 307–10.

[110] Government guidance on the Equality Act 2010 can be accessed at https://www.gov.uk/guidance/equality-act-2010-guidance.

[111] Equality Act 2010, s 193. Charitable trusts have always fared better in that respect. For courts routinely allowed trustees for charities who were disinclined to appoint property on a discriminatory basis to side-step the problematic clause by using the *Cy Pres* doctrine which saves charitable trusts from lapsing when the purpose they were meant to serve becomes unworkable in time: Harding (n 109) 305–07.

declaring them contrary to public policy—as the courts were willing to do with regards to conditions that encouraged divorce or estrangement between parents and children—they resorted to unworkable distinctions and roundabout definitions that enabled them to tackle the problem without being explicit on what they do.[112] But when the House of Lords debated the certainty of a clause that excluded a potential donee who is or becomes Roman Catholic, Lord Wilberforce came clean about the court's attitude to discriminatory clauses:

> It may well be that conditions such as this are, or at least are becoming, inconsistent with standards now widely accepted. But acceptance of this does not persuade me that we are justified, particularly in relation to a will which came into effect as long ago as 1936 ... in introducing for the first time a rule of law which would go far beyond the mere avoidance of discrimination on religious grounds. To do so would bring about a substantial reduction in another freedom, firmly rooted in our law, namely that of testamentary disposition. Discrimination is not the same thing as choice: it operates over a larger and less personal area, and neither by express provision nor by implication has private selection yet become a matter of public policy.[113]

We argue that, with respect, neither Lord Wilberforce, nor the judges who sought to introduce a 'public policy' voidance mechanism by the backdoor, got it quite right. Testamentary freedom does not entail a freedom to create a legal mechanism for distributing benefits on a discriminatory basis, and there is no need for an external criterion like 'public policy' to achieve this result.[114] While no attempt has been made to use the sections of the Equality Act which prohibits discrimination in the 'disposal' of property to strike down private trusts or gifts,[115] we claim that the same *property*-justification for the prohibition of discriminatory uses of the power to sell or lease, also renders discriminatory dispositions *ultra vires* the powers of owners in a liberal system of property.[116]

To see why, consider first the implicit reliance of Lord Wilberforce's speech on the dominion conception of property. Lord Wilberforce *presupposes* that owners' right to

[112] The courts used a fine distinction between 'condition precedent' (that rules out an interest from the start) and a 'condition subsequent' (which amounts to a forfeiture of an interest which already (at least partly) materialised). The latter was deemed to require a particularly high standard of certainty, and many discriminatory clauses were interpreted as falling into this forfeiture-like group even when they could just as easily be interpreted as falling under the 'condition precedent' category. See, for example, the string of cases which involved a condition of belonging to 'the Jewish Faith' discussed in Davina Cooper and Didi Herman, 'Jews and Other Uncertainties: Race, Faith and English Law' (1999) 19 LS 339, 346–50; the authors conclude: 'for the most part... [r]ather than asking whether the conditions are in the public interest, the courts have asked instead, the narrower more formal question: are the exclusions sufficiently precise to constitute legally acceptable conditions?' (343); see also Harding (n 109) 308. For a sharp criticism of the distinction see the respective judgments in *Tuck* of Whitford J (([1976] 1 All ER 545, 551–52) and Lord Denning ([1978] 1 All ER 1047 (CA), 1054).

[113] *Blathwayt v Baron Cawley* [1976] AC 397, 426.

[114] By the same token, our analysis is not dependent on the question of whether the 'limited horizontal effects' of the Human Rights Act 1998 can be interpreted to apply to such dispositions. cf Harding (n 109) 311–13.

[115] Beaudry and Nair (n 109) 4.

[116] cf François du Toit, Matthew Harding, and Andreas Humm, *King Nno v De Jager: Three Perspectives*, Stellenbosch LJ (forthcoming).

sell, lease, or donate their property is unqualified, which explains why he views the application of anti-discrimination law as a 'substantial reduction' of their entitlement. This presupposition seems obviously correct if property is indeed properly understood as structured around a robust core of 'sole and despotic dominion'. But that conception must be inadmissible for liberal law. As we repeatedly emphasise, to be justified, property must rely on the maxim of *reciprocal* respect for self-determination. Taking the constitutive role of this maxim in the legitimacy of property seriously implies that the normative powers law confers upon owners need not only be circumscribed as per their service to owners' self-determination. Rather, they must also be compatible with liberal property's third pillar of relational justice. A genuinely liberal law cannot legitimately authorise owners, as the dominion conception does, to apply their normative powers in a way that clearly *disrespects* others' right to self-determination.

At times, relational justice requires *active* accommodation, as in many workplace instances (that are far afield from our topic) or in the modest affirmative obligations which explain equity's darling rule, discussed earlier. In other cases, such as those dealing with non-discrimination, relational justice implies *not* considering certain characteristics when making decisions. Thus, since deciding on one's residence is a major act of self-authorship, relational justice prescribes that in applying their powers in the context of real estate transactions, private owners must set aside certain considerations, such as racist preferences, which fail to respect the self-determination of others, namely potential buyers or lessees.

This prescription is not grounded only in the Rawlsian duty to support the state's effort to fulfil its duty toward would-be victims of discrimination. Rather, it stands on its own, distinctive ground. Even a public commitment to fully secure—say, through public housing—everyone's equality of opportunity could not redeem a property law that authorises private owners to discriminate against others in applying their normative powers of selling or leasing out their property. This *internal*-to-property foundation of the anti-discrimination rule in real estate transactions applies even where the owner's refusal to engage relies on sincere objections grounded in his or her own conception of the good. The reason for this is that relational justice necessarily constrains the class of choices and conceptions of the good that can legitimately require interpersonal respect only to those that recognise others' equal status. The animating ambitions of the murderer, the racist, and the bigot may be authentic; but since they repudiate their victims' equal standing, they have no valid claim to accommodation.[117]

But is this account of discriminatory sales practices relevant to discriminatory testamentary dispositions? Potential donees, one may still argue, may have *expectations* to such dispositions; but these are—at least according to conventional understanding of English inheritance law—merely expectations. If so, why wouldn't the donors be free to subvert them by applying the power of disposition in a discriminatory fashion? After all, disinheritance can be triggered by benign reasons as well, which means that disrespect to a potential donee's self-determination is incidental to the power to bequest.

[117] For more, see Dagan (n 11) 122–39.

Moreover, the analogy from sale to bequest is further weakened once we appreciate that while the identity of the buyer may at times be important to sellers, choosing a donee is what the power of bequest is all about.

These are real differences between the normative powers to sell and to bequest, but neither of them challenges our claim. For unless one presupposes the dominion model of ownership, the claim that ownership authorises discriminatory applications of the power to bequest is a non-starter. The discretionary nature of owners' right to bequest is indeed not different from their right to sell; non-owners, in both cases, have no valid legal complaint against an owner who simply refuses to exercise this right. But taking relational justice seriously as a constitutive pillar of property nonetheless implies that a regime of liberal property must ensure that *both normative powers that law confers on owners*—the power to sell and the power to bequest—are circumscribed so that they are consistent with the self-determination of other people (prospective buyers/lessees and prospective donees, respectively).

Property's normative powers presuppose that both non-owners and owners respect each other's right to self-determination. Therefore, the application of these powers is legitimate only insofar as it does not deny the equal standing of others due to who they are or how they self-define. A benign motivation on the part of the particular donor (such as her religious convictions or concern for the continuity of minority culture) is simply irrelevant to this prescription, which precedes the decision of any specific owner. Therefore, such benign motivation cannot cure the relational injustice of dominating the beneficiary's constitutive decisions in *either* of these cases.[118] Relational justice does not (and indeed should not) purport to police owners' inner psyche; rather, it is about ensuring that the scope of the private authority, which a liberal system sets up and enforces, remains within its legitimate boundaries. Whatever owners' motivations may be, property law must neither authorise nor facilitate violations of the maxim of reciprocal respect for self-determination that secures its legitimacy.[119]

There is yet another reason for invalidating many—although admittedly not all—discriminatory testamentary dispositions, one that does not affect discriminatory sales practices. Discriminatory testamentary dispositions, like that of the Tuck trust mentioned above, typically imply exactly the kind of interpersonal domination that relational justice proscribes, as they dictate core life choices to their donees. They are, in other words, just as offensive to the donee's self-determination as a forfeiture condition that penalises marriage (eg 'to *A* for life, but if *A* marries, then to *B*'), which English courts are happy to invalidate.[120]

118 *Contra* Beaudry and Nair (n 109).

119 We think that the same reasoning should invalidate a discriminatory condition in a conditional gift. The case of discriminatory gifts which are given without conditions is more complicated because there the violation is not *explicitly* recognised, and without further information, law must be careful not to attribute too quickly a disqualifying feature to an otherwise legitimate transaction. (This means that a different conclusion may be in place if a testator, for example, explicitly provides a discriminatory rationale to the exclusion of a child who married the 'wrong' person.)

120 For example, *Lloyd v Lloyd* (1852) 2 Sim (N.S. 255); for details on the way English law voids conditions that are designed to restrain marriage, induce separation or divorce, or interfere with discharge of parental duties, see Glister and Lee (n 56) 14-007–008.

This means that the fact that beneficiaries of a Tuck-like trust are better-off with the conditional donation than without it, cannot rehabilitate the donor's attempted imposition on their autonomy, just as it cannot validate the forfeiture condition that penalises marriage. In both cases—as in the more general case of coercive claims, where one person *illegitimately* exploits another person's predicament and dependence[121]—donees are asked to 'choose' the lesser of two evils; and in both, sanctioning the request threatens to undermine the donee's autonomy and is therefore unacceptable in a genuinely liberal property law.[122]

The astute reader will notice the way this argument from interpersonal domination may justify the resistance of English law to perpetual trusts and may furthermore suggest that even within the regime of the rule against perpetuities there must be limits to the acceptable control of both the settlor and the trustee over the beneficiary. These potential additional implications of our theory seem significant, but their consideration must await another day.[123]

V. Concluding Remarks

Legal institutions, especially those with a rich legacy such as the express trust, do not always evolve with a particular normative commitment in mind. Often their evolution is path-dependent and their rules not only reflect a mix of normative voices, but also testify to the impact of lawyers' internal (doctrinal) language as well as to the effect of interests and power-struggles, which are all necessary parts of the legal drama.

Yet, like other social institutions—and indeed of people, both individuals and groups—the life of the law also includes moments of soul-searching, in which legal institutions are pushed to refine their telos and adjust their rules accordingly. The causes and dynamics of these moments, which may culminate in a salient case or a defining new piece of legislation, are often complicated. But the threat of a crisis—the possible collapse of a legal institution due to its exploitation in indefensible ways—seems an obvious reason, indeed an opportunity, for rethinking the foundations.

We believe that the current predicament of the express trust offers such an opportunity. Trust sceptics are correct to revolt against the increasing abuses of the trust. But

[121] cf Mitchell N Berman, 'The Normative Functions of Coercion Claims' (2002) 8 Leg Theory 45, 53–54 (coercion also implies choosing the lesser of two evils, which means that the baseline for coercion claims is necessarily normative).

[122] As with other cases of coercive claims, this analysis requires to make *qualitative* distinctions between conditions that overly encumber the addressee's self-determination and those that are acceptable. This feature should not be surprising, as it typifies any autonomy-based legal accounts.

[123] Another, more specific example can come from a critical reading of a case like *Re Streed's WTs* [1960] EWCA Civ 2, which suggests that where the pertinent trust *res* is constitutive, rather than fungible, for the beneficiary's life story (that includes, of course, her relationships with others), she should have a voice in the trustee's decision-making process, and where her view is unreasonably ignored (eg if the financial stakes are not sufficiently high to override it), a court may reverse the trustee's decision.

they are wrong to deem it beyond redemption. A charitable interpretation of trust doctrine and of the legacy of the trust offers a happy *raison d'être* around which it can, and should, be reconstructed. The trust plays a distinctive important role in a system of liberal property.[124] Pushing it to live up to this (implicit) promise offers an exciting reformist agenda in which many of its weeds are properly cleared.

124 We hope to have clarified the precise power of our thesis. We acknowledge that there is more than one way to address the function we attribute to the express trust; in fact, as we've claimed it is in some senses a second-best. Moreover, the autonomy-enhancing service of the trust (or any other such residual category), while distinctive, is less fundamental to autonomy than the availability of a proper menu of property types.

7

Freedom of Testamentary Disposition

*Paul B. Miller**

I. Introduction

American law is notoriously solicitous of property owners' freedom of disposition.[1] That freedom is, of course, not absolute. However, American law has fewer of the constraints prominent in other jurisdictions. For example, whereas English law sharply curtails disinheritance of dependents,[2] American law only occasionally limits disinheritance and the limitations it recognises are comparatively narrow. American trust law is thus reasonably said to be influenced profoundly by a concern to effectuate freedom of disposition.[3] This concern explains the preponderance of rules aimed at making the donative express trust an effective mechanism for disposition subject to fiduciary intermediation, with practices of fiduciary administration and judicial supervision alike being guided by an imperative of respect for settlor intention.

In this context, freedom of disposition is often treated as a given: it is so central to our law that one cannot readily imagine it otherwise. And certainly, as a matter of interpretive analysis, this is true. One cannot understand American trust law without appreciating that it is robustly enabling of freedom of disposition. Though I won't argue as much, one suspects that the same is true of English and Commonwealth law,[4] even if freedom of disposition is in those jurisdictions given a narrower berth.

* I am grateful for comments from Hanoch Dagan, Simone Degeling, Simon Douglas, Joshua Getzler, Jessica Hudson, James Lee, Ben McFarlane, John Mee, Charles Mitchell, Aruna Nair, Irit Samet, Rob Sitkoff, and Lionel Smith, as well as participants at the Philosophical Foundations of Trust Law workshop at King's College London. Comments welcome at: paul.miller@nd.edu

[1] Restatement (Third) of Property: Donative Transfers § 10.1 cmt. a (2003) ('Property owners have the nearly unrestricted right to dispose of their property as they please'); Robert H Sitkoff, 'Trusts and Estates: Implementing Freedom of Disposition' (2014) 58 St Louis U LJ 643, 643 ('the organizing principle of the American law of succession . . . is freedom of disposition') (hereafter Sitkoff, 'Freedom of Disposition').

[2] Inheritance (Family Provision) Act, 1938 (1 and 2 Geo VI, Ch 45). For a contemporaneous account, see Joseph Dainow, 'Limitations on Testamentary Freedom in England' (1940) 25 Cornell LQ 337 (hereafter Dainow, 'Testamentary Freedom in England'). For more recent commentary, see Richard Hedlund, 'The End to Testamentary Freedom' (2021) 41 LS 55 (hereafter Hedlund, 'Testamentary Freedom'). The position at common law was more accommodating of testamentary freedom, even as it was frequently questioned. See *Savage v Taylor* (1736) Cas T Talb 234, 238–39 (' . . . If there is tenant for life, remainder over to some other person, so as to be in contingency, if the tenant for life makes a feoffment, or levies a fine without trustees to preserve the contingent remainders, in point of law they are barred: but it is a most barbarous thing to rob persons unborn of their inheritance, and to give it to one who has no colour of title; yet hard and unjust as it is, I do not remember this Court has ever interfered so far as to direct a conveyance to him in remainder').

[3] Sitkoff, 'Freedom of Disposition' (n 1) 643–44 ('The American law of succession embraces freedom of disposition, authorizing dead hand control, to an extent that is unique among modern legal systems').

[4] See *Ilott v The Blue Cross & Ors* [2017] UKSC 17, para 1, per Lord Hughes ('Unlike some other systems, English law recognizes the freedom of individuals to dispose of their assets by will after death in whatever manner they wish') and para 52, per Lady Hale ('Freedom of testation is . . . the default position in the law of England and

Paul B. Miller, *Freedom of Testamentary Disposition* In: *Philosophical Foundations of the Law of Express Trusts*.
Edited by: Simone Degeling, Jessica Hudson, and Irit Samet, Oxford University Press. © Paul B. Miller 2023.
DOI: 10.1093/oso/9780192844934.003.0008

But the position of freedom of disposition—and, especially, freedom of *testamentary* disposition—in normative theory is strikingly different.[5] It has attracted criticism from moral and political philosophers for centuries. Indeed, it is widely viewed as one of the most tenuous incidents of ownership, receiving, at best, half-hearted defence.

Various social ills are attributed to laws enabling testamentary freedom. They include claims that it promotes dynastic accumulation of wealth, generating distributive injustice and social disutility, and that it generates a host of dead hand control problems (eg interference with markets and/or land-use regulation, and the abusive use of gifts as instruments of dominance). Criticisms like these are prevalent in recent work on egalitarianism and distributive justice.[6] But many are age-old and crop up unexpectedly in the work of natural law theorists, classical liberal philosophers, and classical common lawyers. Pufendorf[7] and Blackstone, for instance, were critical of freedom of testation, with the latter disputing its association with owners' moral or natural rights.[8] Adam Smith treated freedom of testation as a curious artificial right rooted in 'piety to the dead' and argued that it should not be exercisable in favour of strangers.[9] In turn, the great classical utilitarians, Bentham and Mill, recommended that testamentary freedom be abolished or sharply curtailed.[10]

Testamentary freedom is thus widely thought to be morally suspect. Yet it enjoys enduring support in American law. The gap between the law and long settled conventional moral opinion is significant. In this chapter, I aim to advance debate by (a) canvassing leading defences of freedom of testamentary disposition, tallying their insights while highlighting their deficiencies; and (b) providing a new defence, built upon the focal meaning of testamentary disposition as gift-giving.[11]

I will suggest that testamentary disposition, where defensible, is defensible through elaboration of a set of moral reasons embedded in the juridically familiar notion that dispositions are gifts. On this view, testamentary dispositions are gifts enabled by law; hence, the exercise of legal powers of disposition counts as the

Wales, subject to the courts' limited discretionary powers'). I am grateful to Ben McFarlane for bringing this case to my attention.

[5] See generally: Michael B Levy, 'Liberal Equality and Inherited Wealth' (1983) 11 Pol Theory 545; David Haslett, 'Is Inheritance Justified?' (1986) 15 Phil and Pub Aff 122; Stephen R Munzer, *A Theory of Property* (CUP 1990) 380; S Stewart Braun, 'Historical Entitlement and the Practice of Bequest: Is There a Moral Right of Bequest?' (2010) 29 Law and Phil 695; and Daniel Halliday, 'Is Inheritance Morally Distinctive?' (2013) 32 Law and Phil 619.

[6] Haslett ibid 125 ('vast inequality in the distribution of wealth is . . . due at least as much to inheritance as to any other factor').

[7] Cited by Jean-Jacques Rousseau, 'Discourse on Political Economy', in *The Basic Political Writings* (CUP 2012) 263 ('[t]he right of property, by its very abstract nature, should not extend beyond the life of the proprietor, and the moment he is dead, his goods should cease to belong to him') (hereafter Rousseau, 'Discourse on Political Economy').

[8] William Blackstone, *Commentaries on the Laws of England* (UChicago Press 2016) Bk II, ch 23.

[9] Adam Smith, *Lectures on Jurisprudence* (OUP 1978), 63–71, as referenced and discussed in J.W. Harris, 'Inheritance and the Justice Tribunal' in Stephen Munzer (ed), *New Essays in the Legal and Political Theory of Property* (CUP 2007).

[10] See Cornelius Cappelen and Jørgen Pedersen, 'Just Wealth Transfer Taxation: Defending John Stuart Mill's Scheme' (2018) 17 Pol Phil and Econ 317 (hereafter Cappelen and Pedersen, 'Just Wealth Transfer Taxation').

[11] This is, then, an examination of the *critical* rather than *posited* morality of law. See Paul B Miller, 'Juridical Justification of Private Rights' in Simone Degeling, Michael Crawford and Nicolas Tiverios (eds), *Justifying Private Rights* (Hart 2020).

exercise of a particular kind of freedom enabled and protected by law to give gifts. I claim that this focal *legal* sense of testamentary disposition is meant to track—ie be rooted in the normative idea, and social practices of— gift-giving in its focal *moral* sense. And the focal moral sense is one in which gift-giving is understood as a socially mediated ritual whereby a token or thing of actual or sentimental value is freely given to another person or cause out of recognition or affection for the person or identification with a cause, or to provide for a person or segment of the public, whether out of duty or benevolence.

I will not suggest that freedom of testamentary disposition is a natural right nor that it should be unlimited or thinly limited. Rather, my aim is to supply a more plausible account of the value of testamentary freedom such that the import of leading criticisms may be assessed from a more balanced vantage point. The focal moral sense of gift-giving which the juridical notion of donative transfer is meant to track points to moral reasons that sustain, but that also limit, the enabling posture taken by law. I hope to explore these limits in future work.

The argument will unfold as follows. Part II explains freedom of disposition, differentiating *inter vivos* from testamentary dispositions in ways that illuminate criticisms of the latter. Part III critically assesses four leading justifications offered in defence of freedom of testamentary disposition, finding them wanting. Part IV develops a more plausible account of the morality of freedom of testation by identifying its focal sense as a matter of the morality of underlying social practices—ie those which involve the freedom to give gifts—and by canvassing the values that are salient as a matter of motive, character, and ends in practices that exemplify the focal sense of testamentary freedom. Part V concludes.

II. Freedom of Disposition

I have said that I will focus on freedom of *testamentary* disposition. I do so for two reasons: first, because it is the most difficult to justify form of freedom of disposition; and second, because most of the justifications offered in aid of it apply equally to *inter vivos* and testamentary dispositions. In this Part, I begin with some general observations about freedom of disposition that hold across different mechanisms for its realisation (eg wills, will substitutes, trusts, and contracts). I then differentiate *inter vivos* and testamentary disposition, canvassing issues raised in criticism of testamentary freedom. Finally, I briefly summarise American law on freedom of testamentary disposition as effectuated through testamentary express trusts.

A. Its General Nature

Freedom of disposition is the freedom of an owner of property to transfer ownership[12] to a person of their choice. Though the association of freedom of disposition with ownership and private property is not one of conceptual or normative *entailment*, it is one of *extension*. Ownership and private property and the values that undergird them are realisable independently of freedom of disposition, but they conventionally encompass it. Indeed, this convention is so widespread that freedom of disposition is often assumed entailed by the very idea of private property, such that one could not properly be said to own property absent enjoyment of wide freedom of disposition. Be that as it may, there is *a* relationship of entailment here. But it is the obverse of that just noted: in order to enjoy freedom of disposition, one must own property (or have been appointed a fiduciary authorised to exercise an owner's freedom of disposition). One can, with effort, contemplate private ownership absent freedom of disposition, but the same is not true vice versa. Freedom of disposition is a freedom held by owners in relation to property amenable of disposition.

Given this, it should be unsurprising that freedom of disposition is constrained by property law's delineation of the rights of owners and its recognition of objects of ownership. Freedom of disposition may be enjoyed only in relation to things relative to which the law recognises property rights.[13] This comports with Smith's and Penner's analyses of the impact of 'thingness' on the content and formal definition of property interests.[14] Freedom of testamentary disposition is marginally wider than that of *inter vivos* disposition.[15] But laws enabling freedom of disposition by and large reproduce constraints the law of property places on the kinds of resources in which one can have property, and the kinds of property interest one can have in those resources. Equally, freedom of disposition is contingent upon property in that it is determined by the specific alienable interests held by owners. One is free to dispose only that which one owns, subject to whatever *in rem* burdens encumber one's ownership.

A *disposition* is a legally effective intentional transfer of ownership. Hence, the enjoyment and exercise of freedom of disposition turns on the existence and nature of legal mechanisms[16] for the intentional transfer of ownership. Dispositions are, of course, not the only mechanisms for the transfer of ownership. Ownership of land and appurtenances can be transferred unintentionally through prescription and otherwise (eg accession). Ownership of chattel can be transferred in accordance with principles on

[12] By reference to 'ownership' I mean to encompass lesser alienable interests in property (ie interests other than the full vested interest held by an owner of property).

[13] See generally: David Horton, 'Indescendibility' (2014) 102 Cal L Rev 543, 543.

[14] J.E. Penner, *The Idea of Property in Law* (OUP 1997); Henry E Smith, 'Property as the Law of Things' (2012)125 Harvard L Rev 1691.

[15] For example, while one cannot dispose of one's body or body parts by sale in life or upon one's death, one can make an *inter vivos* gift of certain bodily tissues, organs, or fluids and a testamentary gift of these materials or one's entire body for science or another recognised purpose.

[16] As outlined in pt II.B, below.

abandonment and the rights of finders. And real and personal property can also be transferred through default estate plans established by laws on intestacy. None of these mechanisms involves a disposition because none implies an owner-transferors' intention that ownership pass to a designee.

In turn, *freedom* of disposition implies that an owner is (by virtue of their ability to invoke different legal mechanisms for disposition) generally free to decide whether, when, how, in respect of what property (or severable interest therein), and for whose benefit, to make a disposition.

B. *Inter Vivos* and Testamentary Dispositions

Freedom of disposition is effectuated through laws that enable *inter vivos* and testamentary disposition, respectively. Enabling law implicates the conjoint operation of the law of property, contract, wills, trusts, and estates.

Inter vivos dispositions are transfers that will take effect—-if, where conditional, at all—at some point during the life of the owner-transferee.[17] The mechanisms are familiar. They include contracts for the sale of land, intangibles, and chattel, as well as various legislative frameworks meant to secure the fairness and integrity of those transactions. They also include mechanisms for donative disposition, including express trusts and gifts made in writing. The integrity of donative transfers—and the importance attached to intentional and uncoerced disposition—is secured by a variety of doctrines, from the maxim that equity will not perfect an imperfect gift to the presumptive rule establishing the purchase money resulting trust. Taken collectively, these mechanisms enable contractual freedom and social practices of gift-giving and philanthropy.

Testamentary dispositions are intentional transfers executed during the life of the owner-transferee but taking effect upon their death. They are central to the law of succession, where they are flanked by rules governing probate, intestacy, and the administration of estates. The primary mechanisms of testamentary disposition are wills, trusts, and will substitutes. These mechanisms enable social practices of family provision, gift-giving, and philanthropy that are, for individuals of ordinary means, distinguished by the value of the disposition(s) and extent of their intended impact on recipients.[18]

As noted earlier, *inter vivos* disposition is relatively uncontroversial. By that, I don't mean to suggest that there is no controversy about how law goes about enabling disposition; I mean, rather, that the *freedom as such* is widely accepted as morally sound.[19] The contrast with testamentary freedom of disposition is stark. As noted earlier, it has been widely criticised for centuries. Leading criticisms, in no particular order, are that: (1)

[17] I here exclude will substitutes that function as mechanisms of testamentary disposition but that enable avoidance of probate through formal transfer of title before the death of the grantor. I thank Rob Sitkoff for encouraging this clarification.

[18] Testamentary disposition usually provides for the distribution of the entirety of a decedent's life savings, real property, and other holdings.

[19] Setting Marxist critiques to one side. See Karl Marx, 'The Right of Inheritance' in *Report of the Fourth Annual Conference of the International Working Men's Association* (1869).

people, once dead, have no moral interests such as might ground a duty to enable or to respect testamentary dispositions; (2) wide freedom of testamentary disposition is objectionable in respect of property that is scarce, management of scarce resources being a problem that confronts living and future generations and that ought, morally, to be addressed by them without impediment by those now deceased; (3) freedom of testamentary disposition is autonomy-enhancing, if at all, only for persons who enjoy it—for everyone else, it implies autonomy-inhibiting dead hand control; (4) limits of foresight mean that testamentary dispositions are inefficient or wasteful; (5) testamentary disposition facilitates dynastic accumulation of wealth, generating widening and persistent socioeconomic inequality; and (6) testamentary disposition undermines the incentives of heirs to be socially mindful and productive.[20]

The above-noted criticisms are general. But some are more cutting, contemplated in light of characteristics of express trusts. Consider, for instance, uses of trusts in estate planning for the wealthy to facilitate tax arbitrage, exacerbating socioeconomic inequality through testamentary disposition.[21] Consider, too, that trusts enable property to be subjected to fiduciary administration for private purposes for extended periods of time.[22] And consider how rules governing the conduct of trustees and protectors extend the reach, and thus the practical effect, of settlor control over property settled on trust.[23] Whereas settlor intention is realised, and property is disbursed, under wills (outright gifts) within a relatively short period of time, trusts often extend the impact of settlor intention temporally for decades or even centuries.[24] Amplified concerns about intergenerational fairness and equity arguably mean that the burden of justifying testamentary freedom reaches its apogee in respect of the express trust as a mechanism for the realisation of that freedom.

C. Freedom of Testamentary Disposition in American Trust Law

As noted earlier, freedom of testamentary disposition is a pillar of American trust law.[25] Comprehensive analysis has been provided by Robert Sitkoff.[26] But, briefly, testators

[20] See works cited at note 5. On the notion that the people have no pre- or post-mortem moral interests such as might ground freedom of testation, see Hillel Steiner, *An Essay on Rights* (Wiley 1994) 250–58 and Cecile Fabre, 'Posthumous Rights' in Matthew Kramer and others (eds), *The Legacy of H.L.A. Hart: Legal, Political and Moral Philosophy* (OUP 2008). For criticism of freedom of testation on egalitarian grounds, see Michael Otsuka, *Libertarianism Without Inequality* (OUP 2003), 35–39.

[21] For discussion, see Paul B Miller, 'Conscience and Justice in Equity' (2020) 21 Jerus Rev Leg Stud, 37, and H Dagan and I Samet, 'Express Trust: The Dark Horse of the Liberal Property Regime' in this book (hereafter Dagan and Samet, 'Dark Horse').

[22] As emphasised by Sitkoff, 'Freedom of Disposition' (n 1) 653 ('the trust implements the principle of freedom of disposition by projecting the donor's will across time').

[23] ibid 658 ('By making a transfer in trust rather than outright, a settlor ensures that the property will be managed and distributed in accordance with his or her wishes as expressed in the terms of the trust rather than the whims of the beneficiaries').

[24] Adam J Hirsch and William KS Wang, 'A Qualitative Theory of the Dead Hand' (1992) 68 Indiana LJ 1, 5 ('The testator's right to control property along the plane of time builds on a more essential right—namely, her right to bequeath property outright to beneficiaries') (hereafter Hirsch and Wang, 'Dead Hand').

[25] See Sitkoff, 'Freedom of Disposition' (n 1); see also Restatement (Third) of Property: Wills and Other Donative Transfers § 10.1 cmt. a (2003) ('The organizing principle of the American law of donative transfers is freedom of disposition').

[26] Sitkoff, 'Freedom of Disposition' (n 1).

enjoy wide freedom in making an effective disposition though an express trust due to the relaxation of formalities. While most states have a writing requirement, contemporaneous witness and notarisation requirements have been foregone in many jurisdictions. Provided that the three certainties obtain,[27] the question whether a disposition was made by way of trust or otherwise is treated as one of deciphering the testator's actual, objectively manifested, intention.[28] In turn, testators enjoy wide freedom in determining which property to dispose of, to whom, when, and in what proportions. Many states grant surviving spouses a substantial 'forced share', but 'in the American legal tradition a surviving child has no rights to a mandatory share'.[29] American law thus tolerates disinheritance of dependents with a morally good claim to support.[30]

American law tracks that of other jurisdictions in permitting donative trusts for purposes only where they are charitable.[31] But its conception of charity is wider and realisation of settlor intention is lent aid by courts' more willing invocation of the *cy près* doctrine.[32]

Furthermore, freedom of disposition undergirds routine administration by trustees as well as judicial supervision and review. Evidence of settlor intention does not exhaust discretion wielded by trustees or judges, but it is the lodestar according to which that discretion is exercised and evaluated. A trustee is to focus first and foremost on settlor intention in interpreting and acting on her mandate.[33] A judge asked to provide direction to a trustee or to resolve a claim of misuse of trust powers will, in turn, be guided by textual and other evidence of settlor intention.

Given that several leading criticisms of testamentary freedom are more pointed in respect of trusts by virtue of their potentially long duration, it is also notable that many American states have abolished or attenuated the rule against perpetuities.[34] These reforms prolong the impact of testamentary dispositions on beneficiaries and third parties while significantly extending the power of testators to shape the lives of others by settling property on trust.

This brief summary omits much yet suffices to establish two things: first, that testamentary freedom in American law is extraordinarily broad, and second, and partly in consequence of its breadth, that it undergirds much trust law and practice.

[27] Certainty of intention, objects, and subject matter.

[28] Restatement (Third) of Prop.: Donative Transfers § 10.1 (2003) ('[The] donor's intention is given effect to the maximum extent allowed by law').

[29] Sitkoff, 'Freedom of Disposition' (n 1) 657.

[30] Adam J Hirsch, 'Freedom of Testation / Freedom of Contract' (2011) 95 Minn L Rev 2180, 2233 ('In most countries, bequests to children are compulsory. Not so in the vast majority of American states, where parents remain free to disinherit children, even while they are minors') (hereafter Hirsch, 'Freedom of Testation').

[31] Subject to limited exceptions. See Richard Ausness, 'Non-Charitable Purpose Trusts: Past, Present, and Future' (2016) 51 Real Property, Trusts and Estates LJ 321.

[32] See generally: Eric G Pearson, 'Reforming the Reform of the Cy Pres Doctrine: A Proposal to Protect Testator Intent' (2006) 90 Marquette L Rev 127; Richard Hyland, *Gifts: A Study in Comparative Law* (OUP 2009).

[33] Sitkoff, 'Freedom of Disposition' (n 1) 659.

[34] David Horton, 'Testation and Speech' (2012) 101 Georgetown LJ 61, 63–64 ('American testators and settlors ... enjoy broad dead-hand control ... In fact, over the course of the last two decades, dead-hand power has expanded dramatically, as twenty-one jurisdictions have abolished the Rule Against Perpetuities ... Settlors in these states can now write their estate plans on a canvas the size of eternity') (hereafter Horton, 'Testation and Speech').

Testamentary freedom is subject to some important limitations. But in elevating the limitations,[35] one misses the policy of the law and the opportunity to consider whether it is sound. Especially in respect of American law, there is a persistent gap between the law and scholarly wisdom as to its morality. This, in itself, is puzzling. The demerits of testamentary freedom have been presented forcefully. But what moral case has been, or might be, made for it?

III. Leading Justifications

As noted earlier, leading defences of testamentary freedom are half-hearted or implausible. Some offer explanation rather than justification, simply reframing or restating the freedom and its entailments (eg increased autonomy for owners). Others offer justifications but the latter are unfocused in their normative implications or insufficiently robust to bear the burden of justifying wide testamentary freedom. These weaknesses make half-hearted presentation rational. But they also raise the stakes for the development of an alternative account of the value of testamentary freedom.

A. From Property (and Natural Right)

Perhaps the most common of arguments offered in justification of testamentary freedom are those rooted in convention, and, more specifically, the conventional juridical constitution of private ownership.[36] Appeals to convention are, for example, reflected in accounts emphasising that testamentary freedom has been recognised for centuries,[37] and in prominent conceptual analyses of private ownership, such as that of Tony Honoré, who claimed that ownership includes incidents of transmissibility and absence of term.[38]

Appeals to testamentary freedom as conventional are probably meant to carry the further implication that the convention is *morally sound*. But appeals to convention are placeholders and not substitutes for argument.[39]

[35] See Melanie Leslie, 'The Myth of Testamentary Freedom' (1996) 38 Arizona L Rev 235.

[36] Most famously, Hugo Grotius, *De Jure Belli Ac Pacis Libre Tres* 265 (Francis W Kelsey tr, Legal Classics 1925); John Stuart Mill, 'Principles of Political Economy' in JM Robson (ed), *The Collected Works of John Stuart Mill*, vol II (Liberty Fund 2006) 218 (asserting that 'the ownership of a thing cannot be looked upon as complete without the power of bestowing it, at death or during life, at the owner's pleasure'). For a contemporary restatement, see Richard A Epstein, 'Past and Future: The Temporal Dimension in the Law of Property' (1986) 64 Washington U L Rev 667, 696–97 (arguing that the integrity of the system of private property in land turns on recognition of 'absolute ownership of infinite duration', which implies in 'the owner of property unfettered discretion in choosing his successor in title').

[37] *Hodel v Irving*, 481 US 704, 716 (1987) (per Justice O'Connor, for the majority 'In one form or another, the right to pass on property—to one's family in particular—has been part of the Anglo-American legal system since feudal times'). Whether this is true is another matter. See Dainow, 'Testamentary Freedom in England' (n 2) 339–44, and his conclusion, at 339 that 'traditional freedom of testation is not an immemorial practice'.

[38] AM Honoré, 'Ownership' in AG Guest (ed), *Oxford Essays in Jurisprudence* (OUP 1961) 107, 120–22. For criticism of Honoré, see Robert Lamb, 'The Power to Bequeath' (2014) 33 Law and Phil 629, 630.

[39] As emphasised by Harris (n 9) 125 (criticising 'dogmatic insistence on a supposedly uncontestable and supra-temporal concept of ownership').

An alternative is to argue that freedom of testation is grounded in considerations of natural right or that it is justified derivatively by moral considerations that support private ownership.[40] The most influential argument of this sort was supplied by John Locke.[41] Locke defended an abridged freedom of testation as entailed by a labour/desert-based natural right to private property. Just as one has a natural right to the exclusive use and enjoyment of resources with which one has mixed one's labour, so too, Locke claimed, one has a right to determine whether, when, how, and to whom to dispose of one's property, subject to the countervailing right of dependent children to inherit property needed for their survival and reasonable maintenance.[42]

The difficulties with Locke's argument are well known. Independently of those that afflict his labour/desert-based account of natural rights to private property generally[43] are problems in extending those arguments to the testamentary disposition of *certain* kinds of property (eg investment funds), and receipt by a beneficiary of *all* kinds of property, where one, the other, or both of the testator and beneficiary have neither toiled nor troubled.

It might be telling that few since Locke have argued for a natural right to testamentary freedom. Blackstone, for instance, flatly denied that testamentary freedom has a basis in natural law.[44] He treated it as a matter of artificial right, being founded on considerations of public convenience,[45] and hence as severable—conceptually and normatively—from the idea of ownership.

[40] Hirsch and Wang, 'Dead Hand' (n 24) 6 ('The traditional rationales for testamentary freedom are as varied as they are controversial. Perhaps the oldest is the notion that testators have a natural right to bequeath'). Waldron suggests that Locke was close to contradiction in endorsing both wide testamentary freedom *and* a right to inheritance in children because he assumed that wide powers of disposition inhere in the idea of private property. Jeremy Waldron, 'Locke's Account of Inheritance and Bequest' (1981) 19 J Hist Phil 39, 44 ('What explanation ... can be given for Locke's ranking bequest ahead of inheritance ... ? One possible explanation is that Locke ... regarded the right of bequest as part of the very idea of property') (hereafter Waldron, 'Locke's Account').

[41] For commentary, see David P Gauthier, 'The Role of Inheritance in Locke's Political Theory' (1966) 32 Can J Econ and Pol Sci 38; Waldron ibid; and Leslie Kendrick, 'The Lockean Rights of Bequest and Inheritance' (2011) 17 Leg Theory 145.

[42] John Locke, 'First Treatise of Government' in Peter Laslett (ed), *Two Treatises of Government by John Locke* (CUP 1988), para 87 ('But if anyone had began and made himself property in any particular thing ... that thing, that possession, if he dispos'd not otherwise of it by his positive Grant, descended Naturally to his Children, and they had a right to succeed to it, and possess it'); John Locke, 'Second Treatise of Government', ibid para 190 ('Every man is born with a double right: first, a right of freedom to his person ... Secondly, a right, before any other man, to inherit, with his brethren, his father's goods'). The right of inheritance is a right to the necessaries beyond which, Locke believed, testators enjoy wide testamentary freedom. ibid para 65 ('A Father may dispose of his own Possessions as he pleases, when his Children are out of danger of perishing for want').

[43] Waldron, 'Locke's Account' (n 40) 39–40 ('If a right of property is essentially *earned* by an individual, then one would expect that right to die with the man who earned it. To vest the earner's right in somebody else as a result of his death would amount to the creation of an *unearned* right of property ... At death, according to the purest version of this kind of theory, there should be no succession, no bequest, no inheritance').

[44] '[N]aturally speaking ... if [one] had a right to dispose of his acquisitions a moment beyond his life, he would also have a right to their disposal for a million of ages after him; which would be highly absurd and inconvenient'. William Blackstone, *Commentaries on the Laws of England* (UChicago Press 2016) vol II, 10.

[45] 'We are apt to conceive at first view that it has nature on its side; yet we often mistake for nature what we find established by long and inveterate custom. It is certainly a wise and effectual, but clearly a political, establishment; since the permanent right of property, vested in the ancestor himself, was no natural, but merely a civil right'. ibid 11.

B. From Autonomy

Another leading argument is that wide testamentary freedom is defensible on the basis of the value of autonomy. This strategy seems promising given that we're concerned with the justification of a particular kind of freedom enabled by law. One might reasonably think that the moral value of autonomy, to the extent that it is served by testamentary freedom, is sufficient also to ground it.[46]

Autonomy-based arguments vary, but they include observations and/or claims that testamentary freedom: enhances the scope of authority and thus freedom enjoyed by owners in pursuing their ends through ownership of property; generates a limited but existentially important measure of control for people facing their own mortality; enables self-authorship through identification with persons or causes supported by benefaction; and is inherently valuable insofar as testamentary dispositions are richly expressive acts.[47]

It is not for nothing that most think first of autonomy when considering how to defend testamentary freedom. However, many appeals to autonomy provide, at most, weak support for testamentary freedom. That is because they simply assume the moral value of autonomy and think of it as singular and inherent (ie as the value of autonomy as such) and not as a complex of inherent and derivative values (the latter being activities, states of being, relationships, and other goods of objective moral value advanced *through* autonomous choice). Perhaps in consequence, arguments from autonomy have been wanting. Indeed, some invoke autonomy without making a recognisable argument. For instance, from the observation that testamentary freedom enhances autonomy (ie of owners), one is invited to conclude that the overall moral good of testamentary freedom is that it enhances autonomy.[48] The latter is a contestable normative claim, the former an observation about something obvious.

There are other difficulties. One is the difficulty of establishing that people have autonomy interests that survive their death, and hence can support laws enabling choices that take effect post-mortem and that significantly impact others. It is precisely this difficulty that makes freedom of disposition more controversial relative to testamentary dispositions than it is for *inter vivos* dispositions. We may alight upon good moral reasons for laws that enable testamentary freedom, but it is odd to think that those reasons are entailments of autonomy, understood as something inherently and

[46] See Dagan and Samet, 'Dark Horse' (n 21) [ms] 5 ('The trust is autonomy-enhancing because it dramatically increases the settlor's scope of options') and at 17 (claiming that the express trust is a 'residual category allowing autonomous individuals to "invent" their own private forms of interaction').

[47] Horton, 'Testation and Speech' (n 34) 65–66 ('Testators and settlors do not merely arrange for their possessions to be managed and distributed after they die. They do something else: they make a statement. Testation is a form of speech ... By rewarding some people, snubbing others, and attaching conditions to their bequests, they offer a final assessment of their lives, their loved ones, and the world').

[48] ibid 66 ('recognizing testation's expressive function militates against current efforts to narrow the scope of testamentary autonomy').

singularly valuable. It is odd because the dead are not autonomous embodied beings when their choices are to be given effect.[49]

Another difficulty is that of showing that appeals to autonomy are capable of justifying freedom of testamentary disposition in view of the ways in which it is customarily exercised. Consider the argument that testamentary freedom advances autonomy interests in expression. David Horton has said that we should treat instruments like wills as richly expressive media for statements by testators about the persons and causes that matter to them, whether by virtue of inclusion or exclusion from a benefaction.[50]

Now, it is certainly true that testamentary dispositions are expressive acts.[51] But the same may be said of most legally recognised intentional actions, whether they be words or deeds. One is taken to own, in the sense of having authored, one's intentional action for the law's purposes:[52] thus are social narratives developed through the attribution of intended meaning to all manner of intentional conduct. Of course, intentional actions vary significantly in the extent to which an actor can be reasonably understood to have specifically intended certain meanings. And they vary, too, in terms of what—if anything—we intend to accomplish through them. Some are purely expressive (eg writing a poem or love letter). Others are performatively expressive; that is, they count as recognised ways of *doing something* (eg whistling for a taxi). One question about the viability of Horton's argument is whether the expressive dimension of testamentary freedom is essential or incidental to its justification. But another, more basic, question goes to the kind of expressive act testamentary freedom implicates. Answering the latter question enables one to respond to the former. The words and other intentional actions of testators in exercising testamentary freedom are predominantly *performative*. They are meant to accomplish that which the freedom enables: legally effective disposition. Rarely are the same actions undertaken in a *purely expressive* manner (eg to convey love, approval, care, or, conversely, animus). And that is borne out by Horton's own observations.[53] Dispositions are primarily made through unadorned—yet, crucially for performative expression, predictably effective—boilerplate.[54] It is very infrequent that one finds contextualising text that has no legal (performative) effect but is instead in the nature of a personal communication to persons within and/or excluded by the disposition.

How, then, ought one to think about the imperative of attending to the expressive acts of testators? Not as Horton would have it. As a matter of law, we attend to the testator's *performative* utterances by treating them as presumptively authoritative

[49] 'Freedom of contract and of gift-giving fit snugly within a libertarian ethic, but freedom of testation, narrowly defined, carries that ethic into new existential territory: Must we respect persons' autonomy embodied in a last will, even after they have become *dis*embodied?': Hirsch, 'Freedom of Testation' (n 30) 2186.

[50] Horton, 'Testation and Speech' (n 34). See also Lamb (n 38) 647.

[51] As Horton puts it, testators' 'choices' may be 'seen as statements'. ibid 78.

[52] One is also often made to 'own' (in the sense of being made to take responsibility for) one's unintentional acts, but for different reasons.

[53] Horton, 'Testation and Speech' (n 34) 81 (acknowledging that 'the vast majority of testamentary instruments do not openly communicate the testator's or settlor's views') and at 88 ('Admittedly, many testators and settlors reveal little in their estate plans').

[54] ibid 85 ('most testamentary instruments are bleached clean of an owner's actual voice').

indication of their intentions for a disposition. That is, we attend to them by rendering them performatively effective. We don't, as lawyers, look beyond semantics germane to legal function. In this, wills and trusts are no more morally significant as mechanisms for expression than are contracts, consent forms, and other legal instruments. These instruments are valuable not in what they allow us to *say to one another* but in what they enable us to *do* (eg exercise legal capacities, incur new obligations, and waive or insist upon our rights). When one considers this and the existence of other means through which testators can make purely expressive 'final statements', it is difficult to believe that expressive autonomy makes an appreciable contribution to the justification of testamentary freedom.

C. From Social Utility

Almost as common as the above two lines of argument—and sharing a tendency to blur descriptive and normative claims—are suggestions that wide testamentary freedom is justified on the basis of social utility.[55] These suggestions are prevalent in theoretical economic analysis of law, but are also evocative of a casual consequentialism that characterises much contemporary legal thought.

One approach is to infer justification from general observations about how investment savings, stimulated by the prospect of exercising testamentary freedom, contribute to prosperity through the virtuous cycle of the ready supply of capital, socially and economically productive use of capital, and robust long-term returns on investment. Observations about what *is* usually the case economically result in impressionistic but intuitive suggestions about what *ought* to be the case for laws that undergird markets. In this context, one might begin with the observation that investment (on the order of trillions of dollars, in the United States) of personal savings in publicly traded securities is a pillar of capitalism and associated welfare advantages. Add the observation that investment savings accounts are a very substantial class of assets subject to testamentary disposition, with many testators accumulating savings with mind to plans for testamentary disposition. And consider the inference that wide testamentary freedom incentivises savings significantly and does so independently of other incentives, increasing the likelihood, frequency, and sum of savings invested, in turn increasing substantially the capital available for productive use in a market economy.[56] If one is disposed to casual consequentialism on normative issues, it might (setting, with equal casualness, Hume's dictum that one cannot derive evaluative conclusions from correct descriptive statements) be thought a very short leap to the normative

55 For an overview, see Daniel B Kelly, 'Restricting Testamentary Freedom: Ex Ante versus Ex Post Justifications' (2013) 82 Fordham L Rev 1125, 1127–28.

56 Hirsch and Wang, 'Dead Hand' (n 24) 7–8 ('One argument ... holds that freedom of testation creates an incentive to industry and saving ... persons derive satisfaction out of bequeathing property to others. To the extent that lawmakers deny persons the opportunity to bequeath freely, the subjective value of property will drop, for one of its potential uses will have disappeared. As a result, thwarted testators will choose to accumulate less property, and the total stock of existing wealth at any given time will shrink').

inference that wide freedom of testamentary disposition is justified in that it promotes social utility.

Another line of argument holds that testamentary freedom advances social utility by enabling effective private provision for dependents and charitable causes. Both objects will, absent adequate private provision, either be unmet or a drain on the public purse. If the dependents of a decedent are not provided for, assuming no one voluntary undertakes the burden of private provision, it will often fall upon the government to provide for dependents through guardianship and/or social welfare programmes.[57] In turn, if charities were precluded from estate gifts they would be left to rely on (ordinarily, more modest) *inter vivos* donations, limiting their ability to advance causes of public benefit with any deficiency to be met by public provision. Given that private provision for dependents and charities minimises public expenditures and can be more efficient than public provision, considerations of social utility that bear on its *exercise* are thought to support wide testamentary freedom independently of those noted immediately above that bear on the incentive effects of its *anticipated* exercise.

Of the four leading justifications for testamentary freedom, arguments from social utility provide it with its strongest support. It is difficult to deny the moral importance of considerations of social utility even if one rejects the notion that the principle of utility is a grundnorm. Likewise, the plausibility of speculation about positive contributions to social utility associated with the anticipation and exercise of testamentary freedom. But how well have these arguments fared under the critic's torchlight? Not well, it turns out.

It cannot help that contemporary proponents of arguments from social utility find themselves opposite of Bentham *and* Mill. Bentham wrote critically of testamentary freedom and advocated its curtailment, especially in respect of dispositions beyond the family.[58] Mill was scarcely less critical, though he favoured limitation through inheritance taxes and redistribution.[59] Both worried about the disutility of the incentive effects of inheritance on heirs (eg the likelihood that large bequests generate sloth, waste, conflict, and unhappiness).

There are other difficulties, too. The first is that arguments from social utility are largely speculative: most rely on a complex set of empirical assertions that, while plausible, have not been established.[60] So, for example, we simply don't know to what extent wide testamentary freedom incentivises savings, or how it stacks up relative to other incentives to save (eg economic security or retirement). We don't know which

[57] As observed by Dainow, 'Testamentary Freedom in England' (n 2) 337 (explaining that the passage of the 1938 Inheritance (Family Provision) Act in England marked 'the first breach in the doctrine that a testator may, through mere caprice, turn loose his dependents upon the public for support').

[58] Jeremy Bentham, 'Supply Without Burthen. Escheat Vice Taxation' in W Stark (ed), *Jeremy Bentham's Economic Writings* (Allen and Unwin 1952).

[59] Cappelen and Pedersen, 'Just Wealth Transfer Taxation' (n 10) 318.

[60] For example, assertions about the positive incentive effects of testamentary freedom on savings and investment behaviour by testators ignore the negative incentive effects of inheritance on heirs. Hirsch, 'Freedom of Testation' (n 30) 2183 n 7 (2011) (noting that '[e]conomic studies have found that a large fraction (possibly in the range of 80 percent) of household wealth in the United States traces to gifts and inheritances, as opposed to participation in the labor economy').

curtailments of testamentary freedom would undermine its positive incentive effects on investment, and to what extent. We don't know whether and to what extent abolition or curtailment of testamentary freedom would increase costs of public provision for dependents and charitable causes, partly because of counterfactual problems: we don't know whether and to what extent individuals would make use of other avenues of private provision (eg insurance and *inter vivos* disposition) or whether, absent wide testamentary freedom, novel informal or formal mechanisms might develop in response to unmet social needs. In turn, bearing in mind concerns about the disutility of inheritance, we don't know the extent to which these risks are offset by gains in social utility. In short, the justificatory power of arguments from social utility turns on a complex set of unproven factual assumptions about existing and counterfactual scenarios and the impact of the same on owners' decisions about the acquisition, investment, use, and disposition of their property. Absent such evidence, their justificatory power is thus weak.

The second problem is that arguments from social utility overclaim. What we need are arguments for wide testamentary freedom. What we have to hand falls short. So, for example, arguments pointing to the incentive effects of testamentary freedom on investment ignore the fact that testamentary freedom is not cabined by asset class. It extends to real property and chattel as well as to intangible property. Likewise, arguments pointing to savings on public expenditures realised through private provision for dependents ignore the fact that wide testamentary freedom permits the disinheritance of dependents and provision for those without need. As Bentham and Mill recognised, the breadth of testamentary freedom makes it paradoxical, if not objectionable, as a means by which to advance social welfare.

D. From Moral Obligation

At least since Locke, another popular line of argument seeks to ground testamentary freedom in a moral obligation of provision for dependent family members.[61] This strategy is importantly different from the argument about provision grounded in considerations of social utility. The latter argument focuses on the aggregate welfare advantages of private provision. The argument from the obligation of provision is, by contrast, rooted in the deontic morality of partiality and care in family relationships.[62]

[61] But see Waldron, 'Locke's Account' (n 40) 44 ('[I]s there any reason to suppose that [a parent] should be able to alienate his property from his family deliberately by gift or bequest? Surely the answer must be no. The child's title to the father's property is not a mere privilege dependent on the will of the father, but a *right* [quoting Locke]: "For Children being by the course of Nature, born weak, and unable to provide for themselves, they have by the appointment of God himself, who hath thus ordered the course of nature, a Right to be nourish'd and maintained by their Parents ... "'). See also Rousseau, 'Discourse on Political Economy' (n 7) 263 ('The spirit of these laws [enabling testamentary freedom] ... is that from father to son, and from relation to relation, the goods of a family should go as little out of it and be as little alienated as possible').

[62] Hirsch, 'Freedom of Testation' (n 30) 2189 ('only the stoniest of hearts views an estate plan exclusively as a medium of exchange'). Blumenthal suggests that American lawyers of the founding generation were confident that testamentary freedom would be exercised in cognizance of obligations of family provision. Susanna L Blumenthal, 'The Deviance of the Will: Policing the Bounds of Testamentary Freedom in Nineteenth Century America' (2006) 119 Harvard L Rev 959, 970–76 (hereafter Blumenthal, 'Deviance of the Will').

For the sake of simplicity, we shall assume that the obligation of provision extends to meeting the reasonable needs of a testator's dependents. On this relatively narrow conception of the obligation, testamentary freedom of disposition is justified insofar as it enables one to recognise and to meet one's obligation to satisfy the needs of dependents (persons for whom one is subject to assumed or imposed burdens of care).

Several things may be said in favour of this strategy of argument. The first is that it is plausible that there is a moral obligation of provision for dependents. The second is that testamentary disposition is one way in this obligation can be discharged in the face of an eventuality that imperils dependents. The third is that it is consonant with the argument from social utility, and so can draw strength from it. A fourth observation is that the first two points—on the existence of the obligation and possibility of it being discharged through testamentary disposition—have shaped and are reflected in contemporary law and policy.[63] Indeed, it is in respect of a norm of family provision that benefactions are conventionally characterised as customary or deviant, respectively.[64]

For these reasons, we might appear to have arrived at last at a robust basis of justification for wide testamentary freedom. Most testamentary dispositions are made in favour of immediate family members, and many have thought that the moral basis of enabling law is found in the obligation of provision. So far, so good. But it is not good enough. The apparent strengths of the argument are betrayed by the breadth of testamentary freedom. For instance, the argument does not support recognition of freedom of disposition in testators who do not have dependents for whom to provide. Nor does it support freedom in selection of beneficiaries and specification of their shares (as noted earlier, under American law a testator can blithely ignore obligations of provision for dependent children by disinheriting them and/or by making grossly unequal provision for dependents who are equal in moral desert). There is also the difficulty that testators are free to give amounts that grossly exceed the needs of their beneficiaries, however liberally defined. Finally, the argument ignores charitable bequests and testators' freedom to rank morally supererogatory ends above morally obligatory ones. Put simply, wide freedom of testamentary disposition enables testators to ignore, much as it enables them to meet, obligations of provision.

IV. A Fresh Start

To this point, we've canvassed leading defences of testamentary freedom and found each hobbled by significant deficiencies. I leave open the possibility that testamentary freedom might be unjustifiable. But I don't think that we should assume that, simply because familiar arguments are unavailing. Instead, we might reconsider our approach. If an alternative identifies a genuinely robust basis of justification for testamentary

[63] Dainow, 'Testamentary Freedom in England' (n 2) 347.

[64] See generally: Blumenthal, 'Deviance of the Will' (n 62). See also Hedlund, 'Testamentary Freedom' (n 2) 59 ('The courts have always been more skeptical of the validity of wills that disinherit family; for instance, testamentary capacity is only presumed if the will "appears rational". If not, the executor must prove capacity').

freedom, we will be better positioned to consider how far it reaches in future work. I'll sketch such an alternative in what follows.

I begin by revising our framing of the problem. I believe that efforts to unearth and explain the moral value of wide testamentary freedom have been bedevilled by preoccupation with its excesses; ie with practices of testamentary choice that are deviant[65] and/or pernicious.[66] Malicious or neglectful disinheritance are examples, as are bequests aimed at entrenching dynastic wealth or emblematic of invidious discrimination. Because these important but exceptional practices are hard to justify, so too, it is supposed, is the freedom that underlies them. The latter supposition is fallacious. But it is understandable if one's thinking about the morality of freedom is skewed by preoccupation with cases that test its limits.

In what follows, I will approach our problem differently, relying on a methodological device that is familiar in general jurisprudence. The device is that of orienting one's analysis of law by attending to the *focal* moral and legal senses of legal concepts (including the concept of law as such) and to *typical* social practices in which reliance is placed on these concepts.[67] The motivation for use of the device is the recognition that one is more likely to develop a sound understanding of legal concepts and associated practices, in positive and in normative terms, if one attends first to what is focal and typical and only later to what is peripheral and deviant. Deployed in this context, our approach to the problem of justifying wide testamentary freedom will require that we determine its focal conceptualisation and typical exercise.

Briefly, I suggest that the focal meaning of testamentary freedom is that which treats it and associated legal mechanisms and concepts (eg donative intention, delivery, and acceptance) as a species of *gift*, shaped by the morality of a wider genera of gift relationships. On this view, testamentary freedom is, as a matter of legal semantics, necessarily concerned with—being enabled by—the effectuation of transfers upon death animated by *bona fide* donative intention (ie an intention to convey property to another without consideration and for their benefit).[68] Put otherwise, the focal moral sense of testamentary freedom is that which treats it as a matter of the freedom to make legally effective gifts of property that will take effect upon death, consistent with one's donative intentions (the latter being directed, in the main, to the subject matter, objects, time of vesting, and lawful conditions upon conveyance of alienable interests). On this view, testamentary gifts are a subspecies of legal gift, belonging within the genus of gift relationships. The genus includes formal and informal gift exchange, associated mechanisms and rituals, and a shifting complex of legal, social, and moral norms, and associated enabling rules or practices. And, significantly, the focal moral sense that joins species (testamentary gift, made effective by law) with genus (gift) is moderately

[65] Deviant empirically, relative to customary practice, and normatively, relative to morally salubrious testamentary choice.

[66] Blumenthal, 'Deviance of the Will' (n 62) 964.

[67] See John Finnis, 'Drawing on Aristotle', in *Natural Law and Natural Rights* (OUP 1980), 9.

[68] Notice that while donative intention, relational reciprocity (delivery and acceptance), and property (ie the requirement that one has a transmissible interest in property) are constitutive elements of the legal concept of a gift, economic value is not.

controlling—semantically and normatively—of our invocation of normative concepts (eg laws enabling gift-giving, and associated social rites and rituals laden with expectations in relation to gift-giving and gift-receipt).[69] That sense is one which treats gift-giving as a socially mediated ritual whereby a token of sentimental value, money, or thing with market value is freely given to another person or cause out of recognition or affection for the person or identification with a cause, or to provide for a person or segment of the public, whether out of duty or benevolence.

Typical practice in the exercise of testamentary freedom of disposition comports well with its focal moral sense. Testamentary freedom is predominantly exercised by way of dispositions for the benefit of the decedent's surviving family members, intended as gifts. Less common, but still typical, are dispositions for charitable causes, and these dispositions are likewise intended and treated as gifts. The economic value of estates subject to disposition, while significant, is not as high as one might expect. The median values of estates devolved by inheritance (intestacy or will) and by trust in the United States are $76,200 and $92,700.[70] These figures—reflecting the relatively modest means of middle-class Americans—provide a useful benchmark by which to assess the significance of testamentary gifts for testators relative to their likely level of economic security and wherewithal to make substantial gifts by *inter vivos* disposition. They are also a useful corrective to those who associate testamentary freedom with disposition of high-value estates by the wealthy.

Relative to the focal moral sense of testamentary freedom and the practices that typify its exercise, deviant benefactions—including those that entail disinheritance of dependents—are deviant empirically and normatively.[71] The same is true of so-called 'eccentric' benefactions: those that, though not harmful, are of questionable benefit to anyone other than the testator.[72] While tolerated as valid, these dispositions are not 'gifts' in a focal or conventional sense. They are striking precisely because they are difficult to square with the focal moral and legal sense of testamentary disposition.

Again, an advantage of attending to focal sense is that it enables one to determine how legal concepts are to be understood by dint of a regulative semantics. As deployed here, it directs attention to questions like (a) whether informal gift relationships have a morality that informs or is otherwise apt to that of formal legal gift-giving; (b) whether the morality of testamentary gift-giving differs substantially from that of lifetime gift-giving and if so, how and why; and (c) whether, in light of these considerations and others, we have dispositive (sound and sufficient) moral reasons for laws enabling testamentary disposition.

[69] I say *moderately* in recognition that semantics and normativity are dynamic, and that semantical analysis of legal concepts must allow for ambiguity and imprecision in use where they obtain.

[70] Board of Governors of the Federal Reserve System, *Survey of Consumer Finances* (2019), online: https://www.federalreserve.gov/econres/scfindex.htm. Note that the former figure represents the median value of inheritances for families in which both parents are without a college degree; the latter is the median for families in which at least one parent has a college degree.

[71] Blumenthal, 'Deviance of the Will' (n 62).

[72] ibid 1016: 'Now in the pantheon of "eccentric" but capable testators was Jeremy Bentham, who directed that his body 'be embalmed and kept stuffed in a chair in one of his old apartments"'.

I have suggested that this way of framing the problem of justifying testamentary freedom permits a fresh response to it. In what follows, I develop elements of that response, examining the value of the states of being, of modes of relating, and of goods realised for, or in relation to, others through giving testamentary gifts, and hence, through the enjoyment and exercise of testamentary freedom.

A. Expressing Moral Motivation

To the extent that one is concerned with the morality of choice, one is led naturally to consider intentional and motivational elements of choice. *Intention* is a matter of a choice being purposeful; ie, reflecting conscious, goal-directed, action.[73] *Motivation* is a matter of nature and effect of practical reasons and other causal factors (eg emotions, reactive attitudes, manias) on deliberation and choice. *Moral motivation*, in turn, is a matter of the practical reasonableness of one's choices bearing in mind the practical reasons for which one acted relative to those for which one might and ought to have acted. A concern for morally sound motivation on the part of an actor is one of acting for the right reasons and/or with defensible moral emotions or attitudes; a concern for morally sound motivation on the part of those scrutinising the choices of others is one of determining how they were motivated and whether apparent or likely motivations were proper.

All choice, other than those that which is instinctive, is presumed to be motivated. But deciphering motivation, including moral motivation, is often difficult despite our willingness to infer it from observable behaviour; intentions are more readily communicated though reliable signals of conscious choice.

It is sometimes assumed that, to the extent that the law is concerned with the morality of choice (rather than, say, of outcomes), it is concerned with that of intention. In respect of duty-imposing rules, it shows concern for the morality of intention where intention is an element of fault in defining conditions of breach. In respect of power-conferring rules, it shows concern for the morality of intention by broadening the ambit of intentional choice or by providing new avenues for the same. We are here concerned with power-conferring laws that enable legally effective donative disposition and, accordingly, emphasise donative intention. Thus, an assumption that the law is concerned with the morality of intention and that it displays that concern by broadening the scope for choice enjoyed by owners dovetails with the argument from autonomy discussed in Part II.B; the assumption generates a supposition that morality of choice is exclusively one of determining the extent of respect for the intentions of owners in testamentary dispositions.

In some contexts, the morality of choice pertinent to law is one of intention to the exclusion of motivation. But this is not one of those contexts. Understood in light of its focal moral sense, the morality of testamentary choice encompasses intention *and*

[73] Michael Bratman, *Intentions, Plans and Practical Reason* (HUP 1987).

motivation. Laws that enable testamentary freedom enlarge the scope for intentional choice, but moral reasons for respecting intentional choice *for its own sake* extend only as far as the arguments from autonomy canvassed in Part II.B reach. Remember that those arguments assume that the moral value of autonomy is singular and inherent, being independent of values realised through choice. This stands in contrast with a view that treats the morality of autonomy as complex and contingent, being dependent on the value of particular choices made and what those choices reflect about the moral commitments and character of the chooser.

In suggesting that the morality of testamentary freedom extends beyond intention, encompassing motivation, I'm gesturing towards the latter, richer and more resourceful, and also more demanding, view of the moral salience of autonomous action. On this view, the morality of testamentary freedom is partly a matter of supporting moral motivation in choices through which we provide for others. That is, it is a matter of enabling well-motivated choices that, being that they implicate gift-giving, are oriented towards the well-being of others (beneficiaries of testamentary gifts).

In what follows, I take it that testamentary freedom matters morally for testators in part because it enables them to effectively express morally sound motivations towards persons and causes favoured in a mechanism for testamentary disposition.

This comports with the focal moral sense of testamentary disposition as a species of donative transfer (gift-giving) premised on donative intent. If we are to make sense of dispositions *as gifts* and underlying intention as *donative*, we ought in turn to recognise that enabling law contemplates—and is justified in part by its effectiveness in eliciting—*benevolent* or *righteous* motivation. Benevolently motivated gift-giving encompasses dispositions that reflect animating reasons, attitudes or feelings of love, kindness, gratitude, charity, care, and concern towards one's chosen beneficiaries. Righteously motivated gift-giving encompasses reasoned recognition of a moral obligation to provide for one's beneficiaries. For many, economic insecurity or a fear of burdening loved ones means that testamentary disposition will be the only or most meaningful way in which to express moral motivations through gift-giving.

Against this line of argument, two objections might be raised. The first is that the law appears diffident about moral motivations because it does not compel them. The second is that the law appears indifferent about motivation generally in that it tolerates some immorally motivated gift-giving, including that reflecting *callous motivation* (eg calculative gift-giving) and *malevolent motivation* (gifts motivated by malice, spite, envy, jealousy, etc.).[74]

Neither objection is sound. The premise underlying the first is correct but the conclusion does not follow. It is true that the law does not, because it cannot, compel motivation; again, motivations are not readily amenable of proof to the law's standards, and are sometimes not even open to conscious awareness and control. But one cannot validly infer on this basis that the law is indifferent to, or diffident about, the morality

[74] See cases discussed in Blumenthal, 'Deviance of the Will' (n 62), including *Johnson v Moore's Heirs*, 11 Ky. (1 Litt.) 371 (1822) (testator disinherited immediate relatives out of 'antipathy' towards them).

of motivation. Rather, the law can, and in my view does, facilitate the expression of moral motivations indirectly by enabling conduct in which might reasonably expect such motivation to be prevalent.[75] That the second objection fails should be plain from our response to the first. The law, if it is to enable well-motivated conduct, must provide freedom of choice that can be differently motivated, tolerating a modest risk of amoral or immoral motivation for the sake of securing greater prospects for morally motivated choice. Admittedly, if testamentary dispositions were customarily poorly motivated, the focal moral sense of testamentary disposition as a species of gift relationship would be unsettled by virtue of a divergence between legally sanctioned practice and the moral complexion of gift-giving. But there is no reason to suppose that testamentary dispositions are usually poorly motivated. Furthermore, one can appreciate this *without* supposing that a sound justification of wide testamentary freedom should encompass dispositions that are deviant (immoral) in motivation as well as those that are normal (moral) in motivation.[76] The latter alone comport with and evince the practical point of gift-giving as action through which we demonstrate value and/or recognition of others through material or symbolic provision. Though it may be that the law can often only tame excesses of valid but deviant testamentary 'gifts', one should not suppose that enabling law is justifiable only if justificatory reasons can be supplied for deviant gifts, any more than one should suppose that justificatory reasons that support the institution of contract should also support unfair, exploitative, or otherwise deviant contracts. Rather, again, attention to focal meaning and customary use helps us to understand the moral point of our laws *and* what is wrong or pernicious in their misuse.

B. Practicing Virtue

Intention and motivation inform the moral significance of choice in relationships of responsibility. But choice is also morally significant in what it reveals of the identity and character of an agent. Choices, and what they tell of our intentions and motivations, are often treated as indicative (as the best or only evidence) of person's values and commitments. They are thus morally significant in what they reveal about one's virtue or vice and about the ends one values.

We begin with choice and virtue. We develop and practice virtue and vice through the decisions we make. Indeed, one school of thought on moral motivation—the personalist school—takes it that moral motivations are the product of virtue, immoral motivations of vice.[77] On this view, the relationship between the conventional morality of

[75] See Adam J Hirsch, *Bequests for Purposes: A Unified Theory* (1999) 56 Washington and Lee L Rev 33, 35 ('The beginnings of the purpose bequest in Great Britain lay in the Christian pursuit of piety') (hereafter Hirsch, 'Bequests for Purposes').

[76] *Contra* Hirsch, 'Freedom of Testation' (n 30) 2200 ('Nor is social disapproval of tyrannical conditions an adequate basis for intrusions by government upon freedom of transfer. As one court put the matter arrestingly, "a man's prejudices are a part of his liberty"') (citation omitted).

[77] Timothy Schroeder, Adina L Roskies, and Shaun Nichols, 'Moral Motivation' in John Doris (ed), *The Moral Psychology Handbook* (OUP 2012), cited and discussed by Connie Rosati, *Moral Motivation*, in Edward N Zalta

choice—understood as centred upon intention and motivation—and that of virtue is tight: we develop and practice virtue and vice primarily through our choices and, in turn, the moral upshots of our choices examined longitudinally are the best evidence of our having a particular virtue or suffering a particular vice. But one needn't assume such a tight relationship, excluding other factors that influence intention and motivation, in order to appreciate that character is formed and expressed partly through the choices we make. Our choices, viewed relative to virtue and vice, are expressions of moral identity: media through which we communicate values and thus constitute—and, at the same time, evaluate—ourselves as agents identifiable partly for the values we assert, ignore, or reject.

To the extent that our choices are media through which we forge and express moral motivation and so, in turn, form and practice virtue, we may infer that laws that directly facilitate well-motivated choice[78] thereby enable the practice of virtue. Testamentary freedom thus has added moral value to the extent that laws enabling the practice of benevolently or righteously motivated gift-giving present important opportunities for the practice of virtue.

If testamentary freedom enables the practice of virtue, it remains to identify specific virtues the practice of which might be supported by wills, trusts, and similar devices. As one might expect, they track the moral motivations identified earlier. They include the virtues of dutifulness and practical reasonableness, such as are manifested in righteously motivated choice. The dutiful person is one who can be counted upon to meet genuine moral obligations, and to the extent that this person is also possessed of the virtue of practical reasonableness; they do so through reasoned recognition of obligations as genuinely obligatory (ie as supported by decisive moral reasons for compliance). They also include the virtues of liberality (generosity), magnanimity, kindness, and friendship, such as are manifested in and reinforced by benevolently motivated choice. The generous, kind, magnanimous, and friendly person is one who can be counted on to have caring regard for others and concerned awareness of their needs and interests, manifested in altruistic conduct.

Testamentary freedom enables one to practice these virtues but it is, of course, not the *only* way in which virtue can be cultivated through gift-giving; the analysis provided here applies to donative disposition generally. However, testamentary dispositions hold a special significance, morally and existentially. They are our *final* dispositions and so final opportunity to recognise and provide for persons and causes that mattered to us during our lives. And they are the most economically substantial gifts most of us will make, given that most people lack the economic security and wherewithal to demonstrate equivalent liberality during their lifetimes.

(ed), *The Stanford Encyclopedia of Philosophy* (2016), online: https://plato.stanford.edu/archives/win2016/entries/moral-motivation/

[78] 'Directly' in that the kind of activity or relationship enabled by law is one that, by its nature, is a fulcrum for moral motivation. Gift-giving is one example; adoption, marriage, and the formation of charities are others. Each, in its focal moral sense, entails other-regarding commitment.

Against the notion that cultivation of virtue helps to justify wide testamentary freedom, one might imagine a couple of objections. The first is that testamentary freedom is so wide as to enable the practice of vice as well as virtue. The second emphasises iterated practice—or habit—in the cultivation of virtue. The objection, briefly, is that testamentary dispositions are one-off choices and so unlikely to be significant in cultivation of virtue.

As to the first objection, my reply echoes that developed in response to the objection about badly motivated dispositions. The law must tolerate vice within fairly wide margins if it is to elicit virtue. Here, the law can do no more than nudge; it cannot coerce virtue any more than it can stamp out vice or produce salubrious motivation. But this does not undermine the claim of alignment between the focal moral sense of gift-giving and the focal legal meaning of testamentary disposition. 'Gifts' given by the vicious in vice might sometimes be suffered as legally valid, but we needn't suppose that they exemplify testamentary disposition and so must be given moral justification if testamentary freedom is to be justified at all, much less that they render the law's relationship to virtue paradoxical. Rather, I am wont to say that a vicious testator whose dispositions evince vice has missed a redemptive opportunity supplied by law, his 'gift' standing as a gnarly monument of flawed character. In turn, I think we are inclined to view testamentary gifts that evince the virtue of the virtuous as final confirmation of good character.

As for the second objection, I note that testamentary decisions are not, like other one-off choices, mere ephemera. One cannot isolate these decisions from attendant contexts. It is true that testamentary dispositions take *effect* only once, after a testator's death. However, they usually loom significantly in testators' thoughts and self-concept during their lives. It is hence not unreasonable to think that the contemplation and planning for one's final dispositions figure significantly in the development and expression of personal character.

C. Realising Goods

A significant measure of the value of testamentary freedom lies in its enabling gift-giving as such, understood in its focal moral sense as involving donative transfers premised on moral motivation and inviting of the practice of virtue through recognition of, or provision for, other persons or other-regarding causes. But testamentary freedom is valuable also to the extent that its exercise contributes positively to human flourishing by securing, directly or indirectly, the realisation of human goods in beneficiaries of a benefaction.[79] That gifts can have moral value in promoting human flourishing should, in a way, be obvious given that gift-giving implicates mechanisms for mutual

[79] One might also argue that well-motivated benefactions contribute to the flourishing of the testator while alive, but I shall set that possibility to one side on the basis that the focal moral sense of gift relationships emphasises a gift's intended and actual impact on beneficiaries.

recognition and provision. But the importance of attending separately to the impact of gift-giving on flourishing is best understood in recognition that gifts sometimes fail to realise value in this way. Gifts occasionally reflect well on the giver's intention, motivation, and character and yet (whether due to insufficiency or problematic terms) prove morally trifling or worse in light of their intended purpose and actual impact. In short, some gifts fail to advance, or end up impeding, the flourishing of their recipients. These donative transfers are defective as gifts to the extent of these deficiencies.

In arguing that we need still to attend to the value of gifts in analysing the morality of testamentary freedom, I mean to emphasise *moral value* assessed in terms of the benefaction's predictable impact on the flourishing of the gift's recipients or ultimate beneficiaries. The moral and economic value of gifts can come apart: often, a gift of significant economic value will also, partly by virtue of that, contribute significantly to the flourishing of its recipient. But a gift might be of great, moderate, trifling or no moral value, whatever its economic value. The moral value of a gift, again, is a matter of its advancement of one or more goods—experiences, relationships, endowments, opportunities, or states of being conducive to human flourishing—and economic value is ordinarily only of derivative significance to the moral value of a gift (ie it is important to the extent incidental to the realisation of goods of inherent value).

There are, obviously, differences of opinion on which goods have moral value and how that value is made manifest in states suggestive of human flourishing. John Finnis, Martha Nussbaum, and Amartya Sen, among others, offer importantly different views on these questions. However, we need not brook any controversy here. There is broad consensus across classical and contemporary sources on the value of several goods—eg those of family, friendship, community, education, research, freedom of conscience and belief, of vocational fulfilment, leisure, the arts, health, and practical reasonableness—and this suffices for our purposes. That is, it suffices to establish that: (a) it is consistent with the focal moral sense of gifts as *benefactions*; (b) it is important (morally) that gifts generally *actually are* benefactions insofar as they realise moral value; (c) the moral value of a good is a matter of its contribution to flourishing; and (d) testamentary gifts promote flourishing, and so have moral value in this sense, insofar as they realise or enable the realisation of goods for beneficiaries.

In view of the above, testamentary freedom has moral value—and, likewise, express trusts and other legal mechanisms that facilitate it—to the extent that testamentary gifts enable testators to contribute to the flourishing of others. This underscores what should be obvious from lived moral experience. Many benefactions contribute to the realisation of goods of love and friendship, being a final, tangible remembrance of a loving bond and act of devotion. Most benefactions also advance goods the achievement or maintenance of which requires money or other resources. Consider gifts for maintenance of dependents, the terms of which usually permit or require that resources be devoted to meeting specific needs or supporting opportunities conducive to flourishing (eg provision for life's necessities and for education). These gifts, disbursed and used responsibly, are capable of securing the realisation of important goods for beneficiaries. And that capacity is part of their moral point.

I have, thus far, focused on testamentary gifts for persons. But much the same is true of gifts for purposes. Indeed, recognition of the potential of testamentary gifts to advance flourishing is evident from the history of charities law.[80] The law recognises as charitable those purposes that promise to enhance flourishing through provision, for instance, of education or relief from its expense, of aid to the poor, or of care for the sick. The moral value in gifts for charitable purposes lies in their contribution to the flourishing of members of the general public or a segment thereof.

In saying that testamentary freedom has moral value, in part, to the extent that it enables its bearer to provide effectively for the flourishing of others, I am not claiming that testamentary freedom is always exercised so as to advance flourishing, nor do I deny or underestimate concerns of distributive justice where private provision generates or exacerbates inequality in access to goods or opportunities essential to flourishing.

As to the first point: as was true of our reflections on motivation and virtue, here, too, I mean to emphasise the focal moral sense of testamentary disposition as gift-giving while allowing for imperfection in its realisation. As noted earlier, it is possible—if uncommon—for a gift to be of trifling moral value (no appreciable positive impact on flourishing) or to be of disvalue (negative impact on flourishing).[81] For example, a benevolent testator who provides lavishly for a beneficiary might undermine their flourishing by inducing dependency and malaise. But a null or negative impact on the flourishing of recipients is just another way in which a gift might prove defective relative to its focal moral sense.

As to the latter point: it is inevitable that testamentary disposition, being a mechanism of private ordering in the allocation of property, can generate or exacerbate social inequality. The exercise of testamentary freedom might typically contribute to the flourishing of beneficiaries but it does so without being directly regulated by a norm of distributive equality. When one pairs this realisation with the recognition that beneficiaries are not equal in moral desert relative to windfall gains, one can appreciate the moral and policy importance of allowing for the public benefits of private provision while adjusting for distributional inequality through taxation and redistribution. Notice, though, that the question whether and to what extent inheritance should be taxed is one that goes to the moral *limits* of testamentary freedom such as might follow from its *justification*.

[80] Hirsch, 'Bequests for Purposes' (n 75) 34 ('Historically, lawmakers have differentiated the rules applicable to bequests for purposes depending upon the sort of purpose the testator had in mind. Bequests for "charitable" purposes... are "favored creatures of the law", and courts see to it that they are given effect').

[81] ibid ('At the opposite extreme [from the favorable treatment shown to charitable purposes] lie bequests for objects found to *dis*serve the public interest, originally known as "superstitious" purposes; courts take a dim view of these, refusing to allow them to be carried out') and at 70 ('Though the cases are few, courts have invariably invalidated bequests for purposes that they identify as injurious to members of the community').

V. Conclusion

This chapter has examined leading arguments offered in defence of wide testamentary freedom and, finding them wanting, offers an alternative. Viewed, as it has been, within conventional frames of analysis of the *morality of property*—and its central preoccupations with autonomy, need, scarcity, and equality—testamentary freedom is widely considered beyond the pale. Arguments from property, autonomy, social utility, and obligations of provision each failed to show that laws enabling testamentary freedom are morally defensible.

I've suggested that testamentary freedom can be defended more robustly on the footing of the *morality of gift relationships*, with particular attention to the moral value of testamentary benefaction in enabling the expression of moral motivation, the practice of virtue, and realisation of goods essential to the flourishing of testators' intended beneficiaries. An advantage of this approach is that it recognises moral complexity, allowing one to appreciate the moral significance—indeed, touching beauty—of dispositions that comport with the focal moral sense of benefactions as gifts, while at the same time pinpointing ways in which other dispositions prove morally defective despite their legal validity. Hence, the approach endorsed here is not quietist or apologetic. It acknowledges that specification of the scope of testamentary freedom must mitigate inherent risks of moral deficiency (eg of spiteful or malicious disinheritance, or wasteful or harmful inheritance) while accommodating side constraints responsive to concerns surfaced within the morality of property (eg regarding the interests of future generations, and the impact of inheritance on distributive justice). Precisely how these tradeoffs are to be made raises questions that I must leave for future work.

8

A Fresh Look at Purpose Trusts

*Matthew Harding**

In this chapter, I argue for a fresh look at purpose trusts. The main thesis I seek to defend is that purpose trusts represent a distinctive legal form that enables settlors to organise their affairs in a way that is not fully achievable using other legal forms. At the same time, I aim to unsettle assumptions about purpose trusts that are grounded in contestable conceptions of the nature of the trust and in understandings of the demands of public policy that are difficult to defend. Once these assumptions are cleared away, the overall picture that emerges is one in which purpose trusts have a useful role to play in a legal system grounded in liberal commitments, but a role that must be carefully circumscribed in view of the relevant demands of public policy.

In Part I of the chapter, I consider purpose trusts in contrast to other elements of dispositive arrangements, viz beneficiary trusts, powers for objects, and purpose powers. I emphasise that, as is the case with other legal forms, the existence of purpose trusts depends on acts of interpretation about which reasonable minds might disagree. In Part II, I argue that purpose trusts offer settlors a distinctive facility because, in addition to enabling settlors to deploy the benefit of property as all trusts do, they entail a particular mode of governance that cannot be accessed fully using other legal forms. Part II also offers some brief reflections on purpose trusts from a liberal standpoint that is interested in the autonomy-enhancing capacity of facilitative private law. In Part III, I turn to the distinction often drawn between valid charitable purpose trusts and invalid non-charitable purpose trusts, arguing that this distinction, as currently drawn, is difficult to defend. In Part IV, I consider where to draw the limits when it comes to the recognition of private purpose trusts, and I discuss how such trusts might be appropriately enforced. Part V concludes.

* My sincere thanks to Sinead Agnew, Murray Baird, Hanoch Dagan, Simone Degeling, Simon Douglas, Lusina Ho, Jessica Hudson, John Mee, Charles Mitchell, Rosemary Langford, Ying Khai Liew, Alec Morris, Ian Murray, Irit Samet, and Matthew Turnour, each of whom helped me to think through, test, and refine the ideas in this paper. I have not come close to doing justice to their many helpful and insightful comments, and of course all errors remain mine alone. Thanks are also due to Tom Fletcher and Louise Ellis for their outstanding research assistance in preparing this chapter for publication.

Matthew Harding, *A Fresh Look at Purpose Trusts* In: *Philosophical Foundations of the Law of Express Trusts*. Edited by: Simone Degeling, Jessica Hudson, and Irit Samet, Oxford University Press. © Matthew Harding 2023. DOI: 10.1093/oso/9780192844934.003.0009

I. Identifying Purpose Trusts

The possibility of a purpose trust typically arises in the setting of what, for want of a better description, I will call a dispositive arrangement. A dispositive arrangement is one in which a disponee enjoys dispositive powers or is under dispositive duties in respect of assets.[1] Such an arrangement will usually entail a composite, or package, of such powers and duties.[2] When looking at a dispositive arrangement, identifying a purpose trust revolves around two key questions. First, is any part of the arrangement purpose-oriented in the sense of oriented to an articulated abstract end?[3] And second, does the purpose-oriented part of the arrangement entail a dispositive duty or is it composed only of dispositive powers? In some cases, the answers to these questions will be clear. But in others they will not. In all cases, the questions demand the application of interpretive tools to ascertain, from an objective standpoint, the intention of the disponor who brought the dispositive arrangement into being.[4] Thus, purpose trusts do not come to be recognised in law because they present themselves as instances of some ideal form. Rather, as with other legal forms in which terms must be given meaning, they emerge from acts of interpretation that might be contested or revised. And what to one reasonable interpretive mind is a purpose trust might appear to another as something quite different.

One important question that might arise in a given case is whether some part of a dispositive arrangement is purpose-oriented. In many cases, it will be evident, as a matter of interpretation, that this is so. For example, where a disponor seeks to establish a charitable purpose trust, the objective meaning of the trust terms is likely to unambiguously disclose a purpose-oriented arrangement.[5] This is because the settlor of a charitable purpose trust will usually be at pains to articulate, in the trust terms, abstract purposes that demonstrably fall within the legal conception of charity. Failure to achieve this clarity about purposes might cause the trust to fail.[6] At the same time, it will often be clear that a disposition is not purpose-oriented, for example, where it takes the form of a power to dispose of assets to certain named objects. It may even be

[1] On dispositive powers and duties, see Geraint Thomas, *Thomas on Powers* (2nd edn, OUP, 2012), paras 1.14, 10.82–10.95, 10.153, 10.168.

[2] See further Lionel Smith, 'Massively Discretionary Trusts' (2017) 70 CLP 17, 19–20 (hereafter Smith, 'Massively Discretionary Trusts').

[3] See *Attorney-General (NSW) v Perpetual Trustee Co (Ltd)* (1940) 63 CLR 209, 222 (Dixon and Evatt JJ): 'A charitable trust is a trust for a purpose, not for a person. The objects of ordinary trusts are individuals, either named or answering a description, whether presently or at some future time. To dispose of property for the fulfilment of ends considered beneficial to the community is an entirely different thing from creating equitable estates and interests and limiting them to beneficiaries.'

[4] On the objective standpoint, *Byrnes v Kendle* (2011) 243 CLR 253, 273–75 [53]–[59] (Gummow and Hayne JJ), 290–91 [113]–[117] (Heydon and Crennan JJ); *Twinsectra Ltd v Yardley* [2002] 2 AC 164 [17], [71] (Lord Hoffmann) (hereafter *Twinsectra*); *Legal Services Board v Gillespie-Jones* (2013) 249 CLR 493, 525 [119] (Bell, Gageler and Keane JJ); see also the discussion in Ying Khai Liew and Charles Mitchell, 'The Creation of Express Trusts' (2017) 11 J Eq 133, 137–41.

[5] On terms and their role in dispositive arrangements, see J Hudson and C Mitchell, 'Justificanda' in this book.

[6] *Morice v Bishop of Durham* (1804) 9 Ves 399, 404–05 (Sir William Grant MR) and *Morice v Bishop of Durham* (1805) 10 Ves 521, 533–34 (Lord Eldon).

clear, as an interpretive matter, that a dispositive arrangement is not purpose-oriented even though it refers to purposes. For example, James Penner discusses arrangements in which a beneficiary's interest in trust assets is limited with reference to the cost of carrying out some specific purpose such as educating that beneficiary.[7] Such an arrangement is clearly a trust for a beneficiary even though its terms refer to a purpose.

Nonetheless, in some cases, reasonable minds might simply disagree on whether some part of a dispositive arrangement is purpose-oriented. This is one way to understand the longstanding debates about the well-known case of *Re Denley's Trust Deed*.[8] Trustees were placed under a dispositive duty to maintain land as a sports ground for the benefit of employees of a company and others selected by the trustees. The trust deed made clear that 'the employees of the company shall be entitled to the use and enjoyment of the said land'.[9] In finding the arrangement to be a valid trust, Goff J distinguished between purpose trusts generating excessively 'indirect or intangible' benefits for persons and those which, 'though expressed as a purpose, [are] directly or indirectly for the benefit of an individual or individuals'.[10] For Goff J, arrangements meeting the latter description were 'in general outside the mischief of the beneficiary principle' according to which a trust must be enforceable and capable of being controlled by the court.[11]

Some have argued that, in *Denley*, Goff J recognised a species of non-charitable purpose trust at odds with orthodox English trusts law.[12] Others insist that Goff J's reasoning is consistent with the recognition of a trust to benefit an ascertainable class of beneficiaries, coupled with a power to benefit others.[13] For present purposes, I want to emphasise a different, anterior, point. Given that the trust in *Denley* was expressed to be in furtherance of a purpose, and that the trust terms also indicated that an ascertainable class of beneficiaries was to benefit from the arrangement, it is hardly surprising that there is disagreement as to whether or not the trust was purpose-oriented. From an objective standpoint, more than one interpretation of the trust terms seems reasonably available. Moreover, the fact that the trust was expressed to be in furtherance of a purpose does not necessarily determine the question how to interpret those terms. This is because, according to the prevailing interpretive approach in trusts law, it is necessary to have regard not only to the words used by a settlor, but also the context in which those words figure, the settlor's conduct, and other relevant circumstances.

[7] JE Penner, 'Purposes and Rights in the Common Law of Trusts' (2014) 48 Revue juridique Themis de l'Universite de Montreal 579, 587.

[8] [1969] 1 Ch 373.

[9] ibid 376.

[10] ibid 383–84.

[11] ibid 384. For the principle, see *Morice v Bishop of Durham* (1804) 9 Ves 399, 404–05 (Sir William Grant MR) and *Morice v Bishop of Durham* (1805) 10 Ves 521, 539–40 (Lord Eldon).

[12] See, eg, Alec J Morris, 'Private Purpose Trusts and the Re Denley Trust 50 Years On' (2020) 34 Trust Law Int 165.

[13] See, eg, PJ Millett, 'The Quistclose Trust: Who Can Enforce It' (1985) 101 LQR 269, 281–82; Paul Matthews, 'From Obligation to Property, and Back Again? The Future of the Non-Charitable Purpose Trust' in David Hayton (ed), *Extending the Boundaries of Trusts and Similar Ring-Fenced Funds* (Kluwer Law International 2002), 222 (hereafter Matthews, 'From Obligation to Property').

Now consider the question whether an element of a dispositive arrangement is a duty requiring the application of assets in furtherance of a purpose, or a power to apply assets in such a purpose-oriented way. Once again, as with any legal form in which terms must be given meaning, there might be more than one reasonably available interpretive possibility. The difficulty discerning whether terms disclose a duty or a power was on display, beyond the setting of purpose trusts, in the landmark case of *McPhail v Doulton*.[14] There, terms contemplated a discretionary distribution of income in making grants, and then an accumulation and further distribution of any income not distributed in making those grants. At first instance, Goff J interpreted the terms as setting up a power to make the grants coupled with a duty to accumulate and distribute income not applied to the grants.[15] A majority of the Court of Appeal agreed.[16] However, in the House of Lords, a different interpretation was preferred, according to which the duty was to make the grants and the power was to accumulate and distribute any surplus once grants had been allocated. Lord Wilberforce was aware of the subtlety of the interpretive question to which the case had given rise:

> It is only necessary to read the learned judgments in the Court of Appeal to see that what to one mind may appear as a power of distribution coupled with a trust to dispose of the undistributed surplus, by accumulation or otherwise, may to another appear as a trust for distribution coupled with a power to withhold a portion and accumulate or otherwise dispose of it. A layman and, I suspect, also a logician, would find it hard to understand what difference there is.[17]

A similar point might be made about purpose-oriented dispositive arrangements. In cases of 'trusts of imperfect obligation', testamentary dispositions in furtherance of certain non-charitable purposes have been recognised and upheld as valid. These purposes include building and maintaining a testator's grave, maintaining a testator's domestic animal, and saying private masses for a testator's soul.[18] There is also a case about a disposition to further the purpose of fox-hunting.[19] On one view, expressed in *Re Astor's Settlement Trusts* and *Re Endacott*, trusts of imperfect obligation are dispositive duties, enforceable by those who would take in default their performance.[20] On this view, trusts of imperfect obligation are exceptional examples of valid non-charitable purpose trusts. However, an alternative view is that trusts of imperfect obligation are in fact dispositive powers enforceable by takers in default.[21] And as purpose powers,

[14] [1971] AC 424 (hereafter *McPhail v Doulton*).

[15] *Re Baden's Deed Trusts* [1967] 1 WLR 1457, 1466, 1468–69.

[16] *Re Baden's Deed Trusts* [1969] 2 Ch 388, 400 (Harman LJ), 402–03 (Karminski LJ).

[17] *McPhail v Doulton* (n 14) 448. The interpretations preferred in the lower courts may have been influenced by a desire to uphold the arrangement, given that the test for certainty of objects was at that time markedly different for dispositive duties than for dispositive powers: *Inland Revenue Commissioners v Broadway Cottages Trust* [1954] 1 Ch 20. Of course, that changed following the House of Lords' decision in *McPhail v Doulton* itself.

[18] *Pettingall v Pettingall* (1842) 11 LJ Ch 176; *Mitford v Reynolds* (1848) 16 Sim 105; *Mussett v Bingle* [1876] WN 170; *Re Dean* (1889) 41 Ch D 552; *Pirbright v Salwey* [1896] WN 86; *Re Hooper* [1932] 1 Ch 38.

[19] *Re Thompson* [1934] Ch 342.

[20] *Re Astor's Settlement Trusts* [1952] Ch 534 (hereafter *Re Astor's Settlement Trusts*); *Re Endacott* [1960] Ch 232.

[21] See, eg, Paul Matthews, 'The New Trust: Obligations without Rights?' in AJ Oakley (ed), *Trends in Contemporary Trust Law* (Clarendon Press 1996), 8 (hereafter Matthews, 'The New Trust'); Kelvin FK Low,

they are perfectly valid as a matter of orthodox English trusts law, so long as they satisfy certainty requirements, perpetuity rules, and the demands of public policy.[22] The point to note is that this interpretive debate has arisen at all. And that there seems no compelling reason to prefer one interpretation over the other. Both interpretations seem reasonably available within the parameters of the prevailing approach to ascertaining disponor intention.[23]

The interpretive difficulties that can arise when purpose trusts are in view are not distinctive to purpose trusts. The same difficulties arise routinely in relation to all trusts, as well as contracts and other facilitative legal forms whose existence and incidents depend on acts of interpretation. Nonetheless, I think it is important to emphasise that such interpretive difficulties arise in purpose trust settings. Orthodox trusts law draws sharp and far-reaching distinctions between purpose trusts and beneficiary trusts, and between trusts for charitable purposes and trusts for non-charitable purposes. The validity of dispositive arrangements turns on these distinctions. To the extent that the distinctions themselves depend on contestable interpretive acts in individual cases, we might wish to question their existential consequences.

II. Purpose Trusts: A Distinctive Mode of Governance

In their chapter in this collection, Hanoch Dagan and Irit Samet present a sympathetic reconstruction of trusts law that views trusts as an important element in a liberal property regime.[24] For Dagan and Samet, trusts serve the autonomy-enhancing objects of such a regime to the extent that they enable settlors to craft bespoke arrangements (within limits) under which they and others may enjoy the benefits of property in a multitude of ways.[25] On this view, trusts are useful to settlors because they supplement the menu of stable default arrangements reflected in property law's numerus clausus with a residual category in which settlors can create their own arrangements according to their own lights. Elsewhere, Dagan and Samet notice that trusts not only make available a multiplicity of self-chosen options, but also—and significantly—enable property-sharing arrangements to be crafted around stable norms of fiduciary stewardship.[26] Their account thus highlights in several ways that trusts make their own distinctive contribution to facilitative private law.

'Non-Charitable Purpose Trusts: The Right to Forgo Enforcement' in Richard C Nolan, Kelvin FK Low and Tang Hang Wu (eds), *Trusts and Modern Wealth Management* (CUP 2018), 498–99 (hereafter Low, 'The Right to Forgo Enforcement').

[22] *Twinsectra* (n 4) [81], [101] (Lord Millett); *Re Shaw (deceased)* [1957] 1 WLR 729, 743–46.

[23] In some jurisdictions, the interpretive debate is rendered academic by more prescriptive approaches: in the United States, see the Restatement (Second) of Trusts § 124 (1959), and in Ontario, see the *Perpetuities Act*, RSO 1990, c P.9, s 16, providing that non-charitable purpose trusts are to be upheld and enforced as powers.

[24] H Dagan and I Samet, 'Express Trust: The Dark Horse of the Liberal Property Regime' in this book (hereafter Dagan and Samet, 'Dark Horse').

[25] ibid 20–24.

[26] See, eg, Hanoch Dagan and Irit Samet, 'The Beneficiary's Ownership Rights in the Trust Res in a Liberal Property Regime' (2023) 86 MLR 701.

In this part of the chapter, I want to argue that, in addition to the distinctive contribution that all trusts make to facilitative private law, purpose trusts make a further distinctive contribution as well: they enable a relatively pure form of what Rosemary Teele Langford calls 'purpose-based governance'.[27] In order to understand this further contribution, it is necessary first to explore further what the notion of purpose-based governance entails. According to Langford, purpose-based governance requires a certain mindset on the part of fiduciaries with governance duties; it demands that fiduciaries frame questions, challenges, plans, and actions with the furtherance of abstract purposes, and not the competing claims of interest-holders, in mind.[28] Similarly, Paul Miller and Andrew Gold have distinguished the 'fiduciary governance' of purpose trusts from the 'fiduciary service' that is demanded of the trustees of trusts for beneficiaries.[29] In fiduciary service, the trustee must administer the trust in the best interests of the beneficiaries. In fiduciary governance, the central task is not to maximise benefit for interest-holders. It is, rather, to 'determine or advance certain abstract purposes'.[30]

Purpose trusts thus require trustees to approach matters of governance within a certain conceptual framework, one that is interested in the application of trust assets in the furtherance of purposes rather than for the benefit of interest-holders. This sets them apart from beneficiary trusts, in which the question of how best to benefit interest-holders animates governance. Settlors of purpose trusts are thereby enabled not only to achieve desired dispositive outcomes, but also to provide for the pursuit of those outcomes via a particular modality. Yet while the modality of purpose-based governance helps to locate purpose trusts as distinctive facilities when contrasted with other trusts, it does not bring the distinctiveness of purpose trusts fully into view. This is because disponors have available to them purpose-oriented legal forms other than the purpose trust. A disponor with charitable intentions might settle assets on charitable purpose trust. But equally she might found a charitable company, or make a gift to an unincorporated association pursuing the charitable purpose in question. Each of these options offers purpose-based governance because charities are required by law to be purpose-oriented irrespective of their legal form.

In order to understand the distinctiveness of purpose trusts when contrasted with legal forms other than the trust, we must explore further the implications of the fact that purpose trusts are trusts, as opposed to companies or associations, to name two other legal forms that might be purpose-oriented. The key is in apprehending that, as trusts, purpose trusts demand not only purpose-based governance but also a high degree of fidelity to settlor's intentions. This expectation of fidelity may be seen in several different ways. First, as the purpose trust has no legal personality, it cannot hold

[27] Rosemary Teele Langford, 'Purpose-Based Governance: A New Paradigm' (2020) 43 UNSWLJ 954.

[28] ibid 956–57. This difference between the purpose-based governance demanded in purpose trusts and the concern for interest-holders required in trusts for persons is well expressed in s 26 of New Zealand's Trusts Act 2019: 'A trustee must hold or deal with trust property and otherwise act (a) for the benefit of the beneficiaries, in accordance with the terms of the trust: (b) in the case of a trust for a permitted purpose, to further the permitted purpose of the trust, in accordance with the terms of the trust.'

[29] Paul B Miller and Andrew S Gold, 'Fiduciary Governance' (2015) 57(2) William & Mary L Rev 513.

[30] ibid 517.

interests that might stand at odds with the application of trust assets to the purposes for which it has been settled.[31] The settlor who sets up a purpose trust may therefore do so with confidence that the trustee will never be presented with circumstances in which a choice must be made between the interests of the trust and the pursuit of the settlor's stipulated purposes. Matters seem more complicated where a purpose-oriented arrangement is incorporated. A company has a legal personality and, at least as far as law is concerned, holds interests.[32] And while recent scholarship on purpose-based governance has argued persuasively that the interests of a purpose-oriented company lie in the pursuit of its purposes,[33] there seem to be exceptional circumstances in which this alignment of interests and purposes might not obtain.

To illustrate, consider *Lehtimaki v Cooper*.[34] A married couple founded a charitable company limited by guarantee, Children's Investment Fund Foundation (CIFF). Its purposes related to the welfare of children in the developing world. The company had more than US$4 billion in assets. When the couple separated, they agreed that the wife should resign as a member and trustee of CIFF and that US$360 million should be transferred from CIFF to a charity founded by the wife so that she could continue her philanthropic work using a new vehicle. This agreement had to be approved by CIFF's members. The husband and the wife were both members but they were unable to participate in this approval thanks to their conflicts of interest. This left the decision to be made by the only other member of CIFF, Dr Lehtimaki. The case turned on the question whether the court could order Dr Lehtimaki to exercise his discretionary voting power as a member of CIFF to approve the agreement to transfer US$360 million out of CIFF and into the wife's other charity. Dr Lehtimaki had not fully disclosed how he intended to exercise his voting power if left undisturbed to do so by the court.

Dr Lehtimaki's caution seems appropriate. It seems clear enough that approving the transfer was consistent with the intentions of the founders of the charity, who were the married couple. Approving the transfer might also have been consistent with the furtherance of the purposes for which CIFF was established, given that the purposes of the wife's other charity were largely in alignment with CIFF's own purposes.[35] Nonetheless, the purposes of the wife's other charity were not identical to those of CIFF, and this leaves open the possibility that the purposes of CIFF were not optimally served by making the transfer. Moreover, when attention is paid to CIFF as an interest-holder,

[31] Note that in some jurisdictions, the trustees of a charitable purpose trust may incorporate for certain legal purposes: see Charities Act 2011 (England and Wales), s 251; Charitable Trusts Act 1957 (NZ), s 7. However, such incorporation does not affect the purpose-based governance associated with the trust form: see Charities Act 2011 (England and Wales), s 254.

[32] See, eg, *Corporations Act 2001* (Cth), s 181(1)(a) ('A director or officer of a corporation must exercise their powers and discharge their duties ... in good faith in the best interests of the corporation').

[33] See Ian Murray and Rosemary Teele Langford, 'The Best Interests Duty and Corporate Charities: The Pursuit of Purpose' (2021) 15 J Eq 92 (hereafter Murray and Langford, 'Best Interests Duty'). Note also ss 220 and 221 of the Charities Act 2011 (England and Wales), expressing the duties of trustees and members of a Charitable Incorporated Organization (CIO) in terms of purpose-based governance (trustees and members must exercise powers in the way they decide, in good faith, 'would be most likely to further the purposes of the CIO').

[34] *Lehtimaki v Cooper* [2020] UKSC 33 (hereafter *Lehtimaki v Cooper*).

[35] Compare Children's Investment Fund Foundation, https://ciff.org/, accessed 7 October 2022, and Big Win Philanthropy, https://www.bigwin.org/, accessed 7 October 2022.

matters become murkier still. As Sir Geoffrey Vos put it in his judgment at first instance, 'it is not entirely clear why disposing of assets of US$360 million should be regarded as being in the best interests of CIFF'.[36] Of course, this latter problem might be surmounted by arguing that CIFF has no interests apart from the furtherance of its purposes, but this is the very question in issue. If nothing else, the facts of *Lehtimaki v Cooper* demonstrate that this is a live, and potentially difficult, question for purpose-oriented companies. It is not such a question for purpose trusts, because a purpose trust is not a legal person with interests. It is rather a mandate conferred on trustees to further stipulated purposes.

Lehtimaki v Cooper highlights a further way in which the purpose trust demands a high degree of fidelity to disponor intentions when contrasted with other purpose-oriented legal forms. The governance of a purpose trust lies with its trustees, the court exercising supervisory jurisdiction over trusts, and the enforcer of the trust who might be the Attorney-General or a regulatory authority in the case of a charitable purpose trust, and someone else in the case of a non-charitable purpose trust.[37] For these participants in the purpose trust, governance is primarily a matter of ensuring that the trust terms stipulated by the settlor are faithfully carried out.[38] In the exceptional case where fidelity to settlor-stipulated terms is properly overridden by other objectives, it is usually necessary to invoke the court's supervisory jurisdiction or, in the case of charitable purpose trusts, seek the approval of the Attorney-General or a regulator.[39] And the conditions that trigger such approval are not easily satisfied. For example, where the trustees of a charitable purpose trust seek to vary the purposes of the trust, they must obtain a cy-pres order, which will be granted only in certain circumstances. In the law of England and Wales, regard must be had to the 'spirit of the gift', requiring that disponor intentions be taken into account.[40]

In other purpose-oriented legal forms, governance involves not only office-holders such as trustees or directors, and in the case of charitable arrangements State institutions, but also members exercising discretionary powers in general meetings. This interposition of members in matters of governance creates opportunities for purpose-based governance to depart from disponor intentions. In *Lehtimaki v Cooper*, the Supreme Court of the United Kingdom made clear that, at least in some circumstances, the members of a charitable company have fiduciary responsibilities when exercising their governance powers. These fiduciary responsibilities demand that members exercise their powers in what they in good faith believe will best further the charitable purposes of the company in question.[41] This ensures some degree of fidelity to

[36] *The Children's Investment Fund Foundation (UK) v Attorney-General* [2017] EWHC 1379 (Ch) [128]. Nonetheless, the Chancellor considered that, on balance, the transfer was in the best interests of CIFF: at [128]. One factor was that the transfer would bring to an end the governance stalemate that triggered the litigation.

[37] I return to the question of enforcement of purpose trusts in Part IV.

[38] Honest, good faith performance of the trust according to its terms is the 'irreducible core' of trusteeship: see *Armitage v Nurse* [1998] Ch 241, 253 (Lord Millett). See also *Youyang Pty Ltd v Minter Ellison Morris Fletcher* (2003) 212 CLR 484 [32].

[39] Charities Act 2011 (England and Wales), s 115; Charities Act (Singapore, cap 37, 1994 Rev Ed) s 32(2).

[40] Charities Act 2011 (England and Wales), s 62.

[41] *Lehtimaki v Cooper* (n 34) [77], [89]. This decision brought the law relating to the members of charitable companies into alignment with the law relating to members of CIOs: see Charities Act 2011 (England and Wales),

disponor-stipulated purposes over time. Nonetheless, the court was careful to leave open the question of the scope of the fiduciary responsibilities of members of charitable companies, especially where there are large numbers of members.[42] *Lehtimaki v Cooper* is thus consistent with the proposition that, in some circumstances, members are free to exercise governance powers in what they believe will further their own interests, and not in order to further disponor-stipulated purposes at all.[43]

Moreover, in legal forms where members enjoy governance powers, they might reshape the entire arrangement in a way that departs from disponor intentions. Take, for example, a charitable company. In my home jurisdiction of Australia, the *Corporations Act 2001* (Cth) states that the default position for such a company is that the members may change the objects of the company by special resolution in general meeting.[44] A disponor who founds a charitable company might override this default position by articulating provisions in the company's constitution that make it difficult for members to change company objects.[45] However, members' powers to change company objects cannot be removed altogether. To that extent, members with a mind to change company objects may reorient the company away from disponor-stipulated purposes and towards purposes that resonate more with the members themselves. To the extent that members of a charitable company have fiduciary responsibilities, they would not be free to reorient that company towards the purpose of returning profits to themselves.[46] Nonetheless, members might stipulate new charitable purposes for the company that supersede those expressed in the company's founding constitution, and it is difficult to see how members' power to change objects could be constrained by fiduciary responsibilities to remain faithful to the very objects that members are empowered to change. For the disponor who seeks fidelity to her stipulated purposes over time, this might be cause for concern.

The contrast between purpose-based governance in purpose trusts and purpose-based governance in other purpose-oriented legal forms should not be overstated. It is always open to a disponor to vary the default position with respect to any purpose-oriented legal form. The disponor who wishes to empower trustees to stipulate new purposes for a purpose trust may do so. Equally, the disponor founding a charitable company may insert provisions in the company's constitution that place impediments in the

s 220. The decision did not extend to unincorporated associations, but the reasoning would seem to apply to that setting too.

42 ibid [105].

43 Note Lloyd Hitoshi Mayer, 'Fiduciary Principles in Charities and Other Nonprofits' in Evan J Criddle, Paul B Miller and Robert H Sitkoff (eds), *The Oxford Handbook of Fiduciary Law* (OUP 2019), 107–08, and Murray and Langford, 'Best Interests Duty' (n 33) 114, acknowledging that the position of members in US and Australian law, respectively, remains unsettled.

44 *Corporations Act 2001* (Cth) s 136(2) ('[A] company may modify or repeal its constitution, or a provision of its constitution, by special resolution').

45 ibid s 136(3) ('[A] company's constitution may provide that the special resolution does not have any effect unless a further requirement specified in the constitution relating to that modification or repeal has been complied with').

46 See *Grain Technology Australia Ltd v Rosewood Research Pty Ltd (No 2)* [2019] NSWSC 1744 (hereafter, *Rosewood*).

way of members seeking to stipulate new purposes over time. Moreover, as *Lehtimaki v Cooper* made clear, charities of all forms are subject to the court's supervisory jurisdiction and, in England and Wales at least, approval of the Charity Commission is needed where changes to a charity's purposes are in view.[47] Nonetheless, as a matter of default law, purpose-based governance in a purpose trust is more straightforwardly responsive to disponor intentions than in other purpose-oriented legal forms, because in those other forms members exercising governance powers may 're-purpose' arrangements over time.[48]

Before leaving the topic of the purpose trust as demanding a distinctive mode of governance, something should be said about the difference between purpose trusts and purpose powers. Both are purpose-oriented arrangements. Both require purpose-based governance. Does the purpose trust offer anything distinctive to the disponor when contrasted with the purpose power? Kelvin Low argues that well-known problems associated with the enforcement of purpose trusts mean that 'the purpose trust is not a clearly more practically effective device for achieving a settlor's purposes as compared to the power'.[49] I return in Part IV to the enforcement of purpose trusts. For now, I want to emphasise a different point. Even if purpose trusts and purpose powers seem similar when their practical enforcement is in view, they are nonetheless distinctive in important ways. Like any legal form, the purpose trust expresses certain conceptual and normative commitments.[50] These include a commitment to offering disponors the powerful normative instrument of the legal duty, an instrument that is not available in the case of a purpose power. It is this offer that renders the purpose trust distinctive when contrasted with the purpose power. Practical impediments to enforcement of the duties entailed in the offer should not call into question the distinctiveness of the purpose trust. They should rather call attention to the question of how enforcement mechanisms can be designed to ensure that the purpose trust lives up to its promise as a legal form.

Earlier, I referred to Dagan and Samet's contribution to this collection, which emphasises the importance of trusts to facilitative private law in view of the multiplicity of settlor-devised arrangements in which trusts might figure. My account of the distinctive mode of governance embedded in the purpose trust as a legal form highlights another sort of contribution that purpose trusts might make to a facilitative private law inspired by a liberal commitment to enhancing personal autonomy. The conditions of personal autonomy include what Joseph Raz refers to as an 'adequate range' of options for individuals to choose from when pursuing their goals and life plans.[51] Plainly, an

[47] *Lehtimaki v Cooper* (n 34) [69]; Charities Act 2011 (England and Wales), ss 198 and 275.

[48] Note that the United Kingdom Parliament has recently enacted legislation seeking to harmonise procedures for changing a charity's purposes irrespective of its legal form: Charities Act 2022 (England and Wales). For the reasons given in the text, such efforts at harmonisation should be viewed with caution. See further the excellent discussion in John Picton, 'Mapping Bad Charity' in S Farran, R Hewitson and A Ramshaw (eds), *Modern Studies in Property Law*, vol 11 (Hart Publishing 2020).

[49] Low, 'The Right to Forgo Enforcement' (n 21) 503. See also Low, 'The Right to Forgo Enforcement' (n 21) 504–05: the purpose trust 'offers no countervailing advantage whatsoever to existing, conceptually sound legal devices'.

[50] On legal forms, see further: Larissa Katz, 'Legal Forms in Property Law Theory' in James Penner and Michael Otsuka (eds), *Property Theory: Legal and Political Perspectives* (CUP 2018).

[51] Joseph Raz, *The Morality of Freedom* (OUP 1988), 373.

adequacy of options demands that individuals enjoy a sufficiency in respect of the ends that they might freely pursue. Thus, for example, an individual whose career options were limited to labouring on a family farm in one or another capacity could not be said to enjoy the conditions of autonomy to that extent. However, and crucially, an adequacy of options is also a matter of sufficiency in the modalities or pathways that individuals might adopt in the pursuit of ends. For example, an individual might choose the end of making music in a variety of ways, from forging a career as a recording artist to joining a community choir to playing the piano for family and friends in the privacy of the home. This sort of diversity and difference in modalities by which ends are pursued enables a range of distinctive and dependable engagements with value, irrespective of the ends for which the modalities are deployed, and to this extent it makes a material contribution to the conditions of autonomy in itself.

A focus on modalities when thinking about the adequacy of options leads quite naturally to facilitative private law as an important social site for the articulation and organisation of modalities by which individual ends might be pursued.[52] Thus, a liberal case begins to emerge for distinctions to be maintained between different private law forms, such as contracts, corporations, and trusts, insofar as those forms reflect different modalities. Moreover, the case extends to distinctions between sub-forms that reflect different modalities again: standard form versus bespoke contracts, private versus public corporations, beneficiary trusts versus purpose trusts, to name a few. In this light, purpose trusts, which embody a distinctive mode of governance and, to that extent, the promise of a distinctive sort of engagement with value, might find their place in autonomy-enhancing facilitative private law. This, of course, assumes that all else is equal. As I will explain in Part IV, that assumption is problematic. Nonetheless, the prima facie case for purpose trusts as part of autonomy-enhancing facilitative private law seems worth highlighting, especially as purpose trusts have long been viewed with suspicion at least in onshore jurisdictions.[53]

III. The Distinction Between Charitable and Non-Charitable Purpose Trusts

Common law jurisdictions usually draw a distinction between charitable and non-charitable purpose trusts, treating the former as valid, and the latter (on the whole) as invalid. In different jurisdictions, the distinction is drawn in different ways depending

[52] In a book chapter critiquing autonomy-inspired accounts of private law, James Penner is arguably insufficiently sensitive to the possibility that private law might make this sort of contribution to the conditions of personal autonomy. James Penner, 'Taking Raz Seriously: On the Value of Autonomy and its Relation to Private Law' in *Oxford Studies in Private Law Theory*, vol II (2022) <http://dx.doi.org/10.2139/ssrn.4150144>, accessed 7 October 2022.

[53] See, eg, James P Webb, 'An Ever-Reducing Core? Challenging the Legal Validity of Offshore Trusts' (2015) 21(5) Trusts & Trustees 476. See also Adam S Hofri-Winogradow, 'The Stripping of the Trust: A Study in Legal Evolution' (2015) 65(1) UTLJ 1; Lionel Smith, 'Give the People What They Want? The Onshoring of the Offshore' (2018) 103(5) Iowa Law Rev 2155.

on the content of the prevailing legal conception of charity. In some jurisdictions, the distinction continues to be more or less as articulated by Sir William Grant MR in *Morice v Bishop of Durham* early in the nineteenth century: charitable purposes are public benefit purposes within the 'spirit and intendment' of the preamble of the Statute of Charitable Uses 1601.[54] In other jurisdictions, statutory restatements of the legal conception of charity aim to depart from the Elizabethan preamble but at the same time keep faith with the tradition of finding as charitable only those public benefit purposes sufficiently analogous to purposes recognised as charitable in past judicial decisions or legislation.[55] In all jurisdictions, a legal conception of charity is maintained, with the implication that purpose trusts are treated as valid where their purposes are within that conception and are highly likely to be treated as invalid where their purposes lie beyond it.

Some examples might help to illustrate the effects of the distinction between charitable and non-charitable purpose trusts that is maintained across the common law world. In the Australian case of *Royal National Agricultural and Industrial Association v Chester*,[56] a testator sought to bequeath assets to the Association for the purpose of 'breeding and racing of Homer Pigeons'.[57] The High Court of Australia found that, although the purpose might generate public benefit, and although the Association had addressed any concern about uncertainty by preparing a scheme setting out in detail the ways in which it would carry out the purpose, the purpose was not within the spirit and intendment of the Elizabethan preamble. For this reason, the trust was invalid.[58] In *Oppenheim v Tobacco Securities Trust Co Ltd*, a trust for the purpose of educating the children of employees and ex-employees of a group of companies was struck down on the basis that the children who stood to benefit from the purpose being carried out were all connected to a single propositus, the parent company, and to that extent the trust could not be said to be for the public benefit.[59] And in *Gilmour v Coats*, a trust for the purpose of maintaining a cloistered order of nuns was declared invalid on the basis that it could not be demonstrated on the evidence that the intercessory prayer of the nuns was efficacious and therefore benefited the public.[60]

In these cases, settlors tried to unlock the potential of purpose trusts and failed. From a liberal standpoint interested in the autonomy-enhancing capacity of facilitative private law, this seems to demand further investigation. Why should settlors seeking to

[54] *Morice v Bishop of Durham* (1804) 9 Ves 399, 405, and see also *Morice v Bishop of Durham* (1805) 10 Ves 521, 542–43 (Lord Eldon). The preamble refers to the following purposes: the relief of aged, impotent, and poor people; the maintenance of sick and maimed soldiers and mariners, schools of learning, free schools, and scholars of universities; the repair of bridges, havens, causeways, churches, sea banks, and highways; the education and preferment of orphans; the relief, stock or maintenance of houses of correction; marriages of poor maids; supportation, aid, and help of young tradesmen, handicraftsmen, and persons decayed; the relief or redemption of prisoners or captives and the aid or ease of any poor inhabitants concerning payments of fifteens, setting out of soldiers, and other taxes. Recourse to the spirit and intendment of the preamble when working out whether a purpose trust is valid is the current practice in Canada, New Zealand, and (to an extent) Australia.

[55] See, eg, Charities Act 2011 (England and Wales), s 3.

[56] [1974] 48 ALJR 304 (hereafter *Chester*).

[57] ibid 304.

[58] ibid 305–06.

[59] *Oppenheim v Tobacco Securities Trust Co Ltd* [1951] AC 297.

[60] [1949] AC 426, 446 (Lord Simonds).

further their chosen purposes by employing the distinctive mode of governance embedded in the purpose trust be prevented from doing so? Indeed, in the Australian *Chester* case, having declared that the purpose trust in view was invalid because it fell beyond the spirit and intendment of the Elizabethan preamble, the High Court expressed disquiet with 'what now appears as an unnecessary restriction imposed by law upon the capacity of a testator to support with his bounty purposes which seem good to him and do not offend against the law'.[61] What reasons could there be for enabling only those settlors whose purposes fall within the legal conception of charity to access the facility of the purpose trust?

One answer to this question points to the fact that the enforcement of charitable purpose trusts lies with the State, through the office of the Attorney-General, and argues that this enforcement mechanism is justified only in respect of trusts formed for the public benefit purposes that fall within the legal conception of charity. On this view, for trusts with purposes that fall beyond that conception, enforcement is problematic and for this reason such trusts should not be recognised. I will return to the question of purpose trust enforcement in Part IV. For the moment, I want to focus on another argument that might be made in support of a distinction between valid charitable and (largely) invalid non-charitable purpose trusts. This argument points to the fiscal and other benefits that are extended to charities, along with the regulatory burdens that charities bear. The idea is that, so long as the State extends fiscal and other benefits to charities, and imposes particular regulatory burdens on them, there are strong public policy reasons for policing the boundaries of the legal conception of charity, to ensure that the relevant benefits and burdens are allocated in a defensible way.

Ensuring a defensible allocation of benefits and burdens seems a strong argument for maintaining some sort of distinction between arrangements in furtherance of endorsed purposes that stand to generate public benefit and arrangements in furtherance of other purposes. However, when thinking about the relevance of this argument to the distinction between valid charitable and (largely) invalid non-charitable purpose trusts, a couple of points must be made. First, even if it is accepted that a distinction between endorsed public benefit purposes and other purposes is justified as a matter of public policy, it does not follow that the distinctions currently drawn in common law jurisdictions between charitable and non-charitable purposes are drawn in the right place. There can be no doubt that the legal conception of charity has developed in a highly path-dependent and historically contingent way and it would be surprising if it had reached an optimal state in any common law jurisdiction. Indeed, judges have repeatedly emphasised that the legal conception of charity must develop and adapt as social, economic, political, and cultural circumstances change.[62] In that ongoing

[61] *Chester* (n 56) 306.

[62] *Bathurst City Council v PWC Properties Pty Ltd* (1988) 195 CLR 566, 582 [34] (Gaudron, McHugh, Gummow, Hayne and Callinan JJ); *Taylor v Taylor* (1910) 10 CLR 218, 238 (Isaacs J). See also *Scottish Burial Reform and Cremation Society Ltd* [1968] AC 138, 154 (Lord Wilberforce); *Inland Revenue Commissioners v McMullen* [1981] AC 1, 15 (Lord Hailsham); *National Anti-Vivisection Society v Inland Revenue Commissioners* [1948] AC 31, 69–70 (Lord Simonds).

process of development and adaptation, there is always a risk that the legal conception of charity will be over-inclusive, under-inclusive, or both.

On one view, the legal conception of charity remains unacceptably under-inclusive for as long as it entails a requirement that charitable purposes be within the 'spirit and intendment' of the Elizabethan preamble or even analogous to extant charitable purposes. At times, something like this view appears to have animated judicial decision-making. For example, in *Incorporated Council of Law Reporting for England and Wales v Attorney-General*, Russell LJ did not seek to establish that the purpose of producing and disseminating law reports was within the spirit and intendment of the Elizabethan preamble. Instead, he found that the purpose was charitable because it stood to generate public benefit and there was no reason to think that it was beyond the spirit and intendment of the Elizabethan preamble.[63] A similar approach was taken by the New Zealand Court of Appeal in *Re Greenpeace of New Zealand Inc*. There, the court ruled that a public benefit purpose should be presumed charitable unless a similar purpose had been found non-charitable in an analogous case.[64] That said, such departures from established practice and principle are unusual. They are also at odds with unambiguous statements from apex courts in various jurisdictions,[65] and with recent legislative interventions across the common law world,[66] affirming that not all public benefit purposes are to be recognised as charitable in law.

A more radical view sees the legal conception of charity as under-inclusive insofar as it incorporates a requirement that, in addition to being public, charitable purposes must be approved by the State as beneficial to people. On this view, purposes should be recognised as charitable where they have a public character and are not contrary to law or fundamental public policy. This view is unusual but not without its proponents. In his concurring opinion in the well-known US case of *Bob Jones University v United States*, Powell J expressed unease with the operation of the benefit test embedded in the legal conception of charity, arguing that the test assumes that the proper function of charities is to 'act on behalf of the Government in carrying out governmentally approved policies'.[67] In expressing this unease, Powell J emphasised the value of a charity sector independent from the State as a site for diversity, and he stated that '[f]ar from representing an effort to reinforce any perceived "common community conscience", the provision of tax exemptions to non-profit groups is one indispensable means of limiting the influence of government orthodoxy on important areas of community life'.[68]

[63] *Incorporated Council of Law Reporting for England and Wales v Attorney-General* [1972] Ch 73, 88–89. See also Sachs LJ at 94.

[64] *Re Greenpeace of New Zealand Inc* [2013] 1 NZLR 339 [43]. See also *Commissioner of Inland Revenue v Medical Council of New Zealand* [1997] 2 NZLR 297.

[65] See, eg, *Williams' Trustees v Inland Revenue Commissioners* [1947] AC 447, 455 (Lord Simonds); *Vancouver Society of Immigrant and Visible Minority Women v Minister of National Revenue* [1999] 1 SCR 10 [175]–[177] (Iacobucci J, Cory, Major and Bastarche JJ concurring); *Re Greenpeace of New Zealand Incorporated* [2015] 1 NZLR 169 [18]–[21], [27]–[31] (Elias CJ, McGrath and Glazebrook JJ), [120] (William Young and Arnold JJ).

[66] Charities Act 2005 (New Zealand), s 5; Charities Act 2009 (Ireland), s 3; Charities Act 2011 (England and Wales), s 2; *Charities Act 2013* (Cth) s 12.

[67] 461 US 574 (1983), 609.

[68] ibid

One way, then, in which the legal conception of charity could be brought more into alignment with underlying liberal commitments is through recognition that all public purposes are charitable so long as they are lawful and consistent with fundamental public policy. However, such a move might have significant ramifications for the revenue. A less disruptive line of argument might seek to put pressure on the proposition that a single legal conception of charity should apply in trusts law, tax law, and regulatory settings. The proposition has not gone untested. Indeed, in the landmark case of *Commissioners for Special Purposes of Income Tax v Pemsel*,[69] the central question was whether the meaning of the word 'charitable' in section 61 of the United Kingdom Income Tax Act of 1842 was the same as the meaning developed by English Chancery judges administering the law of trusts over centuries and rationalised in *Morice v Bishop of Durham*. A majority of the House of Lords ruled that the tax statute picked up the trusts law meaning, a ruling that has since informed the orthodox approach to interpreting the meaning of 'charity' and its cognates in tax statutes across the common law world.[70] But equally significantly, two of the six Law Lords presiding over the appeal thought that the word 'charitable' in section 61 bore something closer to the 'lay' meaning of charity as poor relief.[71]

The Australian experience is even more instructive. In the early days of the Australian federation, in *Chesterman v Federal Commissioner of Taxation*,[72] the High Court of Australia had to consider the meaning of the word 'charitable' in a provision of a Victorian statute making available exemptions from death duties. A majority of the court gave the word a narrow meaning, along the lines adopted by the minority in *Pemsel*.[73] That decision was overturned by the Privy Council.[74] Australia's federal parliament subsequently legislated to restrict the availability of tax deductions for charity donors to only those donors making gifts to charities with benevolent purposes focused on the relief of distress or disadvantage.[75] That legislative reform decoupled the availability of fiscal benefits for public benefit purposes from the legal conception of charity that applied, and continues to apply, in the trusts law of the states and territories of Australia. A further decoupling occurred in 2013, when Australia's federal parliament enacted the *Charities Act 2013* (Cth). That Act sets out a legal conception of charity that applies for the purposes of Australian federal tax and regulatory law,[76] but because of constitutional limitations on the powers of the federal parliament the Act does not apply for the purposes of state and territory trusts law. As a result, in Australia at the present time, there is one legal conception of charity for the purposes of federal

[69] [1891] AC 531.

[70] ibid 563 (Lord Watson), 573 (Lord Herschell), 589 (Lord Macnaghten, Lord Morris agreeing at 592). It was in the course of describing the trusts law meaning that Lord Macnaghten articulated the famous four 'heads' of charity that have since figured in the legal conception of charity around the common law world: at 583.

[71] ibid 552–53 (Lord Halsbury LC), 565 (Lord Bramwell).

[72] (1923) 32 CLR 362.

[73] ibid 384 (Issacs J), 397–98 (Rich J), 399–400 (Starke J).

[74] *Chesterton v Federal Commissioner of Taxation* (1925) 37 CLR 317.

[75] *Income Tax Assessment Act 1922* (Cth) s 23, as amended by *Income Tax Assessment Act 1927* (Cth). See the discussion in Ann O'Connell, 'The Tax Position of Charities in Australia – Why Does it Have to be so Complicated' (2008) 37 Aust Tax Rev 17.

[76] *Charities Act 2013* (Cth) ss 5–6 and 12.

tax and regulatory law, and an overlapping but different conception for the purposes of trusts law.[77]

The Australian experience shows that the legal conception of charity in trusts law does not necessarily have to apply for the purposes of tax and regulatory law, despite the interpretive move made over a century ago in *Pemsel*. And not only is it possible to decouple trusts law from tax and regulatory law in this way; it seems straightforwardly desirable to do so.[78] The policy objectives underpinning tax and regulatory law seem manifestly different from those underpinning trusts law. In the case of tax law, the policy objectives presumably have to do with securing the revenue and ensuring an equitable allocation of associated benefits and burdens across society as a whole. In the case of regulatory law, the policy objectives might focus more on ensuring that organisations that are endorsed and supported to carry out public benefit purposes adhere to standards of conduct and remain accountable to the public in certain ways. It is not readily apparent why these various policy objectives should in any way affect the position taken in trusts law on the validity or otherwise of a purpose trust. They seem extraneous to trusts law and better pursued via other means.

This then leaves the question: if trusts law's approach to purpose trusts should be unaffected by the policy objectives of tax and regulatory law, then to what policy objectives should that approach be sensitive? This brings us back to the liberal standpoint. From that standpoint, the policy objectives of trusts law seem to have something to do with securing the autonomy of settlors by making available particular modalities distinctive to trusts, including the mode of governance that purpose trusts make possible. It then follows that the policy objectives informing trusts law do not depend on the maintenance of any sort of distinction between valid charitable and (largely) invalid non-charitable purpose trusts. Indeed, it seems arguable that they might be frustrated by such a distinction. On the other hand, I have argued elsewhere that there may be a liberal case for maintaining a public benefit requirement along the lines found in charity law across the common law world insofar as it signals the State's endorsement of a certain kind of altruistic action.[79] If that argument holds, it may be defensible to maintain a distinction between public and private purpose-oriented arrangements—including trusts—to highlight those altruistic arrangements that the State considers worthy of its endorsement, quite apart from any tax or regulatory settings.

That said, a policy objective of endorsing certain public purpose-oriented arrangements does not support an approach to purpose trusts that considers them valid or invalid depending on whether they fall within the legal conception of charity. The

[77] Indeed, the picture is even more complex because in some instances state and territory tax statutes use legal conceptions of charity that depart from both trusts law and federal tax and regulatory law: see further: Ian Murray, 'Regulating Charity in a Federated State: The Australian Perspective' (2018) 9(4) Nonprofit Policy Forum 20180034 <https://doi.org/10.1515/npf-2018-0034>, accessed 7 October 2022.

[78] See Gino Dal Pont, 'Why Define "Charity"? Is the Search for Meaning Worth the Effort?' (2002) 8(1) Third Sect Rev 5.

[79] Matthew Harding, *Charity Law and the Liberal State* (CUP 2014), especially ch 3; Matthew Harding, 'Independence and Accountability in the Charity Sector' in John Picton and Jennifer Sigafoos (eds), *Debates in Charity Law* (Hart Publishing 2020); Matthew Harding, 'Charity and Law: Past, Present and Future' [2020] Sing JLS 564.

better approach, bearing in mind liberal commitments to autonomy-enhancing facilitative law, might be one in which all public purpose trusts are recognised as valid in law and endorsed by the State along with other public purpose-oriented arrangements. In drawing such a distinction between public and private purpose trusts, the State might maintain its commitment to supporting altruistic action, but without at the same time adhering to the historic conception of 'charity'. Meanwhile, policy objectives informing the tax and regulatory treatment of public benefit organisations might be pursued through tax and regulatory law. In such a world, tax and regulatory law might affect the legal position of public purpose trusts, just as it might affect public purpose-oriented arrangements of other descriptions. But it would not affect the anterior question whether a public purpose trust is valid.

IV. Private Purpose Trusts: Limits and Enforcement

If there is a liberal argument for recognising public purpose trusts as valid, what about private purpose trusts? The proposition that private purpose trusts might be valid in law seems dramatically at odds with the current treatment of such trusts at least in onshore jurisdictions. What reasons might be offered for limiting the recognition of purpose trusts to only those purpose trusts with a public character? One type of argument for recognising only public purpose trusts stems from what might be called the 'deficit model' of purpose trusts. According to the deficit model, purpose trusts lack core characteristics of the trust as a legal form as they do not entail a jural relationship between trustee and beneficiary. On this view, public purpose trusts (whether charitable purpose trusts or some more encompassing category as outlined above) might be recognised in law because they are normatively desirable despite the fact that they are conceptually lacking as trusts. However, the view goes, there is no normative argument for the recognition of private purpose trusts that might overcome the problem posed by the fact that such trusts do not instantiate jural relationships. Overall, the deficit view is that beneficiary trusts are both 'true' and normatively desirable trusts, endorsed public purpose trusts are normatively desirable even though they are not 'true' trusts, and private purpose trusts are neither 'true' trusts nor normatively desirable.[80]

The deficit model might be challenged on the basis that it rests on a contestable assumption about the core characteristics of the trust as a legal form. According to some scholars, the trust is not best conceived as a jural relationship between trustee and beneficiary but rather as a governance arrangement in which a trustee has binding obligations to hold and steward assets in certain ways.[81] This latter conception of the trust has

[80] James Penner, 'Justifying (or Not) the Office of Trusteeship With Particular Reference to Massively Discretionary Trusts' (2021) 34(2) Can J Law Jurisprud 365, 368–70. See also JE Penner, *The Law of Trusts* (11th edn, OUP 2019), 243–45; Matthews, 'From Obligation to Property' (n 13); Matthews, 'The New Trust' (n 21).

[81] The debate as to the proper conceptualisation of the trust relationship is far from settled. See Matthews, 'From Obligation to Property' (n 13) 206–13 for an overview of the debate between those who view the trust through the lens of property and ownership, and those who see the trust as a species of personal obligation. For detailed arguments in favour of the latter conceptualisation of the trust, see John H Langbein, 'The Contractarian Basis of the Law of Trusts' (1995) 105 Yale L J 625; David Hayton, 'Developing the Obligation Characteristic of the

the theoretical advantage of explaining how approved public purpose trusts (whether or not limited to charitable purpose trusts) can be understood as central cases of trusts, as opposed to trusts in some partial, lesser, or different sense. Given that such arrangements have been described as trusts for hundreds of years, this theoretical advantage seems a significant one. In any event, the fact that the deficit model is closely connected to a contestable conceptual account of the trust as a legal form suggests a need to look beyond arguments against the recognition of private purpose trusts that rely on the deficit model. Moreover, we saw earlier that a liberal argument seems available for purpose trusts as part of facilitative private law, whether those trusts are for public or private purposes. The possibility of this argument should motivate us further to look beyond the deficit model in trying to establish boundaries around the recognition of private purpose trusts.

Once we look beyond the deficit model, considerations of public policy come squarely into view. If such considerations demand the recognition of beneficiary trusts and approved public purpose trusts, but not private purpose trusts, then this might justify the traditional scepticism towards private purpose trusts in English law, notwithstanding that there is a prima facie liberal argument for purpose trusts of all types given the distinctive mode of governance they entail. From a liberal standpoint, some public policy considerations seem straightforwardly applicable to all trusts. For example, in their chapter in this collection, Dagan and Samet discuss trusts that in their terms discriminate against historically disadvantaged groups. They argue that such trusts should be treated with caution in any legal system that seeks to maintain autonomy-enhancing facilitative private law.[82] In other work, I have also explored this topic, arguing that trusts that discriminate in their terms should not be facilitated in liberal private law to the extent that they demean historically disadvantaged groups in ways that undermine autonomy.[83] Thus, to take a couple of examples, a trust to promote some viewpoint that is discriminatory in racial or gender terms should not be enabled in liberal private law;[84] nor should a trust to further the purposes of a political party whose agenda is bigoted in some way. To the extent that discriminatory terms are more likely to shape purpose trusts than beneficiary trusts, the public policy against harmful discrimination is likely to apply with particular force to purpose trusts. However, and significantly for present purposes, such public policy considerations do not ground any sort of argument against private purpose trusts specifically, but instead touch all trusts whatever their formal character.[85]

Trust' (2001) 117 LQR 96 (hereafter Hayton, 'Developing the Obligation Characteristic'); Patrick Parkinson, 'Reconceptualising the Express Trust' (2002) 61 CLJ 657. For a defence of the view that trust beneficiaries should be regarded as the beneficial owners of trust property, see JE Penner, 'The (True) Nature of a Beneficiary's Equitable Proprietary Interest under a Trust' 27(2) Can J Law Jurisprud 473.

[82] Dagan and Samet, 'Dark Horse' (n 24) 48–55.

[83] Matthew Harding, 'Some Arguments against Discriminatory Gifts and Trusts' (2011) 31(2) OJLS 303; Matthew Harding, *Charity Law and the Liberal State* (CUP 2014), ch 7.

[84] See, eg, *Attorney-General v Family First New Zealand* [2022] NZSC 80 [135]–[140].

[85] *King NO v De Jager* [2021] ZACC 4. See also Francois du Toit, Matthew Harding and Andreas Humm, '*King NO v De Jager* 2021 4 SA 1 (CC): Three Perspectives' (2022) 33 Stellenbosch L Rev 501.

A similar point might be made about the public policy considerations that trusts scholars sometimes raise against settlor uses of trusts to shield assets from the legitimate claims of others. There can be no doubt that in offshore jurisdictions private purpose trusts are used routinely to achieve such objectives. As Paul Matthews has argued, such trusts allow beneficial interests in trust assets simply to disappear from view, leaving legitimate claims against those beneficial interests with nowhere to go.[86] To the extent that private purpose trusts are used for asset shielding, it is strongly arguable that they should not be recognised in facilitative private law. The liberal argument for recognising purpose trusts and their entailed distinctive mode of governance seems weak at best when the purpose for which trustees are given a mandate by the settlor is contrary to public policy. However, once again, this argument from public policy is not confined to private purpose trusts, even if it applies with particular force to such trusts. Problematic asset shielding is not confined to private purpose trusts, as is evidenced by the recent literature criticising the use of 'massively discretionary trusts' by settlors seeking to enjoy the benefit of ownership of assets while shielding those assets from legitimate claims.[87] Indeed, recent cases highlighting some of the relevant public policy concerns have not involved purpose trusts at all, but rather beneficiary trusts coupled with wide powers of appointment.[88] Public policy considerations should be deployed against private purpose trusts where these are used for asset shielding, but the same considerations should be deployed with equal force against all trusts used for such ends, irrespective of the form they happen to take.

This brings me to the question of enforcement. Challenges relating to the enforcement of private purpose trusts are often spoken of as one of the biggest impediments to their recognition in law.[89] In *Morice v Bishop of Durham*, both Sir William Grant MR and Lord Eldon spoke of the deep connection between the recognition of trusts and the extent to which trustees may be held accountable in a court in matters relating to the performance of the trust.[90] On the deficit model of private purpose trusts, this deep connection takes the form of a conceptual truth about trusts as jural relationships between trustees and beneficiaries in which beneficiaries have rights against trustees and standing to enforce those rights. On this view, private purpose trusts are unenforceable because they lack beneficiaries. As we have seen, the deficit model rests on contestable claims about the conceptual character of trusts. But even if we reject the deficit model, the lesson of *Morice v Bishop of Durham* seems hard to ignore: a trust is not viable as a legal form unless trustees are accountable. And trustees are not accountable unless there is someone with standing to bring before the court questions relating to that

[86] Matthews, 'The New Trust' (n 21) 19–22.

[87] Hanoch Dagan and Irit Samet-Porat, 'What's Wrong with Massively Discretionary Trusts' (2022) 138 LQR 649; Smith, 'Massively Discretionary Trusts' (n 2).

[88] *Clayton v Clayton* [2016] 1 NZLR 551; *JSC Mezhdunarodniy Promyshlenniy Bank v Pugachev* [2017] EWHC 2426 (Ch); *Webb v Webb (Cook Islands)* [2020] UKPC 22.

[89] See Low, 'The Right to Forgo Enforcement' (n 21). See also *Leahy v The Attorney-General for New South Wales* [1959] AC 457, 478–79; *Re Astor's Settlement Trusts* (n 20) 547–49 (Roxburgh J); *Re Wood* [1949] Ch 498.

[90] *Morice v Bishop of Durham*(1804) 9 Ves 399, 404–05, and see also *Morice v Bishop of Durham* (1805) 10 Ves 521, 532–33, 539–40 (Lord Eldon).

accountability. In the case of beneficiary trusts, beneficiaries have this standing. In the case of approved public purpose trusts (whether or not limited to charitable purpose trusts), the State, acting through the office of the Attorney-General and also through charity regulators in several jurisdictions, has standing to hold trustees accountable in the public interest. Matters are much less clear in the case of private purpose trusts. Who has standing to enforce such trusts?

As David Hayton has made clear in his seminal work on the topic, once the deficit model of private purpose trusts is put to one side, the settlor of such a trust may address enforcement by simply appointing an enforcer who, according to the trust terms, has the standing to hold the trustee to account.[91] This enforcer might be the settlor herself or someone else whom the settlor trusts to ensure that the trustee carries out the settlor's stipulated private purpose. In the absence of a dogmatic insistence that a trust must be a jural relationship between trustee and beneficiary, the existence of a settlor-appointed enforcer is not conceptually difficult. Rather, it is one available response to an open question about the enforcement of purpose trusts that might be answered in a variety of ways. Indeed, we already see alternative responses in the sphere of charitable purpose trusts, where the Attorney-General is the traditional enforcer, but standing is extended in several jurisdictions to regulators and members of the public as well.[92] Indeed, once the understanding of the trust as a jural relationship between trustee and beneficiary is set aside, it might even be possible to imagine the conceptual possibility of a beneficiary trust with a non-beneficiary settlor-appointed enforcer who enjoys standing to hold the trustee to account.

While the enforcement of private purpose trusts raises no special conceptual problems, it might nonetheless raise practical problems grounding public policy reasons against recognising such trusts. At least two considerations seem relevant to the question of practical problems associated with enforcement. One is that, unlike the beneficiaries of a beneficiary trust, the enforcer of a private purpose trust has no interest in the trust assets and, to that extent, lacks a motivation to enforce that beneficiaries might ordinarily be expected to have. Another consideration is that, unlike the Attorney-General, the enforcer of a private purpose trust has no duties arising from public office that bear on the exercise of her enforcement powers. The Attorney-General is accountable to the public in the exercise of her enforcement powers in relation to charitable purpose trusts, while the enforcer of a private purpose trust lacks this public accountability. Indeed, as Kelvin Low has argued, the enforcer of a private purpose trust may be accountable to no-one in the exercise of her enforcement powers. For Low, this lack of accountability in enforcement sets private purpose trusts apart from other trusts in a way that shows them to be of particular concern.[93]

[91] Hayton, 'Developing the Obligation Characteristic' (n 81) 103–04.

[92] Charities Act 2011 (England and Wales), ss 114 and 115; Trustee Ordinance (Hong Kong) cap 29, s 57A(a)(iii); *Trustee Act 1925* (ACT) s 70(5)(e); *Trustee Act 1936* (SA) s 36(1c)(e); Charities Act (Singapore, cap 37, 1994 Rev Ed) s 32. In the United States, standing is extended to those who have a 'special interest' in the charity, see, eg, *Lucker v Bayside Cemetery*, 979 NYS 2d 8 (NY, 2013).

[93] Low, 'The Right to Forgo Enforcement' (n 21) 489–94.

Worries about lack of motivation and accountability should not be overstated. The beneficiaries of 'massively discretionary trusts' might lack motivation to exercise powers of enforcement given that trustees enjoy wide powers of appointment in favour of others that, in practice, mean dispositions of trust assets will never be made to the beneficiaries.[94] In many jurisdictions, the Attorney-General is under-resourced, under-staffed, and lacks the political will to exercise enforcement powers in respect of charitable purpose trusts.[95] At the same time, Hayton points out that the settlor of a private purpose trust might choose an enforcer because the enforcer already holds an office or role in which she has legal duties to pursue the purpose specified by the settlor quite apart from the trust.[96] In these circumstances, extant duties generate motivations to exercise enforcement powers in respect of the trust. And a settlor might appoint an enforcer who has professional responsibilities demanding that she takes seriously her role when exercising her enforcement powers.[97] In these ways, private purpose trust enforcers might be motivated and made accountable notwithstanding that they lack interests in trust assets and are not subject to public law duties.

Nonetheless, concerns about the practical enforcement of private purpose trusts are sufficiently weighty to raise the question whether some new enforcement model might be desirable if such trusts were ever to be recognised in the onshore world. One possible model is foreshadowed by section 115 of the English Charities Act conferring standing, in respect of charitable purpose trust enforcement, on 'any person interested in' the trust.[98] In a similar way, enforcement powers could be conferred on individuals 'interested in' private purpose trusts. A provision such as this has the potential to enable those with the requisite motivation to ensure that the trustees of private purpose trusts are held accountable before the court. However, how such a provision might operate turns in large part on how courts interpret 'interested in' in the setting of the provision.

As Hui Jing points out in his recent study of section 115 of the English Charities Act 2011, being 'interested in' a purpose trust might mean being in a position to benefit from the exercise of dispositive powers by the trustees, or it might mean being concerned in a more abstract way for the furtherance of the purpose for which the trust exists.[99] Jing argues that English courts have tended to favour the latter interpretation in the Charities Act 2011 setting but notes that the matter is not beyond dispute.[100] I want to suggest here that adopting this latter understanding of 'interested in' is desirable in cases of charitable purpose trusts and would be equally desirable if such a provision were enacted in respect of private purpose trust enforcement. Recall that a

[94] Smith, 'Massively Discretionary Trusts' (n 2) 29–30.
[95] See, eg, *Rosewood* (n 46).
[96] Hayton, 'Developing the Obligation Characteristic' (n 81) 99–100.
[97] Under s 1(1)(c) of the Isle of Man's Purpose Trusts Act 1996, a purpose trust must have at least two trustees, at least one of whom must be a 'designated person'. A 'designated person' must either be a trustee corporation or a person with certain professional responsibilities: s 9(1). While these provisions relate to trustees, there is no reason why similar provisions or terms could not work in respect of enforcers.
[98] Charities Act 2011 (UK), s 115.
[99] Hui Jing, 'Enforcing Charitable Trusts: A Study on the English Necessary Interest Rule' (2022) 42(2) iesLeg Stud 228, 232–36.
[100] ibid 234–36.

purpose trust entails a particular modality that demands of trustees that they approach questions of governance within a certain intellectual framework. It is the furtherance of abstract purposes, not the (potentially competing) interests of persons that should be given priority in purpose-based governance. This is the case not only for trustees but also for others charged with the governance of purpose trusts, including enforcers. The ideal enforcer of a purpose trust, then, is one who will readily think in terms of the furtherance of the abstract purpose for which the trust has been settled, and not with reference to the ways in which she herself might benefit from that purpose being carried out. Reflection on the distinctive character of purpose trusts thus generates some insights into desirable models of enforcement of purpose trusts of all types. However, it does not fully answer the difficult questions about motivation and accountability that Low and others have highlighted.

V. Conclusion

A fresh look at purpose trusts reveals that in some ways trusts law operates on the basis of distinctions that, once subjected to scrutiny, seem difficult to defend. The maintenance of a distinction between beneficiary trusts and purpose trusts depends on interpretive acts about which reasonable minds might sometimes disagree. The distinction between charitable purpose trusts and non-charitable purpose trusts cannot be reconciled easily with relevant public policy objectives and might be better replaced with a distinction between public purpose trusts and private purpose trusts. Finally, the conceptual distinctions underpinning the view of the trust as a jural relationship between trustee and beneficiary come under pressure once it is acknowledged that charitable purpose trusts are not jural relationships and yet have been regarded as trusts for hundreds of years.

In other ways, however, a fresh look at purpose trusts demands that legal distinctions be taken more seriously than is arguably the case currently. For example, the distinction between purpose-oriented trusts and purpose-oriented corporations seems significant once all the incidents of the distinctive modality of purpose trusts are brought into view. For the same reason, the distinction between purpose duties and purpose powers is meaningful, even if problems of practical enforcement arise in respect of both. But perhaps the most important lesson that emerges from a fresh look at purpose trusts is that such trusts offer settlors something distinctive that cannot be accessed fully using other legal forms. This grounds a prima facie liberal argument for recognising purpose trusts in facilitative private law. If limits are then to be drawn around the recognition of purpose trusts, those limits must be justified by clear arguments of public policy, and not extrapolated from conceptual claims about trusts that turn out to be contestable.

9

Administrators as Trustees of Australian Class Action Settlements

Simone Degeling[*]

I. Introduction

This chapter is about trusts of the proceeds of class actions. Finality in an Australian Federal class action[1] may be achieved via settlement or judgment. This chapter considers the position in relation to settlement, by far the most common route to finality.[2] If the settlement includes a fund of settlement monies, these funds ('the recovery') will be held pursuant to a court-sanctioned private express trust.[3] The court appoints an 'Administrator' who holds the recovery on trust for eligible group members according to the terms of the settlement. The office of Administrator is not provided for in the *Federal Court of Australia Act 1976* (Cth) Part IVA ('Part IVA') nor any equivalent state legislation. Rather, the office is one recognised or created by the parties in their settlement agreement and recognised and approved by the court in approving the terms of any class action settlement where a trust is contemplated or declared in the settlement distribution scheme ('SDS'). This chapter seeks to understand the distinct contribution

* ORCID id 0000-0001-7498-8590. I am indebted to Scott Donald, Rebecca Gilsenan, Matthew Harding, Jessica Hudson, The Hon Justice Jeremy Kirk JA, Michael Legg, Paul Miller, Charles Mitchell, and Irit Samet for their comments and generously discussing some of the ideas in this chapter with me. I thank Jack Zhou for his research assistance. All remaining errors are my own.

[1] Statute provides for opt-out class actions in the Federal Court of Australia and the Supreme Courts of Victoria, New South Wales, and Queensland: *Federal Court of Australia Act 1976* (Cth) Part IVA (hereafter Part IVA); *Civil Procedure Act 2005* (NSW) Part 10; *Supreme Court Act 1986* (Vic) Part 4A; *Civil Proceedings Act 2011* (QLD) Part 13A. The *Civil Procedure (Representative Proceedings) Bill* 2019 (WA) has been introduced to the Western Australian Parliament but has yet to be made law. The state regimes are similar, but not identical, to Part IVA. This chapter proceeds by reference to Part IVA, drawing on other state examples where relevant. Unless otherwise indicated, all class action statutory references are to Part IVA.

[2] In the period 2004–17, 60 per cent of all Part IVA actions were resolved by judicially approved settlement agreement. 10.6 per cent of proceedings were dismissed and over 20 per cent were discontinued. A trial is rare. See Australian Law Reform Commission, *Integrity, Fairness and Efficiency-An Inquiry Into Class Action Proceedings and Third Party Litigation Funders* (ALRC Report No 134, December 2018) table 3.6.

[3] The only situation in which the settlement recovery will *not* be held on trust is a class action settled on terms incorporating a so called 'process' settlement distribution scheme. According to this approach, the class action settles by agreeing a method of determining liability and compensation in relation to each group member. The total settlement amount may or may not be capped. Gilsenan and Legg describe this approach as 'a form of adversarial alternative dispute resolution'. There is no fund of settlement monies held by an administrator and hence no trustee or trust. Instead, funds are held by the respondent pending resolution of liability and quantum of compensation in relation to each group member. See R Gilsenan and M Legg, 'Australian Class Action Settlement Distribution Scheme Design – Deciding Who Gets What' (2019) 38 UQLJ 15, 24 (hereafter Gilsenan and Legg, 'Australian Class Action Settlement Distribution Scheme Design').

Simone Degeling, *Administrators as Trustees of Australian Class Action Settlements* In: *Philosophical Foundations of the Law of Express Trusts.* Edited by: Simone Degeling, Jessica Hudson, and Irit Samet, Oxford University Press. © Simone Degeling 2023. DOI: 10.1093/oso/9780192844934.003.0010

made by the express trust relationship to the administration of class action settlements. It asks what is the value added by the use of an express trust of the recovery or how may its use be justified?

A trust of the recovery ensures that any monetary award agreed in the settlement and approved by the court is assured; that it is actually delivered to the hands of group members. Group members exercise their autonomy in deciding to remain in a Part IVA proceeding instead of opting out. However, in real terms, this is not simply a choice to be part of a class action: group members desire a meaningful remedy or redress. In providing the apparatus of justice, courts must ensure that any settlement funds reach group members. The use of the trust form ensures that this happens. The objectives of Part IVA are '(1) to promote the efficient use of court time and the parties' resources by eliminating the need to separately try the same issue; (2) [t]o provide a remedy in favour of persons who may not have the funds to bring a separate action, or who may not bring an action because the cost of litigation is disproportionate to the value of the claim; and (3) [t]o protect defendants from multiple suits and the risk of inconsistent findings'.[4] The trust presents a means of keeping faith with these objectives via a structure of delegated authority and decision-making. The Administrator is the court's delegate and permits the Administrator to assume responsibility for administering the recovery. The trust offers a direct line of reporting and responsibility which permits close supervision by the court yet also permits the delegation of appropriate powers to the Administrator. Correlatively, the trust also facilitates the enrolment of suitable actors as Administrator. Finally, the stable yet flexible character of the trust form permits the ability to craft bespoke terms reflecting the terms of a particular settlement, while also permitting asset segregation and partitioning, enrolment, and delegation. However, the trust is not simply a structure of delegated decision-making. Crucially, it also carries with it a set of rules which ensure that the Administrator as trustee adheres to the terms of the SDS and the ability of the court directly to carry into execution the terms of the SDS should the Administrator fail to do so. The trust thus offers a more perfect or absolute form of the administration of justice, because equity's default posture is to supervise and compel the Administrator as trustee to perform the trust. This is important precisely because the Administrator is the court's delegate in administering the SDS.

The discussion in this chapter proceeds as follows. Section II sets out aspects of the Federal class actions regime as the procedural context in which the trust terms exist. Section III considers the above justifications which may be offered for the use of a trust of the recovery and Section IV briefly concludes.

[4] *Bright v Femcare Ltd* [2002] FCAFC 243; (2002) 195 ALR 574 [152] (Finkelstein J).

II. Procedural Context

This section briefly sketches the Australian Federal class actions regime to provide the statutory context in which the Administrator, and the terms on which any recovery is held, operate. Consistent with its objectives,[5] Part IVA permits the claims of many to be aggregated and pursued by a representative applicant on behalf of group members. Part IVA regulates the initiation,[6] conduct, and settlement of proceedings.

A. Forming a Class

A representative proceeding may be commenced where seven or more persons have claims against the same person, the claims of all those persons are 'in respect of, or arise out of, the same, similar or related circumstances' and these claims give rise to 'a substantial common issue of law or fact'.[7] The representative applicant is a party to the proceedings and pursues those proceedings on behalf of the represented class.[8] The pleadings need not name individual group members but must 'describe or otherwise identify the group members to whom the proceeding relates',[9] specify the nature of the claims and the relief sought and the common questions of law or fact common to the claims of the group members.[10] Members of the represented class are not parties to the proceeding but are nonetheless bound by the judgment of the court. Res judicata therefore applies on the common questions litigated in the class action.[11] The applicant's lawyer has carriage of the litigation on behalf of all group members.[12]

A class action may have multiple respondents and it is not necessary for all group members to have a claim against all respondents.[13]

Unlike the position in some other jurisdictions, there is no certification requirement.

[5] ibid

[6] There are limits to the scope of Part IVA. For example, the statute does not directly regulate the solicitation of potential group members to the claimant class.

[7] Part IVA (n 1) s 33C(1). There is no requirement that the relief sought for each group member be identical, the proceeding may include claims for damages which require individual assessment, and the action may involve separate acts or omissions of the respondent done or omitted to be done in relation to individual group members: Part IVA (n 1) s 33C(2).

[8] ibid s 33D confirms that the representative party has a 'sufficient interest' to commence and continue a proceeding against the respondent, and bring an appeal from a judgment in the proceeding, on behalf of those referred to in s 33C(1)(a).

[9] ibid s 33H(1)(a).

[10] ibid ss 33H(1)(b) and (c).

[11] ibid s 33ZB provides that a judgment in a representative proceeding binds all affected group members other than those who have exercised their right to opt out of the proceeding. *Anshun* estoppel also applies to the common issues in the proceeding: *Timbercorp Finance Pty Ltd (in liq) v Collins* [2016] HCA 44; (2016) 259 CLR 212.

[12] Some group members may have entered a retainer with the applicant's lawyer and some may not.

[13] *Cash Converters International Limited v Gray* [2014] FCAFC 111; (2014) 223 FCR 139, [13], [22], [28] (the Court).

B. Open and Closed Class Actions and the Right to Opt Out

Class actions may be pursued either as open or closed class actions. In an open class action, consistent with the position that group members are required to be described but not individually identified,[14] group members, or those on who behalf a representative proceeding has been commenced,[15] are not generally required to consent to being in a representative proceeding.[16] Therefore, in an open class action, the individual identity of most group members will not be known.[17] A class action may also be pursued as a closed class action in which named group members consent to participation prior to the commencement of proceedings.[18] In this category, despite consent not being required under Part IVA, it is not forbidden.[19] The identity of group members in a closed class action will therefore be known.

However, irrespective of whether the proceeding is an open or closed class action, all group members have a right to opt out of the proceedings.[20] This right is required to be drawn to the attention of group members via a statutory opt out notice.[21] The court supervises this process[22] and typically requires that group members receive notice of the commencement of the proceeding and of their right to opt out. Group members may opt out by giving written notice,[23] relevantly by returning the opt out notice by the date ordered by the court.

Group members who have opted out are no longer group members and do not participate in the recovery. Those who opt out retain their individual rights, if any, against the respondent. However, group members who have not exercised their right to opt out are bound by any judgment[24] given in the proceedings.[25] However, despite not opting out, not all group members are necessarily entitled to participate in the recovery. This is because the court may approve a class closing procedure as part of,[26] or subsequent to, opt out.

[14] Part IVA (n 1) s 33H(1)(a).

[15] ibid s 33A.

[16] ibid s 33E(1). Section 33E(2) sets out the exceptions, all of whom must give written consent to being a group member: (a) the Commonwealth, a State or a Territory; (b) a Minister or a Minister of a State or Territory; (c) a body corporate established for a public purpose by a law of the Commonwealth, of a State or of a Territory, other than an incorporated company or association; or (d) an officer of the Commonwealth, of a State or of a Territory, in his or her capacity as such an officer.

[17] The identity of the representative applicant, and any other group members who individually retain the applicant's lawyer, will be known.

[18] See, eg, *P Dawson Nominees Pty Ltd v Multiplex Limited* [2007] FCA 1061; (2007) 242 ALR 111, [49] (Finkelstein J); *Multiplex Funds Management Ltd v P Dawson Nominees Pty Ltd* [2007] FCAFC 200; (2007) 164 FCR 275, [141]–[142] (Jacobson J).

[19] ibid

[20] Part IVA (n 1) s 33J.

[21] ibid s 33X(1)(a).

[22] ibid ss 33X(1)(a), 33Y.

[23] ibid s 33J(2).

[24] Which captures a settlement, and binds group members who did not opt out, via s 33V and s 33ZB: *Dyczynski v Gibson* [2020] FCAFC 120; (2020) 381 ALR 1 [247] (Murphy and Colvin JJ), [391] (Lee J).

[25] Part IVA (n 1) s 33ZB(b).

[26] See, eg, *Kelly v Willmott Forests Ltd (in liquidation) (No 4)* [2016] FCA 323; (2016) 335 ALR 439.

Class closure is a procedure whereby the identity of individual class members is ascertained in order to facilitate finality in the proceeding. Class closure is not required by Part IVA, but either the applicant or the respondent may seek orders[27] requiring group members to register by a specified date in order to identify themselves as having an interest in any judgment or settlement obtained.[28] Failure to register for class closure will not constitute opting out of the proceeding, but will mean that the group member will not be entitled to participate in the recovery. In consequence, a non-registered group member is bound by any settlement or judgment[29] but is not entitled to any payment or benefit under the SDS.

C. Obtaining Finality and Court Approval of Settlement

When a class action is settled s 33V is engaged which provides:

> (1) A representative proceeding may not be settled or discontinued without the approval of the Court.
> (2) If the Court gives such an approval, it may make such orders as are just with respect to the distribution of any money paid under a settlement or paid into the Court.

Court approval of the terms of the proposed settlement deed, and the proposed SDS (settlement distribution scheme) which sets out the terms by which any recovery will be distributed to group members, is therefore a condition precedent to the coming into effect of the settlement and SDS. An application for the court's approval is made by interlocutory application[30] and prior notice of the application for settlement approval must be given to group members[31] who may lodge an objection to the terms of settlement.

The settlement deed is entered into by the representative applicant on behalf of group members, the respondent, the litigation funder, and the lawyer for the representative party. The funder and the lawyer are parties to the settlement as their costs will be paid out of the recovery. The court considers both the terms of settlement, as well as the 'structure and workings of the scheme by which [the settlement] sum is proposed to be distributed amongst group members'[32] (ie the SDS), asking whether these are 'fair and reasonable having regard to the claims made by group members who will be bound

[27] Part IVA (n 1) s 33ZF (power to make any order to do justice in the proceeding). In Victoria, this general power (also s 33ZF) is supplemented by *Supreme Court Act 1986* (Vic) s 33ZG (order may specify a date by which group members must take a step).

[28] See, eg, *McMullin v ICI Australia Operations Pty Ltd (No 6)* [1998] FCA 658; (1998) 84 FCR 1, 3–4 (Wilcox J); *Hodges v Waters (No 5)* [2014] FCA 965 [6] (Perram J); *Inabu Pty Ltd v Leighton Holdings Pty Ltd* [2014] FCA 622 [17] (Jacobson J); *Farey v National Australia Bank Ltd* [2014] FCA 1242 [11] (Jacobson J).

[29] Part IVA (n 1) s 33ZB.

[30] Class Actions Practice Note (GPN-CA), Federal Court of Australia, 2019 [15.1] (hereafter Practice Note).

[31] Part IVA (n 1) s 33X(4). This notice may be dispensed with where 'it is just to do so'.

[32] *Darwalla Milling Co Pty Ltd v F Hoffman-La Roche Ltd (No 2)* [2006] FCA 1388; (2006) 236 ALR 322 [41] (Jessup J).

by it'.[33] This is a complex evaluative exercise, taking into account the interests of group members inter se as well as the balance of justice as between the applicant and group members and the respondent. Added to this is the phenomenon of the unknown group member. Particularly where there has not been class closing, in an open class action there will likely be unidentified and unrepresented group members. Therefore, pursuant to s 33V, the court's role 'is protective. It assumes a role akin to that of a guardian, not unlike the role a court assumes when approving infant compromises.'[34] The court also reviews the amounts to be paid out of the recovery to the litigation funder, both as costs and commission, and also to the lawyer.

Assuming that the court approves the deed of settlement and SDS, it will typically make orders which include the following (or similar):

- pursuant to s 33V, approve the settlement of the proceedings on the terms set out in the deed of settlement and the SDS;
- pursuant to s 33ZF, authorise the applicant nunc pro tunc for and on behalf of all group members to enter, and give effect to the transactions contemplated by, the deed of settlement;
- pursuant to s 33ZF, [named person] be appointed as Administrator of the SDS and be given the powers and immunities contained in the SDS, subject to further directions and orders of the Court; and
- [named person] as Administrator under the SDS to have liberty to apply to the Court in relation to any matter arising under the SDS.

D. Administrator as Trustee under the SDS

The Administrator is pursuant to the SDS appointed or otherwise constituted an express trustee of the recovery. The Administrator administers the SDS not the court. The mechanics are that by the terms of settlement, the proceeds of the litigation are paid by the respondent or its insurer into the account identified in the SDS. Legal title to the account is held by the Administrator. The SDS contains the declaration and terms of the trust, which terms also include relevant statute (eg a state trustee act) and equitable principle. For example, the SDS may state that the Administrator will hold the fund containing the recovery on trust.[35] Alternatively, the SDS and court orders may contemplate that the recovery be paid to a nominated legal person, such as a solicitor

[33] *Australian Securities and Investments Commission v Richards* [2013] FCAFC 89, [7] (the Court).

[34] ibid [8]. See also Practice Note (n 30) [15.2] and [15.3].

[35] See, eg, *Endeavour River Pty Ltd v MG Responsible Entity Limited (No 2)* [2020] FCA 968, Annexure A to Orders (hereafter Endeavour River SDS), cl 1.2. *Cantor v Audi Australia Pty Limited (No 5)* [2020] FCA 637 and Settlement Scheme VW, Audi and Skoda Class Actions in the Federal Court of Australia (*Maurice Blackburn*, 11 November 2020) cl 9.3 (held on file with author) (hereafter VW, Audi and Skoda SDS).

for the applicant, and held in the trust account of that solicitor pursuant to the terms of the SDS.[36]

The analysis in this chapter assumes that a private express trust has been validly declared and properly constituted. The trust property is the balance of the account or a specified sum to be held as a traceably identifiable part of a mixture already held by the Administrator on trust.[37] Although we may formally identify the respondent as settlor, the intentions of this party are in this context not particularly significant. This is because the funds are paid pursuant to the terms of a settlement agreed by the claimant and respondent which has received the imprimatur of the court. Nonetheless, it is not in doubt that the respondent evinces an intention to declare a trust as part of the settlement. The potential beneficiaries or objects of the trust are the group members entitled to participate in the recovery who are described but not necessarily identified. In many cases, the court will also at a prior stage have ordered class closing requiring an act of individual registration by group members. While an application under s 33V is not directed to certainty of objects, it is tolerably secure that the trust meets the requirements of conceptual certainty[38] and mechanisms such as class closing provide the means of obtaining evidential certainty such that list certainty is satisfied. However, the Administrator is not able to tell by the class closing or group description the share of each group member's interest in the fund. This turns on the particular terms of each SDS. Depending on the terms, group members may be beneficiaries or objects.

However, as foreshadowed in the Introduction, it is not invariably the case that the recovery will be held on trust. The exception is a process SDS. Part IVA imposes no limit on how an SDS may be designed, so long as it receives court approval under s 33V. In a process SDS,[39] no trust is required as the SDS may contemplate a structure pursuant to which title to the recovery (or a part of it) is held by the respondent or, on payment, held by the group member. A mechanism to distribute the recovery from a fund, and a means to supervise that mechanism, is therefore not required. An example is *Casey v DePuy International (No 2)*[40] which concerned implants used as components in knee replacement surgery. The applicant commenced a class action against the

[36] *Lenehan v Powercor Australia Ltd (No 2)* [2020] VSC 159; Orders of The Honourable Justice Nichols' (Supreme Court of Victoria, 6 April 2020) <https://www.supremecourt.vic.gov.au/sites/default/files/2020-04/Lenehan%20orders%20of%20the%20Honourable%20Justice%20Nichols%206%20April%202020.pdf>, accessed 20 July 2021.

[37] See, eg, 'Terang/Cobden Bushfire Class Action Settlement Distribution Scheme' (Supreme Court of Victoria, 6 April 2020) <https://www.supremecourt.vic.gov.au/sites/default/files/2020-04/Terang%20Settlement%20Distribution%20Scheme.pdf>, accessed 20 July 2021 (hereafter Terang SDS), where the definition of Settlement Sum 'means ... $17,500,000 plus interest ... in the Settlement Distribution Fund' where the Settlement Distribution Fund was a controlled moneys account 'to be established by [lawfirm] with [named bank] for the purpose of the Scheme'.

[38] See, eg, Endeavour River SDS, Annexure A, cl 11 (Definitions): 'Group Member means all persons who acquired an interest in fully paid units in the Murray Goulburn Unit Trust in the period 29 May 2015 to 26 April 2016 (inclusive), are alleged to have suffered loss or damage by reason of the [respondent] ... and have entered into a litigation funding agreement with [named litigation funder by date] ... and have not otherwise opted out of [the class action].'

[39] See Gilsenan and Legg, 'Australian Class Action Settlement Distribution Scheme Design' (n 3) 24. In a 'process settlement distribution scheme' the proceeding settles by agreeing a method of determining liability and compensation in relation to each group member. The total settlement amount may or may not be capped. The authors describe this approach as 'a form of adversarial alternative dispute resolution'.

[40] [2012] FCA 1370 (hereafter *Casey*).

manufacturer alleging breach of the statutory warranties in the *Trade Practices Act 1974* (Cth) and negligent manufacture in respect of implants used in her 2008 bilateral knee replacement surgery.[41] The action was subject to class closure and settled on the basis that the agreed Liability Protocol[42] and Compensation Protocol[43] would be applied. These protocols received the necessary imprimatur of the court.[44] The scheme contemplated that individual group members would individually be legally represented or self-represented in the administration of the SDS. Crucially, there was no settlement fund or global amount approved in the settlement. Therefore, no Administrator of a fund was required, and no trust was declared. Process SDSs therefore necessarily fall outside the ambit of this chapter and will not further be discussed.

III. Evaluating the Use of Trusts in Administering Class Action Recoveries

Justifications for the use of trusts of the recovery may be made on the grounds that the trust: (A) delivers the settlement approved by the court and assures any monetary award reaches the hands of group members; (B) provides necessary legal infrastructure in the sense that it facilitates the supervision of the administration of the recovery; (C) permits the enrolment of actors with the necessary capacity to administer the recovery; (D) is autonomy enhancing; and (E) is a source of default law or a device for importing default law. As will be seen, these justifications are mutually supporting and interlinked.

Importantly, although we may identify one or some of these qualities in other institutional forms, none of these other forms carries the whole package, ie *all* of the benefits of a trust.

A. The Trust Delivers the Justice and Monetary Award Approved by the Court

The claims brought in class actions are diverse and include civil wrongs and statutory claims, which together may be understood as legal wrongs.[45] Leading legal theorists have sought to explain why it is that law imposes liability on those who commit legal wrongs. It lies beyond the remit of this chapter to give detailed accounts of these theories. Of relevance is the observation that all rest on the role of courts in providing the apparatus of justice and the means to vindicate rights and remedy wrongs. Moreover, all

[41] ibid [4] (Buchanan J).
[42] 'Casey v DePuy Liability Protocol' (on file with author).
[43] 'Casey v DePuy Compensation Protocol' (on file with author).
[44] *Casey* (n 40) [19] (Buchanan J).
[45] Peter Birks, 'Definitions and Divisions: A Meditation on *Institutes* 3:13' in P Birks (ed), *The Classification of Obligations* (Clarendon Press 1997) 1, 23–27; P Birks, 'Equity in the Modern Law: An Exercise In Taxonomy' (1996) 26 UWALR 1, 10–11.

observe that the justice dispensed must be taken to be meaningful justice, in the sense that whatever remedy is awarded is actually delivered or acquitted. As explained below, a trust of the recovery ensures that, to the extent that a monetary remedy is agreed in the settlement and approved by the court under s 33V, it is delivered to the hands of group members. I take corrective justice and civil recourse theories to illustrate.

Corrective justice theorists emphasise the relational nature of legal liabilities. Corrective justice lies in the parties having what 'lawfully belongs to them'.[46] Injustice arises when, compared to this standard, 'one party realizes a gain and the other a corresponding loss'.[47] The law corrects this injustice by restoring the parties to their prior position. There is correlativity between the parties. The defendant's liability 'reflects the conclusion that the defendant and the [claimant] have respectively done and suffered the same injustice'.[48] Thus, the defendant has an obligation to restore or repair the particular claimant. Leaving aside the limited possibility of self-help, this will involve the work of courts. Consider, for example, John Gardner's account. He argues that the effect of designating conduct as a wrong (specifically, a tort), entails 'creating a legal right to corrective justice in favour of those who are wronged'.[49] This legal right to corrective justice is actually a bundle of rights which 'include not only the wrongdoer's duty to repair, but also a largely undirected legal power for the person wronged to determine whether that legal duty is concretized and enforced through the courts, with a consequent duty on the courts to assist, when that power is validly exercised by the issue of proceedings'.[50] Thus the wronged party is given not only against the wrongdoer but also a right to 'conscript the court (and its officers) in . . . [the wronged party's] quest for corrective justice'.[51]

The central claim of civil recourse theories[52] is that legal wrongs (specifically torts) are those things 'for which courts provide victims a right of civil recourse-a right to sue for a remedy'.[53] Civil recourse theorists rest their accounts on the view that 'those who have been wronged are entitled to some avenue of civil recourse against the

[46] Ernest Weinrib, 'Legal Formalism' in D Paterson (ed), *A Companion to Philosophy of Law and Legal Theory* (2nd edn, Blackwell 2010) 327, 330.

[47] ibid 330.

[48] Ernest J Weinrib, *Corrective Justice* (OUP 2012), 10.

[49] John Gardner, 'What is Tort Law For? pt 2. The Place of Distributive Justice' in John Oberdiek (ed), *Philosophical Foundations of the Law of Torts* (OUP 2014) 335, 340.

[50] ibid

[51] ibid. Thus, Gardner further observes (at 341, 344), that *access* to corrective justice is being allocated or distributed.

[52] See generally: Andrew S Gold, 'The Taxonomy of Civil Recourse' (2011) 39 Florida State U L Rev 65. As Gold observes, there are now various schools of civil recourse theory. The foundational work was that of Zipursky, who has also written more recently with Goldberg. See generally: Benjamin C Zipursky, 'Rights, Wrongs, and Recourse in the Law of Torts' (1998) 51(1) Vanderbilt L Rev 1; Benjamin C Zipursky, 'Civil Recourse, Not Corrective Justice' (2003) 91 Georgetown LJ 695 (hereafter Zipursky, 'Civil Recourse, Not Corrective Justice'); Benjamin Zipursky 'Philosophy of Private Law' in Jules Coleman and others (eds), *The Oxford Handbook of Jurisprudence and Philosophy of Law* (OUP 2004) 623; John CP Goldberg and Benjamin C Zipursky, 'Torts as Wrongs' (2010) 88(5) Texas L Rev 917 (hereafter Goldberg and Zipursky, 'Torts as Wrongs'); John CP Goldberg and Benjamin C Zipursky, 'Rights and Responsibilities in the Law of Torts' in Donal Nolan and others (eds), *Rights and Private Law* (Hart Publishing 2011) 251; John CP Goldberg and Benjamin C Zipursky, 'Tort Law and Responsibility' in John Oberdiek (ed), *Philosophical Foundations of the Law of Torts* (OUP 2014) 17 (hereafter Goldberg and Zipursky, 'Tort Law and Responsibility'); and Benjamin C Zipursky, 'Civil Recourse Theory' in Andrew S Gold and others (eds), *The Oxford Handbook of the New Private Law* (OUP 2020) 53 (hereafter Zipursky, 'Civil Recourse Theory').

[53] Goldberg and Zipursky, 'Torts as Wrongs' (n 52) 985.

wrongdoer'.[54] The contemplated 'avenue' is state provided, being a court and its infrastructure. Thus, the granting to individuals who have been 'injuriously wronged a legal power to exact a remedy from the wrongdoer through the courts',[55] for example through the existence and provision of tort law, is not relying on a pre-existing duty of repair.[56] Rather, it fulfils a political duty that the state owes its citizens.[57] As explained by Zipursky, in providing private rights of action and empowering individuals to enforce those right through the courts, the state is fulfilling basic preconditions for a just liberal democracy.[58] Private rights and the right to enforce those rights, shielded from the state's choice as to which rights should be enforced[59] and underlining non-violent and civil exercises of power, are critical to the protection of our security and dignity.[60]

So how does this advance our understanding of the justifications for, advantages of, using a private express trust of a class action recovery? First, that the class actions regime, as embodied in Part IVA, exists at all is in fulfilment of the state's role in providing the means to obtain justice. When we speak of access to courts, that implicitly carries with it a need for a body of civil procedure. Further, as demonstrated by Matthew Shapiro[61] in his discussion of civil recourse theory, theories of justice also presuppose the existence of a body of civil procedure and different theories may emphasise different aspects of procedure. For example, as discussed by Shapiro, civil recourse theorists rely on a relatively '"thick" conception of adjudication that ties the resolution of private law disputes to the state's authority'.[62] Other accounts, including corrective justice accounts, may permit a thinner conception where adjudication is a state-provided means of dispute resolution which is one of a menu of options including, for example, arbitration, mediation, or other privately administered means. Thus, as stated in the objectives of Part IVA,[63] the class action procedure itself is part of the apparatus of justice and one means through which potential group members may obtain repair and redress via the courts.

Second, assuming the use of the Part IVA procedure, that procedure must be capable of delivering whatever outcome or decision is determined in the class action or settlement. The potential remedial consequence of participation in the procedure must be assured, such that any settlement approved by the court will be carried out. The outcome of the class action must be meaningful and tangible. From the perspective of group members, participation in a class action is not only about a determination of rights but, when approved, delivery of a financial settlement to the hands of eligible group members.

[54] Zipursky, 'Civil Recourse Theory' (n 52) 56.
[55] Goldberg and Zipursky, 'Tort Law and Responsibility' (n 52) 27.
[56] Zipursky, 'Civil Recourse, Not Corrective Justice' (n 52) 699.
[57] Goldberg and Zipursky, 'Tort Law and Responsibility' (n 52) 28.
[58] Zipursky, 'Civil Recourse Theory' (n 52) 68.
[59] ibid 66.
[60] ibid 67.
[61] Matthew A Shapiro, 'Civil Wrongs and Civil Procedure' in Paul B Miller and John Oberdiek (eds), *Civil Wrongs and Justice in Private Law* (OUP 2022) 87.
[62] ibid 95.
[63] Above note 4.

Consistently with these objectives, the trust ensures that the recovery will be paid to group members in accordance with the terms of the SDS. As outlined below, group members do not take the risk that the Administrator will use or apply the recovery other than as specified in the SDS and have the right to approach the court for orders seeking specific enforcement of the terms of the SDS. As trustee, the Administrator has a positive obligation to obey the trust terms[64] and, at minimum, to exercise the reasonable care that an 'ordinary prudent [person] of business' would exercise.[65] The powers given to the Administrator in the SDS must be exercised for the purposes for which they were given and not to achieve an improper or ulterior purpose.[66] The Administrator as trustee is not in general permitted to delegate their trust, except where specifically permitted by the SDS, by statute or where it is necessary for the trustee to employ another party as agent.[67] This strong commitment to the intentions of the settlor, as recorded in the SDS and approved by the court, is not replicated in other institutional forms. As observed by Matthew Harding,[68] unlike a corporation, a trust has no separate legal personality, so that the trust cannot hold its own ends which might stand 'at odds' with the mandate of the trustee.

Crucially, the significance of the use of the trust is not simply the bundle of particular duties owed by the Administrator as trustee. Group members have, in addition to the court's general power under Part IVA, the benefit of equity's supervision of the Administrator. Use of the trust form carries with it a right in beneficiaries to the court's assistance in enforcing the trust terms via an administration action seeking orders that the trust be carried into execution by the court.[69] 'Appurtenant'[70] to this right is the court's ability, in appropriate circumstances on application by the trustee, to advise the Administrator[71] and to compel the provision of information by the Administrator as trustee.[72] To this list should be added the Administrator's duty to account which encompasses a duty to keep records, to report to beneficiaries and the court and to pay the amounts required to be paid to group members.[73] The duty to account is reinforced

[64] *Youyang Pty Ltd v Minter Ellison Morris Fletcher* [2002] HCA 15; (2003) 212 CLR 484 [32] (the Court) (hereafter *Youyang*).

[65] *Re Speight* (1883) 22 Ch D 727, 739–58 (Bacon VC); *Speight v Gaunt* (1883) 9 App Cas 1, 19 (Lord Blackburn). An Administrator may well be held to a higher standard of care given their expertise and that they are likely remunerated for their services. See *Bartlett v Barclays Trust Co Ltd (No 1)* [1980] Ch 515, 534 (Brightman J); *Australian Securities and Investments Commission v Drake (No 2)* [2016] FCA 1552; (2016) 340 ALR 75, [272]–[276] (Edelman J).

[66] *Cowan v Scargill* [1985] Ch 270, 288 (Sir Robert Megarry VC); *Karger v Paul* [1984] VR 161.

[67] *Re Bellamy and Metropolitan Board of Works* (1883) 24 Ch D 387, 403–04 (Bowen LJ); *Buckby v Speed* [1959] Qd R 30, 35 (Philp J).

[68] Matthew Harding, 'A Fresh Look at Purpose Trusts' in this book.

[69] *McLean v Burns Philp Trustee Co Pty Ltd* (1985) 2 NSWLR 623; 635 (Young J); *Palmer v Ayres* [2017] HCA 5, (2017) 259 CLR 478, [84]–[85] (Gageler J). This right also accrues to a discretionary object *Blenkinsop v Herbert* [2017] WASCA 87; 51 WAR 264 [72] (the Court).

[70] *Palmer v Ayres* [2017] HCA 5; (2017) 259 CLR 478 [84] (Gageler J).

[71] *Macedonian Orthodox Community Church St Petka In v His Eminence Petar Diocesan Bishop of Macedonian Orthodox Diocese of Australia and New Zealand* (2008) 237 CLR 666 [71]–[74] (Gummow ACJ, Kirby, Hayne and Heydon JJ) and *Trustee Act 1925* (NSW) s 63.

[72] The basis and scope of this right is contested. See J Campbell, 'Access by Trust Beneficiaries to Trustees' Documents and Reasons' (2009) 3 J Eq 1; *Hartigan Nominees Pty Ltd v Rydge* (1999) 29 NSWLR 405 (NSWCA) 421–22 (Kirby P); *Schmidt v Rosewood Trust* [2003] 2 AC 709 (PC) [36], [54] (Lord Walker).

[73] *Byrnes v Kendle* (2011) 243 CLR 253, [42] (Gummow and Hayne JJ); *Hancock v Rinehart* [2015] NSWSC 646, [338]–[341] (Brereton J).

by equity's accounting procedures and ability to give consequential relief,[74] all of which enforce the 'essential nature of the position of a trustee'.[75] As argued by Jessica Hudson and Charles Mitchell in their chapter in this book,[76] the use of the trust form thus carries with it a set of rules which facilitate supervision of the trustee and may assist in preventing a breach of trust by ensuring that the Administrator adheres to the terms of the SDS in the first place, or addressing deviations when these occur. Most significantly, through the availability of the administration action, the trust confers a standard default through which group members may obtain specific relief; a means of ensuring that the settlement approved by the court in the class action is actually delivered to the hands of group members. Other institutional forms do not carry this apparatus of supervision and enforcement packaged with the standard default. For example, it might be possible to craft bespoke contractual arrangements to distribute the recovery, including a suite of reporting requirements to group members. However, as contractual arrangements, these would carry an entitlement to compensatory damages in default of performance, not a right to actual performance.[77] Moreover, such damages would also be subject to the risk that the Administrator might go insolvent and are thus not a proxy for actual performance. Further, it would not by contract be possible to create a right to receive judicial advice.

Additionally, a trust of the recovery uniquely offers as part of the package the proprietary quality of asset segregation and protection. The Administrator holds title to the recovery and is bound by an obligation enforceable in equity to hold that title for the benefit of eligible group members.[78] In consequence, group members do not take a solvency risk on the Administrator. The Administrator does not hold the recovery as part of her personal estate. Contrast the case of a non-class action procedure, where a claimant pursues an individual claim against the defendant. While the claimant may take a solvency risk on *the defendant*, in the case where damages are paid into court, the claimant does not take a solvency risk on *the court*. However, in Part IVA proceedings, without a trust of the recovery, this is the result which obtains. For reasons of practicality, in Part IVA proceedings, the court does not administer the fund of the recovery, it is paid to the Administrator. Thus, unless this money is held by the Administrator in trust, group members take a solvency risk on the Administrator and cannot be assured of that their monetary remedy will be delivered to their hands. This outcome cannot be guaranteed by other potential structures delegating distribution of the recovery. Additionally, this protection does not stop with the Administrator. Group members may also assert a range of personal and proprietary remedies against third party knowing recipients

[74] See generally: *Libertarian Investments v Hall* (2013) 16 HKCFAR 681 [167]–[172] (Lord Millett NPJ); *Agricultural Land Management Ltd v Jackson [No 2]* [2014] WASC 102 [333]–[349] (Edelman J); E Elliott, 'Personal Monetary Claims' in John McGhee (ed), *Snell's Equity* (34th edn, Sweet & Maxwell 2020) ch 20.

[75] *Spellson v George* (1987) 11 NSWLR 300, 316 (Powell J).

[76] J Hudson and C Mitchell, 'Justificanda' in this book.

[77] Group members may potentially have an equity for specific performance for such contracts. However, this might be difficult to establish given the nature of the contract being for payment of a money sum and the requirement that damages not be adequate. Additionally, the availability of specific performance would be subject to any bars to relief.

[78] *DKLR Holding Co (No 2) Pty Ltd v Commissioner of Stamp Duties* [1980] 1 NSWLR 510, 518–20 (Hope JA).

of trust property or its traceable substitutes,[79] and those who attract accessorial liabilities.[80] Further, group members or the Administrator may assert a claim for recovery of misapplied assets or their traceable substitute which can be asserted against any former Administrator, their trustee in bankruptcy and third-party recipients.[81]

B. The Trust as Infrastructure

A trust creates a single line of reporting and responsibility in relation to the distribution of the recovery according to the terms of the SDS. This permits and facilitates close supervision of the distribution of the recovery according to Part IVA and the orders made in the proceeding. As identified by Scott Donald, a distinctive feature of trusts is that they have an 'infrastructure role'[82] which includes that trusts focus responsibility for administration of the trust on the office of trustee. As Donald describes, the trustee sits at the apex of a complex 'matrix of accountabilities'[83] which arise in two senses. First, with respect to the administration of trust assets, '[n]o other private party can assert authority over the administration of the trust'.[84] Leaving aside the case where specific trust terms in the trust instrument reserve powers to others or require consultation with others, the trustee alone is empowered to take decisions, exercise discretions, and act with respect to the trust property and the trust terms. Moreover, as noted above, these duties are not delegable. Second, as Donald describes, the 'law of trusts makes the trustee accountable in the event of specific types of deficiency in the administration of trust'.[85] For example, the trustee owes duties to the beneficiaries which are enforceable in equity.

In consequence, despite the presence of other actors, a regulatory body or court is able to focus on the trustee as a 'primary object of regulation'.[86] This is via equity's administrative jurisdiction discussed above and also pursuant to Part IVA. The trust as a device is therefore uniquely compatible with Part IVA. The trust focuses the trustee as the primary object of the court's supervision and orders in administering the SDS under that legislation. Following orders under s 33V approving the SDS, the court continues to supervise the implementation of the SDS. The Administrator is required to report to the court during the life of the SDS and at its conclusion. As in other regulatory contexts, the 'placing of ... powers and obligations in a single central location [the

[79] *Barnes v Addy* (1874) LR 9 Ch App 244, 252 (Lord Selborne); *Farah Constructions Pty Ltd v Say-Dee Pty Ltd* (2007) 230 CLR 89.

[80] ibid; *Consul Developments Pty Ltd v DPC Estates Pty Ltd* (1975) 132 CLR 373.

[81] *Foskett v McKeown* [2001] 1 AC 102; *Grimaldi v Chameleon Mining NL [No 2]* (2012) 200 FCR 296; *Independent Trustee Services Ltd v GP Noble Trustees Ltd* [2013] Ch 91.

[82] M Scott Donald, 'The Pension Trust: Fit For Purpose?' (2019) 82(5) MLR 800, 805 ff (hereafter Donald, 'The Pension Trust').

[83] ibid 807.

[84] ibid 806–07.

[85] ibid 807.

[86] ibid 808.

trustee] simplifies'[87] the setting of required conduct and the supervision of that conduct. Moreover, this outcome is consistent with the objectives of Part IVA in promoting the efficient use of court time and the parties' resources.[88]

By contrast, other institutional forms, for example, the corporation, do not have this single line of direct reporting and responsibility. For example, in a corporate structure, the primary organ of decision-making is the board of directors. Regulation and court supervision may be directed to a corporate board and liability is that of the corporate entity. However, decision-making in the board is necessarily collective. While directors exercise their powers collectively, they may also individually be held accountable[89]. Moreover, in other contexts, where a corporate trustee is employed, it has been observed that the use of the corporate form may render complex the otherwise relative direct accountability offered by the use of a trust.[90]

C. The Trust as an Enrolment Device

Despite the office of Administrator not being contemplated in Part IVA, the functions performed by Administrators support and put into effect the court's orders in implementing the terms of the settlement. The Administrator is, within the terms of the SDS, the court's delegate. In understanding this it is important to appreciate that an SDS is not 'self-executing'. A myriad of decisions is required to be made and powers exercised. Some of the matters delegated to the Administrator under the SDS are matters which would otherwise have had to be decided by the judge in the proceeding had the trust not been employed. For example, the Administrator might be required to determine the quantum to be paid to particular group members, taking into account their unique circumstances. Thus, the Administrator performs a role which is essential to achieving finality and in this sense is fundamental to the class action. In addition, the Administrator will likely be required to deal with a very large number of group members who are entitled under the SDS, all of whom have suffered loss or other reason for remedy and may potentially be litigious. The Administrator will often be the lawyer for the applicant, who resigns from this office prior to taking up their role as Administrator.[91]

While the infrastructure role of the trust focuses on the direct line of reporting and accountability that it offers, a key aspect of the Administrator's role is to carry out the court's mandate. It is also vital therefore to consider the position from that of the putative Administrator. Is being Administrator an attractive option? Leaving aside the obvious point that Administrators are remunerated (subject to the supervision of the

87 ibid 808.

88 Above note 4.

89 *Re Westmid Packing Services Ltd (No 2)* [1998] 2 All ER 124, 130 (CA) (the Court).

90 See M Scott Donald 'Delegation by Superannuation Fund Trustees' (2020) 37 Companies and Securities LJ 319, 329–31.

91 Resignation may be required by the SDS. See, eg, DePuy Hips SDS cl 2.1(b).

court), as an institution, why is this office filled? One answer may come from the work of Julia Black. In the financial services context, Black[92] has written about regulatory systems, observing the challenges that the fragmentation and hybridisation of governmental regulation has brought. In response, Black suggests that a more nuanced understanding of regulatory systems should be employed, which recognises the phenomena of non-state actors who have been involved in the regulatory system and, in other instances, whose participation could be *elicited* to perform regulatory functions. Central to Black's argument is the notion of 'enrolment' of actors in regulatory processes as a regulatory strategy. Enrolment may be formal or informal or a combination of the two,[93] and refers to the enlisting of one actor to regulate others. Arguably the trust as a device offers the capacity to enrol or enlist the putative Administrator into the process of administering the class action. In this way, a structure of delegated decision-making and administration by the court is able to leverage off those with relevant expertise in delivering the outcomes of the class action. Enrolling Administrators thus permits the court to maintain fidelity with the objectives of Part IVA in promoting the efficient use of time and resources, providing access to justice, and protecting defendants from the risk of a multiplicity of suits.[94]

Empirical research is necessary to determine the particular motivations and attitudes of individual Administrators. However, high-level observations are nonetheless possible which show that the trust device facilitates enlisting Administrators. The use of the trust permits bespoke terms which confer on the Administrator the necessary 'authority and legitimacy, strategic position and organisational capacity'[95] to be part of the system of regulation, or, in this case, the supervision and administration of the class action recovery. In particular, as discussed below in Section III.D.2 (The Trust as Autonomy Enhancing), terms articulating an overriding duty to the court and a high degree of protection to the Administrator from potential suits from group members are relevant. These are examples taken from a review of the terms of publicly available SDS. However, the underlying conceptual point is that, subject to the overall institutional constraints of the trust form, the terms may be adjusted to suit the particular requirements of the particular settlement. In this way, the flexibility of the trust form permits the participation of suitable actors to be elicited such that being an Administrator will not be 'too unattractive'[96] and a structure of delegated decision-making and administration by the court put into place.

[92] Julia Black, 'Enrolling Actors in Regulatory Systems: Examples from UK Financial Services Regulation' [2003] PL 63 (hereafter Black, 'Enrolling Actors in Regulatory Systems'); Julia Black, 'Paradoxes and Failures: "New Governance" Techniques and the Financial Crisis' (2012) 75 MLR 1037 (hereafter Black, 'Paradoxes and Failures').

[93] Black, 'Enrolling Actors in Regulatory Systems' (n 92) 86, 89.

[94] Above note 4.

[95] Black, 'Enrolling Actors in Regulatory Systems' (n 92) 73.

[96] Simon Gardner, *An Introduction to the Law of Trusts* (3rd edn, Clarendon Press 2011) 187–89, noting that there must be an adequate supply of willing trustees.

D. The Trust as Autonomy Enhancing

Autonomy refers to our ability to self-determine or to lead a 'self-directed life'.[97] As is well known, Joseph Raz identified three conditions for autonomy: appropriate mental abilities, an adequate range of options, and independence.[98] First, in relation to a person's mental abilities or capacities, a person must possess the necessary physical and mental health and well-being, intellectual ability and emotional capacity to decide on their own ends, and the capacity to make plans on how to achieve those ends. Second, a person must have an adequate range and variety of options to choose from, and these options must be meaningful in the context of their lives. As argued below, it is this second condition for autonomy which is significant in illuminating the use of the trust of class action recoveries. The role of the liberal state is to '"enable individuals to choose valid conceptions of the good" by providing a "multiplicity of valuable options"',[99] including property arrangements which accommodate an individual's needs and circumstances.[100] Finally, a person must be independent in the sense that they live a life free from 'coercion and manipulation by others'.[101] This discussion proceeds (1) by considering the context in which a trust of the recovery operates. It is artificial to consider whether the trust form may be autonomy enhancing without also considering the broader locus of choice for group members; and (2) narrowing our focus, and considering the extent to which the trust form may be considered autonomy enhancing by reference to the evidence of particular bespoke terms which may be included in an SDS.

1. A trust of the recovery is the end point of a matrix of choices

When we think about autonomy in the context of a trust of the recovery under Part IVA, arguments from autonomy come in at many levels. In an overall sense, a trust of the recovery is the end point of the group member's decision in the first instance to vindicate their right, to seek a legal remedy via participation in the class action, and to agree to the trust structure embodied in the SDS. This outcome itself rests on many factors including the existence of the Part IVA procedure, the group members' decisions not to opt out and the mechanics of settlement of the claim. It is artificial to consider whether the use of the trust may be justified by arguments from autonomy without considering the broader matrix of choice for the group member.

That the Part IVA procedure is available at all, as part of the menu of available legal options, is itself in service of the existence of the range and variety of procedures which may be engaged by victims of legal wrongs and is thereby autonomy enhancing.

[97] Hanoch Dagan, 'Autonomy and Pluralism in Private Law' in Andrew S Gold and others (eds), *The Oxford Handbook of the New Private Law* (OUP 2020) 177, 182.

[98] Joseph Raz, *The Morality of Freedom* (OUP 1986) 372 (hereafter Raz, *Morality of Freedom*).

[99] Hanoch Dagan, 'The Challenges of Private Law: A Research Agenda for an Autonomy-Based Private Law' in Kit Barker and others (eds), *Private Law in the 21st Century* (Hart Publishing 2017) 67, 72 quoting Raz, *Morality of Freedom* (n 98) 133, 162, 265.

[100] ibid 79.

[101] Raz, *Morality of Freedom* (n 98) 373.

Reflecting on the objectives of Part IVA,[102] the procedure is designed to increase access to justice, *inter alia*, by providing a remedy for those who may not have the financial resources to bring a separate action or for whom the cost of the action is disproportionate to the value of their individual claim.

Further, as observed by Paul Miller in this volume, the value of autonomy is not simply its inherent moral value, but is 'a complex of inherent and derivative values'[103] such as 'activities, states of being, relationships and other goods of objective moral value advanced *through* autonomous choice'[104]. In other words, it is useful to identify the choices made in the exercise of autonomy. Focusing on the group member's actions, it may seem counter-intuitive to speak of a group member's exercise of autonomy in an *opt-out* class action as provided for in Part IVA. As described in Section II above, in an open class action group members are described not identified. Class actions may also be closed in which group members are named. However, in both instances, group members who meet the group description (open class) or are named (closed class) are bound by any judgment[105] given in the proceedings unless they exercise their right to opt-out.[106] So the autonomous choice in question is the group member's decision not to opt out. To the extent that the default position under consideration is one of coercion via auto enrolment in the class, we may therefore question whether the Part IVA procedure does not, after all, add to the adequate range of options for redress, and whether the trust of the recovery correlatively fails to add to the multiplicity of valuable options for group members?

A similar phenomenon of auto enrolment was examined by Amanda Cooke in her study of UK private pensions.[107] Since 2012, all employers must 'automatically enrol eligible employees into a qualifying pension scheme, pay contributions on behalf of the employee and deduct employee contributions to the scheme from the employee's pay'.[108] The objective of auto pensions enrolment is, at the societal level, to increase saving for retirement and reduce reliance on the state pension, which is said to be designed only as a supplement to private arrangements.[109] Crucially, employees may leave the scheme after auto enrolling. However, the autonomy of employees is arguably curtailed to the extent that they are, initially at least, automatically enrolled in a pension fund and, moreover, in a default investment fund. Cooke maintains that nonetheless auto enrolment may be justified from autonomy as a form of paternalistic intervention. Arguably, had the employees had perfect knowledge and perfect motivations to save, they would themselves decide to enrol in a pension scheme. However, absent such perfect conditions, auto enrolment puts the employee in the position they would have been in had the information, circumstances, and self-discipline been optimal.[110] Further,

[102] Above note 4.
[103] P Miller, 'Freedom of Disposition' in this book.
[104] ibid.
[105] Which includes any settlement. See above note 24.
[106] Part IVA (n 1) s 33J.
[107] Amanda Cooke, *Pensions and Legal Policy* (Hart Publishing 2021).
[108] ibid 1.
[109] ibid 21–22.
[110] ibid 43–45.

employee autonomy is ultimately protected via the employee's right to exit[111] which requires adequate information to be a meaningful autonomous choice. Similar arguments may be made in relation to class membership under Part IVA where group members also have the statutory right to opt out. Auto enrolment in the class replicates the position that group members may well have come to, had their decisions about seeking redress been rational and well informed. In addition, the existence of the particular class action and the right to opt out[112] are required under Part IVA to be widely publicised[113] including by means of press advertisement, radio or television broadcast, or any other means. This has been broadly interpreted, such that it also includes, for example, via social media.[114] Further, Part IVA and Federal Court Guidance[115] specifies the broad range of information which must be included in an opt out notice. Therefore, although auto enrolment characterises membership of the class, meaningful choice for group members is still in play. Group members effectively get to decide whether to pursue their claim independently or as part of the Part IVA procedure.

Finally, we come to settlement. As described in Section II above, all who have not opted out of the class action are bound by the terms of the deed of settlement and SDS. Being bound by both the structure of Part IVA proceedings, and the outcome of the proceedings, is the inevitable consequence of the group member's earlier decision not to opt out. At settlement, the remaining locus for group member decisions is as to the terms of settlement, including that the Administrator will hold the recovery on trust or a process SDS employed. This will be negotiated by the representative party and their lawyers on behalf of group members. Court approval of the terms of any settlement and SDS is a condition precedent to their coming into effect[116] and prior notice[117] of the application for settlement approval must be given to group members who may lodge an objection to the terms of settlement with the court.

2. The trust form is itself autonomy enhancing

The trust is a stable legal form which carries with it a high degree of certainty about how the structure will operate and interact with other legal principles, yet is sufficiently flexible to respond to the particular circumstances and conditions of the settlor.[118] This is a key observation made in this volume by Hanoch Dagan and Irit Samet, who argue that, in a liberal property regime which subscribes to the *numerous clauses* principle, property law should nonetheless also subscribe to a form of structural pluralism in order that the autonomous choice of parties as to the variety of property arrangements available to them might be maintained.[119] Dagan and Samet suggest that the private express

111 ibid 43–45.
112 Part IVA (n 1) s 33X.
113 ibid s 33Y(4).
114 See, eg, *Wotton v Queensland* [2017] FCA 406 (order 7) where Mortimer J ordered that the opt out notice be publicised via Facebook.
115 Part IVA (n 1) s 33Y; Practice Note (n 30). Per s 33(Y)(2) the form and content of a notice must be approved by the court.
116 Part IVA (n 1) s 33V.
117 ibid s 33X(4).
118 H Dagan and I Samet, 'Express Trusts and Liberal Property' in this book.
119 ibid.

trust offers this flexibility as a residual category in which, within the boundaries of an institutionally stable form, the settlor may tailor arrangements to suit their ends.[120] In this way, the trust form ensure that parties have an adequate range and variety of options to choose from, and these options are meaningful in the context of parties' lives, enabling them to pursue a good life.[121]

It is this flexible yet stable character of the trust which is arguably its strongest card in arguments from autonomy in favour of the use of an express trust of the recovery. This version of the autonomy argument also underpins and supports many of the other arguments above. It is precisely because the trust offers the package of asset separation and a single line of direct reporting and responsibility *in combination* with the ability to craft bespoke terms which is vital. In particular, the ability to design terms which permit the Administrator to be enrolled or enlisted into the work of the court in supervising and administering the class action recovery. In this respect it is crucial to observe that the Administrator is the court's delegate, *but not on standard terms*. Compare the position of say, a trustee in bankruptcy, which is also a delegate of the court but acts according to the terms of the relevant bankruptcy legislation and a statutory trust.[122] While the trust in the SDS is declared pursuant to Part IVA, the statute does not mandate or prescribe any terms. Of course, a non-trustee independent decision-maker could be employed to make relevant decisions and exercise relevant powers. The point is that the trust offers the unique package of default characteristics which in combination facilitate this outcome.

Given these parameters, the following bespoke terms may be included in the SDS. However, as discussed below and in Section IV, this flexibility has limits and carries risk. In particular, it creates opportunities for gaming and distorting the trust form. This is not a novel observation.[123] However, the particular potential distortions perhaps reflect the Part IVA context.

(a) Duty to court

In recognition of the Administrator's role as the court's delegate, and the trust as part of the apparatus of justice, the SDS may give primacy to the Administrator's duty to the court. Thus, the SDS may provide that the Administrator will '[implement the SDS] fairly and reasonably ... with the Administrator's duty to the Court to take priority over any obligations or duties to individual Group Members, including duties that arise from any existing solicitor-client relationship between the Administrator and their clients'.[124] Such drafting is not without difficulty. There are two immediate questions,

[120] ibid.

[121] Raz, *Morality of Freedom* (n 98) 373, 412.

[122] See John Langbein, 'The Secret Life of the Trust: The Trust as an Instrument of Commerce' (1997) 107 Yale LJ 165, 168 (hereafter Langbein, 'Secret Life of the Trust').

[123] See, eg, Lionel Smith, 'Massively Discretionary Trusts' (2017) 70(1) CLP 17.

[124] VW, Audi and Skoda SDS (n 35) cl 2.1(a). See also 'Kilmore Bushfire Class Action Settlement Distribution Scheme' (Supreme Court of Victoria, 10 November 2014) cl A3.2(a) <https://www.supremecourt.vic.gov.au/sites/default/files/assets/2017/09/a5/aa2765adb/settlement%2Bdistribution%2Bscheme.pdf>, accessed 8 November 2022 (hereafter 'Kilmore SDS'); 'Endeavour River SDS' (n 38) annexure A, cl 1.3; DePuy ASR Hip Implants Class Action Settlement Distribution Scheme' (Maurice Blackburn Lawyers, December 2020) cl 2.1(a) <https://www.depuyclassaction.com.au/>, accessed 8 November 2022 (hereinafter 'DePuy SDS').

which can only be flagged in the context of this chapter. However, as highlighted in the Conclusion, their resolution may have implications for the identity and recruitment of Administrators.

First, what does this mean for the existing fiduciary obligations owed by the Administrator as the lawyer for the applicant. Are these released? This problem is potentially magnified when it is realised that that lawyer may also owe fiduciary obligations to other group members.[125] In apparent recognition of the pre-existing fiduciary obligations owed by the lawyer, and that the Administrator is appointed by the court, such a term attempts to limit or negate the extent to which any such fiduciary obligations continue once the role of Administrator is assumed. As has been said, the enforceability of such a clause against the applicant and other group members lies beyond the scope of the present discussion.[126] However, withdrawal from a fiduciary relationship may itself constitute breach of a fiduciary obligation of loyalty.[127] Much will turn on the disclosures by the Administrator, in their capacity as lawyer for the applicant, about the nature and extent of any conflict, and the ability of the applicant and other group members to give a discernible signal of agreement, as may constitute informed consent to any such breach.[128] Second, what is the nature of the obligations owed by the Administrator to the group members under the SDS. As trustee, does the Administrator owe fiduciary duties, albeit of a different scope that was owed as solicitor?

(b) Indemnity

The tension here is to permit the Administrator to recover their reasonable costs, while keeping these as low as possible in order that the value of the recovery for group members will be maintained. The court tightly supervises payments out of the fund. The Administrator may therefore have no right of indemnity for cost incurred in the Administration. Rather, the SDS will likely provide that the Administrator has power to appoint to itself from the recovery the administration costs. The SDS will specify the priority of this payment in relation to other claims on the recovery, for example the order of payment of the Administrator in relation to group members, the litigation funder, and the lawyers. Further, the SDS will likely set out the method by which the costs of the Administrator are to be calculated and that they are subject to the review of the court. For example, the Administrator may be required to submit costs to an independent costs assessor prior to approval by the court[129] or may be at liberty to pay the costs from the recovery,[130] subject to the overall supervision of the court. The SDS procedure may therefore be more tightly controlled than

[125] See further: Simone Degeling and Michael Legg, 'Fiduciary Obligations of Lawyers in Australian Class Actions: Conflicts Between Duties' (2014) 37 U of New South Wales LJ 914.

[126] *ASIC v Citigroup (No 4)* [2007] FCA 963; (2007) 160 FCR 35; *UDC v Brian* [1985] HCA 49; (1985) 157 CLR 1.

[127] See, eg, *Dealer Support Services Pty Ltd v Motor Trades Association of Australia Ltd* [2014] FCA 1065; (2014) 228 FCR 252 [59]–[60] (Beach J).

[128] *Farah Constructions v Say-Dee Pty Ltd* [2007] HCA 22; (2007) 230 CLR 89 [107] (Gleeson CJ, Gummow, Callinan, Heydon and Crennan JJ).

[129] Terang SDS (n 37) cl 14.1.

[130] Kilmore SDS (n 124) cl A4.

that provided for under the state trustee acts[131] or equitable principle.[132] In equity, recourse to trust funds depends on the trustee's expenses having been 'properly incurred'.[133] Given the breadth of this category it is tolerably secure that it is unlikely a court charged with approving an Administrator's costs under an SDS would depart from the same understanding of the expenses which in substance would be permitted under equitable principle.

Of significance however is the possibility that under an SDS an Administrator may not be entitled to recoup expenses without court approval. Under the *Trustee Act 1925* (NSW) prior court approval is similarly not required before the trustee exercises their power to recoup expenses. However, as explained in the *Macedonian Church Case*[134] doing so carries with it the risk that subsequent judicial review of the recoupment may determine that the 'costs might be outside the indemnity'. This risk is counterbalanced by the availability of judicial advice under s 63 *Trustee Act 1925* (NSW) pursuant to which the trustee may 'take advice before embarking on any course which might carry a risk of incurring costs that might be outside the indemnity'.[135] However, the SDS advice provisions do not necessarily carry this advantage.

(c) Directions from court

As the court's delegate, it is unsurprising that the SDS may provide that Administrator is entitled to approach the court for advice and direction. This right may be unfettered[136] or apparently only engaged, for example, where the Administrator considers the 'procedures' to be followed in 'implementing' the SDS are 'in doubt or uncertain' or it is 'appropriate' for advice on 'implementation or administration' or 'it is necessary to provide a report to the Court in relation to the administration' of the SDS.[137] The SDS may further specify that it is not necessary to inform group members of the advice application[138] or that notification need only be given if ordered by the court.[139]

In relation to the terms of the SDS providing that the Administrator has the liberty to apply to the court for advice in the event of uncertainty or doubt in the administration of the settlement arrangements, it is unclear whether this is intended to replace the right to judicial advice under *Trustee Act 1925 (NSW)* s 63 or whether both are

[131] For example, *Trustee Act 1925* (NSW) s 59(4) provides that a trustee may reimburse themselves out of trust property 'all expenses incurred in or about execution of the trustee's trusts or powers'.

[132] See Jessica Hudson and Charles Mitchell, 'Trustee Recoupment: A Power Analysis' (2021) 35 Trust L Int 3.

[133] *Nolan v Collie* [2003] VSCA 39; (2003) 7 VR 287; *Gatsios Holdings v Kritharas Holdings (in liq)* [2002] NSWCA 29; *Re Raybould* [1900] 1 Ch 1; M Scott Donald, 'The "proper" approach to a trustee's right to indemnity out of trust assets' (2014) 8 J Eq 283.

[134] [2008] HCA 42; (2008) 237 CLR 66.

[135] ibid [69] (Gummow A-CJ, Kirby, Hayne and Heydon JJ).

[136] Terang SDS (n 37) cl 12.1.

[137] VW, Audi and Skoda SDS (n 35) cl 15.1.

[138] VW, Audi and Skoda SDS cl 15.1 (n 35); DePuy SDS (n 124) cl 14.1.

[139] Kilmore SDS (n 124) cl J1.2.

intended to be available.[140] Section 63 is broader than the SDS in that it permits the trustee to apply to the court for its 'opinion, advice or direction' and, if the trustee acts in accordance with the advice or direction, is deemed under s 63(2) to have acted in discharge of their responsibility as trustee, so long as they have not been guilty of 'any fraud or wilful concealment or misrepresentation in obtaining the advice, opinion or direction'.[141] The SDS does not so deem.

SDS terms may vary as to whether or not group members are required to be given notice of the advice application.[142] However, presumably any advice given would have force as an 'order in the proceeding' and would bind group members. This largely replicates the position under the *Trustee Act 1925* (NSW) which provides that, although interested parties such as group members may be served, and will therefore are bound as parties, they are not required to be served. All interested parties are nonetheless bound by the advice, direction, or opinion given.

There is however an important difference between the two procedures. The SDS procedure appears to be directed to resolving uncertainty in implementation or instructions for the Administrator. While these mechanical matters obviously reflect the beneficial entitlements of group members, the statutory procedure is identified as being for the protection of the trustee and the interests of the trust. As stated in *Macedonian Orthodox Community Church v His Eminence Petar the Diocesan Bishop of Macedonian Orthodox Diocese of Australia and New Zealand*,[143] s 63 'affords a facility for giving "private advice". It is private advice because its function is to give personal protection to the trustee'.[144] Further, given that the particular question for advice may be whether a trustee should incur the cost of prosecuting or defending litigation (eg in relation to an alleged breach of trust), and acknowledging that a trustee is 'entitled to an indemnity for all costs and expenses *properly* incurred in performance of the trustee's duties',[145] the judicial advice procedure also has 'another and no less important purpose of protecting the interests of the trust'.[146]

[140] In *Hodges v Waters (No 7)* [2015] FCA 264; (2015) 232 FCR 97 [47] (hereafter *Hodges*), Perram J held that '*any* claim for judicial advice in relation to the compromise of federal causes of actions is in federal jurisdiction' (emphasis added) and therefore that the Federal Court of Australia had jurisdiction to hear an application by a trustee of a unit trust who brought an application for judicial advice in the Federal Court under *Trustee Act 1925* (NSW) s 63 in relation to whether it should settle a class action brought for breaches of *Corporations Act 2001* (Cth) and the *Australian Securities and Investments Act 2001* (Cth). More complex is the question whether an Administrator would have liberty to apply to a state Supreme Court for advice. The resolution of this question lies beyond this chapter, but application of *Judiciary Act* 1903 (Cth) s 39B and, for example, *Jurisdiction of Courts (Cross-Vesting) Act 1987* (NSW) s 6(1) and s 6(3) suggest that it may be difficult to maintain an argument against transfer of any proceedings to the Federal Court of Australia. See also *Richards v Macquarie Bank Ltd [No 5]* [2013] FCA 1442 [41] (Logan J), who stated without deciding: 'It is said that there may nonetheless be an ability to approach a State Court under State legislation providing for trusts. A nice question may well be raised as to whether the scheme for which Pt IVA . . . provides is a code not admitting of the intrusion of State Courts into a compromise approved by this court.'

[141] *Trustee Act 1925* (NSW) s 63(2).

[142] In VW, Audi and Skoda SDS (n 35) cl 15.1 and DePuy SDS (n 124) cl 14.1(b) there is no obligation on the Administrator to inform group members. In Terang SDS (n 37) (cl 12) and Endeavour SDS (cl 8.1) the SDS is silent on the question. In the Kilmore SDS (n 124) (cl J1.2) the Administrator is not obligated to give notice to group members except where the court orders otherwise.

[143] [2008] HCA 42; (2008) 237 CLR 66 (hereafter *Macedonian Church*).

[144] ibid [64] (Gummow A-CJ, Kirby, Hayne and Heydon JJ).

[145] ibid [71] (Gummow A-CJ, Kirby, Hayne and Heydon JJ).

[146] ibid [72] (Gummow A-CJ, Kirby, Hayne and Heydon JJ).

Particularly in those SDS which do not contain a broad 'judicial' immunity from suit,[147] or if that immunity is read down, there is thus an obvious tactical advantage to relying on the statutory advice procedure. It provides a means by which the Administrator is deemed to have discharged their duty in relation to the subject matter of the advice. Further, s 63 advice has significance for whether the trustee may rely on *Trustee Act 1925* (NSW) s 85 (Excusable Breaches of Trust) which provides that where a trustee may be personally liable for any breach of trust, the court may relieve the trustee in whole or in part from personal liability,[148] to the extent that the trustee has acted honestly and reasonably, and ought fairly to be excused for the breach *and* for omitting to obtain the direction of the court in the matter which the trustee was committing the breach.[149] Advice pursuant to the terms of the SDS will not suffice for the purposes of *Trustee Act 1925* (NSW) s 85.

(d) Immunities

The SDS may provide that the Administrator, in relation to the SDS, 'shall have the same immunities from suit as attach to the office of a judicial officer of the Court [referring to a judicial officer of the Supreme Court of a State or, presumably, the Federal Court of Australia]'.[150] This is an extremely wide immunity. However, from the perspective of the Administrator this may be desirable given that the Administrator is interacting with a large class of group members who may be aggrieved and potentially litigious. It also reflects the role of the Administrator as the court's delegate and in implementing the SDS and arguably removes a barrier to enrolling potential Administrators to the office.

A judge of a Supreme Court has a common law immunity from suit[151] which precludes civil liability[152] and has been described as 'absolute'[153] and 'indefeasible'.[154] The immunity accrues when the judge acts, within jurisdiction, in the performance of their judicial function or capacity and other actions sufficiently connected or 'intimately

[147] See, eg, VW, Audi and Skoda SDS (n 35).

[148] *Trustee Act 1925* (NSW) s 85(1).

[149] ibid s 85(2). See *Macedonian Church* (n 143) [35]–[36] (Gummow A-CJ, Kirby, Hayne and Heydon JJ).

[150] Terang SDS (n 37) cl 10.3. See also Kilmore SDS (n 124) cl A3.2(b); DePuy Hips (n 124) cl 2.1(c). In the VW, Audi and Skoda SDS this immunity did not attach to the Administrator, but a Review Assessor charged by the Administrator with independently arbitrating a dispute as to a group member's entitlement, cl 8.8(c).

[151] *Re East; Ex parte Nguyen* [1998] HCA 73; (1998) 196 CLR 354 [30] (Gleeson CJ, Gaudron, McHugh, Gummow, Hayne and Callinan JJ); *Fingleton v The Queen* [2005] HCA 34; (2005) 227 CLR 166 [36] (Gleeson CJ) (hereafter *Fingleton*), approving *Sirros v Moore* [1975] QB 118, 132 (Lord Denning MR); *Gallo v Dawson* (1988) 63 ALJR 121, 122 (Wilson J) (hereafter *Gallo*), also approving *Sirros v Moore* [1975] QB 118, 132 (Lord Denning MR).

[152] Judicial officers also enjoy limited immunity from criminal responsibility where the breach of the criminal law occurs as part of the performance of their judicial functions. The position was considered in *Yeldham v Rajski* (1989) 18 NSWLR 48 (hereafter *Yeldham*) where Kirby P stated (at 58) that, as with the immunity from civil liability, it is necessary to determine whether the conduct was performed as part of judicial function, and whether or not there is a 'clear absence of jurisdiction'. See also at 69 (Hope A-JA). Thus, a speeding offence in a 'private car on a highway' will not attract immunity from criminal liability, nor will accepting a bribe. See also *Fingleton* (n 151) [40] (Gleeson CJ).

[153] *Donaldson v State of New South Wales* [2019] NSWCA 109 [8] relying on *Mann v O'Neill* [1997] HCA 28; (1997) 191 CLR 204, 238 (Gummow J).

[154] *Donaldson v State of New South Wales* [2019] NSWCA 109 [8] quoting *Gibbons v Duffell* [1932] HCA 26; (1932) 47 CLR 520, 528 (Gavan-Duffy CJ, Rich and Dixon JJ).

associated'[155] with this function, such as administrative functions.[156] Statute extends this immunity to ministerial duties.[157] As explained by Fitzgerald JA in *Wentworth v Wentworth*[158] a judge acts 'within jurisdiction for this purpose if [they are] exercising a jurisdiction which the court of which [they are] a member possesses'. The relevant jurisdiction of a court is a question of construction and interpretation of the relevant constitutional and statutory arrangements,[159] and the Supreme Court of a state is a superior court with a broad 'general jurisdiction and responsibility'.[160] So long as the judge acts within jurisdiction, the immunity applies even if the judge acts maliciously, with a want of good faith[161] or was 'under some gross error or ignorance'.[162] However, if the judge acts in bad faith, in the sense that they do 'what they know ... [they have] no power to do'[163] there is no immunity. Similarly, if the relevant conduct is 'purely a personal escapade'[164] the immunity is not engaged.[165] Within the terms of judicial immunity, judicial accountability is preserved via the requirements to work in public, give reasons for decisions, the availability of appellate review, and the possibility of removal from office by parliamentary action.[166]

Given that this immunity removes civil liability, except where the Administrator knowingly acts where they have no power to do so, the question must be asked whether this term contradicts the necessary intention to declare a trust at all? Assuming for the moment this immunity within an SDS is valid, it potentially protects the Administrator against equities for relief held by group members to ensure proper performance and administration of the trust. For example, group members seeking: an account and possibly consequential relief against the trustee,[167] review of the trustee's power to recoup expenses,[168] access to trust information,[169] or to review the trustee's exercise of power

[155] *Yeldham* (n 152) 62 (Kirby P), 69 (Hope AJA). The *Crimes Act 1900* (NSW) s 341(1) required the leave of a judge in order to prosecute a witness for perjury. Earlier authority had held this power to be ministerial and therefore without the immunity. However, the court reasoned that the power under s 341(1) was ancillary to the criminal proceedings in which the perjury was alleged to have occurred and, therefore, that any judicial action under s 341(1) was covered by the immunity.

[156] *Fingleton* (n 151) 190–92 (Gleeson CJ).

[157] *Judicial Officers Act 1986* (NSW) s 44A.

[158] [2000] NSWCA 350; (2000) 52 NSWLR 602, [28].

[159] ibid [25] (Fitzgerald JA).

[160] ibid

[161] *Fingleton* (n 151) 185 (Gleeson CJ).

[162] *Gallo* (n 151) 122 (Wilson J).

[163] *Re McC (A Minor)* [1985] AC 528, 540 (Lord Bridge of Harwich), approved in *Fingleton* (n 151) 185 (Gleeson CJ). See also *Wentworth v Wentworth* [2000] NSWCA 350; (2000) 52 NSWLR 602, 613 (Fitzgerald JA); *Rajski v Powell* (1987) 11 NSWLR 522, 531 (Kirby P).

[164] *Fingleton* (n 151) 189 (Gleeson CJ).

[165] For example, *Yeldham* (n 152) Kirby P gave as an example of conduct potentially falling outside a judge's judicial functions a judge who dismisses his court secretary and is then sued for wrongful dismissal. In this case, the judge 'could not ordinarily invoke, as a defence, his judicial immunity' (at 58) as the dismissal would not likely relate to the judicial functions of the judge.

[166] *Fingleton* (n 151) 166, [39] (Gleeson CJ) and *Scanlon v Director—General, Department of the Arts, Sport and Recreation* [2007] NSWCA 204; (2007) 70 NSWLR 1 [57] (Tobias JA). See, eg, *Constitution Act 1902* (NSW) s 53 (Removal from judicial office) on the ground of 'proved misbehaviour or incapacity' s 53(2), *Judicial Officers Act* 1986 (NSW) pt 7 (Suspension of judicial officers).

[167] *Youyang* (n 64) *Pty Ltd v Minter Ellison Morris Fletcher*; (2003) 212 CLR 484.

[168] *Carter Holt Harvey Woodproducts Australia Pty Ltd v The Commonwealth* [2019] HCA 20; (2019) 268 CLR 524.

[169] JC Campbell, 'Access by Trust Beneficiaries to Trustees' Documents, Information and Reasons' (2009) 3 J Eq 97.

to appoint trust property and any consequential relief.[170] By placing the Administrator beyond the reach of the court it may be argued that the settlor (subject to the court's approval under s 33V(2)), whether the respondent or the Administrator if a trust by self-declaration, has no intention to bind the Administrator to the trust terms.

The 'maxim' of Lord Eldon in *Morice v Bishop of Durham* sets out the core principle of trust formation, that the trust must be capable of performance by the court and will correlatively be supervised and, if necessary, administered by the court:[171]

> 'that the execution of a trust shall be under the controul of the Court, it must be of such a nature, that it can be under that controul; so that the administration of it can be reviewed by the Court; or, if the trustee dies, the Court itself can execute the trust; a trustee, therefore, which in case of maladministration could be reformed; and a due administration directed; and then, unless the subject and the objects can be ascertained, upon principles, familiar in other cases, it must be decided, that the court can higher reform maladministration, nor direct a due administration.'

The paramount obligation of a trustee is to obey the terms of the trust.[172] As set out by Lord Eldon, in default of execution by the trustee the court will itself exercise the power reposed in the Administrator such that the office is performed.[173] The intention to create a trust may be externally manifested and proved by words which are interpreted by reference to their objective meaning.[174] Taking the objective meaning of the SDS, it may be argued that the breadth of the immunity signals the intention of the settlor that the Administrator is beyond the supervision of the court and therefore that the Administrator holds the recovery free of terms. On this interpretation, the settlor is indicating that the Administrator is not subject to any duty to perform the terms on which the recovery is held, including those derived from equitable principle and any relevant legislation. Therefore, if given broad effect, this term 'would in effect destroy the trust'.[175]

Independently of the impact on intention, assuming validity, trust terms which 'have the object and effect of preventing a beneficiary from having recourse to the Courts ... for the protection and ascertainment of his rights'[176] may be void as against public policy.[177] Such clauses 'would have the effect of preventing any questions of administration without limit, and would prevent the beneficiaries from securing the due administration of the trusts ... by the trustees ... and is an attempt

[170] *Karger v Paul* [1984] VR 161.

[171] (1805) 10 Ves 522; (1805) 32 ER 947, 954 (Lord Eldon LC). As emphasised by Ho and Nolan, the 'rules about "certainty of objects" and "the beneficiary (or enforcer) principle" are consequences of this foundational axiom, not themselves foundational of the law of trusts': Lusina Ho and Richard C Nolan, 'The Performance Interest in the Law of Trusts' (2020) 136 LQR 402, 404.

[172] *Youyang* (n 64) [32] (the Court).

[173] See further: Daniel Clarry, *The Supervisory Jurisdiction Over Trust Administration* (OUP 2018) 27–39.

[174] *Byrnes v Kendle* [2011] HCA 26; (2011) 243 CLR 253 [53]–[55] (Gummow and Hayne JJ).

[175] *Rinehart v Welker* [2012] NSWCA 95; (2012) 95 NSWLR 221 [139] (Bathurst CJ) (hereafter *Rinehart*).

[176] *Permanent Trustee v Dougall* (1931) 34 SR (NSW) 83, 86–87 (Harvey CJ in Eq) (hereafter *Dougall*).

[177] *Rinehart* (n 175) [140] (Bathurst CJ).

to oust the jurisdiction of the Court'.[178] On the basis that the immunity conferred on the Administrator appears to cover, for example, actions for the appointment of a new Administrator (noting that the Administrator is a necessary defendant to such actions) and actions for wilful default, it may similarly be argued that the immunity similarly offends against this policy.[179]

Therefore, despite the limited judicial consideration in favour of this immunity from suit stating that '[it] is appropriate, given that [Administrators] are administering a Court approved scheme'[180] if a trust of the recovery is intended, careful consideration needs to be given to the immunity from suit such that it mirrors the position currently conferred under *Trustee Act 1925* (NSW) s 63 and equitable principle.

E. The Trust as Default Law

Finally, we come to the trust as a source of default law or device for importing default law. The use of the trust form carries with it a body of established and understood legal principles which are available to address unanticipated or novel 'dilemmas'. Relevantly, the particular situation is not one which will necessarily have been provided for by the terms of the SDS or Part IVA yet may be provided for in this broader body of principle. Donald describes this as trust law's 'default role'.[181] Similarly, John Langbein famously identifies 'one of the great advantages of the trust for the transaction planner ... is the convenience of being able to absorb [trust law principles] into the ground rules for the deal, merely by invoking the trust label'.[182] Both the court and the Administrator may have recourse to this body of default principle. A particular example of a 'dilemma', which has already been the subject of judicial consideration, is where a surplus remains in the fund after distribution according to the terms of the SDS. There is some evidence that courts have either made cy-près orders or, in the alternative, used the models of judicial reasoning and action in cy-près cases as a template for the exercise of their discretion under s 33V(2), which empowers the court in approving a settlement of a representative proceeding to 'make such orders as are just with respect to the distribution of any money paid ...'.

The surplus in the fund may arise, for example, where cheques are not presented by group members or provided account details are not accepted by the bank clearing system in order to permit an inter-bank transfer of the group member's share of the recovery. The terms of the SDS may provide for this eventuality via a gift over in default, such that there is never an unallocated surplus.[183] For example, the Terang SDS

178 *Dougall* (n 176) 87 (Harvey CJ in Eq).

179 cf *Leerac Pty Ltd v Garrick E Fay* [2008] NSWSC 1082 [14]–[16] (Brereton J).

180 *Johnston v Endeavour Energy* [2016] NSWSC 1132 [37] (Hoeben CJ at CL). See also *Rowe v AusNet Electricity Services Pty Ltd* [2015] VSC 232 [32] (Emerton J) cited in *Watson as trustee for the Murrindindi Bushfire Class Action Settlement Fund v Commissioner of Taxation* [2020] FCAFC 92; (2020) 277 FCR 253 [12] (the Court).

181 Donald, 'The Pension Trust' (n 82) 809–11.

182 Langbein, 'Secret Life of the Trust' (n 122) 166.

183 *Evans v Davantage Group Pty Ltd (No 3)* [2021] FCA 70 [101] (Beach J) (hereafter *Evans*).

(a bushfire class action) required the Administrator to distribute any surplus to group members,[184] subject to the Administrator's 'absolute discretion' to pay 'BlazeAid' (a volunteer based organisation providing assistance to communities after bushfires) if particular financial caps were engaged.[185] However, in other instances, the SDS does not provide terms governing a surplus and the Administrator may seek directions from the court[186] about what to do with this surplus. There is some evidence of 'relief in the nature of some form of *Cy-près* order'[187] being made in relation to these amounts.[188]

Strictly speaking, *cy-près* is available only in relation to charitable trusts[189] and involves a permitted variation of the original charitable purpose. Where the charitable trust has exhausted its original purpose and a surplus remains the surplus is held on substantially the same terms, such that the court 'execute that *cy-près*, ... carry out the general paramount intention in some way as nearly as possible the same as that which the [settlor] has particularly indicated without which his intention itself cannot be effectuated'.[190]

The trusts declared in an SDS are trusts for objects or beneficiaries, not purposes, or even charitable purposes. However, in *Simpson v Thorn Australia Pty Ltd trading as Radio Rentals (No 5)*[191] Lee J held:

> 'equity provides some flexibility within these bounds when it comes to designing and applying cy-près schemes. Extending this principle to ordering schemes in the current class action context, particularly in the light of the well-established position in the United States, seems to me to fulfil the requirement that the principled application of equitable remedies "must be shown to have an ancestry founded in history and in the practice and precedents of the courts administering equity jurisdiction" [citing *In re Diplock; Diplock v Wintle* [1948] Ch 465, 481–482; *Gee v Pritchard* (1818) 36 ER 670, 674] That is, provided it is only applicable in circumstances consistent with the doctrine's ordinary operation, being circumstances of *impossibility or impracticality* of distribution to those entitled to the relevant fund. ... It follows I consider that the Court presently possesses sufficient power to fashion a remedy to allow a distribution of a settlement sum pursuant to a form of cy-près scheme if it is *impracticable*

184 Terang SDS (n 37) cl 9.6.

185 Terang SDS (n 37) cl 9.7: BlazeAid could be paid if less than $5,000 left overall or if an amount to be distributed to an individual group member is less than $100, that amount.

186 Note this is an example where *Trustee Act 1925* (NSW) s 63 judicial advice may provide an advantage over advice under the SDS.

187 *Clark v National Australia Bank Limited (No 2)* [2020] FCA 652 [26] (Lee J).

188 See generally: Rachael Mulheron, *The Modern Cy Près Doctrine: Applications and Implications* (UCL Press 2006); Jeff Berryman and Robyn Carroll, 'Cy près as a class action remedy– justly maligned or just misunderstood?' in K Barker and others (eds), *Private Law Key Encounters with Public Law* (CUP 2013) 320.

189 There is some limited evidence for the use of cy près orders in relation to trusts for persons rather than purposes. See David Foster, 'Construction and Execution of Trusts in Chancery, c. 1660–1750' (2019) 40 J of Legal History 270, 289–96.

190 *Attorney-General for NSW v Adams* (1908) 7 CLR 100, 125 (Isaacs J) quoting with approval *Re Taylor* (1888) 58 LT 538, 543 (Kay J).

191 [2019] FCA 2196, [23]–[24] (hereafter *Simpson*). See also *Clark v National Australia Bank Limited (No 2)* [2020] FCA 652 [26] (Lee J).

or impossible to distribute all or some of the settlement sum to group members individually (being circumstances directly analogous to there being a trust which has exhausted its original purpose and a surplus remains).'

With respect, in the absence of acceptance of a non-charitable purpose trust, this statement is rather wide. It appears to miss the point that the intention of the settlor in the trusts declared in the SDS is to benefit the group members as beneficiaries or objects, not for the advancement of purposes. In default of the position in equity, his Honour also relied on s 33V(2) which empowers the court in approving a settlement of a representative proceeding to 'make such orders as are just with respect to the distribution of any money paid ... '.[192] Application of s 33V(2) to a surplus will depend on construction of 'just', to which Lee J suggests *cy-près* may be employed as an equitable analogue in giving guidance in identifying 'a charity or cause closely related to those persons to whom the money is owed'.[193] The order would therefore be pursuant to s 33V(2) rather than 'a cy-prés order as such'.[194] However, even taking the point that the reasons in these cases reflected the arguments put to the court,[195] what both of the above solutions apparently ignore is a possibility that the surplus will be held on resulting trust for the settlor. This will most likely be the respondent in the class action.

IV. Conclusion

A trust of the proceeds of a class action ensures that the monetary settlement approved by the court actually reaches the hands of group members. This is because the trust permits a particular structure of court supervised delegated decision-making and distribution, pursuant to which not only may group members enforce the terms of the SDS against the Administrator, but crucially also have recourse to equity's supervisory jurisdiction. This chapter explores how the trust form (A) delivers the settlement approved by the court and assures any monetary award reaches the hands of group members; (B) provides necessary legal infrastructure in the sense that it facilitates the supervision of the administration of the recovery; (C) permits the enrolment of actors with the necessary capacity to administer the recovery; (D) is autonomy enhancing; and (E) is a source of default law or a device for importing default law. The decision by courts to adopt an arrangement whereby implementation of an SDS is delegated to a court-supervised Administrator also carries structural risk. Enrolling Administrators, here via the trust, creates significant vulnerabilities and dependencies,[196] which can in turn lead to potential distortions in the trust form.

192 ibid [25]–[26].
193 *Simpson* (n 191) [26]. See also *Evans* (n 183) [106] (Beach J).
194 *Evans* (n 183) [106] (Beach J).
195 *Hsiao v Fazari* [2020] HCA 35; (2020) 270 CLR 588 [53] (Kiefel CJ, Bell and Keane JJ).
196 Black, 'Paradoxes and Failures' (n 92) 1051–52.

Further work, beyond the scope of this chapter, is required more fully to understand the office of Administrator and the equitable supervision of that office. First, the fiduciary responsibilities of the Administrator are vital. The tasks delegated to Administrators are varied and may, for example, include determining a particular group member's entitlement to recovery on a particular head of loss and the quantum of that recovery. While ensuring that the terms of the SDS are an 'attractive option', in adopting a delegated structure, courts require a pool of suitably qualified Administrators. The former lawyer for the claimant class may well be appointed as Administrator, not least because 'they have a close familiarity with the subject matter of the proceeding and class members' claims so that the claims can be assessed and finalised as quickly as possible ... and enjoy the trust of a large number of class members'.[197] However, it is not the case that the applicant's former solicitor is automatically appointed. A court makes an independent determination as to whether another professional or entity could perform the office at a lesser cost.[198] The potential breach of the fiduciary prohibition against conflict or the 'real or substantial possibility of a conflict'[199] which arises from this appointment loom large. In this context, the need for fiduciary constraint, as an additional equitable control beyond those imposed through the use of the trust form, is relevant.

The second observation requires empirical work about the culture and attitudes of Administrators to be secure. However, based on the legal drafting of publicly SDS, we may tentatively suggest that Administrators regard themselves as primarily supervised by Part IVA and do not necessarily act by reference to the relevant *Trustee Acts*. For example, it is not clear the extent to which Administrators invoke the judicial advice procedure under the state *Trustee Acts*. Further, we may speculate that the community of class action lawyers who act in these proceedings, and who may draft the terms of SDS, are accustomed to working primarily within the confines of Part IVA. However, it is also tolerably secure that the general law of trusts applies to an SDS. More work must be done to determine the precise interaction between particular SDS terms, Part IVA, and the default package of trust law.[200] Administrators who regard themselves as solely regulated by Part IVA face a compliance risk if they ignore equity's independent remit.

[197] *Wotton v State of Queensland (No 10)* [2018] FCA 915 [42] (Murphy J).
[198] *Lifeplan Australia Friendly Society Limited v S&P Global Inc (Formerly McGraw-Hill Financial, Inc) (A Company Incorporated in New York)* [2018] FCA 379 [54] (Lee J).
[199] *Hospital Products Ltd v United States Surgical Corporation* [1984] HCA 64; (1984) 156 CLR 41, 103 (Mason J).
[200] See, eg, *Hodges* (n 140).

10

Illegality, Tax in Another Jurisdiction, and an Express Trust

Ann Mumford[*]

I. Introduction

In a 2016 High Court case, *Hniazdzilau v Vajgel*, a businessman was countered in his attempt to establish a claim to beneficial ownership of a company with a defence of illegality.[1] The court found that the unlawful act was not central to the claim; in other words, he had not relied on the unlawful act to establish his petition. As the law stood in 2016, the simple commission of unlawful acts by one party was not enough for the illegality defence to adhere.

There is an old-fashioned feeling in this holding. The decision was reached after two important cases addressing illegality, and before another.[2] Responding to a sense of unease that the law was unsettled, the *Hniazdzilau* court followed the line of reasoning in one case, but also considered the implications of another.[3] As it turns out, the court was right to feel uneasy as, just three years later, the Supreme Court produced another important decision;[4] and, indeed, it is possible that, were the *Hniazdzilau* case decided today, as opposed to 2016, the issues might be approached differently.[5]

There is a twist to *Hniazdzilau*, that renders it, perhaps, a bit more modern. The illegality alleged in this case involves tax—either avoidance[6] or evasion,[7] the terms used

* With sincere thanks to Peter Alldridge, Jane Henderson, Adam Hofri-Winogradow, Peter Maggs, Colm McGrath, Louis Triggs, the participants in the London Tax Work in Progress Series, the participants in the workshop supporting this collection, and the editors of this collection.

1 [2016] EWHC 15 (Ch).

2 The case was decided after *Tinsley v Milligan* [1994] 1 AC 340 and *Allen v Hounga* [2014] UKSC 47, but before *Patel v Mirza* [2016] UKSC 42.

3 The court followed *Tinsley v Milligan*, and considered the implications of *Allen v Hounga*.

4 *Patel v Mirza*, [2016] UKSC 42. See also *Stoffel & Co v Grondona* [2020] UKSC 42, clarifying the common law approach to illegality established in *Patel*.

5 It is plausible that the court's holding that, for a claim to establish legal ownership to succeed, there should be a close link between illegal acts and a claim for beneficial ownership, might be approached differently after *Patel's* impactful change of direction from *Tinsley*. The decision in *Hniazdzilau* seemed to turn on the principle that, where money transferred into a trust lawfully belonged to the settlor (at the time of the transfer), then beneficiaries should retain beneficial interest in those funds. If the funds did not belong to the settlor lawfully, the reasoning ran, then the outcome should be different, and the illegality defence should succeed. It is also important to note that this case was decided several years before the War in Ukraine, the implications of which are considered later in this chapter.

6 See *Hniazdzilau* (n 1) [122], where 'avoid the payment of tax' is mentioned.

7 See ibid [195], where 'tax evasion' is referenced; and [122]: '[t]he exercise, he asserted was to optimise tax, and it involved nothing criminal in any country; he denied that there was anything dishonest in having use the process of the Russian court in this fashion'.

Ann Mumford, *Illegality, Tax in Another Jurisdiction, and an Express Trust* In: *Philosophical Foundations of the Law of Express Trusts*. Edited by: Simone Degeling, Jessica Hudson, and Irit Samet, Oxford University Press. © Ann Mumford 2023.
DOI: 10.1093/oso/9780192844934.003.0011

interchangeably[8] in a presumed allusion to the lack of distinction between the concepts in Russian law.[9] The tax avoidance/evasion occurred not in the UK, but in Russia. The modern twist is that counsel for Mr Hniazdzilau aimed to frame the issue as a question of the UK courts' support (or not) for global tax justice, or, more specifically, Russian tax law.[10] He also argued that, in UK criminal law, the Proceeds of Crime Act[11] allows the entirety of undeclared income to be confiscated through an assessment (ie to tax), and not simply that portion of the sum which otherwise would have been liable to taxation.[12] This would indicate broad support from Parliament for an expansive (perhaps even extra territorial) approach to crimes involving taxation, especially on the point of thwarting financial benefit.[13]

This chapter considers justifications for the argument that tax abuse is sufficiently terrible that it should defeat a claim of beneficial ownership to an express trust.[14] The possibility that tax abuse is particularly harmful to the state, and it may be objectionable that an actor may rely on the protections of the very state that has been harmed, is

[8] A classic account of the difference between the two terms is provided in Robert Walker, 'Ramsay 25 years on: Some Reflections on Tax Avoidance' (2004) 120 LQR 412, 412. As Lord Walker explains, '[i]t goes like this: tax evasion—illegal and criminal; tax avoidance—legal but unacceptable; tax mitigation—legal and acceptable'. He reassures that this is too 'complex' an area for such a 'crude' classification (ibid).

[9] As Mikhail Khodorkovsky, in a famous case, learned to his cost. He was sentenced in May 2005 to nine years' deprivation of freedom for fraud and tax evasion. A claim in the Moscow Commercial Court against YUKOS for non-payment of VAT in 2001 had led to consideration by the Constitutional Court of the statute of limitations in relation to tax offences. Legislation sets this as three years but the Court controversially ruled in July 2005 that such time limitation does not extend to deliberate tax evasion. There were two strong dissenting opinions. See Jane Henderson (forthcoming) *The Russian Constitution in Context* (2nd edn). See also Peter Maggs and others, *Law and Legal System of the Russian Federation* (7th edn, Juris Publishing 2020), 55; *OAO Neftyanaya kompniya YUKOS v Russia*, ECHR Judgment of 31 July 2014 (Application no 14902/04); and, the discussion of 'strict liability' in 'Tax evasion and other criminal tax offences', in Maxim Rovinskiy, 'Tax litigation in the Russian Federation: overview', Thomson Reuters Practical Law (1 February 2018). This is not to imply that all tax disputes lead to criminal charges; but, rather, that criminal charges are exceptionally difficult to defend. For a discussion of tax schemes in the Russian courts, see a post from a blog run by a prominent Russian tax lawyer, Sergey Pepalaev: Sergey Budylin (author) 'End of Tax Schemes. FTS Review', https://zakon.ru/blog/2019/07/15/konec_nalogovyh_shem%C2%A0_obzor_obzora_fns, accessed 26 July 2021. Finally, for the basics of tax crime in Russia, see Resolution of 26 November 2019 N 48, Concerning the Practice Application of Liability Laws by Courts for Tax Crimes, Plenum of the Supreme Court of the Russian Federation.

[10] *Hniazdzilau* (n 1) [194].

[11] 2002 (Ch 29) ('POCA').

[12] *Hniazdzilau* (n 1) [195]. This is the argument:

> As a matter of public policy, Mr Roe submitted, Parliament, in this context, has provided that all undeclared income constitutes the proceeds of crime, not merely such part of it as would otherwise have been taxed: see *R v William* [2013] EWCA Crim 1262, concerning the Proceeds of Crime Act 2002. There is, therefore, he submitted, no reason for the court to take an approach which is more generous to Mr Hniazdzilau than this. It would, therefore, be irrelevant, if the money provided for the purchase of the Property was, as Mr Hniazdzilau suggested (and Mr Bronovets denies), his own money, since a substantial part of it was only available to him (on his evidence) because he avoided paying it over to the tax authorities by pretending that it was being used for trade, and further because, again, on Mr Hniazdzilau's evidence, the whole purpose of the manner of completion of the transaction was tax evasion.

This claim somewhat confuses POCA pt 1 (confiscation upon conviction) and pt 6 (where the law enforcement body takes over the taxpayer's relationship with His Majesty's Revenue and Customs and makes an assessment), and, possibly, pt 5 (civil recovery, which requires a court order). Additionally, treating the extent to which somebody is enriched by evasion as property in their hands confuses issues about identifying the property with the purposes of laundering law. See Peter Alldridge and Ann Mumford, 'Tax Evasion and the Proceeds of Crime Act 2002' [2006] Leg Stud 353.

[13] ibid

[14] The centrality issue will be dealt with by investigating the argument that tax evasion may be so terrible that when a trust is involved, even tangentially, then unlawfulness has the potential to permeate the entire trust.

addressed. Simply because someone has harmed the state, of course, it does not follow that that person is not entitled to the protections of law. The difficulty lies in balancing the freedom of choice afforded by trusts law with the broadly drawn obligations of taxation law. This difficulty is considered within the contexts of leading arguments within the literature (in particular, Dagan, and Murphy and Nagel). The chapter concludes that while inconsistencies in UK law might exist, they are less challenging than those found in the idea of the 'comity of nations'[15] that the *Hniazdzilau* case considered.

II. The Challenge of Responsibility for Another State's Tax System, and the Relevance for Trusts

An express trust sits at the heart of the facts in *Hniazdzilau*, wherein illegality (involving tax abuse) was raised as a defence to a claim to benefit. Tax abuse is not a new topic in the illegality jurisprudence, generally, but references to a global sense of tax justice, with consequences for the reach of an express trust, present a new twist on existing arguments,[16] especially when considered in light of the implications of new directions in illegality forged by the Supreme Court.[17] Even without these twists, the relationship between taxation and express trusts has always been complicated. Express trusts, for example, are reliant upon the state (which itself depends on taxation) both for recognition and enforcement.[18] They are also quite varied in reach, and broadly defined. Express trusts can arise in a number of different ways, over a reach of many years. Although clearly a genus of property law, considering express trusts as only a 'species' of property inevitably misses the point that express trusts have many different forms.[19] Thus, arguments concerning the relationship between taxation law, and trusts, may well differ depending upon the nature of the express trust at issue.

Where a beneficiary profits from tax abuse that was made possible by an express trust, as occurred in *Hniazdzilau*,[20] there will be arguments that the trust, itself, may be immoral. These arguments will depend on a presumption that it is immoral to interfere with the ability of a specific state to collect taxes. If the state at issue is (as in *Hniazdzilau*) Russia (before the war in Ukraine), this may be quite a complicated presumption. The presumption might be based, first, on expediency—in other words, given that, in the twenty-first century, cooperation between countries to facilitate tax collection appears

[15] *Hniazdzilau* (n 1) [194].

[16] See discussion in James SF Lee, 'Tax, Equity and Artificiality' (2018) 31(4) Trust L Int 219.

[17] Considered below, 'A case decided after *Tinsley* ...'

[18] Hayton emphasises the importance of the existence of someone to enforce it as a key feature of the express trust: D Hayton, 'Developing the Obligation Characteristic of the Trust' (2001) 117 LQR 96. That enforcer will depend upon the State for their power.

[19] Focusing on the need for enforcement does raise the Parkinson/Hayton debate (if tangentially): Patrick Parkinson, 'Reconceptualising the Express Trust' (2002) 61(3) CLJ 657, 682–83. This debate is discussed below; but, briefly, Hayton places a great deal of emphasis on the fact that an express trust relies upon another person to enforce it (as part of an attempt which attempts to define what a trust is), and Parkinson agrees that focusing on enforcement helps one to understand 'the irreducible core of the trust concept'. Parkinson, however, then offers a definition of an express trust as an 'equitable obligation' with different categories of legal consequences (ibid).

[20] See discussion below.

completely necessary, then, if the UK is going to be able to collect enough taxes to fund itself, it will have to engage in cooperation.[21] Alternatively, the presumption might be based on a judgment, or assessment, of the other country's law: so, in 2016, the UK might have assessed the Russian state as being a state meriting cooperation, and might have been happy enough to assist it in the collection of its taxes.[22] The motivation for expediency might also lie somewhere in between, as perhaps these questions tend to be avoided by the international community as much as possible, even during times of heightened international tax cooperation,[23] until, perhaps, disruptive events occur, as with the war in Ukraine, at which point cooperation is suspended. Before then, tax co-operation is facilitated, as much as possible.

Arguments in *Hniazdzilau* of a 'comity between nations'[24] present another way (when considered alongside the changes in the doctrine of illegality) in which this case now appears quite dated. The disruptive impact of the war in Ukraine has isolated Russia from many other nations, including the UK. A number of questions follow from this. In the context of the doctrine of illegality, is it right to wait for disruptive events, or should closer analyses be triggered by an earlier threshold? Additionally, what are the criteria that should be used to assess the justice of tax *and* trusts policies in the context of another country's tax system? Should public conscience be part of that criteria, and which 'public' should be included?

The last question is particularly difficult. Consider a different example: trusts which are offshore to the UK. If an assessment of the public conscience in reaction to the Panama Papers[25] had been undertaken,[26] then the result of the assessment might have been that there was little faith that there were many, or any, good reasons for the persons whose identities were revealed to keep their money offshore. So, *any* use of offshore trusts might be found necessarily to offend (the UK's) public conscience, in that context. Different views might well be taken by other countries. To develop this analysis, it is worth explaining the historic vista of international tax justice. In the traditional view, bilateral treaties rest at the heart of international tax law. These treaties were negotiated, it has been presumed, with active advocacy by both parties, each hoping to achieve the best possible deal for themselves.[27] These treaties rest somewhat apart from the questions of distributive justice in each state, the point being that the question of whether or not a state is spending sufficient money on social programmes is viewed as a quite

[21] And it does. See, *inter alia*, the Global Forum on Transparency and Exchange of Information for Tax Purposes, and the OECD/G20 Inclusive Framework on BEPS, https://www.oecd.org/ctp/international-tax-co-operation-map.htm, visited 31 July 2022.

[22] The UK did cooperate with Russia for tax purposes in 2016. In March 2022, the UK suspended cooperation. See https://www.gov.uk/government/news/uk-suspends-tax-co-operation-with-russia, accessed 31 July 2022.

[23] These issues are touched upon in Tsilly Dagan, 'The costs of international tax cooperation' in Eyal Benvinisti and Georg Nolte, *The Welfare State, Globalization, and International Law* (Springer 2004) 49–77.

[24] *Hniazdzilau* (n 1) [194].

[25] See generally: James O'Donovan, Hannes F Wagner and Stefan Zeume, 'The value of offshore secrets: Evidence from the Panama Papers' (2019) 32 Rev Financ Stud 4117; Usman W Chohan, 'The Panama Papers and Tax Morality' (2016), available at SSRN 2759418; and Paul Beckett, *Tax Havens and International Human Rights* (Routledge 2017).

[26] In line with the sort of assessment suggested in *Hounga*, discussed below, 'A case decided after *Tinsley*...'

[27] The classic source for this assessment is John F Avery Jones, 'The David R. Tillinghast Lecture—Are Tax Treaties Necessary?' (1999) 53 Tax L Rev 1.

separate issue from the matter of a bilateral tax treaty that that state has with another country. This is because the questions of taxation and spending in one state are considered to be domestic issues, and strictly not the concern of other states. Other states, within this view, are essentially competitors—for investment, and for tax revenues.[28]

International tax competition frustrates theories of justice which presuppose the statist approach upon which the traditional view rested—put very simply, the idea that redistributive justice is the responsibility of the state, and individual states are not compelled by the demands of justice to consider what is fair in the context of global justice.[29] Within the literature exploring philosophies of taxation, Dagan recommends looking beyond the statist approach (the idea that the state is responsible for justice for its citizens), in favour of a global view of justice, because tax competition undermines the state's capacity to provide justice to its citizens. In reaching this conclusion, she reviews arguments which address whether the state or global approach is best, and points out how tax undermines the statist argument. Significantly, she engages Nagel's arguments that states should only be responsible for persons to whom they have a strong connection.[30] She describes Nagel as a 'strong statist'.[31]

Nagel (and Murphy) posit that tax policy cannot be considered separately from other legal institutions, and it is important to engage in consolidated analysis of economic and legal justice.[32] It is not enough, they argue, to consider justice in taxation from the perspective of pre-existing entitlements based in property law. For example, it is incorrect to think of taxation as taking from people what they already own. One area of law supports, and enables, others. It is therefore important to consider legal and political justice from an institutional perspective, or, in a joined up way. The real challenge, as this chapter will argue, is justifying the extension of this holistic perspective beyond the boundaries of the nation state. So, for example, in some instances, tax abuse might be sufficiently harmful that it should defeat a claim of beneficial ownership to a trust, even where the tax abuse is not central to the claim. That is, as Dagan has proposed, notions of *tax* justice, specifically, no longer should be considered solely *within* the boundaries of the nation state,[33] given that tax justice has acquired a global dimension.

If trusts law is portrayed as underpinned by agreements concerning ownership of property, or, essentially, deals about something,[34] then that portrayal will rest somewhat comfortably within a traditional view of international tax. In that traditional view,

[28] Today, projects such as Base Erosion and Profit Shifting (BEPS) programme suggest much closer cooperation. For a discussion of the history of international, coordinated efforts against harmful tax competition, see E Traversa and A Flamini, 'The Impact of BEPS on the Fight Against Harmful Tax Practices: Risks and Opportunities for the EU' [2015] 3 BTR 396.

[29] As Tsilly Dagan explains, in 'International tax and global justice' (2017) 18 Theor Inq Law 1.

[30] ibid citing Thomas Nagel, 'The Problem of Global Justice' (2005) 33 Philos Public Aff 113.

[31] ibid 8.

[32] Liam Murphy and Thomas Nagel, *The Myth of Ownership: Taxes and Justice* (OUP 2002).

[33] Dagan (n 29).

[34] This is also Langbein's central argument (in other words, that trusts are similar to contracts): John H Langbein, 'The contractarian basis of the law of trusts' (1995) 105 Yale LJ 625 628. It is a controversial one. This is an argument that should be approached cautiously, and I am particularly grateful to Adam Hofri-Winogradow for the insight that Langbein's argument is perhaps best suited to commercial trusts. Perhaps 'consensus' is more suitable here, than contract.

international tax law is also basically a deal—a collection of treaties. The fact that taxation and trusts are allowed to interact as they do will imply that both that states endorse this, and that there is a normative basis for this.

The global consensus on taxation, specifically, however, has moved away from the traditional view, as the tax system has come to be viewed as one that is navigated by global companies that encourage countries to compete for the economic privileges of hosting them. The cost of hosting is the undermining of taxation, and, as Dagan emphasises, the frustration of what states aim to accomplish for their citizens.[35] So, as no state is immune from this threat, it is appropriate to treat exploitative tax acts in one jurisdiction as a potential threat to all jurisdictions. This line of reasoning might justify what could be described as the expediency approach; ie it is expedient for countries to cooperate with each other on taxation, despite a certain level of concern about the choices of some of these countries, until disruptive acts—such as war—render this untenable.

Dagan also explains that tax systems will be unable to fulfil their end of the social contract, with their own citizens, if tax law is treated as the concern only of each state for its own citizens. In a similar vein, Murphy and Nagel argue that the amount of resources that are available for redistribution will depend upon protections found within private law. Both arguments emphasise the importance of not viewing tax in a vacuum, but approach this from different points of comparison—Dagan worries about the international aspect, and Murphy and Nagel worry about (among other things) trusts, or, more specifically, the intersection between tax and private law. The greatest potential for social justice occurs when their arguments are put together—so, when we consider the interlinked nature of tax to other areas of law (Murphy and Nagel), *outside* the boundaries of the nation state (Dagan).

Justice requires attention both to the perspectives of the individual taxpayer, and the collective. From the perspective of the individual taxpayer—so, from the perspective of the litigants in the *Hniazdzilau* case—the basic starting point of a just tax system would be that taxpayers should only have to pay what their legislature requires. If the amount required by their law is too little, then that is not for the courts to remedy. What if a taxpayer deliberately seeks to challenge or test the law with a series of arrangements that are forever one step ahead of the legislature? The classic rule of law response to this might be that citizens always should have notice of what the law says, so that they might plan their behaviour accordingly. And yet, to what extent is it appropriate to adopt the response of the English legal system to what might be named the 'testing taxpayer' in the international context? This rule of law argument might be recast as a question of the norms developed by a *community* of states (as opposed to a single state). In *Hniazdzilau*, this recasting is complicated because the court has been asked not to enforce the laws of another state (so, the UK has not been asked to serve as a tax collector for Russia), but to decline to allow someone to benefit from undermining the laws of another state. Before considering this issue, the next section considers the problem in a domestic context.

[35] Dagan (n 29) 35.

III. The Integration of Public with Private Justice: The Importance of Appreciating the Entire Story of Trusts

The key text for the question of the interconnectedness of tax with other areas of law in a single state's legal system is Murphy and Nagel's 2002 book, *The Myth of Ownership: Taxes and Justice*,[36] which prompted a significant shift in taxation scholarship, and in many ways introduced a new way of thinking about tax justice.[37] The 'main message' of this book is that:

> ... societal fairness, rather than tax fairness, should be the value that guides tax policy, and that property rights are conventional: they are to a large extent the product of tax policies that have to be evaluated by standards of social justice; so they cannot be used to determine what taxes are just.[38]

One of the implications of this argument is that justice in taxation should not be assessed simply by reference to the extent to which it is worthwhile, or not, to deprive somebody of something they are described as otherwise owning, were it not for tax. The implications of the extension of this argument to another country are complicated.

Social justice, beyond the boundaries of the state, may be approached in a broad way—broader than, for example, not only economic efficiency analyses (which are common in tax), but also broader than simply distributive justice. The distinction is important, largely because it is notoriously difficult to explain how principles of distributive justice may provide a normative foundation for private law.[39] Distributive justice analyses in taxation law tend to be based on economic efficiency, and to centre around differing forms of welfare maximisation,[40] although there can be variations in this approach. Some theories of distributive justice will treat questions surrounding the advancement of equalities as incidental by-products of the pursuit of maximum welfare for all, for example, whereas other theories place equality and fairness at the forefront, and argue that welfare cannot be maximised without equality for all.[41] Both views might be viewed as the within the purview of the traditional, public law analyses of taxation (which begin, and end, at the borders of the nation state).

Murphy and Nagel argue that the public-private division should be disregarded when one is assessing whether tax is just.[42] They explain this point as follows. Taxation determines which of society's resources will be kept in private control, and which will

[36] (n 32).

[37] Wenar argued that this book '... established the importance of tax policy as a field of philosophical enquiry and defines the bounds within which the debate should proceed': Leif Wenar, 'The Myth of Ownership: Taxes and Justice' (2005) 114 Philos Rev 285, 285.

[38] Murphy and Nagel (n 32) 173.

[39] Willliam Lucy, *Philosophy of Private Law* (Clarendon Law 2007), ch 9.

[40] Murphy and Nagel (n 32) 56.

[41] ibid

[42] ibid 76–77.

be available for public distribution. It also determines how public resources are distributed (the entry point of distributive justice analyses). It is difficult to assess the successfulness of either, unless we know how resources will be distributed privately, if they are not available for public distribution.[43] The reasons for preferring public distribution, over private control, as matters of general, theoretical approaches to justice, are kept distinct, just so that the justifications for preferring one over the other are kept 'clear'.[44] It is therefore appropriate to consider how the normative principles underpinning different areas of law interact, support each other, and, yes, undermine each other.

The issue becomes even more difficult in the context of the interconnectedness of law. Murphy and Nagel would argue that tax is at the heart of private law, and, indeed, connected to all other areas of law. And it is in the context of trusts law, specifically, that it is perhaps time to talk about the importance of tax. A simple reminder of the history of this area of law is telling. Trusts developed in the Court of Chancery in response to claimants' dissatisfaction with the remedies of the common law courts. These developments in equity were particularly useful for tax purposes. Famously, an early form of trust known as 'the use' enabled one person (who was not required to pay tax) to hold the title of land for the use of another. Essentially, one person held the land in common law (the non-taxpayer), and another held it in equity. The Statute of Uses in 1536 addressed this, by making the beneficial owner of the land liable for feudal duties.[45] The cost of this was almost wholly to take away the power of land owners to control what happened in the future through wills.[46] Nonetheless, the Statute of Uses certainly achieved its aims. It enabled the collection of a great deal of revenue, and was long admired for its drafting style.[47] It was also deeply unpopular.[48] It significantly reduced land owners' autonomy, and had the effect of reimposing a system of primogeniture on landowners who had become accustomed to using wills.[49] Lawyers threatened to search for loopholes unless the law was changed, and the King 'loftily' (in Baker's telling) dismissed the threats of commoners.[50] Nonetheless, by 1540, the government retreated, and reintroduced powers to dispose of freeholds by will.[51]

Trusts law thus developed as a response against the desire of the sovereign to control too much. It enables landholders to resist the wishes of the king. In this way, trusts law responds to the desires of the people,[52] and enables and protects autonomy of choice within legal systems. Perhaps clashes between different areas of law (so, between taxation and trusts) are inevitable. Any time the law affords the possibility of specific

[43] ibid 77.
[44] ibid
[45] Statute of Uses, c 10, 27 Hen. VIII (1536).
[46] Sir John Baker, *Introduction to English Legal History* (5th edn, OUP 2019), 274.
[47] ibid 275.
[48] ibid 276.
[49] ibid
[50] ibid
[51] ibid. See also ibid 305–07.
[52] Lionel Smith, 'Give the People What They Want: The Onshoring of the Offshore' (2017) 103 Iowa L Rev 2155, 2156. In other words, trusts law responds to the desires of the people to manage their property as they wish.

choices for the individual in one area of law, the possibility of utilising that choice to respond to obstacles in another area of law naturally will follow.

It is important to remember, however, that to argue that trusts are nothing more than vehicles for the avoidance of tax, or other obligations, would be to miss the 'idea' of trusts.[53] Consider, as a basic starting point, that if somebody is pursuing tax advantages through trusts, at a minimum there will be certain requirements that need to be fulfilled before the trust is established.[54] These requirements mean that a motive of tax avoidance will not be the entire story. The legal requirements are at least as important a part of the story as the motive.[55]

The needs and the rights of the individual are not often considered in tax policy literature, where it is far more common to consider tax from a broader perspective. Individuals are viewed relationally. Traditional tax analyses may be consider whether one additional person, in one of two groups, is better off as a consequence of tax policy (and no one is in a worse position).[56] The challenge, however, with any relational analysis is that, for every tax policy, some people will benefit, and some people will not.[57] Economic efficiency and relational analyses, generally, are therefore unlikely to provide information that will help in the assessment of different policy choices that involve an individual, and the collective.[58]

The narrow, efficiency-based focus stops at the borders of the nation state. So, it not only fails to provide the framework for discussing autonomy (so integral to the idea of trusts), but it also is not really designed for dealing with the difficult topic of international tax equity. Indeed the *Hniazdzilau* case provides an example of arguments designed for one area of law being deployed in another. As the next section will emphasise, the sense here is that clashes between different areas of law are perhaps best revealed by actors determined to undermine it.

IV. The Case: Enter, International Testers of Law

A. '... just an ordinary tale of Belarusian folk ...'[59]

Questions concerning clashes between tax and trusts law are challenging, but not nearly as difficult as those that arise when another jurisdiction is involved. For example: for a state to continue to function, it may be important for its courts not to extend too much legitimacy to tax protest. If, say, too many taxpayers were to refuse to pay tax until a controversial activity (an unpopular war, for example) stopped, then money would not be available for the basic functions of the state (hospitals, schools, etc.). How is it fair,

[53] Lionel Smith, 'Mistaking the Trust' (2011) 40 HKLJ 747, 790.
[54] ibid 789.
[55] ibid
[56] Murphy and Nagel (n 32) 50. Specifically, this is a description of Pareto efficiency. ibid
[57] ibid
[58] And this is why 'moral and political theorists' are likely to use a wider range of criteria; ibid
[59] Clifford Darton, 'Trusts and the law of illegality' (2016) 22 Trusts & Trustees 729, 729.

then, to prioritise tax collection in a domestic context, and not to extend the same favour to another country?

So, for example, should Russian tax law be enforced by other states? Should an express trust be allowed actively to undermine Russian taxation law? These are complicated questions; and, indeed, the facts of the case in question *Hniazdzilau v Vajgel* are no less complex. A simple summary of the dispute is that illegality was raised as a defence to a claim to beneficial interest in property. The court considered whether a foreign businessperson should claim beneficial ownership of shares which were held in the name of another person simply for the purposes of tax abuse. The court also explored arguments that claimants should not be allowed to place reliance on their own illegal actions, and that public policy requires that victims of exploitation merit protection. The decision of the court ultimately turned on the fact that the *Tinsley v Milligan* approach to illegality (then) still stood, despite the decision in *Allen v Hounga*.

It is worth noting the extent to which all of the litigants had attempted to use the law to confuse and to obfuscate. It could be suggested that no one arrived to court with clean hands, and it was the court's role to consider a balance between immorality and illegality. Mr Hniazdzilau, the claimant, had asserted that he was the beneficial owner of shares in a company, named Bennet Invest Limited, which was incorporated in England in 2006. He was challenged by Mr Bronovets,[60] who argued that the company had been established entirely on *his* behalf. Mr Hniazdzilau submitted that Mr Bronovets was in fact his lawyer from Belarus, whom he had instructed to arrange for a company called Fitton, which had incorporated Bennet Invest Limited, to acquire funds to purchase a property in Minsk. At a standoff, Mr Hniazdzilau and Mr Bronovets each denied that the other had any claim to the company.

The motivation for the dispute was ownership by Bennet Invest Limited of the property in Belarus, which had become quite valuable, and was estimated to be worth between $3 and $6 million USD. Mr Hniazdzilau claimed that Bennet had funded the purchase of that property through business assets that Mr Hniazdzilau personally owned, whereas Mr Bronovets countered that the funding came from Bennet's trading activities.[61] The facts of the case, largely, thus, appeared to turn on what the judge, Jeremy Cousins QC, described as 'factual disputes',[62] until Mr Bronovets somewhat dramatically applied to amend his defence, and asserted illegal acts by Mr Hniazdzilau.

The drama was heightened because, until that point, a great deal of the court's efforts had been invested in attempting to keep the trail of defendants straight. Mr Vajgel, the first defendant, was an employee of Fitton, and Bennet's sole shareholder. Mr Hniazdzilau alleged that Mr Vajgel held the shares in Bennet on trust for him. He also claimed that Mr Vajgel had been acting contrary to the terms of the trust. The difficulty was exacerbated by the court's challenge in deciding, not quite who was the most credible witness, but, rather, who was the least untrustworthy. Mr Bronovets, for

[60] Who is more important to this case than the named defendant, Mr Vajgel, who plays a comparatively minor role, and largely is unaddressed by the court.
[61] *Hniazdzilau* (n 1) [1].
[62] ibid [2].

example—who raised the illegality claim against Mr Hniazdzilau—is described as 'profoundly unsatisfactory and unreliable'.[63] For that matter, the evidence provided by Mr Hniazdzilau was denounced by the court as 'extremely unsatisfactory in a number of important respects'.[64] There is a strong sense in the decision, although it is not explicitly stated, of an element of surprise that any single element of the arrangements might be identified as more immoral, or offensive to a test of public conscience,[65] than another.

Mr Hniazdzilau conceded that he had misled a Moscow court about the purpose of a loan, in order to facilitate tax abuse in that jurisdiction. Specifically, he testified that he had produced 'completely fictitious invoices' in order to fund Bennet's acquisition of the valuable property in Belarus.[66] Thus, although purchasing the property was always part of his plan, the reason for the deception was to reduce the amount of tax that he otherwise would have been required to pay. As the judge explained:

> Unattractive as Mr. Hniazdzilau's 'tax optimisation' explanation for the invoicing and receipt of funds was, I found it to be entirely credible, and I accept it. It may demonstrate that Mr. Hniazdzilau is a man with scant regard for paying his due share of tax, and the keeping of honest business records; whether or not this is a consideration which should preclude his being granted relief is for consideration later in this judgment in connection with the topic of illegality.[67]

The plan was more complex than the simple production of fictitious invoices. The invoices themselves related to the fees charged by banks for money transfers.[68] The transfers involved a 'group' of companies, and were effected 'around the world'.[69] The point of the deception was somehow to 'trigger' payments to Bennet, and it was the receipt of these payments which enabled the 'optimisation of tax'.[70]

The property (if the court were so to decide) was Mr Hniazdzilau's property only as a consequence of the tax 'optimisation'. Thus, if Mr Hniazdzilau were to be successful, this might be viewed by people in Russia as an indication that the English courts 'somehow … approve[d]' of his actions, although it was conceded (the court noted) that this argument was not very 'clear'.[71] Any application of equitable remedies to tax fraud would carry the risk of undermining 'the integrity of the legal system', despite that fact that the tax fraud occurred in another country, because of '[c]omity between

[63] ibid [21].
[64] ibid [18].
[65] Which is important given *Allen v Hounga*, discussed below.
[66] *Hniazdzilau* (n 1) [18].
[67] ibid [158].
[68] ibid [103].
[69] ibid
[70] ibid. In particular, Mr Hniazdzilau caused Bennet Invest Limited to sue a company called Koluchingo, in which he had a controlling interest. When asked during examination why he would do such a thing, Mr Hniazdzilau responded that he hoped to disguise a sale and purchase agreement for Koluchingo as a loan that failed to be repaid. The reason for this was that Russian taxes would have been due on a sale and purchase. He insisted that there was nothing criminal about this, in either Russia or Belarus. See [122–24], 'The Koluchingo Loan'.
[71] ibid [104(ii)].

nations'.[72] Additionally, Parliament, through the Proceeds of Crime Act, had determined that '... *all* undeclared income constitutes the proceeds of crime, not merely such part of it as would have been taxed'.[73] This meant that evidence submitted by Mr Hniazdzilau that the purchase of the Belarus property was funded not from money connected to the tax evasion in Russia, but from money connected to tax avoidance in the UK, was irrelevant. This was argued as both a foundational principle of equity, and as an approach that Parliament implicitly (through POCA) had endorsed.[74] The justification for this approach would be to ensure balance in the law, such that actions which would be 'condemned' in one area of the law are not rewarded in another.[75]

Finally, the attempted avoidance of tax *in the UK* did not escape further notice—and, indeed, counsel cited dicta from *Piper v Kirk*,[76] where the deputy judge observed that, if an element of a transaction had been upheld as valid (in the end, it was not), he nonetheless would have declined to enforce it, as it appeared that its purpose was to enable the avoidance of tax.[77] Mr Hniazdzilau's lawyers responded, among other points, that applying what could be described as the confiscation principle to him might actually serve to undermine the legal system, as it would leave him without funds to pay tax penalties, should they occur.[78] In response, counsel for Mr Bronovets argued that allowing Mr Hniazdzilau to succeed in this action ran the risk of rewarding bad behaviour. The suggestion that success for Mr Hniazdzilau would give the impression that English courts implicitly sanctioned bad behaviour faltered, however, when one considered that Mr Bronovets was little better—[79] unless, of course, there is something particularly terrible about tax abuse.

The judge, considering the question of illegality, held that the 'rule-based approach' of *Tinsley v Milligan* continued (at that time) to be relevant. The issue, in his view, was whether *Tinsley* had been overruled by *Hounga*,[80] which allowed consideration of the preservation of the 'integrity of the legal system', and thus permits enquiries into the

[72] ibid [194(iii)]. In other words, that nations should try to help each other with their tax laws. This is a somewhat shaky argument in the context of the Revenue Rule (on which see, *inter alia*, Brenda Mallinak, 'The Revenue Rule: A Common Law Doctrine for the Twenty-First Century' [2006] DJCIL 79, 79), which, historically, mandated that countries should not enforce each others' tax laws. This is a lightly argued point in the decision, however; and, additionally, in this area, much has changed over the years.

[73] ibid [195] (emphasis in original), citing *R v William* [2013] EWCA Crim 1262, and the Proceeds of Crime Act 2002 (Ch 29). But cf discussion at note 12, above. Perhaps, as with the 'comity' point (see note 72, above) the POCA references were also meant as a lightly argued reference to the spirit of legislation and legal practice, as opposed to the substance of the law.

[74] See discussion in note 12, above. It is worth noting, however, that equity might say that one should not profit from crime, but it need not follow that one should lose everything.

[75] *Hniazdzilau* (n 1) [195], citing *Hall v Herbet* [1993] 2 SCR 159, 176 and *Les Laboratoires Servier* [2015] AC 430, [24].

[76] [2010] EWHC 23 (Ch).

[77] *Hniazdzilau* (n 1) [196]. *Piper v Kirk* was otherwise distinguished from applicability to the issues in *Hniazdzilau* by the facts.

[78] ibid [206]. This is a difficult argument to follow. It is a principle of POCA that confiscation should not bankrupt anyone (hence the 'recoverable sum'). Additionally, there has not been a conviction here, and confiscation follows conviction. Additionally, why should this disadvantage be treated any differently from any other tax penalties? They all render one poorer. Again, perhaps this all can be resolved by assuming that the spirit of POCA is being alluded to here, rather loosely, as opposed to the letter.

[79] ibid [206(d)].

[80] *Hounga v Allen* [2014] UKSC 47.

public policy basis of illegality. He held that although there might be a debate as to whether the approach to the illegality defence in *Tinsley* should (then) continue to be followed, the case in any event had not been overruled or supplanted by *Hounga*. Thus, Mr Cousins, the judge, was able to dismiss the illegality defence as a bar to Mr Hniazdzilau's interests. Mr Hniazdzilau, as a consequence, was found to be the beneficial owner of Bennet Invest Limited, and won the case.[81]

B. A Case Decided After *Tinsley*, and Before *Patel*

This was not the first time that a court dealt with the illegality defence and tax avoidance, although the twist of the tax law at issue being foreign does make *Hniazdzilau* interesting. Even without the factor of Russian tax law, the intersection of tax avoidance and illegality, generally, merits attention in this discussion. Both illegality and tax avoidance involve activity which a court might conclude is immoral, but the challenge is that the court is actually being asked to decide whether it is illegal.[82]

The challenge was perhaps particularly difficult in the pre-*Patel* era. Indeed the uncertainty then surrounding the illegality defence was viewed by the judge, Mr Cousins, to be so acute that it was prudent to consider the issues raised under both the *Hounga* and *Tinsley* approaches,[83] which perhaps serves to emphasise how unsettled this period was. Interestingly, *Hniazdzilau* predates not only *Patel*, but also the Criminal Finances Act 2017,[84] which created the offence by a corporation of failing to prevent tax evasion. This offence includes a territorial scope outside of the UK. This does hint at the possibility of perhaps even a further shift in approach towards tax evasion as a matter of public policy, and the prospect of harsher outcomes for fact patterns with an international tax element.

If this is to be the case, then the question of *whose* moral standards[85] in international tax and trusts disputes should dominate would be a challenging one. In the context of

[81] The decision ultimately turned on the court's acceptance of Mr Hniazdzilau's claim that he had both given instructions to yet another defendant, Mr Enriquez, to establish Bennet, and also had provided funds for that purpose. The shares in Bennet therefore were held by Mr Vajgel on express trust for Mr Hniazdzilau. *Hniazdzilau* (n 1) [181], Mr Cousins explains that 'Mr Vajgel and Mr Enriquez were never more than bare trustees who cannot assert interests contrary to those of the true beneficial owner of the Shares. There is no basis for supposing that anyone other than Mr Hniazdzilau or Mr Bronovets has such an interest. As between them, for reasons considered in relation to Mr Hniazdzilau's fiduciary claim, Mr Bronovets cannot dispute that Mr Hniazdzilau is the beneficial owner because of the common intention which they shared, and because the circumstances would make it unconscionable for Mr Bronovets to defeat that intention.' The judge rejected almost all of the evidence presented by Mr Bronovets.

[82] This idea is explored in Michael W Poulsom, 'Acquiring property rights ex turpi causa' (2019) 2 Conv 149, 158–60.

[83] Darton (n 59) 729.

[84] s 46.

[85] The eighteenth-century case of *Holman v Johnson*, a famous 'starting point' (Toby and David Russell, 'Illegal Trusts' (2016) 22 Trusts & Trustees 721, 721) for illegality, contains the principle that '[n]o court will lend its aid to a man who founds his cause of action upon an immoral or an illegal act. If, from the plaintiff's own stating or otherwise, the cause of action appears to arise from *ex turpi causa*, or the transgression for a positive law of this country, there the court says he has no right to be assisted': (1775) 1 Cowp 341, 343. After *Patel*, however, it is important to recall Lord Toulson's admonition that 'although Lord Mansfield made it clear in *Holman v Johnson* that the illegality defence operates as a rule of public policy and is not designed to achieve justice between the parties, that does not mean that any result, however arbitrary, is acceptable': *Patel v Mirza* [2016] UKSC 42, [91]. The

the development of the doctrine of *ex turpi causa* in UK courts, public morality analyses largely have been confined to the domestic sphere, with the possible exception (as will be discussed) of references to settled, international consensus (for example, against human trafficking, as in the *Hounga* case).[86] Given that the *Hniazdzilau* court decided the case by turning to *Tinsley*, the question of how the post-*Patel* era will deal with international tax issues is an interesting one.

Tinsley, at the least, offered the possibility of a court deciding what a case is *about*. Is it, for example, *about* social security, or is it *about* contract law? The well-known facts of *Tinsley* concerned a couple, Ms Tinsley and Ms Milligan, who lived together in a house for which they both paid. The house was registered only in Ms Milligan's name, however, to facilitate Ms Milligan's false claims with the Department of Social Security. When Ms Tinsley and Ms Milligan ended their relationship, Ms Tinsley asserted *ex turpi causa* precluded Ms Milligan's claims on the house. The House of Lords famously held that Ms Tinsley held the house in trust for Ms Milligan.[87] The court appeared to decide that this was a contract case, and not a case about the distributive justice concerns of social security law.[88]

If the facts of *Tinsley* had somehow involved an international element, might the House of Lords have placed the emphasis elsewhere? Eleven years after *Tinsley*, the case of *Hounga v Allen* explored some issues involving a foreign law element, but in a different context. The case involved an employer, who offered a position to a fourteen-year-old girl from Nigeria. It was illegal for the girl to be employed in the UK. The offer proposed that, in exchange for education, a small monthly payment, and the acquisition of false documents which would enable her to enter the UK under a six-month visa,[89] the girl would provide childcare and housework. She was aware that it was illegal for her to work in the UK. She worked for the employer for eighteen months, during which she was neither enrolled in a school, nor paid any wages. She also suffered 'serious physical abuse' from the employer, who regularly threatened her that, as she worked in the UK illegally, she would be sent to prison if she approached authorities.[90] After leaving the employer's household, she brought an action to recover for unfair dismissal.

'maxim' that one should come to a private law claim with clean hands is believed to have developed from Lord Mansfield's statements: Nicholas Strauss, 'Illegality decisions after *Patel v Mirza*' (2018) 134 LQR 538, 538. So important is this principle that, in *Patel*, [[2016] UKSC 42], Lord Toulson opened his opinion for the majority with these very words.

[86] Not wholly because of the inclusion of the possibility of an international public conscience—which would be reaching too far—but this did play a part.

[87] A comparison of the facts of *Tinsley* with *Hniazdzilau* invokes the comparisons of Dee Cook's important studies in *Rich Law, Poor Law* (OUP 1989) where she explained that 'poor' crimes (like social security fraud) tended to receive harsher treatment in law than 'rich' crimes (like tax fraud). This dichotomy does not extend to the *Hniazdzilau* (rich crime) and *Tinsley* (poor crime) comparison, as illegality defeated neither claim. For discussion of the instances in which tax avoidance might provide a ground for denying equitable relief, see Steve Evans, 'It's Clean Hands Again: the dirtiness of not paying tax considered in the Supreme Court' (2015) 1 Conv 61–6; and Lee (n 16). Both articles consider (among other issues) the implications of Lord Walker's comments on tax avoidance in *Pitt v Holt* [2013] UKSC 26, 135, where he described 'artificial' tax avoidance as 'a social evil'.

[88] Nelson Enonchong, 'Illegality: The Fading Flame of Public Policy' (1994) 14 OJLS 295, 296. This is because the majority in *Tinsley* relied upon a principle known as the *Bowmaker* rule, which allows a party to recover where the essence of the claim itself does not rely upon illegality: *Bowmaker v Barnet Instruments Ltd* [1944] 2 All ER 579.

[89] *Hounga* (n 2) [10].

[90] ibid [14].

Writing for the majority in *Hounga*, Lord Wilson reviewed the cases that had been decided since *Tinsley*. He emphasised the international and domestic advances in the efforts against modern slavery, and held that '[t]he *public policy* in support of the application of … [the] defence [of illegality] … , to the extent that it exists at all, should give way to the public policy to which its application is an affront'.[91] And what of the reliance test? Would there be a reversion to a test of public conscience? Lord Wilson acknowledged that '[i]n the wake of the *Tinsley* case the reliance test has inevitably taken hold … '.[92] Nonetheless, public conscience also was relevant here, as people would be offended by any decision that prevented this victim from recovering in private law, simply because her own illegal acts had been a key part of the wrongs she had suffered.

The status of the illegality defence after the *Hounga* decision was criticised as deeply 'unsatisfactory'.[93] The Law Commission's decision to allow the defence to develop in common law was dismissed as unwise, and there were calls for intervention.[94] Lords Mance and Sumption joined the call for reform.[95] Lord Mance, in particular, worried that, after producing 'several penetrating reports', the Law Commission appears to have given up on reform.[96] He also warned that he did not share the Law Commission's 'optimis[m]' that the courts would develop a coherent and fair case-by-case approach to illegality.[97]

This was the context within which the *Hniazdzilau* decision occurred. Mr Cousins avoided the difficult question of public conscience by retreating to the *Tinsley* holding, and identifying the source of the claimant's interest. After the *Patel* decision in 2016, however, the rejection of the 'no reliance' principle makes it less easy for a court to take this approach, and to decide what a case is 'about'. In *Patel*, the Supreme Court held that a claimant who satisfies the requirements of a claim for unjust enrichment should not be prevented from enforcing this claim simply because the money which he seeks to recover was paid for an unlawful purpose. Considering the proportionality of the application of the illegality defence, a court might consider a number of issues, including the seriousness of the conduct, its centrality to the dispute, whether it was intentional and whether there was any difference in the parties' respective blameworthiness.

The courts will have some significant issues to address as the effects of the *Patel* holding develop in years to come. Consider, for example, that it is possible for the Proceeds of Crime Act 2002 to recover the proceeds of crime, even in the absence of a conviction. In the *Patel* case, the Supreme Court decided that Mr Patel should be able to recover money paid to Mr Mirza, despite the fact that Mr Patel was attempting to benefit from insider information in trading securities.[98] In theory, Mr Patel might have

[91] ibid [52] (emphasis added).
[92] ibid [29].
[93] James Goudkamp and Mimi Zou, 'The defence of illegality in tort law: Beyond judicial redemption?' (2015) 74 CLJ 13, 16. Perhaps, it might be said, as Cotterrell would have predicted. See note 115, below.
[94] ibid
[95] James Goudkamp, 'The Doctrine of Illegality: A Private Law Hydra' (2015) <https://papers.ssrn.com/sol3/papers.cfm?abstract_id=2693358>, accessed 1 July 2021.
[96] Jonathan Mance, 'Ex Turpi Causa—When Latin Avoids Liability' (2014) 18 Edinb Law Rev 175, 176.
[97] ibid. Cases continued to come before the courts, including, and in particular, the case of *Patel*, although not exclusively: see also *Les Laboratoires Servier & Anor v Apotex Inc* [2014] UKSC 55.
[98] An offence under s 52 of the Criminal Justice Act 1993.

found that the money he recovered nonetheless was confiscated by the state under the Proceeds of Crime Act.[99]

The confiscation of Mr Patel's money in this way might satisfy the need of funding the state, but the implications of the Proceeds of Crime Act for the express trust, in particular, are complicated. It is not surprising that counsel in *Hniazdzilau* reached for the Proceeds of Crime Act when attempting to justify a broad approach to a global tax 'comity', as few pieces of legislation reach further than POCA. Its powers are regularly reconsidered, and broadened.[100] Within these powers, a confiscation order under POCA 2002 is an order *in personam*, on the basis that defendants are deprived of the value of the benefit they received from their conduct.[101] Civil recovery is a remedy *in rem*, granted in respect of identifiable and recoverable property.[102] What of express trusts? Parkinson famously argued that the ' ... language of trusts is the language of property rights, not personal rights',[103] but proposed that the express trust can be a broader, equitable obligation, certainly founded in property rights, but not unconnected from the possibility of rights *in personam*.[104]

As both parties in *Patel* were described by the court as 'liable to conviction',[105] confiscation (*in personam*) might be possible. Presumably, convictions might be possible under Russian law in *Hniazdzilau* as well, but section 6 of POCA refers to convictions before the Crown Court, and in any case the morality of enforcing this aspect of Russian law would be questionable both on its own terms, and more broadly, in the aftermath of the war in Ukraine.[106] In any event, where convictions have not occurred, civil recovery actions *in rem* are possible (relying, in a further layer of complication, upon the tax assessment power).[107] All of these questions might be clarified and addressed within the context of UK law, but would remain much more complex when considered within an argument that advances a global idea of tax justice.

V. A Philosophy for International Tax, and Trusts

A guiding principle for international tax justice might approach this question simply: if it is a tax law, it should be enforced by all states. And if the tax law emanates from a State which does not respect human rights? Criteria may then be developed as a prerequisite to domestic tax law becoming a matter of international concern.

99 'Such a solution might be regarded as the fairest of them all ... ': Graham Virgo, '*Patel v Mirza*: one step forward and two steps back' [2016] 22(10) Trusts & Trustees 1090, 1096.

100 See Frederick Cram, 'Understanding the Proceeds of Crime Act 2002: Cash seizure and frontline policing' (2013) 52(2) Howard J Crime Justice 121.

101 See *Faichney and another v Vantis HR Ltd and others* [2018] EWHC 565 (Ch), [2018] All ER (D) 151 (Mar).

102 s 245A(3) POCA 2002.

103 Parkinson (n 19) 657.

104 ibid 683.

105 For conspiracy: *Patel* (n 2) [267].

106 See discussion in note 9, above.

107 See discussion in note 12, above.

Should the content of taxation law itself be considered, apart from other human rights issues? On one view there might not be too much divergence between the underlying norms or values in taxation as between different states, unless of course a taxation law itself violates some norms accepted by some states as sacrosanct, eg if there were a tax law that taxed according to race or gender for example (so, facially, was not neutral). Leaving those examples aside, however—so it is not so much a question of what tax law is, but what it facilitates—it is difficult to develop an argument based on taxation law, alone, and separate from other areas of law. Attention seems naturally to turn to the entirety of a state's laws, as a whole; or, perhaps, to the depths of its worst laws. Considering states in this way, as a whole, can lead to contradictory results.

For example, in a domestic context, for the state to continue to function, it may be important for the courts not to extend too much legitimacy to tax protest. If too many taxpayers were to refuse to pay tax until a new Prime Minister were elected, for example, then money would not be available for the basic functions of the state (hospitals, schools, etc.). Is it fair, then, to downplay tax protest in a domestic context, and not to extend the same favour to another country?

Criteria might be developed to deal with these questions, and, in any case, they are simply modern, tax twists on old debates. For example, they are similar to the questions that arise when the normative values of international law, *jus cogens*, interact with domestic legal systems that do not offer a basic minimum of rights to some persons. In this context, *jus cogens* is either quite undemocratic (because international norms trump the domestic law), the product of a wider consensus (ie given that the international community has agreed that the rights in question should be available), or perhaps even simpler questions of treaty interpretation. The complaint that allowing the international consensus to dominate is anti-democratic only succeeds if the country is either excluded from the concept of the international community (so, it never signed up to this value), and, perhaps more forcefully, if the international community is viewed as incapable of sustaining consensus indefinitely.[108]

This discussion also might be approached from a rather more universal perspective, and one which is not as embedded in the traditions of Western constitutional democracies (and, thus, which inevitably slides into a classic effort to resolve positivist/natural law tensions).[109] For example, Kant argued that the 'civil state', when viewed solely as a 'legal state', is based upon, roughly, freedom, equality, and independence.[110] These are not necessarily rights that are guaranteed by the state (so, not a product of the classic constitutional system), but, instead, are essential principles which make it possible to *found* a state.[111] They are values of the international community.[112] This is a form of

108 Aspects of this example are analysed more thoroughly in Gianluigi Palombella, 'The Rule of Law, Democracy and International Law: Learning from the US Experience' (2007) 20(4) Ratio Juris 456.

109 ibid 475.

110 Immanuel Kant and others, 'On the Relation of Theory to Practice in Constitutional Law: (Contra Hobbes)', in *On the Old Saw: That May Be Right in Theory But It Won't Work in Practice* (University of Pennsylvania Press 1974) 57–74, 58.

111 ibid

112 See also Palombella's (n 108) engagement with Kant.

natural law which is based on consensus, among all persons, regardless of country (or sovereign). The conflict with positivist law does not arise, because one could argue that, if a state in Kant's argument created a law which offended equality, it has sacrificed its right to exist. The question, then, would be whether it is possible to identify the constituent parts—the implementing rules of freedom, equality, and independence—of the international rule of law? The answer cannot be all domestic laws, of all states, as simply transposing domestic rules to international problems is unlikely to provide a framework for addressing international challenges.[113] The challenge here lies in the fact that it is difficult to articulate an international rule of tax law in a coherent way.[114] *Hniazdilau* is a potent example of this.

The numerous difficulties of globalisation will not escape familiar conundra of what might be described as traditional (domestic) law.[115] There will be some aspects of this problem that are particular to tax and internationalisation, and some that are not. So the question is not only what should happen, for example, when there is a clash between an express trust, and tax; but, also, whether the answer should differ when the tax is international?

The *Tinsley* approach of deciding what a case is *about* might be replaced, in the post-*Patel* era, with a proportional consideration of a variety of public policy factors. The risk is that this might lead to a clash between the fundamental principles surrounding express trusts, and any consensus reached on international tax cooperation. For example: trusts law affords autonomy to individuals in finance, family care, and more. It is possible to construct a domestic system of rules which prevents the freedom that trusts law affords from taking too much from the state, and from becoming exploitative. The reach of the protections of the domestic system, however, might not stretch overseas.

The possibility of an international consensus on the best resolution for this kind of conflict appears limited; yet, even in the unlikely event that a consensus was reached, the terms of the consensus might be too broad. For example, there might well be good reasons for keeping a trust offshore, and it is at this point that, traditionally, arguments engage references to the value of privacy in one's affairs, and even the risk of kidnap that some people, in some jurisdictions, face.[116] To add an additional layer of complication: moving back to the facts of *Hniazdzilau*, the UK probably counts as the 'offshore' jurisdiction. These questions return us to the discussion of what does, and does not, count as an overly broad approach in social justice assessments of tax and trusts. So,

[113] Paul Burgess describes this as 'derivation', in 'Deriving the international Rule of Law: an unnecessary, impractical and unhelpful exercise' (2019) 10(1) Transnatl Leg Theory 65.

[114] See Roger Cotterrell, 'Transnational Communities and the Concept of Law' (2008) 21(1) Ratio Juris 1, which provides a (not optimistic) account of some of the challenges.

[115] And, thus, a return to Hart, and some controversies. See, eg, Roger Stumpff Morrison, 'Law Is the Command of the Sovereign: HLA Hart Reconsidered' (2016) 29(3) Ratio Juris 364, 381–82 (criticising the fundamental tenets of Hart's thesis that coercion is not central to law on the grounds that Hart misunderstood, for example, Holmes's famous 'bad man' argument in 'The Path of the Law' (1897) 10 Harvard L R 457, 459, by incorrectly assuming that, in Holmes's view the content of law changes according to whether the bad or the good man is asking the question. Morrison argues that it does not.) The question of coercion, or enforcement, in the international context is even more complicated. As Cotterrell (n 114) might argue, attempting to transpose Holmes and Hart into the international context would prompt a reconsideration of basic points of reference in theories about the content of law.

[116] Such arguments are considered throughout the three sources listed in note 115.

in our first example, the offshore trust case, it might be possible to identify some kind of tax abuse, and to connect that abuse to the existence of the trust, for the defence of illegality appropriately to cause some aspect of the trust to fail, or otherwise to block claims of beneficial ownership.

What next for *international* tax and trusts? It may be that the Kantian concept of the international rule of law, and its strong reliance on a natural justice framework, provide hints of a useful way forward. The 'tax justice' argument in *Hniazdzilau* would still fail, but not because tax is excluded from the 'comity of nations'. Kant would argue that if each community builds its state properly, then a functional international community follows.[117] The history of trusts might be presented as part of a narrative in which the UK has built its own laws properly, so as to ensure autonomy, and privacy. The effort of balancing interests in illegality cases might need to consider: has another country built their own laws properly?

So tax justice need not be defended blindly, and disruptive events, like war, will be part of the discussion. This is not an argument in defence of the statist approach (with an exception for war), but rather a call for balancing exercises with nuance. So, for example, many aspects of trusts law may make perfect sense in the UK, but have unexpected and undesirable consequences elsewhere. The fact that, in some circumstances, they also lead to abusive tax arrangements need not be the entirety of the story, but it is important that it is part of the story.

VI. Conclusion

It is tempting to imagine that the decision in *Hniazdzilau* was viewed with a great deal of interest by businesspersons overseas. Had the court decided differently, perhaps English trust law might have been viewed as considerably less attractive for the formalities of international investment. Mr Cousins' concern about the litigants he faced in that case perhaps should not be dismissed lightly. Simply because litigants may be unappealing, of course, it does not follow that they should be deprived of the protections of law. But the very fact that this case arose in the first place, with these defendants, and their choices of law and jurisdiction, hints at the emergence of important questions in the trajectory of trusts, taxation, and the expectations of law.

Trusts law attracted the defendants in *Hniazdilau* to the UK. An objective of the chapter was to ask why, and what follows—were they attracted to the UK because they hoped to undermine Russian taxation law (clearly, yes), and, if so, what should the response to that be? Should tax always be uncoupled from the quality of the state it funds? Possibly, yes, as long as the state in question satisfies a global consensus as to basic human rights assurances (given the possibility of voting governments out of power)—but should this also be encouraged for another country with a history of abuses of

[117] As explained in P Capps and J Rivers, 'Kant's Concept of International Law' (2010) 16 Leg Theory 229.

human rights? Even then, should the 'good' things accomplished by tax in those countries be taken into account?

Accounts of the international rule of law tend to proceed along the lines of identifying exceptions to the domestic laws of countries, based on different justifications (of global consensus, of natural law, of morality). In the context of international taxation and trusts, a more integrated approach (considering the impact of rules domestically, internationally, and, indeed, from a variety of different perspectives) would appear to be necessary, so as to support the development of a new taxonomy entirely.

Index

For the benefit of digital users, indexed terms that span two pages (e.g., 52–53) may, on occasion, appear on only one of those pages.